Hannah Arendt

Modern European Thinkers

Series Editors: Anne Beech and David Castle

Over the past few decades, Anglo-American social science and humanities have experienced an unprecedented interrogation, revision and strengthening of their methodologies and theoretical underpinnings through the influence of highly innovative scholarship from continental Europe. In the fields of philosophy, post-structuralism, psychoanalysis, critical theory and beyond, the works of a succession of pioneering writers have had revolutionary effects on Anglo-American academia. However, much of this work is extremely challenging, and some is hard or impossible to obtain in English translation. This series provides clear and concise introductions to the ideas and work of key European thinkers.

As well as being comprehensive, accessible introductory texts, the titles in the 'Modern European Thinkers' series retain Pluto's characteristic radical political slant, and critically evaluate leading theorists in terms of their contribution to genuinely radical and progressive intellectual endeavour. And while the series does explore the leading lights, it also looks beyond the big names that have dominated theoretical debates to highlight the contribution of extremely important but less well-known figures.

Also available

Alain Badiou
Jason Barker

André Gorz
Conrad Lodziak and Jeremy Tatman

Georges Bataille
Benjamin Noys

Félix Guattari
Gary Genosko

Jean Baudrillard
Mike Gane

Jürgen Habermas
Luke Goode

Walter Benjamin
Esther Leslie

Guy Hocquenghem
Bill Marshall

Pierre Bourdieu
Jeremy F. Lane

Julia Kristeva
Anne-Marie Smith

Gilles Deleuze
John Marks

Slavoj Žižek
Ian Parker

HANNAH ARENDT

A Critical Introduction

Finn Bowring

PlutoPress
www.plutobooks.com

First published 2011 by Pluto Press
345 Archway Road, London N6 5AA

www.plutobooks.com

Distributed in the United States of America exclusively by
Palgrave Macmillan, a division of St. Martin's Press LLC,
175 Fifth Avenue, New York, NY 10010

British Library Cataloguing in Publication Data
A catalogue record for this book is available from the British Library

ISBN   978 0 7453 3142 3   Hardback
ISBN   978 0 7453 3141 6   Paperback

Library of Congress Cataloging in Publication Data applied for

This book is printed on paper suitable for recycling and made from fully managed
and sustained forest sources. Logging, pulping and manufacturing processes are
expected to conform to the environmental standards of the country of origin.

10   9   8   7   6   5   4   3   2   1

Designed and produced for Pluto Press by Chase Publishing Services Ltd
Typeset from disk by Stanford DTP Services, Northampton, England
Simultaneously printed digitally by CPI Antony Rowe, Chippenham, UK and
Edwards Bros in the United States of America

To Chris,
for his friendship,
good humour, and common sense.

Contents

A Note on Referencing and Abbreviations

For this study of Arendt's work, I have drawn generously on all her posthumously published texts. To simplify the referencing system, which in Arendt's case, given her penchant for essays, would otherwise require scores of separate bibliographical entries, I have restricted my Arendt references largely to her books, including the edited collections. Where the articles in these collected volumes span several decades, this is clearly an unsatisfactory way of dating Arendt's arguments and ideas. But my intention is to present Arendt's work as an organic whole, so in my view the loss of detail in referencing the dates and titles of Arendt's essays is a small price to pay for improved readability. The system of abbreviations I use is as follows (in alphabetical order):

CR   *Crises of the Republic*. San Diego: Harcourt Brace, 1972.
EJ   *Eichmann in Jerusalem: A Report on the Banality of Evil* [1963]. Revised and enlarged edition. Harmondsworth: Penguin, 1977.
EU   *Essays in Understanding 1930–1954: Formation, Exile, and Totalitarianism*. New York: Schocken, 1994.
HC   *The Human Condition* [1958]. Second edition. Chicago: University of Chicago Press, 1998.
JP   *The Jew as Pariah*. New York: Grove Press, 1978.
JW   *The Jewish Writings*. New York: Schocken, 2007.
LA   *Love and Saint Augustine*. Chicago: University of Chicago Press, 1996.
LK   *Lectures on Kant's Political Philosophy*. Chicago: University of Chicago Press, 1982.
LM1/2   *The Life of the Mind*. Volumes 1 and 2. San Diego: Harcourt, 1978.
MD   *Men in Dark Times* [1968]. London: Jonathan Cape, 1970.
OR   *On Revolution* [1963]. Revised edition. Harmondsworth: Penguin, 1990.
OT   *The Origins of Totalitarianism* [1951]. Third edition. New York: Harcourt, 1973.

OV   *On Violence.* San Diego: Harcourt Brace, 1970.
PF   *Between Past and Future: Eight Exercises in Political Thought* [1961]. Second edition. Harmondsworth: Penguin, 1968.
PP   *The Promise of Politics.* New York: Schocken, 2005.
RJ   *Responsibility and Judgement.* New York: Schocken, 2003.
RV   *Rahel Varnhagen: The Life of a Jewish Woman* [1957]. Revised edition. San Diego: Harcourt Brace Jovanovich, 1974.

Introduction: Time for Action

The work of Hannah Arendt is well known to students and scholars of political science and philosophy, but in the discipline of sociology, and its more imaginative sibling, social theory, her name often stirs only faint recognition. As an academic who teaches social theory in a social science department, my own interest in Arendt arose from studying debates on the labour process and the future of work. The 'sociology of work', as it used to be called, has become a rather unfashionable field in recent years, partly because the concept of work, finally having escaped the grip of political economy, now has many rival definitions and meanings. Today the term is used to draw attention to the previously neglected endeavours of a multitude of individuals performing all manner of socially and economically relevant activities, from childrearing to the performance of gender, from 'identity work' to 'emotional labour'. Used to confer sociological status on any activity that requires effort, inventiveness, initiative or perseverance, 'work' is a concept that has been haemorrhaging significance.

In contrast to the increasingly promiscuous use of the term, Arendt's well-known division of human activities into three distinctive types – labour, work and action – suggested something less capricious and more essential. It offered an anthropologically grounded set of categories with which to look again at, amongst other things, the trials and frustrations of paid employment, and above all it helped answer a question that had been bothering me for some time. What are we going to do when there is not enough work to occupy most of us most of the time? Or, as the late André Gorz used to put it: how can we humanise the free time which capitalist economies, despite their most strenuous and destructive efforts, cannot help but keep producing? Arendt's answer is partly Aristotelian in flavour: we are political beings ('animals', in Aristotle's formulation, though Arendt would regard this as a contradiction in terms), and political action is the highest manifestation of the human condition. But of course, politics takes time.

As I shall show later in this book, Arendt emphasised the political dimension of human activity in explicit opposition to Marx's definition of our species as quintessentially productive in nature.

1

This same opposition also influenced Habermas's reconstruction of historical materialism, and his insistence that we recognise the significance of both instrumental labour and communicative interaction in understanding the development of modern society and the modes of human flourishing. Arendt's dialogue with Marx is more or less explicit, but her work has relevance to other thinkers, both classical and contemporary, in the sociological tradition. Her intellectual struggle to marry freedom with stability, the initiation of something new with the continuity of a common world, would immediately prompt a reference to Durkheim, were it not for Arendt's hostility to the idea of the 'social', and indeed her deep suspicion of the sociological obsession with the normal and predictable rather than the unexpected and the extraordinary. Intellectually, Arendt's own outlook appears to have more in common with the neo-Kantian tradition inherited by Max Weber, though again we shall see that there are some curious divergences, such as their different conceptualisations of bureaucracy and their opposing theories of power. In the course of this book I shall explore how Arendt's thought relates to a number of other perspectives and thinkers in contemporary social theory, including feminist epistemology, political ecology, Foucault's post-structuralism, and the work of Richard Sennett and Zygmunt Bauman.

Let me preview a couple of important themes here. Arendt's intellectual standing has risen in some quarters over the last two decades as the anti-foundationalist critique of Enlightenment rationalism has gathered pace. Arendt's argument is that politics is always an exchange of opinions, and truth has no central role to play in it because, like violence, truth has a coercive force which is incompatible with free deliberation and judgement. Perhaps most interestingly, Arendt suggests that a kind of common truth – a sense of there being a common world which we share and care about – becomes tangible to us only when we exchange different perspectives on it. The 'objectivity' of the world, in other words, cannot be grasped from a single standpoint, as the objects in this world are three-dimensional, and show their full dimensions only when seen from many sides. Arendt's position here converges with the idea of 'triangulation' in social science research, a concept which, since Cicourel (1974), has increasingly been framed in constructivist terms, referring less to the validation of data by means of different methods, and more to the provision of rich composite descriptions of the world through the eliciting of different perspectives on it (Seale 1999).

Arendt's emphasis on the importance of a world which lies between separate individuals, and which they care about enough to want to guarantee its preservation beyond their own individual lifespans, also has ramifications for the disposable society we are currently living in, where an obsession with the self and its identity combines with an increasingly careless attitude towards the world of things. If Bauman is correct in designating this an age of 'liquid modernity', then the loss of worldly stability is also the loss of that which, standing in between different people, binds and separates them at the same time. When this in-between world is destroyed, people find themselves pressed together so tightly that both self and world lose their integrity, and a lonely indifference to public life becomes the norm. Bauman originally argued that totalitarianism was a permanent possibility in a bureaucratic modernity founded on rational hierarchy, organised obedience and rule-governed order. In his more recent characterisation of liquid modernity, this danger is consigned to the past. But if, as Arendt argues in *The Origins of Totalitarianism*, it is worldless instability which sweeps people into the arms of ideological fanaticism and totalitarian rule, then the break with an earlier era may have been exaggerated. In contemporary societies, the seemingly unstoppable force of economic and technological expansion may be the only bastion of certainty in a world of unpredictability and risk. But as with the forces of history or race, to which the totalitarian movements of the last century appealed, we are at the mercy of this certainty not the masters of it.

The continuity between this and the previous century can also be articulated in terms of the increasing prominence given to life, the body and its natural appetites, in the realm of public affairs. Received wisdom has it that while totalitarianism germinated under conditions of acute scarcity, the consumer paradise of the post-Second World War Western democracies progressively neutralised the fanatical passions that arise from abject poverty and need. But critics of capitalism have long argued that this is a system which does not settle people's needs so much as continually provoke them at ever higher levels of abundance. These reinvented needs are not necessarily sublimated aesthetic or spiritual desires, but are typically the crude extension of an unrefined animal existence. Arendt believed that when the public realm becomes devoted to the satisfaction of physical needs, politics surrenders its autonomy, thereby also losing the ability to bestow life with human dignity, to guarantee it those 'artificial' human rights which protect individuals from being treated like animals. It is not just that politics has become a powerless pawn in an unstoppable process of economic growth, but that all public activities are now entangled with the imperatives of life – from the performances of the most loyal customers of the cosmetic surgery industry, whose public careers last only so long as their youthful looks, to the medical management of death, and to the scientific innovations of those biotech revolutionaries who want to accelerate the evolutionary adaptation of the human species by eliminating the bottlenecks of cumbersome and ambiguous speech, the asking of unanswerable questions, the purposeless search for meaning. How else can we make sense of the incongruous combination in the contemporary world of meaningless life and abundant death, of plenty and starvation, of the fetishisation of health and the military terrorising of defenceless bodies – if not by a thoroughgoing banalisation of life, where the worshippers of eternal youth already wear the frozen countenance of the living dead, and the cyborg enthusiasts already assume themselves to be reprogrammable machines.

There is another thing about Arendt's work which really stands out for me. Arendt possesses the surprisingly rare, and rather unsettling, ability to make you, or rather to make you want to, think. This sounds like an anodyne observation. After all, aren't we all, academics, intellectuals and students, in the full-time business of thinking? Universities are full of very clever people, but Arendt makes clear – first in the style of her writing and reasoning, and second in the explicit analysis of humans' mental faculties that she developed in her later work – that cognition and thinking are not the same thing. What she seemed to learn most from her study of Adolf Eichmann is that intelligent people are able to do the most awful things, and that cleverness does not immunise us against thoughtlessness and the temptation to do wrong. Arendt's own determination to think through, clarify, and then judge the human component in the most inhuman of events and deeds is perhaps the most challenging and controversial of her intellectual gifts – what Stephen Whitfield aptly called her 'feline capacity for seeing in the dark' (1980: 256).

In the final chapters of this book I explore the surprising suggestion in Arendt's later writings that there may be a positive relation between the life of the mind and the ability to make moral and political judgements (surprising because, for most of her intellectual career, she saw the philosophers' elevation of thinking over doing as partly responsible for the jaundiced view of public life that is commonplace today). In Arendt's view it is the ability of the mind, the thinking self, to de-centre itself, to assimilate new opinions and entertain a plurality of competing perspectives, that makes possible both the art of persuasion and the practice of judgement.

I am not spoiling the conclusion when I say that I am still not sure how successful is Arendt's adventurous engagement with moral philosophy. But uncertainty is the enemy neither of politics nor of thinking, for the dream of an incontestable truth can only be realised by bringing to an end the need for dialogue and thinking. This book is written for the wakeful rather than the sleepy, its aim being to show how Arendt's work can enliven the debate between politics, philosophy and sociology.

THE STRUCTURE AND PURPOSE OF THIS BOOK

Although the primary purpose of this study is to introduce Arendt to readers with a limited knowledge of her work, this is not a short book, and nor is it merely introductory. As well as engaging with the debates that have arisen around Arendt's writings over the last thirty years, I have tried to start or continue some new debates, discussing the relevance of her ideas to consumer society, for example, and considering whether her distinction between 'nature' and 'world' is compatible with a solution to the ecological crisis we now face. When I pictured the future reader of this book, I thought of a student or scholar with a social science background, perhaps with an interest in Marxism, feminism, post-structuralism, or Critical Theory, and who has a political outlook – that is, who is interested in the interface between theory and practice, and in the theory *of* practice. I also hope this book will have some selective interest to established Arendt scholars who have not yet exhausted their involvement with her writings, and who are curious to see how Arendt looks from a more sociological perspective.

The chapters that follow can be roughly divided into four parts. The first three chapters concentrate on Arendt's analysis of human activities. Chapter 1 explains the categories of labour, work and action; Chapter 2 describes Arendt's account of the perversion of the hierarchy of activities in the modern age; and Chapter 3 explores Arendt's theory of action and power. For the first two chapters, *The Human Condition* is the primary reference point, while *On Revolution* figures most prominently in the third one. But I draw freely on the full range of Arendt's writings whenever they help me clarify or elaborate on her arguments, and have resisted the temptation to divide her work into discrete chronological phases.

Chapters 4 and 5 offer a more critical engagement with Arendt's writings. Chapter 4 examines three themes: her critique of Marx, her understanding of nature, and her theory of culture. Chapter 5 reinvestigates Arendt's controversial distinction between the social and the political, using feminist analyses of her work as a starting point for a wider discussion about the history of the public sphere and its contemporary ailments.

Chapters 6 and 7 make up the third section of the book, which focuses on Arendt's study of totalitarianism. Although *The Origins of Totalitarianism* was published seven years before *The Human Condition*, and is often studied in isolation from her more theoretical works, I use the former to help illustrate some of the key concepts in Arendt's political philosophy, such as worldlessness and action. Chapter 6 explores Arendt's account of the structural and ideological precursors to totalitarianism, notably imperialism, racism and bureaucracy. Chapter 7 concentrates on what Arendt believed were the defining features of totalitarian rule, highlighting the challenge these features pose to conventional social scientific explanations, and ending by looking at some of the tensions in, and continued relevance of, Arendt's analysis.

The central theme of the final two chapters is moral and political responsibility. Chapter 8 explores how Arendt's understanding of human wickedness evolved from her book on totalitarianism to her report on the trial of Adolf Eichmann a decade later, and how her account of evil's 'banality' bears some comparison with functionalist theories of social behaviour. Reflecting on Zygmunt Bauman's critique of Durkheim's sociological treatment of morality, I also note the kinship – as well as the contrasts – between Bauman and Arendt's understanding of moral autonomy. Chapter 9 continues this theme by reviewing Arendt's incomplete writings on the life of the mind, and her attempt to recruit Kant in order to produce a theory of judgement that is principled but not rule-governed, and which is attuned to the particular without being subservient to it.[1]

A BIOGRAPHICAL SKETCH

Arendt was born in Hannover in 1906. Her parents, who were educated, well-travelled and politically progressive secular Jews, took their only child back to their home city of Königsberg when she was still an infant. After both her father and grandfather died in 1913, the otherwise precocious Arendt suffered several years of infectious illnesses and emotional malaise. Expelled from her school for organising a boycott of a disagreeable teacher's classes, she attended Greek, Latin and theology lessons at the University of Berlin, avidly reading Kant, Kierkegaard and Jaspers, then returning to her school to complete the *Abitur* exam a year ahead of her peers in 1924.

Starting at Marburg University later in the year, Arendt enrolled on Heidegger's ground-breaking seminars on Greek philosophy. Her classmates included Hans Jonas, Karl Löwith and Günther Stern, and had she arrived a few years later she would have had Herbert Marcuse for company. Moving to Freiburg in 1925 to work for a semester under Heidegger's former mentor, Edmund Husserl, Arendt then followed Heidegger's recommendation that she study with Karl Jaspers in Heidelberg. There she became part of an intellectual milieu which gravitated around the Weber salon that Marianne Weber had re-established after her husband's death, with Gertrud Simmel and Gertrud Jaspers also playing prominent roles.

Arendt completed her doctorate on 'Saint Augustine's Concept of Love' in 1929, and saw it published by Springer later that year. Moving to Berlin, she met again and married Günther Stern. While Stern worked on his *Habilitationsschrift* for Frankfurt University, Arendt began a study of German Romanticism which crystallised into a biography of the Jewish *salonnière* Rahel Varnhagen. During this period she became increasingly politicised, reading Marx, Lenin and Trotsky, writing review articles for German sociology journals, and moving closer to the Zionism of her charismatic friend Kurt Blumenfeld. Meanwhile her husband's efforts to qualify as a *Privatdozent* had been obstructed by Theodor Adorno's unsupportive comments on his *Habilitationsschrift*, and he too had become radicalised, in this case by the Communist Party, and was now writing political journalism under the pseudonym Günther Anders. When the Reichstag was set ablaze in February 1933, prompting the mass arrest of German communists, Stern fled to Paris. For a time Arendt remained in Berlin, using her apartment to hide political refugees looking to escape from Hitler's Germany, and, at the bequest of the German Zionist Organisation, spending time in the Prussian State Library covertly collecting documentary evidence of anti-Semitism in German public and private life. Arousing the authority's suspicions, Arendt was detained by the police, but released eight days later after she had charmed the officer who arrested her into believing the accusations were groundless.

Arendt's appetite for risk-taking was quenched, however, and she fled with her mother to Prague and then Geneva, with her mother returning to Königsberg, and Arendt joining her husband in Paris, in the Autumn of 1933.

In Paris Arendt's political enthusiasm was matched only by her disdain for the cowardice and self-deception of German intellectuals who, like Heidegger, had found philosophical justification for siding with the Nazis. With her contempt for philosophy and academia growing, she threw herself into Zionist social work, first as a secretary for *Agriculture et Artisanat*, and then as a director of Youth Aliyah, both organisations that trained and educated young Jewish refugees and assisted in their visa applications in preparation for emigration to Palestine. She also researched and wrote on anti-Semitism and the 'Jewish Question', though the most important manuscripts from this period have only recently been translated and published. In her Parisian social circle she befriended Walter Benjamin, Raymond Aron, Erich Cohn-Bendit, whose future son, Daniel, would play a leading role in the Paris student movement of 1968, and the self-educated former Spartacist Heinrich Blücher, whom she would later marry after she and Stern divorced in 1937. When Youth Aliyah, alarmed at the growth of fascist sympathies among the French population, moved to London in 1938, Arendt stayed in Paris working for the Jewish Agency, helping refugees from Austria and Czechoslovakia.

In May 1940, four months after they had married, Arendt and Blücher were transported by the pre-Vichy French government to separate internment camps for 'enemy aliens' in the foothills of the Pyrenees. When France surrendered to the Nazis later that summer, Arendt was able to secure her release from the camp at Gurs, and was later reconciled with Blücher, whose own captors had fled amidst the chaos, fortuitously meeting him in unoccupied Montauban. With Günther Stern, who had emigrated to the US in 1936, petitioning on their behalf, Arendt and Blücher were granted emergency American visas. Making the most of a rare relaxation of the Vichy exit permit rules, they escaped to Portugal in January 1941, arriving by boat in New York in May 1941, with Arendt's mother luckily joining them a few weeks later.

Arendt found work as a regular columnist for the German-language newspaper *Aufbau*, which soon became an important touchstone for German-Jewish intellectuals around the world. There Arendt stressed the need for a Jewish army to fight against Hitler and reverse the political naivety, philanthropic idealism, and blind faith in their 'chosenness', that she believed was the most fateful historical affliction of the Jews. After the Biltmore Conference in May 1942, Arendt became increasingly concerned about the nationalist demand, led by Ben-Gurion, for a Jewish state in Palestine, where the majority Arab population would be given minority status. She saw this as an ugly repetition of the fascism from which the European Jews had fled, and a long way from the system of mixed Arab-Jewish municipal councils which was her own political ideal. She also saw, with notable prescience, that a small Jewish state surrounded by Arab peoples would inevitably find itself, in exchange for military and economic protection, taking care of American or British interests in the Middle East, thereby betraying its original claim to autonomy and perpetuating the imperialist dynamics that had contributed to the collapse of the European comity of nations.

In 1944 Arendt became research director for the Conference on Jewish Relations, and then its off-shoot, the Commission on European Jewish Cultural Reconstruction, helping to track down and recover Jewish cultural treasures that had been lost or stolen during the Nazi occupation of Europe. This enabled her to visit Europe in 1949–50, where she renewed her relationships with Heidegger and Jaspers. She combined her work for the Commission with a four-year stint as senior editor at Schocken Books, which specialised in texts by Jewish authors. English had quickly become Arendt's primary writing medium, and she was soon contributing articles to, amongst other US publications, *The Nation*, *Review of Politics*, *Commonweal*, *Commentary*, and *Partisan Review*, whilst at the same time conducting extensive research on the book that would be published in America as *The Origins of Totalitarianism*, and in Britain as *The Burden of our Time*. The first edition appeared in 1951, the same year she obtained US citizenship. In recognition of the achievement of the book she was invited to give a series of lectures at Princeton University in 1953.

Funded by a Guggenheim grant, Arendt had also started working on a study of Marxism. Some of her ideas she presented as Foundation lectures at the University of Chicago in 1956, though by then she had already accepted a full-time teaching post at Berkeley. In 1957, two years before it was published in her native Germany, *Rahel Varnhagen: The Life of a Jewish Woman* was translated and published in London, with a revised edition finally appearing in the US in 1974. In 1958, as a by-product of her never-finished project on Marx, Arendt published her most philosophical text, *The*

Human Condition. This was followed, in 1961, with *Between Past and Future*, a collection of philosophical essays on the concepts of freedom, history, culture, tradition and authority. A study of the French and American revolutions, *On Revolution*, appeared two years later, the same year that her account of the 1961 trial of Adolf Eichmann, *Eichmann in Jerusalem*, was published as a book. The latter provoked a storm of controversy, with Arendt accused of defending the man she refused to demonise, and of betraying the Jews whom she refused to exempt from criticism for co-operating with the Nazis. Suffering a campaign of public smears, Arendt endured testing relationships with a number of her friends, including Hans Jonas, with whom the book was never discussed, and Kurt Blumenfeld, a life-long friend since Heidelberg, who died before Arendt could win back his affection.

In 1963 Arendt began teaching part-time for the University of Chicago's Committee on Social Thought, moving to the New School for Social Research in New York four years later to take up a full-time position. Her writing took the shape of essays and review articles, many of them engaging with topical political issues, such as the student and anti-war movements, and the use of violence and lying in politics. *Men in Dark Times*, a collection of essays on exemplary moral, political and intellectual figures, ranging from Rosa Luxemburg and Walter Benjamin to Pope John XXIII, was published in 1968. *On Violence*, an expanded version of an essay Arendt had written for the *Journal of International Affairs*, was published as a short book in 1970, and the essay reappeared in *Crises of the Republic* (1972), along with articles on civil disobedience and lying.

Perhaps because of the growing temptation for political activists to resort to violence in their public protests, Arendt had begun to re-evaluate her attitude to philosophy and the contemplative life that she had repudiated so decisively in the 1930s. She began teaching a course on Kant at the New School in 1970, and worked on an essay, 'Thinking and Moral Considerations', which began to explore the moral faculties of the mind. On the day she delivered this as a lecture to the Society for Phenomenology and Existential Philosophy in October 1970, Heinrich Blücher died of a heart attack. A proposal of love from W. H. Auden several weeks later shocked rather than comforted her. Though Auden was not her only suitor, Arendt mourned the loss of her husband keenly, and became increasingly dejected by what she called the 'deforestation' of her closest peer group.

In the Spring of 1973 she gave the Gifford Lectures at Edinburgh University, focusing on the work she was preparing for a companion volume to *The Human Condition* entitled *The Life of the Mind*. Returning to Edinburgh to resume the Gifford series in May 1974, she herself suffered a heart attack while delivering the first lecture. Despite recovering well and fulfilling a variety of public engagements, she had a second, this time fatal, heart attack on 4 December 1975.

After Arendt's death, her close friend Mary McCarthy prepared the incomplete manuscript of *The Life of the Mind* for publication in two volumes in 1978. In the same year, a collection of Arendt's previously published writings on Jewish issues, *The Jew as Pariah*, was released by Grove Press. This was followed, in 1982, first by the publication of Arendt's *Lectures on Kant's Political Philosophy*, and then by an outstanding biography of Arendt written by her former student and confidante, Elizabeth Young-Bruehl. *Hannah Arendt: For Love of the World*, reignited the public's interest in Arendt, though not just because of its skilful and comprehensive synthesis of her life and work. The book revealed what until then only Jaspers, Blücher, and a handful of Arendt's close friends had always known: that in 1925 she had been the lover of her married teacher, Martin Heidegger, and had kept the secret romance going with visits to Marburg that lasted until 1929. This public revelation prompted a revisiting of Arendt's work, some of it genuinely aimed at re-examining Heidegger's philosophical influence on her thinking, and some of it rather prurient and self-righteous, with Arendt depicted as an apologist for Heidegger's Nazism and a parvenu Jew who was never able to confront the man who refused to treat her as an equal.

A volume of Arendt's early published and unpublished writings, *Essays in Understanding 1930–1954*, was released by Schocken Books in 1994. In 1996, the English translation of Arendt's doctoral study, *Love and Saint Augustine*, which she herself had commissioned and then revised for intended publication in 1964–5, was finally published by the University of Chicago Press. Schocken also released *Responsibility and Judgement* (2003), which includes the texts of some of Arendt's lectures on moral philosophy, and then *The Promise of Politics* (2005), which contains some of the work Arendt had prepared for her intended book on Marx. The Schocken series continued with another volume of Arendt's Jewish writings, the chief value of this book, *The Jewish Writings* (2007), being the inclusion of some important unpublished essays from the 1930s, as well as translations of the articles she wrote for *Aufbau*.

1
The *Vita Activa*

Let me begin, then, with *The Human Condition*, perhaps Arendt's most philosophical study, but also, ironically, the one most likely to be referenced in text-book discussions of the sociology of work. Arendt's analysis of the human condition is founded on a restatement of the ancient distinction between the *vita contemplativa* and the *vita activa*, or what Aristotle called the *bios theōrētikos* and the *bios politikos*. The former is the 'life of the mind' – which is also the title of Arendt's last major work, intended, as she later put it, as a 'second volume' of *The Human Condition* (1979: 306) – and it refers to the activities of thinking, willing and judging that have traditionally been the subject matter of philosophers. The *vita activa* is the practical side of the human condition, the living of the world through doing. *The Human Condition* is almost exclusively devoted to an analysis of the *vita activa*, and it is no coincidence that when Arendt translated the book for its publication in Germany she gave it the more apt title, *Vita activa: oder Vom tätigen Leben* ('Vita Activa or the Active Life').

Arendt divides the *vita activa* into three constituent activities, and the purpose of this chapter is to elucidate these terminological distinctions. The three activities are labour, work and action. They form an ontological hierarchy, in the sense that the limitations of each require, if they are to be surmounted, a 'higher faculty' which is expressed, in the case of labour and work, in a superior form of activity. Work, in other words, offers a solution to the predicaments of labour, and action redeems us from the predicaments of work. If this pattern were continued then of course new levels of activity would accumulate *ad infinitum*, and it would not be possible to divide the *vita activa* into definitive activities, nor to defend their intrinsic importance. So it is unsurprising that Arendt completes her model with the claim that the problems specific to action are resolved 'internally', that is, by means of the faculty of action itself. As the highest form of activity available to men and women, it is action, Arendt claims, which gives meaning to the human condition and which vindicates the passing interval that is each individual life.

THE WORLDLESSNESS OF LABOUR

Arendt reserves the term 'labour' to describe activities that are dedicated to the reproduction of human life. Labour is the lowest form of human activity because it is determined by the necessity of sustaining oneself as an organic being, a necessity faced by all animals, not just the human one. Labour is that 'primordial violence with which man pits himself against necessity' (OR: 114), a kind of biological adaptation to the violence of nature itself. Although labour may produce objects, these are always perishable things; they are produced for consumption, not use, and can never liberate the human being from the necessity of labouring, but only temporarily postpone the insurmountable demands of biological life. Like the nature to which it is bound, labour is thus inherently cyclical and repetitive. Also like nature, labour possesses an inherent fecundity; it can *overproduce* the necessities of life. This surplus, as Arendt believes was demonstrated by Marx's political economy, is what allows ruling groups to exempt themselves from the burden of labour. But since these ruling groups may do little more with their dividend of time than consume the products of others, the fertility of labour, its capacity to yield a surplus, cannot alone raise people above the exigencies of their animal existence.

The lowly status of labour reflects what Arendt calls its 'worldlessness', the meaning of which derives from its opposite, 'worldliness'. It might be tempting, albeit misleadingly so, to draw an analogy between Arendt's concept of worldliness and Weber's description of the *innerweltliche* ('inner worldly') asceticism of the Calvinist. After all, Weber contrasted the 'otherworldly' (*ausser-weltliche*) asceticism of the Catholic monk, for whom 'the holiest task was definitely to surpass all worldly morality', with the puritan who, driven by 'the necessity of proving one's faith in worldly activity', 'substituted for the spiritual aristocracy of monks outside of and above the world the spiritual aristocracy of the predestined saints of God within the world' (1958: 121). But Arendt's use of the term actually harks back to the ancient Greeks, whose determination to defy human mortality by leaving a permanent mark on the world was overturned by the Christian belief in the immortality of the soul. Like Richard Sennett, who viewed the 'worldly asceticism' recorded by Weber as a precursor to the contemporary psychiatric phenomenon of narcissism (1977: 333–6), Arendt actually finds in Weber's study of the Protestant ethic proof that a world*less* care for the purity of the self lay at the origin of our modern, supposedly 'materialistic' culture.

> The greatness of Max Weber's discovery about the origins of capitalism lay precisely in his demonstration that an enormous, strictly mundane activity is possible without any care for or enjoyment of the world whatever, an activity whose deepest motivation, on the contrary, is worry and care about the self. World-alienation, and not self-alienation as Marx thought, has been the hallmark of the modern age. (HC: 254)

The idea that care for or fascination with the self, or 'self-interest' as she sometimes refers to it, suffers a potentially fatal loss of the 'world', is an important theme for Arendt that we shall return to in a moment. The 'worldliness' which is forfeited through preoccupation with the self is the property attributed to things which endure and 'stand still' long enough to be experienced, in different aspects from the perspectives of different people, as a common reality worthy of care and preservation. Arendt sometimes uses the term 'world' synonymously with 'reality', in the sense that the world human beings share is neither imprisoned within, nor indifferently external to, individuals, but is rather that which lies *between* them and which becomes real to them – that is, becomes a shared object instead of a private sense impression – when they talk *about* it and show it their concern (or *caritas*, in the language of St Augustine). Our 'perceptual faith' in the independent existence of objects thus 'depends entirely on the object's also appearing as such to others and being acknowledged by them' (LM1: 46).

'Worldlessness', on the other hand, refers to our estrangement, or retreat, from the objects, customs, laws and institutions which humans produce in their effort to inhabit a common world more lasting than their biological selves. The loss of the world – 'the withering away of everything *between* us' (PP: 201) – may be a consequence of social turbulence, when movement and process undermine permanence and durability so that a subjective inwardness, an interest in the self and its physical or moral survival, takes precedence over care for the common world. Some sociologists influenced by Émile Durkheim have spoken in very similar terms about the way that affluent societies have replaced stable collective representations of social life – such as public buildings, churches and monuments – with disposable tools and commodities whose owners and users are destined to outlast them. 'For the first time in the history of man on this planet', Magda and John McHale observed in 1975, 'we began to make men who lasted longer than things' (cited in Simon and Gagnon 1976: 365). 'Pace Durkheim,' Zygmunt Bauman writes in his account of our contemporary 'liquid' modernity, 'it is now each of us, individually, that is the "longest living" of all the bonds and institutions we have met; and the only entity whose life-expectation is steadily rising rather than shrinking' (2001: 21). It is this focus on life and the self, as opposed to a lasting world, which for Arendt is symptomatic of our degraded civilisation. Worldlessness, or 'world alienation', is in Arendt's view 'always a form of barbarism' (MD: 13).

Labour is worldless, then, partly because it produces no lasting memorials to the labourer, and partly because its origin lies in an experience of bodily irritation which is essentially privative – so much so, in fact, that it may be *word*less as well as worldless, being resistant to public expression and objectification in a shared language. If the reason for labour is physical discomfort, from which labour, often painful in itself, can produce only a temporary respite, then labour is a worldless experience, Arendt argues, because pain *sensitises us to our bodies* rather than to the worldly objects we encounter. 'The pain caused by a sword or the tickling caused by a feather indeed tells me nothing whatsoever of the quality or even the worldly existence of a sword or a feather' (HC: 114). Hence if labour typically depends on the 'proximity senses' of touch, taste and smell, this is because hearing and, in Arendt's view, especially sight, are more 'world-giving' – they refer us to independent objects rather than merely bodily sensations.

Pain may be so worldless, in fact, that by depriving us of a worldly reference point it also allows us to 'forget it more quickly and easily than anything else' (HC: 51). Arendt's account of the worldless character of physical sensations, as well as of the essentially somatic passions and emotions of the 'soul', is to some extent a challenge to the old metaphysical dualism between Being and Appearance, in which that which appears is regarded as superficial or derivative, while the essential truth of things lies beneath the surface that serves and conceals it. This perspective, which is complemented by the functionalist and evolutionary view that outward behaviours and displays are merely vehicles for the performance of essential inner functions, such as societal or genetic reproduction, is reversed in Arendt's phenomenology, so that the function of what doesn't appear is to make possible the sustaining of appearances. Interestingly, this perspective resonates strongly with the way public and private dimensions of life were, according to Richard Sennett's historical analysis, constructed and experienced in the major cities of eighteenth-century Europe, before modernity made the self the locus of freedom and value. There, the private world of the self was regarded as too 'natural' to permit individual distinctiveness, whereas the public world, by contrast, encouraged elaborately codified modes of self-expression and 'a rejection of the idea that behind the convention there lay an inner, hidden reality to which the convention referred and which was the "real" meaning' (Sennett 1977: 87).

As with Sennett's 'public man', Arendt emphasises how human beings, more so than any other species, live in the world of appearances, and how their appearances attain a worldly reality – 'Being' – not when they succeed in displaying an 'inner self', but when the way an individual chooses to present him or herself is sufficiently consistent over time to become a memorable public narrative. In Arendt's account the psychic world of the 'soul' is only a formless flux of sensations and feelings, a 'chartless darkness' of fleeting and shadowy motives which can be individualised as distinctive worldly objects only through neurotic repetition and psychic disorder. 'Emotions and "inner sensations" are "unworldly" in that they lack the chief worldly property of "standing still and remaining" at least long enough to be clearly perceived – and not merely sensed – to be intuited, identified, and acknowledged' (LM1: 40). Although the soul has its natural expressiveness – we may blush with embarrassment, tremor in fear, glow with happiness – these physical signs are natural extensions of our organic existence, and they share the ambiguity and formlessness of the passions. The inner domain of the soul – which for Arendt is part of the physical 'life process', having 'the same life-sustaining and preserving functions as our inner organs' (LM1: 35) – is no more meant to inhabit the world of appearances than the vital organs of a creature are meant to appear on its surface. Only when humans choose, in what is always also an act of concealment, what is fit to be seen – concealing fear, for example, by displaying courage – do they individuate themselves and, by persisting with that choice, give their conscious existence the worldly quality of what we call personality or character. This is why, for those who are keen to avoid the charge of hypocrisy, the solution is not to be faithful to a 'true' inner self but, as Socrates expressed it, to '*Be* as you wish to appear' – even when you are alone (LM1: 37).

So labour fulfils the necessities of human life and, precisely because of this necessity, it is the least human activity of the *vita activa*. For historical clarification of the ontological inferiority of labour, Arendt directs us to two sources. In Greek antiquity, labour was deemed so worldless an activity, so slavish in answering to the imperatives of life, that it merited no place in the public realm and was instead confined to the obscurity of the home, which was accordingly defined as a sphere of violence and tyranny, where the master of the household held nature in abeyance by dominating those who laboured on it. Arendt points out that labour was not treated with contempt in ancient society because it was performed by slaves; rather, slaves were made to labour because such tasks were slavish and because, contrary to the received wisdom that slavery was developed for economic reasons, the citizens of the city-states saw enslavement to necessity as the greatest threat to a truly human life. And what justified the contemptible fate of the people thus enslaved was the fact that, in accepting enslavement in place of death, the slaves displayed the very animal attachment to life which is characteristic of the *animal laborans*. They had proved their natural unfreedom by refusing, as the Greeks believed no free citizen would do, to risk their lives trying to escape (HC: 36).

The second source of evidence that labour has historically occupied an inferior position in the *vita activa* is the etymology of the word itself. Arendt notes that all the major European languages contain two different terms, each with its own etymological history, for an activity which today we tend to think of as a single practice. Thus, for 'labour' and 'work' we have *ponein* and *ergazesthai* (Greek), *laborare* and *facere* or *fabricari* (Latin), *travailler* and *ouvrer* (French), and *arbeiten* and *werken* (German). In each of these cases, Arendt points out, only the equivalents for 'labour' carry the negative meaning of toil and trouble that is made explicit in the adjective 'laborious', with the French word *travailler*, for example, deriving from a form of torture ('*tripalium*').

> All the European words for 'labour' ... signify pain and effort and are also used for the pangs of birth. *Labour* has the same etymological root as *labare* ('to stumble under a burden'); *ponos* and *Arbeit* have the same etymological roots as 'poverty' (*penia* in Greek and *Armut* in German). (HC: 48 n39)

This linguistic distinction is also telling in that only the equivalents for 'work' can be converted into a noun denoting the finished product of this activity. We refer, for example, to 'the work of our own hands', to a student's 'written work', to 'steelworks', to 'needlework' or 'woodwork'. The noun 'work' and its non-English equivalents are also used today to refer to pieces of art.

Because the condition of labour is organic nature, the ideal of the *animal laborans*, Arendt claims, is abundance. Being a direct expression of the fertility that is inherent in living things, the ideal of abundance affirms rather than transcends the natural cycles of growth, multiplication and decay which are characteristic of biological life (HC: 126). By contrast, the use of the term 'work' to refer to objects of production implies an activity which does indeed transcend the unending processes of organic life, since it comes to rest in the creation of a worldly thing.

WORK AND WORLD

The purpose of work is not the survival of life nor the multiplication of nature's own products, but rather the creation of an unnatural 'world'. Although Arendt does refer to worldliness as 'the capacity to fabricate and create a world' (PF: 209), worldliness requires more than mere fabrication, since it implies our attachment to, and care for, an environment of stable and lasting things. In this category of worldly things Arendt appears to include both material objects like buildings, tools and works of art, and the less tangible but not necessarily less durable forms of cultural, legal and political institutions, including the 'web' of human relationships and narratives that pre-exists every individual, sets the context for their activities, and shapes the way actors are understood, responded to and remembered. In this latter aspect, though she would have rejected this terminological construction as an oxymoron, Arendt's theory of worldliness shares elements of the phenomenological concept of the 'lifeworld' (Habermas 1994: 215).

The term 'lifeworld' would have been unsatisfactory for Arendt because she views the worldly environment as 'unnatural' in the sense that it constitutes an objective artifice erected between humans and nature, and between separate individuals themselves. The work which produces this artifice shares the violence of labour, but as work is the means by which 'man measures himself against the overwhelming forces of the elements' and, by his cunning, magnifies nature's products 'far beyond its natural measure', work testifies to humans' capacity for transcendence and is therefore 'the very opposite of the painful, exhausting effort experienced in sheer labour' (HC: 140). By virtue of its products, work rescues us from the worldlessness of labour by surrounding us with things 'whose very permanence stands in direct contrast to life', and which together constitute 'the condition under which this specifically human life can be at home on earth' (HC: 135, 134). This objectified, 'in-between' world of things protects us from the eternal flux of nature, gives us a separate sense of continuity and identity, and militates against the futility of life by surviving the passage of each generation.

The simple erection of a material home, as, for example, nomadic tribes are wont to do, is in Arendt's view an insufficient remedy for the worldlessness of labour. It is only when the things humans have created are preserved beyond the lifespan of those who use and inhabit them that the world truly comes into being. 'Only where such survival is assured do we speak of culture', Arendt claims (PF: 210).

The world that is produced through work also constitutes the material foundation for human sociality, communication, and ultimately politics. Work yields a common topography of things which 'gathers us together and yet prevents our falling over each other' (HC: 52). It was of course their inability to leave behind a permanent mark on the world which made slaves a cursed people in the eyes of the ancients, a sentiment Arendt contentiously extends to the 'savage' lives of primitive African tribes who 'live and die without leaving any trace, without having contributed anything to a common world' (OT: 300). And it is Arendt's view that secular modernity, in rejecting the Christian belief in eternal life, rightly saw in antiquity a precedent for preserving the human-made world. Hence 'the worldliness of men in any given age can best be measured by the extent to which preoccupation with the future of the world takes precedence in men's minds over preoccupation with their own ultimate destiny in the hereafter' (OR: 230).

Work, Arendt argues, fabricates objects according to the standards of either beauty or utility. Works of art, 'the most intensely worldly of all tangible things' (HC: 167), are not created to be 'used', and for this reason they are as protected from degradation by the demands of utility as they are from the corrosive forces of nature. It is precisely because they are not items of utility that works of art can achieve an 'outstanding permanence' that may outlast the lives of countless generations.

Nowhere else does the sheer durability of the world of things appear in such purity and clarity, nowhere else therefore does this thing-world reveal itself so spectacularly as the non-mortal home for mortal beings. It is as though worldly stability had become transparent in the permanence of art, so that a premonition of immortality, not the immortality of the soul or of life but of something immortal achieved by mortal hands, has become tangibly present, to shine and to be seen, to sound and to be heard, to speak and to be read. (HC: 168)

The ability to produce objects of beauty is thus the 'highest capacity' of *homo faber*. The value of this capacity becomes clearer when we compare it with the other standard which guides the activity of work, and to which modern civilisation has given much greater prominence: the standard of utility. Utilitarianism is, in Arendt's analysis, 'the philosophy of *homo faber* par excellence' (HC: 154). From the outlook of the worker, the value of everything is determined by its usefulness and suitability for the achievement of a desired end, with the end itself being subsequently valued only in so far as it is useful for the achievement of something else. The 'world-giving' faculties of the worker are therefore contradictory, for no worldly product can in principle be sheltered from the worker's search for disposable means. This is why people in utilitarian societies like our own may enjoy an extraordinary abundance of manufactured products whilst at the same time doubting the stability and longevity of their acquisitions. This is also why the ancient Greeks, renowned for their love of beautiful things, were simultaneously hostile to, if not contemptuous of, the artists and artisans who fabricated those things (HC: 155–6; PF: 215–7). Where the citizens of the *polis* were concerned, the instrumental mindset necessary even for the creation of aesthetic objects had no rightful place in the public world of actions and appearances, for 'the standards and rules which must necessarily prevail in erecting and building and decorating the world of things in which we move, lose their validity and become positively dangerous when they are applied to the finished world itself' (PF: 216).

The natural utilitarianism of the worker not only threatens a regression to the worldlessness of the labourer, but is also responsible for a crisis in meaning. Max Weber, who equated the process of rationalisation with the unstoppable growth of instrumental rationality (*Zweckrationalität*), the disenchantment of worldviews and the loss of ultimate values, prefigured Arendt's thoughts in this respect. Weber contrasted the peasant who, 'like Abraham, could die "satiated with life"', with 'civilised man', emancipated 'from the organically prescribed cycle of natural life', striving to accomplish what the interminable march of progress will always render obsolete. Hence 'culture's every step forward seems condemned to lead to an ever more devastating senselessness' (Weber 1970c: 356–7; 1970b: 139–40).

Arendt, like Weber, described the fate of modernity as a world 'left with nothing but an unending chain of purposes in whose progress the meaningfulness of all past achievements was constantly cancelled out' (PF: 78). Utilitarianism has conspired with this trend by treating meaning as if it were a goal that could be realised by productive activity. But meaning, Arendt points out, is a far more encompassing and elusive quality of human action than the particular ends that individuals pursue at any one time. The carpenter cuts the wood 'in order to' realise the goal of making a table; but carpentry, as a vocational choice, is pursued 'for the sake of' an ideal whose meaning demands to be honoured, not produced, chased after or acquired (PF: 79). Meaning, in this sense, derives from what Weber called the 'value-rational' character of human activity (1978: 25–6) – something which he implied had been so degraded by the 'mechanical foundations' of modern capitalism that economic activity in such a society no longer sought meaningful justification at all (1958: 181–3). The value in question may be the ideal of comfort that guides a society of labourers, Arendt suggests, or the ideal of acquisition that guides the commercial classes, or for that matter the ideal of 'usefulness' that prevails in a society of makers. In each case it is the ideal which justifies the ordering of choices, judgement and action by that society's members. The practical criteria of judgement and evaluation, in other words, exist 'for the sake of' that particular ideal.

In the world of *homo faber*, however, the instrumental principle of usefulness – the evaluative criterion of 'in order to' – swallows up the underlying ideal, so that it becomes altogether impossible to think in terms of 'for the sake of', and meaning degenerates into mere utility. Utilitarianism substitutes ideals, which transcend the actions they inspire, with 'ends', whose motivating force terminates with their accomplishment. Hence the guiding ideal of usefulness is reflexively transformed by the evaluative criterion of means and ends, or 'in order to', and is inevitably found wanting. For the 'use of use' – the end to which the philosophy of utilitarianism is the means – cannot be established by utilitarianism itself except by treating it as an object which, once acquired, loses all motivating force and dissolves into meaninglessness.

For an end, once it is attained, ceases to be an end and loses its capacity to guide and justify the choice of means, to organise and produce them. It has now become an object among objects, that is, it has been added to the huge arsenal of the given from which *homo faber* selects freely his means to pursue his ends. Meaning, on the contrary, must be permanent and lose nothing of its character, whether it is achieved or, rather, found by man or fails man and is missed by him. *Homo faber*, in so far as he is nothing but a fabricator and thinks in no terms but those of means and ends which arise directly out of his work activity, is just as incapable of understanding meaning as the *animal laborans* is incapable of understanding instrumentality. (HC: 154–5)

ACTION AND WORLD

Arendt writes in *The Human Condition* that work remedies the worldlessness of labour, and action remedies the meaninglessness of work. We have seen that this is not entirely accurate, however, as the products of *homo faber* cannot alone guarantee the stability of the world. This task must also fall on the shoulders of the actor. Arendt says there are two principal conditions for action. The first of these she calls 'natality', the second 'plurality'. It is worth bearing in mind at this point that these two concepts are not the most obvious of allies, and the tension between the two reflects a broader discrepancy in Arendt's thinking between the sometimes competing principles of freedom and worldliness.

Literally speaking, natality is the condition of being born, which Arendt lyrically describes as 'being a new beginning'. The faculty of action depends on the condition of natality because action is 'to begin something new', and only a being which *is* a new beginning is capable of making a new beginning; that is, freedom can only arise from something that is not the determinate product of a causal chain. Arendt stresses how humans have for millennia treated the arrival of every newcomer with reverent awe, and it may well be the case that the obscurity of each individual's pre-existence – an obscurity which, as Habermas (2003) has argued, is today jeopardised by the reach of modern reproductive technoscience – is essential to the survival of the very concept of human freedom.

Because action, like birth itself, is the start of something that did not exist before, it cannot be explained in causal terms; it is essentially spontaneous, unpredictable, and a surprise to the actor as well as the witnesses to the act. The essential autonomy of action is therefore not the same as 'freedom of choice', for the latter always implies rational selection from already-known alternatives (LM2: 32). 'The fact that man is capable of action means that the unexpected can be expected from him, that he is able to perform what is infinitely improbable' (HC: 178). This is why, to eyes adjusted to the regular patterns of natural processes, the automatic functioning of mechanical systems and the cast-iron certainty of statistical laws, action – 'the actualisation of the human condition of natality' – always looks like a miracle.

> In the language of natural science, it is the 'infinite improbability which occurs regularly.' Action is, in fact, the one miracle-working faculty of man, as Jesus of Nazareth, whose insights into this faculty can be compared in their originality and unprecedentedness with Socrates' insights into the possibilities of thought, must have known very well when he likened the power to forgive to the more general power of performing miracles, putting both on the same level and within reach of man.
>
> The miracle that saves the world, the realm of human affairs, from its normal, 'natural' ruin is ultimately the fact of natality, in which the faculty of action is ontologically rooted. It is, in other words, the birth of new men and the new beginning, the action they are capable of by virtue of being born ... It is this faith in and hope for the world that found perhaps its most glorious and most succinct expression in the few words with which the Gospels announced their 'glad tidings': 'A child has been born unto us.' (HC: 246–7)

The second condition of action, 'plurality', means being among others who are recognised as both equal and unique. Arendt regards plurality – 'the fact that men, not Man, live on the earth and inhabit the world' (HC: 7) – as a basic existential condition of human life whose significance the Romans understood when they defined death as '*inter hominess esse desinere*' – 'to cease to be among men' (LM1: 74). That plurality is part of the human condition is in Arendt's view demonstrated by the fact that when people are alone they are able, by entering into a mental dialogue with themselves, to keep themselves company. 'Nothing perhaps indicates more strongly that man exists *essentially* in the plural than that his solitude actualises his merely being conscious of himself, which we probably share with the higher animals, into a duality during the thinking activity' (LM1: 185).

Arendt's notion of plurality probably had its origins in Heidegger's concept of *Mitsein*, or 'being-with'. For Heidegger (1962), however, this was the fundamentally inauthentic, complacent and anonymous chatter of *das Man* (the *'They'*), whose inconspicuous grip could only be resisted by means of the philosopher's withdrawal into solitary thought. Arendt, by contrast, explicitly repudiated her former teacher's perpetuation of what she saw as 'the old hostility of the philosopher toward the *polis*', and his belief that the public sphere, inherently disposed to mediocrity and conformism, 'functions to hide true reality and prevent the appearance of truth' (EU: 432–3, 446 n5).

Plurality, for Arendt, is the hallmark of the political community, and if plurality is a condition of action then it is unsurprising that Arendt defines action as 'political activity par excellence' (HC: 9). Action is distinguished from labour because it is free rather than determined by necessity; and it is distinguished from work because, as Aristotle defined *praxis* as opposed to *poiēsis*, it is an end in itself rather than simply a movement or process towards an external end (*Ethics*: 1139a16–b18, 1174a3–b24). Action resolves the predicament of meaninglessness because it is the highest form of activity available to human beings: it 'cannot be considered a means in some other respect, because there is nothing higher to attain than this actuality itself' (HC: 207). Though the philosophers of antiquity, with their privileging of thinking over doing, failed to understand as much, Arendt asserts that what we learn from the *experience* of the Greek *polis* and the Roman *res publica*, as indicated in ancient literature and in the ancient use of language itself, is that action coincides with freedom, and this freedom is the highest articulation of the human condition.

It should be evident already that Arendt's definition of action is broad and not always precise or consistent, combining the spontaneous initiation of something new with the display of exemplary deeds, the exemplification of noble ideals, and the republican ideal of political exchange in the public sphere. The ambiguity in the meaning of action is perpetuated by her tendency to couple the term with 'speech'. Part of the reason for this seems to lie in the egalitarian force of language, which we always mobilise with the conviction both that others are equals capable of understanding us, and that each actor is unique enough to have to make an effort to be understood (HC: 175–6). Arendt describes speech as 'the actualisation of the human condition of plurality' (HC: 178), and, echoing Aristotle's distinction between 'voice' and 'speech'

(*The Politics*, 1253a7), she implies that failure to participate in speech communities incurs a loss of meaning. For while as private individuals we may know passions and sensations which are forceful and intense, these are always partly incommunicable, representing a 'truth beyond speech'. In contrast, speech, or what Habermas (1980, 1994), reinterpreting Arendt's theory, calls 'communicative action', brings into existence a common objective world which is accounted for and appropriated only when separate individuals are able to articulate and exchange their unique standpoints on it.

> If someone wants to see and experience the world as it 'really' is, he can do so only by understanding it as something that is shared by many people, lies between them, separates them and links them, showing itself differently to each and comprehensible only to the extent that many people can talk *about* it, over against one another. Only in the freedom of our speaking with one another does the world, as that about which we speak, emerge in its objectivity and visibility from all sides. (PP: 128)

When action is coupled with speech it immediately assumes an important relationship to worldliness, for communicative action now appears to be the means by which the world of things becomes tangible and real. On the one hand, the distinctiveness of unique individuals only appears when there is a common objective world – a stable structure of public institutions, spaces and things – which, as the table gathers together those who sit around it, 'relates and separates men at the same time'. On the other hand, the objectivity of the world appears only when it is talked about and shared, only when it is a *public* world 'distinguished from our privately owned place in it' (HC: 52). 'Only where things can be seen by many in a variety of aspects without changing their identity, so that those who are gathered around them know they see sameness in utter diversity, can worldly reality truly and reliably appear' (HC: 57).

We noted earlier how the creation even of the most worldly object – the work of art – always requires an instrumental outlook which, if allowed to rule without limit, puts in jeopardy 'the cultural realm itself'. The utilitarianism of the maker 'leads to a devaluation of things as things which, if the mentality that brought them into being is permitted to prevail, will again be judged according to the standard of utility and thereby lose their intrinsic, independent worth, and finally degenerate into mere means' (PF: 216). Worldliness, the 'taking care' of the world that is the hallmark of the 'cultivated' person, thus resides neither in the maker nor in the thing made, but in the 'space of appearances' where tastes are communicated and decisions about the common world are shared.

In *Love and Saint Augustine*, Arendt commented on the inherent tendency of the makers of things to lose control over their products, an estrangement that can only be remedied by a 'love of the world':

> It is not 'making' as such that ends the strangeness of the world and lets man belong to it, for making still leaves the essence of man outside his product. Rather, it is through love of the world that man explicitly makes himself at home in the world, and then desirously looks to it alone for his good and evil. Not until then do the world and man grow 'worldly'. (LA: 67)

In the case of cultural production, it is therefore the perception and articulation of beauty, not the creation, by the solitary artist, of beautiful things, which truly 'judges the world in its appearance and in its worldliness' (PF: 222). Drawing on Kant in an original and controversial way, Arendt came to argue that the judgement of beauty is in fact a 'political faculty' which belongs to the sphere of plurality, because through the exercise of this faculty we orient ourselves in a common public world, mediate and exchange different perspectives, and disclose ourselves to others. Just as political judgement is always a refusal to be 'coerced' by an incontestable truth, preferring instead that exchange of opinions which 'constitutes the very essence of political life' (PF: 241), so aesthetic judgement is a refusal to be bullied by an indiscriminate and immoderate love of what is self-evidently beautiful. Perhaps with the German intelligentsia in mind, whose commitment to *Bildung* during the 1930s was a feeble antidote to the perverse charms of Nazism, Arendt reminds us that beauty can be barbaric if it promotes 'immoderate love of the merely beautiful' and a tasteless indifference to the world of human affairs. 'Taste debarbarises the world of the beautiful by not being overwhelmed by it; it takes care of the beautiful in its own "personal" way and thus produces a "culture"' (PF: 224).

The same reasoning is apparent in Arendt's enthusiasm, prompted by personal experience, for jury service, which is one surviving legacy of the public decision-making process of the Athenian *polis*. Juries, she suggested, are 'the last remnant of active citizen participation in the republic', where 'different viewpoints' are exchanged on 'a matter of common public interest' (1979: 317).

Jurors are equalised by the task and the place ... They must deal with something which is of no private interest to them at all: they are interested in something in regard to which they are disinterested. What jurors share is an interest in the case – something outside themselves; what makes them common is something that is not subjective. (Arendt 1977: 105)

We can see from this analysis why Arendt's concept of 'world', conceived as a reality that thickens when different perspectives are articulated together, has been likened to a kind of philosophical 'cubism' (Disch 1997: 143), and why Arendt has been rediscovered by a new generation of post-modernist thinkers attracted to her apparent affinity with standpoint epistemology. As Arendt writes: 'the world comes into being only if there are perspectives; it exists as the order of worldly things only if it is viewed, now this way, now that, at any given time'. Worldliness and action complement each other because humans can endure the burden of their own transient existence by gathering in the 'space of appearances' – the public sphere – for 'the more peoples there are in the world who stand in some particular relationship with one another, the more world there is to form between them, and the larger and richer that world will be' (PP: 175–6).

When a person retreats from the public world, on the other hand, 'an almost demonstrable loss to the world takes place; what is lost is the specific and usually irreplaceable in-between which should have formed between this individual and his fellow men.' If the exchange of different views about the world were to completely disappear, 'the world, which can form only in the interspaces between men in all their variety, would vanish altogether' (MD: 4–5, 31). As we shall see in the next chapter, Arendt believed that such a condition of worldlessness is a characteristic symptom of our modern alienation. With an argument that has important implications for our modern culture of self-disclosure, as well as for the growth of the personal service economy and what sociologists call 'emotional labour', Arendt maintains that this alienation cannot be remedied by the romantic belief that we can reveal ourselves truthfully only through heartfelt expressions of intimacy – by talking about ourselves, rather than about a common world. This is why she praised Lessing for the 'vigilant partiality' with which he sought to stimulate debate about the world, rejecting the brotherliness of mutual belonging and concerning himself 'solely with humanising the world by incessant and continual discourse about its affairs and the things in it. He wanted to be the friend of many men, but no man's brother.' He understood with the Greeks that 'friendship is not intimately personal but makes political demands and preserves reference to the world' (MD: 29–30, 25).

Friendship must be distinguished from love as well as from brotherliness. Although Arendt recognised that sexual love possesses 'an unequalled power of self-revelation', it too can only be sustained by withdrawal from the world.

> Love, by reason of its passion, destroys the in-between which relates us to and separates us from others. As long as its spell lasts, the only in-between which can insert itself between two lovers is the child, love's own product ... Through the child, it is as though the lovers return to the world from which their love had expelled them ... Love, by its very nature, is unworldly. (HC: 242)

Arendt also sees worldlessness as a common experience of pariah peoples who have been denied a true public realm, and its intimate connection with the history and culture of the Jews, as Weber's sociological studies of religion bear out, indicates that worldlessness is not an exclusively modern phenomenon. Although Arendt believed Weber was wrong to view Puritanism as a genuinely worldly religion, she shared his view of the Jew as someone who, by contrast, 'could not think of methodically controlling the present world, which was so topsy-turvy because of Israel's sins, and which could not be set right by any human action but only by some free miracle of God that could not be hastened' (Weber 1978: 620–1). For Arendt, the history of the Jews illustrates how the oppressed and the persecuted often seek, as a 'substitute for that light and illumination which only the public realm can cast', the feeling of brotherhood which derives partly from the 'privilege of being unburdened by care for the world', and which typically arises between people whose experiences and perspectives are sufficiently similar to make conflict and dispute a rare occurrence. 'In this as it were organically evolved humanity it is as if under the pressure of persecution the persecuted have moved so closely together that the interspace which we have called world ... has simply disappeared' (MD: 13–4).

This loss of the worldly interspace is, moreover, to some extent a normal attribute of modern societies. It exists in the formation of what Arendt calls the 'social' realm, where individuals routinely suppress their personal differences and the space that separates them in favour of group identity and collective discrimination against outsiders (RJ: 205). At the other extreme to social conformism is self-centred individualism, the seemingly irresistible force of which leads the typical rational choice theorist to argue that the common good can be promoted by appealing to people's 'enlightened self-interest'. This strategy is doomed to failure, Arendt argues, because the latter is a clear oxymoron (*inter est* means precisely that which 'is between', not that which lies within, separate individuals). 'Self-interest is interested in the self', she asserts, and 'because of its changing condition, that is, ultimately because of the human condition of mortality, the self *qua* self cannot reckon in terms of long-range interests, i.e. the interest of a world that survives its inhabitants' (OV: 78).

ACTION AND SPEECH: UNPICKING THE TENSION

From the very beginning of Greek history, Arendt writes in *The Human Condition*, 'speech and action were considered to be coeval and coequal, of the same rank and the same kind' (HC: 26). In the Greece of Homer, 'a doer of great deeds must at the same time always be a speaker of great words', and the propitious use of words was an event that could match the blows of fate or divinity, ensuring that 'our downfall can become a deed if we hurl words against it even as we perish' (PP: 125). This understanding of speech, as the necessary adjunct to the heroic deeds of the Homeric adventurer, as a way of 'talking back and measuring up to whatever happened or was done', changed with the emergence of the *polis* (HC: 26). As the democratic city-state develops, as 'dealing with others in the public space of the agora ... becomes the real substance of a free life', so 'the most important activity of a free life moves from action to speech, from free deeds to free words' (PP: 124). Though the renowned athletic competitions preserved a recognisable place for demonstrations of non-violent strength and physical prowess, it was the exchange of opinions among engaged citizens which eventually took prominence in the life of the city.

This development was, in Arendt's view, an expression and revival of the spirit of impartiality bequeathed by Homer. Homer's account of the Trojan War famously celebrated the actions of both the victors and the vanquished, seeing the war through the eyes of both sides. It was through verbal argumentation, Arendt believes, that the Greek citizens acquired the same ability to free themselves from limited interests and see the world in its many perspectives. 'Greeks learned to *understand* – not to understand one another as individual persons, but to look upon the same world from one another's standpoint, to see the same in very different and frequently opposing aspects' (PF: 51). Freedom of speech in the presence of others thus became the purest 'political' form of human action, contrasting with the sheer spontaneity of the heroic deed to which Arendt ascribes a 'prepolitical' character owing to its independence from the world of others (PP: 163–7, 127–8).

From this it is clear why Arendt sees the Athenian *polis* as providing the best historical model of a public space for free action of the political, communicative kind. This space was the *agora*,[1] and its function, she suggests, was twofold. First, its aim was to maximise the opportunities for individuals to excel and distinguish themselves in the eyes of their equals, 'to make the extraordinary an ordinary occurrence of everyday life' (HC: 197). Second, it served to give to action a chance of immortality, for action and speech, since they do not aim at the creation of finished objects, ironically possess the same characteristics of transience and futility that are definitive of labour. Prior to the founding of the *polis*, it was the task of the fabricator to ensure the remembrance of intangible actions and words.

> If the *animal laborans* needs the help of *homo faber* to ease his labour and remove his pain, and if mortals need his help to erect a home on earth, acting and speaking men need the help of *homo faber* in his highest capacity, that is, the help of the artist, of poets and historiographers, of monument-builders or writers, because without them the only product of their activity, the story they enact and tell, would not survive at all. (HC: 173)

But depending on the presence of the poet to immortalise human greatness was a fragile and uncertain arrangement that offered the inhabitants of the ancient world no reliable guarantee against forgetfulness. Arendt believes that the origins of the *polis* can be understood as a response to this predicament, as an attempt to render permanent the 'space of action' that until that point had made only a fleeting appearance through the deeds and sufferings of heroes and warriors. Guaranteeing a public audience for its citizens, the *polis* allowed for 'a kind of organised remembrance' by which 'the most futile of human activities, action and speech, and the least tangible and most ephemeral of man-made "products", the deeds and stories which are their outcome, would become imperishable' (HC: 197–8).

Though Arendt provides a historical picture that charts the origins of a change in the definition of action, readers of her work can be forgiven for wondering which concept really had her blessing. Maurizio d'Entrèves has argued that there is an 'expressive' and a 'communicative' model of action in Arendt's thinking, suggesting that the former was most prominent in her early writings, whereas after the publication of *The Human Condition*, and perhaps encouraged by the Hungarian Revolution of 1956, it was the latter concept to which she gave most attention (d'Entrèves 1994: 84). The competition between both conceptions is neatly captured in a passage from 'Introduction into Politics', an unpublished essay written by Arendt in German in the late 1950s and finally translated and published in *The Promise of Politics* (2005). Here Arendt writes of political freedom 'as the freedom to depart and begin something new and unheard-of *or* as the freedom to interact in speech with many others and experience the diversity that the world always is in its totality' (PP: 129, my emphasis).

When considered in isolation, the expressive concept supports an 'agonal' (or 'agonistic') theory of politics which is closely aligned to the Homeric, and perhaps elitist, ideal of individuals disclosing and realising themselves through great and glorious deeds, indifferent to their moral or social consequences. When Arendt defines action as the spontaneous initiation of something rare and extraordinary, and when she stresses the strong affinity between politics and the performing arts – 'where the accomplishment lies in the performance itself and not in an end product', and where virtuosity and excellence reign (PF: 153) – then it is this 'expressive' or 'performative' model of action that she is emphasising.

The communicative model, on the other hand, gives prominence to the exchange of perspectives, the pursuit of solidarity through collective deliberation, agreement and promise-making, and the sustaining of worldliness through the telling and re-telling of stories. Arendt's praise for Socrates – who tried, through public dialogue, 'to make friends out of Athens' citizenry', when they were otherwise engaged in 'an intense and uninterrupted contest of all against all' – illustrates this second conception of action.

In this agonal spirit, which eventually was to bring Greek city-states to ruin because it made alliances between them well-nigh impossible and poisoned the domestic life of the citizens with envy and mutual hatred (envy was the national vice of ancient Greece), the commonweal was constantly threatened.

Because the commonness of the political world was constituted only by the walls of the city and the boundary of its laws, it was not seen or experienced in the relationships between the citizens, not in the world which lay *between* them, common to them all, even though opening up in a different way to each man ... Socrates seemed to have believed that the political function of the philosopher was to help establish this common world, built on the understanding of friendship, in which no rulership is needed. (PP: 16–18)

This more democratic, 'associational' conception of action, has a stronger normative component, as indicated by the moral ideal of 'friendship'. The normative content of action is also apparent in Arendt's frequent observation that action, although it is its own *principium* or source, is inspired by universal public 'principles' which become apparent only so long as the action lasts. 'Such principles are honour or glory, love of equality, which Montesquieu called virtue, or distinction or excellence ... but also fear or distrust or hatred' (PF: 152). These principles lend to action a degree of coherence and orderliness, thus appearing to mitigate the moral arbitrariness and unpredictability implied in the expressive conception of action, tempering Arendt's existential philosophy of freedom with a more conservative commitment to the preservation of humans' worldly accomplishments.

THE PREDICAMENTS OF ACTION

It is important to note at this point that Arendt's theory of action, even when restricted to the expressive model, is not an unqualified glorification of human freedom. Arendt is aware that action may set loose processes which, in their irresistibility and forcefulness, bear an uncanny resemblance to the imperatives of nature that rule the life of the *animal laborans*. This is why action, if it is not to jeopardise human worldliness, requires certain moral restraints which are intrinsic to the faculty itself.

The first, and 'perhaps the most fundamental', of the predicaments of action, is what Arendt calls its 'boundlessness', a quality that is inherent in 'all affairs that go on between men directly, without the intermediary, stabilising, and solidifying influence of things' (HC: 182). Again somewhat ambiguously, Arendt points out that the content of most action and speech *refers to* an in-between objective reality that constitutes a common world and engenders common worldly interests, but she stresses how this objective in-between is overlaid by a more inter-subjective in-between which she describes as the 'web' of person-to-person relationships formed, and continually re-formed, when people disclose themselves and communicate directly to one another (HC: 183–4). This intangible web of sedimented interactions, stories and accounts, pre-exists individual action, and it is the ongoing plurality of this web, 'with its innumerable, conflicting wills and intentions', which makes the person who acts both the agent of something new and the inevitable sufferer of unintended consequences and interpretations. 'These consequences are boundless, because action, though it may proceed from nowhere, so to speak, acts into a medium where every reaction becomes a chain reaction and where every process is the cause of new processes' (HC: 190). Action, no matter how generous its intentions, always interrupts and disturbs the expectations and intentions of others, setting off new initiatives, new interpretations, and new courses of action that could never have been anticipated. This is why one can never identify the unequivocal authors or producers of history, for the 'infinitude of intersecting and interfering intentions and purposes ... into which each man must cast his act', means that 'no end and no intention has been achieved as it was originally intended' (MD: 147–8). All that one can hope to find are the agents who 'set the whole process into motion' (HC: 185).

It is because action is ultimately boundless, because history 'is made by men who never know what they are doing' (PP: 57), that action is menaced by the predicament of 'irreversibility' – by the inability to undo, to stop and reverse, what one has done. For this reason, 'moderation' is one of the oldest and most important political virtues, counterbalancing the fact, as Arendt points out, that 'the political temptation par excellence is indeed *hubris*' (HC: 191). Where action lacks the moderating boundaries of laws, institutions, principles and agreements, a uniquely moral form of action becomes critical to the preservation of freedom. Redemption from the predicament of irreversibility then depends on the faculty of *forgiving*, which 'serves to undo the deeds of the past, whose "sins" hang like Damocles' sword over every new generation' (HC: 237). An understanding of the importance of forgiveness is implicit in the Roman principle of *parcere subjectis* (sparing the vanquished), in the modern constitutional right of Western heads of state to commute the death sentence, and in forms of public inquiry, like the Truth and Reconciliation Commission in post-Apartheid South Africa, which may offer amnesty to criminals who are willing to make full public disclosure of their crimes. But, for Arendt, it is above all in the teachings of Jesus of Nazareth that forgiving became a moral prerogative not merely of the divine or the powerful but of human action itself (PP: 57). In the absence of forgiveness, Jesus seemed to understand, we would be so bound to and conditioned by what we had done that our very capacity to begin something new – our capacity to act – would fall victim to its own power.

Arendt explains the superior status of forgiveness, as itself a supreme quality of action, by contrasting it with vengeance. Vengeance is not action so much as passive *re*action. It doesn't break the boundless chain of consequences but simply perpetuates an often predictable course of events. Forgiving, on the other hand,

> is the only reaction which does not merely re-act but acts anew and unexpectedly, unconditioned by the act which provoked it and therefore freeing from its consequences both the one who forgives and the one who is forgiven. The freedom contained in Jesus' teachings of forgiveness is the freedom from vengeance, which encloses both doer and sufferer in the relentless automatism of the action process, which by itself need never come to an end. (HC: 241)

Forgiveness expresses the original character of action both through its unexpectedness and through its revelatory quality. The object of forgiveness is the 'who' of the forgiven, and love, which is most willing to overlook the worldly 'what' of a person's actions and achievements, is clearly the most powerful form of this. Yet love is a private emotion, and in the domain of public affairs it is not love but rather 'respect' which Arendt believes sustains the redemptive role of forgiveness. Arendt describes respect as 'friendship without intimacy': 'it is a regard for the person from the distance which the space of the world puts between us, and this regard is independent of qualities which we may admire or of achievements which we may highly esteem' (HC: 243).

The second major predicament of action is its unpredictability. Again this derives partly from the condition of plurality, which makes it impossible for actors to foretell and master the consequences of what they have initiated, consequences that may 'quite literally endure throughout time until mankind itself has come to an end' (HC: 233). But unpredictability is also inherent in the act of initiation, which is free because it is spontaneous. Try as we might to find an antecedent cause for action – motives, decisions or desires which could be manipulated to produce different effects – our freedom is ultimately protected by the 'darkness of the human heart', and by the fact that any tangible essence of a person is always transcended by the unique 'who' that 'shows itself in the flux of action and speech', but which cannot be satisfactorily made the object of factual knowledge and conceptual categorisation (HC: 181). It is this fundamental obscurity – of the actor to herself as well as to others, for 'no acting person ever knows what he is doing' (MD: 148) – which ensures that the 'basic unreliability of men' is also the condition of their freedom.

The irony is that it is the boundless, incomplete nature of action which gives it its exceptional strength and its capacity to survive the lifespan of individuals. Yet its unpredictable, fragile and potentially chaotic character is also a source of anxiety, and often an excuse for moral nihilism or indifference. This is why, Arendt argues, civilisations have always been tempted to replace acting with making, that is, to handle people in the realm of public affairs in the same way that *homo faber* disposes of things. This temptation has never been greater than in today's technoscientific world, where the startling achievements of technological fabrication have normalised talk 'about "making the future" and "building and improving society" as though one were talking about making chairs and building and improving houses' (PP: 58). Arendt reminds us that this promethean attitude not only endangers the integrity of political action, but also suppresses our ecological appreciation of nature's independence: 'it can result, and has often enough, in the misrepresentation of all naturally given things as mere material for the human artifice – as though trees were nothing but potential wood, material for tables' (EU: 283).

MAKING AND DOING: SOVEREIGNTY AND FREEDOM

One of the oldest versions of this substitution of making for acting, according to Arendt, is apparent in the separation of the concepts of 'beginning' and 'achieving' (*archein* and *prattein*) in Plato's *Statesman*, which seems to be the first appearance of the division between conception and execution in Western political thought (HC: 222–3; PP: 91, 126). Plato, whose distrust of the *polis* is well known, introduced this division into what was previously considered to be a single act composed of two stages, in order to make the initiator of action the undisputed master of its consequences, essentially by reducing other people to the executors of the master's decisions. Since the master, the 'philosopher-king', was to be exempt from worldly action, while those who acted would be denied the opportunity to start something new, in Plato the original twofold sense of action as both beginning and accomplishing was abandoned, and with it 'the most elementary and authentic understanding of human freedom disappeared from political philosophy' (HC: 225).[2] Politics became a regrettable *means*, originating in the pre-political, ultimately biological need for humans to live together and ensure the competent administration and efficient provision of life's necessities, while its *end* was the post-political freedom of philosophical contemplation (PP: 82–3).

Plato thus modelled his proposals for the administration of public affairs on the well-ordered tyranny of the ancient household. By extending the relationship between master and slave from the household to the public sphere he was, if we are consistent with Greek understanding, precluding the very existence of action itself. But Plato's distinction between the rulers and the ruled remained consistent with the philosopher's belief in the superiority of thinking over doing, as well as the craftworker's characteristic experience of perceiving the image of the product-to-be on the one hand, and creating the image in material reality on the other. Both Plato and Aristotle saw legislation and voting as more important than speech and action because the former yielded a tangible result that protected men from the unpredictability of action and the frailty of human affairs (HC: 195).

From Plato onwards, Arendt suggests, the Western understanding of political communities has been menaced by a deep suspicion of the uncertainties of action and by an accompanying desire to substitute making for acting, *poiēsis* for *praxis*, by dividing that community into rulers and ruled. Almost inevitably this has resulted in the steady encroachment of violence into political affairs. Violence, Arendt points out, has always been an intrinsic component of the fabrication process, but in the pre-modern world this violence was limited and circumscribed by the same logic that justified it – political violence, like the *vita activa* as a whole, was the subordinate *means* by which the *vita contemplativa*, the life of thinking and the life of prayer, was secured. As contemplation lost its privileged status, however, the modern age has left us with the conviction that one can know and understand only what one makes, that *homo faber* takes precedence over the *animal rationale*, and that the violent manipulation of the human world is itself the revelation of the world's inner truth.

This has been particularly striking in the series of revolutions, characteristic of the modern age, all of which – with the exception of the American Revolution – show the same combination of the old Roman enthusiasm for the foundation of a new body politic with the glorification of violence as the only means for 'making' it. Marx's dictum that 'violence is the midwife of every old society pregnant with a new one,' that is, of all change in history and politics, only sums up the conviction of the whole modern age and draws the consequences of its innermost belief that history is 'made' by men as nature is 'made' by God. (HC: 228)

Arendt argues that the flight from action in modern political philosophy is also evident in the replacement of the idea of public freedom – which, as we have seen, must coexist with the inability to control or foretell the consequences of what we do – with the concept of individual sovereignty. Sovereignty – 'the ideal of uncompromising self-sufficiency and mastership' – is modelled on the solitude of craftworker, at home with his ideas, materials and tools, and is therefore 'contradictory to the very condition of plurality' (HC: 234). Accepting the principle of sovereignty as a replacement for that of free action can in Arendt's view only result in either the arbitrary domination of a people or else their stoical withdrawal from the sphere of public life.

The concept of sovereignty is dangerous because it reduces the notion of freedom to a purely mental disposition, to what we tend to think of as 'freedom of choice' or 'free will'. In doing so it destroys the republican association of freedom with public acting and performing and, since sovereign action is independent of the presence of others, it dissociates freedom from plurality, from its embeddedness in a community of fellow actors. In presupposing the separation of freedom and politics – 'in holding that freedom begins where men have left the realm of political life inhabited by the many' – the ideal of sovereignty has, Arendt argues, concealed the true character of freedom. In institutional terms, this has meant substituting for public action and speech a political system in which the representatives of private interests bargain in public in order to maximise the consumer satisfactions of their sovereign members. 'If men wish to be free', Arendt argues against this trend, 'it is precisely sovereignty they must renounce' (PF: 157, 165).

For Arendt, then, uncertainty and loss of sovereignty are the price we must pay 'for plurality and reality, for the joy of inhabiting together with others a world whose reality is guaranteed for each by the presence of all' (HC: 244). This price can be reduced, however, by a second faculty inherent in action, which we already encountered, implicitly at least, in Arendt's argument that we avoid hypocrisy by honouring the person we choose to be. This is the pledging and keeping of promises. Whereas the faculty of forgiving has largely been excluded from the realm of public affairs, being deemed fanciful or inappropriate due to its origins in religion and in love, the importance of promise-making is well recognised in the history of Western thought and civilisation, and Arendt suggests that, 'in the realm of politics', it 'may well be the highest human faculty' of all (OR: 175).

Promising shares with forgiving its communicative character and its dependence on the condition of plurality, 'for no one can forgive himself and no one can feel bound by a promise made only to himself' (HC: 237). The purpose of promise-making is to establish, and where necessary to codify in the form of treaties, contracts, and legal statutes, limitations on action which protect the public space from endangering its own existence. The aim is thus to utilise that 'old virtue of moderation' – 'one of the political virtues par excellence' – in order 'to set up in the ocean of uncertainty, which the future is by definition, islands of security without which not even continuity, let alone durability of any kind, would be possible in the relationships between men' (HC: 191, 237). These 'islands of predictability' and 'guideposts of reliability' can only offer guidance and respite, however, otherwise action will be suppressed by the attempt to dominate and control the future, and promises will 'lose their binding power' which arises from the interaction of separate individuals (HC: 244).

It is here, where people gather together and act in concert, that Arendt claims that public freedom and worldliness may be reconciled, and the 'grammar of action' combined with the 'syntax of power'. For when people unify and bind their actions through mutual promise-making – pledges which cannot be explained as habitual conformity to customary standards of behaviour, but which 'are like control mechanisms built into the very faculty to start new and unending processes' (HC: 246) – they acquire a 'limited independence from the incalculability of the future' and begin to constitute a worldly home, a stabilising foundation, for the power of combined action. It is in this sense that Arendt recognises 'an element of the world-building capacity of man in the human faculty of making and keeping promises' (OR: 175). Laws, treaties, constitutions and alliances are all examples of humans' promise-making abilities, providing a stabilising context for the unpredictability of plurality and freedom (PF: 164).

A clear example given by Arendt of humans' capacity to make and keep promises is the 'Mayflower Compact', the document drawn up and signed by 41 of the 102 passengers on the *Mayflower*, as it landed in what is now Massachusetts in November 1620. Fearful of the uncharted wilderness that awaited them, and of the boundless hopes and private fantasies that excited the imaginations of every passenger, the 41 signatories displayed remarkable confidence in their self-appointed power to 'covenant and combine ourselves together into a civil Body Politick, for our better Ordering and Preservation ... And by virtue hereof to enact, constitute, and frame, such just and equal Laws, Ordinances, Acts, Constitutions and Offices, from time to time, as shall be thought most meet and convenient for the General good of the Colony'. This was the first of many covenants made by the inhabitants of the colonies, the most historic of which was the Constitution of the United States. Like the Pilgrim Fathers, and unlike the Rousseau-inspired French revolutionaries who believed that humans are naturally good but corrupted by an unnatural society, the founders of the Constitution could retain the Puritan's suspicion of the darkness of the human heart 'because they knew that whatever men might be in their singularity, they could bind themselves into a community which, even though it was composed of "sinners", need not necessarily reflect this "sinful" side of human nature' (OR: 174). Puritan individualism was thus no obstacle to the capacity to act in concert, and no high-minded belief in the essential goodness or perfectibility of human nature was necessary for the optimism of the Founding Fathers. 'The hope for man in his singularity lay in the fact that not man but men inhabit the earth and form a world between them. It is human worldliness that will save men from the pitfalls of human nature' (OR: 175).

2
Critique of Modernity

We live in a world whose main feature is change, a world in which change itself has become a matter of course to such an extent that we are in danger of forgetting that which has changed altogether. (Arendt 2002: 282)

THE RISE OF THE SOCIAL

What has changed that we are in danger of forgetting? In *The Human Condition* Arendt's diagnosis of the crisis of modernity focuses on what she regards as a calamitous inversion of the rightful hierarchy of human activities, where the highest element of the *vita activa* has been progressively marginalised and devalued. This process is accompanied by what Arendt calls the rise of 'the social'. Although this term, normally appearing as an adjective or as the noun 'society', is familiar to us both as a colloquial commonplace and as the founding idea of the modern discipline of sociology, Arendt points out that it was absent from Greek language and thought. The ancient Greeks distinguished between the household and the public sphere, but they had no conception of a communal world devoted to the fulfilment of either collective or private needs, such as the administration of life or the reproduction of culture. Life beyond the economic functions of the family was political life (*bios politikos*), and because government and citizen are the same thing in the democratic city-state, 'it cannot be expected', Alvin Gouldner writes in his sociological study of the Greek *polis*, 'that clear distinctions will be made between the polity and the society or between the political and the social aspects of the community' (1967: 136). It is because she wants us to sample the strangeness of the modern age as it would have appeared to the free citizens of Greek antiquity, that Arendt deliberately uses the adjective 'social' as a noun, an awkward formulation aimed at de-familiarising what we assume to be a timeless facet of human existence.

So what is 'the social' in Arendt's account? Sociologists are trained to see the social as the intellectual antidote to myopic individualism. They look to place individual behaviour in its proper 'social context' in order to understand the collective forces and established patterns of orientation which are both the lauded foundation of human civilisation and the only plausible target of behaviour-changing interventions in society. For Arendt, however, the highest expression of human association is not the dutiful reproduction of social membership but rather acting with others in new and revelatory ways. The social is a threat to action, according to Arendt, because it constitutes a blurring of the original boundary between the private and the public, between the household and the realm of political affairs, and with it the distinction between nature and world, necessity and freedom. This boundary started to dissolve, she argues, when private interests and the struggle with the imperatives of life, previously confined to the domestic sphere, began to spread into the light of the political community, tainting the latter with the worldless forces of nature and the organic-like processes of reproduction and growth. Arendt says that one distinguishing feature of the social is that it demands 'behaviour' rather than 'action', and she includes in the category of social behaviour both economic and status-oriented conduct.

The first form of the social, she writes, was 'an organisation of property-owners who, instead of claiming access to the public realm because of their wealth, demanded protection from it for the accumulation of more wealth' (HC: 68). The displacement of the public sphere by the market, which accelerated with a vengeance in nineteenth-century Europe, is significant to Arendt because it involved the supplanting of durable public structures with the quasi-biological permanence of a *process*, as fungible wealth disguised its inherently evanescent character by transforming itself into constantly expanding capital. If the purpose of public life is to sustain a common world more lasting than its mortal inhabitants, then the rise of capitalism met this need in the alienated form of process or movement. 'Only when wealth became capital, whose chief function was to generate more capital, did private property equal or come close to the permanence inherent in the commonly shared world. However, this permanence is of a different nature; it is the permanence of a process rather than the permanence of a stable structure' (HC: 68–9).

Another historical form of 'the social' appears, in Arendt's thinking, in the guise of the 'good society' of the salons, which were prominent in France in the seventeenth and eighteenth centuries (though Rahel Varnhagen's later salon in Berlin [see RV; EU: 57–65] was probably the one Arendt was most knowledgeable about), and which probably had their origin in the court societies of Elizabeth I and Louis XIV. In these royal courts, the nobility were obliged to compete for the patronage of their Queen or King, to charm with their use of etiquette and to impress through the display of extravagance and novelty, the spreading of rumours and intrigues, and the strategic and often excitable manipulation of interests, favours, opinions and secrets. The bourgeois classes who later gravitated to the salons, where fashionable writers, thinkers and readers gathered to gossip, amuse and educate themselves, displayed the same traits of corruption and hypocrisy, according to Arendt (PF: 199). Though it is tempting to view Arendt's critique of the court society as an expression of the classical German preference for *Kultur* over Anglo-French 'civilisation' – the former indicating spiritual, artistic and intellectual expression, the latter referring to both technical rationalisation and the display of polite manners and courteous self-restraint (Elias 2000: 5ff) – her position is more complex than this. For both definitions were unsatisfactory to Arendt because they relegated the worldly realm of politics. In both cases the company of others was valued only as a vehicle for private interests, whether these were the interests of self-cultivation, entertainment, or status ascension.

For Arendt the most recent form of the social is 'mass society', which in her view only developed when the majority of the population became incorporated into the excitable bourgeois society of indiscriminate consumption, egoistic self-interest and loneliness (PF: 198–9). Mass society, as Arendt depicts it, is devoid of the worldly structures which normally function to gather individuals together without destroying or concealing their uniqueness. With the spread of the market economy and the rise of the welfare state, mass society became capable of taking over the survival-oriented functions of the private household by integrating individuals, their self-interests, needs and desires, into large-scale economic and administrative systems. In the course of this development, the web of human actions and commitments that earlier comprised the political community steadily atrophied, and in its place emerged a kind of 'super-human family' whose needs are 'taken care of by a gigantic, nation-wide administration of housekeeping' (HC: 28).

To dramatise the significance of this change, Arendt describes the rise of the social – 'a development in which society devoured the family unit until it became a full-fledged substitute for it' (HC: 33 n24) – as a kind of unrestrained proliferation of life beyond the natural checks and balances of the household. It represents, she says, the 'unnatural growth, so to speak, of the natural', the inappropriate extension of life's irresistible imperatives into the domain of public affairs. Arendt thus refers to 'society', or the 'social realm', as a 'hybrid' of the 'more genuine realms' of the public and the private, an arrangement by which the life-process has become publicly organised in order to secure the harmonious and efficient marshalling of individuals' efforts to reproduce themselves (HC: 46–7; OR: 122). 'Society is the form in which the fact of mutual dependence for the sake of life and nothing else assumes public significance and where the activities connected with sheer survival are permitted to appear in public ' (HC: 46).

THE ASCENDANCE OF LABOUR

Although Arendt associates the social with the substitution of behaviour for action, behaviour actually seems to be a term she uses to describe forms of social interaction which display the attributes of labour. The most damaging consequence of the rise of the social is thus a collapsing of the hierarchy of human activities, so that not only is political action displaced, but work itself is also eclipsed by the rise of the lowest, most despised activity to the position of greatest prominence and even highest esteem. Arendt suggests that the ascendance of labour can be witnessed in several different aspects. First of all, the triumph of the social over the public realm coincided with the growth of a society of job-holders – the unfashionable term for which is 'capitalism', and what today is sometimes referred to as the 'employment society'. With the exception of the artist, whom Arendt describes as 'the only "worker" left in a labouring society' (HC: 126), the prevailing motive for the performance of communal activities in the modern age is neither self-revelation through exceptional speech and action nor the creation of fine or useful things, but rather the necessary perpetuation of life (what we fittingly refer to as 'earning a living'). When the task of politics is defined by its professional representatives in terms of maintaining the optimum level of growth and healthy functioning of the societal organism, then the primitive mentality of labour has affected the political aristocracy as much as the urban proletariat: 'Even presidents, kings, and prime ministers think of their offices in terms of a job necessary for the life of society' (HC: 5). Publicly proclaiming their devotion to liberty and freedom, Western politicians just as frequently appeal to the force of necessity: 'the economy' is the hungry master that must be fed and market forces brook no compromise. Even the association between economic rationality and utilitarianism, the latter being the favoured philosophy of the worker, is misleading here, for the outlook of the typical wage-earner is not a strictly instrumental one, aimed at producing, and then dwelling in, a stable world liberated from the repetitive cycles of the labour process. The end pursued by the typical job-holder is, instead, that most fertile, restless and liquid of means: money.

Relations which are thoroughly permeated by money, Arendt suggests, are like the metabolic interactions of the human body with its environment (HC: 124). When money has become the measure of things, then the fitness of things, their use-value, is subordinated to a logic of exchange that is in principle unlimited and therefore incapable of liberating the economic actor, no longer equipped with a notion of fitness or sufficiency, from the process of exchange itself. Though Arendt regards action, not labour, as the gravest casualty of this process, there are similarities here with Marx's theory of the 'fetishism of commodities', where the 'objective conditions essential to the realisation of labour are alienated from the worker and become manifest as fetishes endowed with a will and a soul of their own' (Marx 1976: 1003). Arendt's brief comments on the transformation of stable wealth into liquid money also bear a more obvious kinship with the work of Georg Simmel, who earlier in the century described how the liquefying effects of money, its corrosion of the bonds that tie people to people and people to things, delivered a purely negative form of freedom.

Money, Simmel observed, liberates people from fixed relations of dependence, fealty and obligation. But by transforming the world of things into a realm of interchangeable commodities, money also deprives people of any cumulative grip on what lies before them. The possessor of money faces an infinity of choices, but since every choice is exchangeable for a monetary equivalent, nothing engages the chooser in a productive or transformative way. Money-mediated choices are, by virtue of their quantitative value, fungible, reversible and revocable. Because they do not demand a commitment premised on the forfeiting or sacrifice of incommensurable alternatives, the outcome of such choices is never an advance over the initial point of departure. What money gives us, in other words, is precisely the power to not be who we are. 'Money means more to us than any other object of possession because it obeys us without reservation – and it means less to us because it lacks any content that might be appropriated beyond the mere form of possession. We possess it more than anything else but we have less of it than all other objects' (Simmel 2004: 325, 400–3). Simmel's account of our contingent, superficial relation to commodities, which also resembles Marx's description of the alienating effects of money in the 'Economic and Philosophical Manuscripts' (1975a: 375–9; see also Fromm 1956: 131–7), is exactly what Arendt means by the worldless condition of labour, which can produce no more than the reproduction of its own existence. Money's indifference to the qualitative value of objects, its ability to 'bring together impossibilities' (Marx), and its replacement of the concrete category of the 'sufficient' with the restless and insatiable principle of 'the more the better', undermines the stabilising role of things. In doing so it threatens to overrun the human world with the movement of a process, in the face of which human action is impotent and superfluous. Later we shall see how Arendt relates this development to the rise of totalitarianism.

Accompanying the spread of the money economy was the transformation of craftsmanship into labour (HC: 124). Though she claimed that the target of her analysis – the 'modern age' – ended with the invention of the atom bomb (HC: 6), Arendt's account here converges with some of the sociological debates on the nature of the modern labour process that were influential in the 1970s, and which have reappeared in more recent studies of computerised manufacturing (e.g. Gorz 1989: 73–89, 122–4; Sennett 1998: 64–75). Of particular interest is Arendt's argument that the threat to the worldliness of work comes from nature-like processes of movement and growth, an argument that offers a new and unconventional way of looking at what social theorists regard as the increasingly fluid nature of 'liquid modernity' (Bauman 2000b).

Central to Arendt's reasoning is the distinction she makes between 'specialisation' and 'division of labour'. The former term she reserves for instances where individuals practise a degree of acquired expertise which raises them above the level of common talent and natural ability, leads them into relations of co-operation and technical interdependence, and makes possible a sense of distinction and accomplishment. Division of labour, on the other hand, unites labourers by parcelling out common abilities, so that each performs a narrowly defined task that any other could equally well do. The labour force is then bound together quantitatively, with all recognising in each other their own interchangeableness as generic members of an animal species.

Division of labour, which Arendt suggests is characteristic of the modern work environment, reflects the spread of nature-like imperatives into the domain of worldly making. It represents a 'multiplication of specimens which are fundamentally all alike because they are what they are as mere living organisms' (HC: 212). It 'presupposes the qualitative equivalence of all single activities for which no special skill is required, and these activities have no end in themselves, but actually represent only certain amounts of labour power which are added together in a purely quantitative way' (HC: 123). While specialisation is the expression of acquired skills and talents, division of labour is the reduction of work to the exercise of particular generic abilities. This is what Adam Smith perfectly described in his account of pin-making in the opening chapter of *The Wealth of Nations*, but it is also mirrored in Sennett's contemporary account, referred to above, of 'flexible specialisation' in the baking industry, where 'user-friendly' technology provides no resistance against which workers can fashion their identities and test their achievements. Division of labour, in Arendt's words, functions 'to eliminate from the path of human labour power – which is part of nature and perhaps even the most powerful of all natural forces – the obstacle of the "unnatural" and purely worldly stability of the human artifice' (HC: 126).

This account of the degradation of work into labour helps explain why Arendt views the sociality that arises from the modern labour process, where the biological rhythm of the factory 'eases labour's toil and trouble in much the same way as marching together eases the effort of walking for each soldier' (HC: 214), as both anti-political and worldless. In this respect it differs both from the 'unpolitical' condition of specialised work, and from the pre-eminently 'political' condition of human plurality in which individuals show an equal respect for one another's difference. Because the collective process of labouring requires the suppression of individuality, Arendt claims that it gives rise to an equally undiscriminating culture: 'all those "values" which derive from labouring, beyond its obvious function in the life process, are entirely "social" and essentially not different from the additional pleasure derived from eating and drinking in company' (HC: 213).

One reason given by Arendt to explain why specialisation has been superseded by division of labour, is the mechanisation of the labour process. By facilitating a pace of functioning infinitely quicker than the rhythmic cycles of nature, machinery promises to liberate us from those natural processes. In practice, however, mechanisation has become a kind of second nature, imposing its rhythms as forcibly as the biological imperative of life. Machines, though they are the objective products of *homo faber*, lose their worldly character when they are absorbed into the labour process. They 'are drawn into this rhythm until body and tool swing in the same repetitive movement' (HC: 146).

Arendt's critique of the effects of mechanisation, which treats technology, not as the enemy of a romantically cherished nature, but as a vehicle for the spread of nature-like forces into the human artifice, makes more sense when we remember how for Arendt the creative activity of *homo faber* stands in marked contrast to the fecundity of organic life. In human fabrication, the process of making and the object made are distinct: the process of production comes to an end where the independent existence of the product begins. In the case of natural organisms, on the other hand, the process of coming into existence is inseparable from existence itself: 'the seed contains and, in a certain sense, already *is* the tree, and the tree stops being if the process of growth through which it came into existence stops' (HC: 150–1). Arendt likens automation to nature, and this is why it renders *homo faber* redundant. In continuous production systems the distinction between process and product has become meaningless: the task of the operator is simply to feed and sustain an unceasing apparatus of production. Hence the older ideal of using machines to liberate people from labour, despite levels of production that would have dumfounded our ancestors, now looks like the quaint legacy of an outdated humanism, as whatever labour is saved by the introduction of machines must be reinvested in the labour process to deliver more goods and new pathways to increased efficiency. It is in this sense that the growth of mechanisation facilitates not a mastery of nature, but rather 'the channelling of nature's never-ending processes into the human world'. As the boundary between nature and artifice is dissolved, the result is an 'unnatural nature' and a 'pseudo world'.

> For a society of labourers, the world of machines has become a substitute for the real world, even though this pseudo world cannot fulfil the most important task of the human artifice, which is to offer mortals a dwelling place more permanent and more stable than themselves. In the continuous process of operation, this world of machines is even losing that independent worldly character which the tools and implements and the early machinery of the modern age so imminently possessed. (HC: 151–2)

The final and perhaps most pertinent reason why Arendt believes we are becoming a 'society of labour' concerns both the quality of, and our attitude towards, the objects that are produced. If the economic production of goods is to coincide with the endless life process, the principal ideals of which are physical comfort and abundance, then we would expect those goods to be designed with maximum perishability and built-in obsolescence, and to be consumed with a corresponding indifference to their durability. And this is of course an impeccable description of modern 'consumer society', whose continued growth demands relentless destruction rather than conservation of our worldly surroundings. Hence the 'uncanny phenomenon', soon to provoke the rise of the political ecology movement, 'that prosperity is closely connected with the "useless" production of means of destruction, of goods produced to be wasted either by using them up in destruction or – and this is the more common case – by destroying them because they soon become obsolete' (HC: 253). The tangible character of the public realm – the thing-like in-between which lends worldliness to the actions and words of women and men – is thus replaced by the inherently transient and disposable form of the commodity.

THE PRIVATE REALM

For Arendt, then, the ascendance of labour is inseparable from the rise of the social and the decline of the political, for as long as the *animal laborans* occupies the public realm, 'there can be no true public realm, but only private activities displayed in the open' (HC: 134). Arendt notes how puzzling the modern term 'political economy' would have sounded to the ancients, for whom the 'economic', deriving from the Greek word for 'household' (*oikos*), was by definition a non-political affair of the private sphere (HC: 29). In Greek antiquity, household relationships and activities were driven by wants and needs, and mastering those needs was the precondition for free participation in the *polis*. Politics did not exist for the sake of life, nor, as in later forms, for the protection of 'society' or of individuals' private wealth. Rather, the household, a domain of strict inequality in which slaves and women were subordinate, existed for the sake of the 'good life' of politics. As already noted, entrance into the freedom of the political realm required the very courage to 'risk life' that the Greeks believed was missing from the attitude of the acquiescent slaves, and so justified their enslavement.[1] The violence which sustained the master-slave relationship was also deemed legitimate because the function of the slave was to help the master subdue the violent forces of nature – 'to liberate oneself from the necessity of life for the freedom of world' (HC: 31). What seems curious from our own modern standpoint is that for the Greeks the idea of both governing ('sovereignty') and being governed was seen as relevant only to the pre-political, unfree realm of the private household. 'To be free meant both not to be subject to the necessity of life or to the command of another *and* not to be in command oneself. It meant neither to rule nor to be ruled' (HC: 32). Freedom was always the public interaction of equals – a viewpoint we find hard to decipher when we associate equality with distributive justice and regard freedom as an essentially private affair – and though the slave-owning citizen was certainly happier than those he commanded, he could never be said to be free until he had liberated himself from the sphere in which he ruled.

It is important to stress that household ownership, and the 'sanctity of the hearth' that this implies, was important to the Greeks not because they shared our modern obsession with the accumulation of wealth. Arendt argues that the uncompromising commitment to economic growth in the modern world is a typically 'social' answer to the predicament of mortality that preoccupied the ancients. Today's dominant discourse thus condemns as utterly foolish all criticism of a process of economic expansion 'as infinite as the life process of the species', conceiving of the dynamic of accumulation in societal terms precisely in order to escape 'the inconvenient fact that private individuals do not live forever and have no infinite time before them' (HC: 116). Growth in GDP, in other words, appears to lend permanence to a movement which, when thought of as an individual accomplishment, offers scant remedy to the burden of mortality.

For the Greeks, on the other hand, the privately owned household was important because it provided the free citizen, who was among a minority in the Athenian *polis*, with 'a privately owned share of a common world', this being 'the most elementary political condition for man's worldliness' (HC: 253). Politics was not regarded, as it casually is today, as the means by which property owners protect and consolidate their personal wealth and livelihood. Rather, politics was the end for which a limited amount of private property was seen as a necessary means. This is why Arendt is sympathetic to Locke's conception of private property which, in her reading, helps contain the worldless character of the life process: 'In a society of property-owners, as distinguished from a society of labourers or jobholders, it is still the world, and neither natural abundance nor the sheer necessity of life, which stands at the centre of human care and worry' (HC: 115–6).

By contrast, the treatment of the private realm as a protected sphere of emotional warmth and intimacy is a peculiarly modern phenomenon which Arendt believes can best be understood as a reaction not against the political realm, but rather against the rise of the social. In the theoretical exploration of intimacy and introspection found in Rousseau and the Romantics, Arendt sees a rebellion against the levelling effects and conformism of a society which 'demands that its members act as though they were members of one enormous family which has only one opinion and one interest' (HC: 39). It is, she suggests, the loss of interiority caused by the breakdown of the distinction between the public and private spheres, and the swallowing of the private household by the social, which precipitated the romantic quest to discover, through sentimental self-disclosure and unworldly introspection, a refuge for a subjectivity 'which formerly had been sheltered and protected by the private realm' (HC: 69). An illustration of this cult of subjectivism is presented by Arendt in her study of Rahel Varnhagen, the 'originator' of 'the Goethe cult in Berlin' and a woman who sought 'to live life as if it were a work of art'. Varnhagen was drawn to the limitless freedom of the mind, Arendt argues, in order to escape the real 'demand for action, the consequences of which necessarily impose limits even upon the freest spirit' (RV: xvi, 10–11).

The retreat from a disappearing public realm and the rejection of the worldly affairs of the political community is also detectable, Arendt claims, in the way 'greatness has given way to charm'. In the ancient world, the public sphere was permeated by a spirit of individual achievement, where people sought to reveal their uniqueness through memorable words and deeds. Such demonstrations of excellence, because they depended for their existence on the judgement of the individual's peers, could never be performed in private. The conquering of the public realm by the social, however, transformed the pursuit of individual distinctiveness into a private and lonely affair, typically expressed in terms of a careful and often tender concern not with the great and memorable, but with the small and irrelevant appurtenances of private life, from personal possessions, pets and home furnishings to gardens and flowers (HC: 41, 52).

So for Arendt the ancient division between the public and the private realm reflects an elementary opposition between ontologically distinct activities, some of which require, for their authentic meaning, to be publicly displayed, and some of which need to be hidden from view. Yet she also suggests that, predating the modern discovery of intimacy, there are in fact two 'non-privative traits of privacy' – that is, two virtues of the private realm which transcend its deficient relationship to the political sphere. The first is that our private space and possessions fulfil and validate needs that we experience with an urgency 'unmatched by the so-called higher desires and aspirations of man', and without which we are inclined to descend into apathy and inertia. It is sheer hubris to believe that the biological differences and animal instincts of humans could either be eradicated or perfectly understood and controlled, Arendt argues, and a society which eliminated this 'dark background of difference' would 'end in complete petrifaction and be punished, so to speak, for having forgotten that man is only the master, not the creator of the world' (OT: 302).

The second attribute of the private sphere which Arendt appears to value is that it offers a hiding place from the public world, a refuge which is both a prerequisite for the voluntary character of political life, and a basis for certain meaningful activities themselves. 'Everything that lives, not vegetative life alone, emerges from darkness and, however strong its natural tendency to thrust itself into the light, it nevertheless needs the security of darkness to grow at all' (PF: 186). Hence 'it is by no means true that only the necessary, the futile, and the shameful have their proper place in the private realm' (HC: 73).

A life spent entirely in public, in the presence of others, becomes, as we would say, shallow. While it retains its visibility, it loses the quality of rising into sight from some darker ground which must remain hidden if it is not to lose its depth in a very real, non-subjective sense. The only efficient way to guarantee the darkness of what needs to be hidden against the light of publicity is private property, a privately owned place to hide in. (HC: 71)[2]

A connection with the concept of natality can also be made here. Arendt describes natality as the condition pertaining 'to beings who know they have appeared out of non-being' (PF: 228). This 'non-being' requires a suitable home, a place where it is sheltered from the world of appearances. For action to be possible, the acting being must constitute a new beginning whose origin lies beyond the light of human reason and beyond the disposal of others. Although the household, in Greek antiquity, was hidden because it contained the lowly activities of ministering to and reproducing life, its non-public status also reflected the fact that it was seen to harbour the mysterious events of life and death – 'things hidden from human eyes and impenetrable to human knowledge' (HC: 63). This is why Arendt believes the definitive feature of Marx's communist utopia – which she characterises as the 'invasion of privacy by society', the 'socialisation of man', the 'no less certain "withering away" of the private realm in general and of private property in particular' (HC: 72) – represents as fundamental a threat to the autonomy and greatness of action as the erosion of the public sphere itself.

To illustrate her point that what cannot be seen and known is not always shameful or meaningless, Arendt gives the extreme example of 'goodness' – 'extreme because this activity is not even at home in the realm of privacy' (HC: 78). Arendt's argument here is controversial because it appears to drive a wedge between morality and politics, making a love of goodness 'the most lonely career there can be for man', because it can endure neither the attention of others nor the company of oneself (RJ: 117). Arendt stresses how the moral equation of goodness with selflessness carries with it the otherworldly, Christian hostility to the public realm from which it originates. It is in the nature of goodness, Arendt observes, that it can only be performed for its own sake, and for this reason it loses its quality as goodness as soon as it becomes an object of public interest, which all action must be if it is fit to shine in the world of appearances. Goodness is also destroyed the moment the author becomes aware of his or her work as good, at which point the activity degenerates into an expression of dutifulness or social utility. 'Here nothing counts but "Let not thy left hand know what thy right hand does", and not even "Take heed that ye do not do your alms before man to be seen of them" (Matt.6.2) is enough; I must be, as it were, absent from myself and not be seen by me' (RJ: 117). To be aware of oneself, and to be seen, as good, is no longer to be good – it is to be reliable, obedient and faithful to others' valuations; or it is to be vain and self-satisfied; or, when vanity is consciously resisted, it is to remain preoccupied with one's inner integrity at the expense of doing good itself (LM2: 67). 'Jesus rejects being called "good" by his disciples', Arendt explains, 'in the same way that Socrates refuses to be called "wise" by his pupils' (PP: 137). Neither goodness nor wisdom can declare themselves without succumbing to hypocrisy. Thus 'goodness must go into absolute hiding and flee all appearance if it is not to be destroyed' (HC: 75).

THE PUBLIC REALM AND THE HISTORICAL PROCESS

There are two further aspects of the rise of the social which are important to Arendt. The first of these is the replacement of government by bureaucratic administration. This administration is an extension of the principle of 'housekeeping' that originated in the private realm, although the 'one-man rule' of the ancient household has now become the 'no-man rule' of mass society, an impersonal system based on conformity to the anonymous laws, norms and needs of the social organism (HC: 40). The bureaucrat is the intellectual transformed into a functionary, a 'menial servant' akin to the domestic labourers of antiquity, but one who labours 'less to keep the life process intact and provide for its regeneration than to care for the upkeep of the various gigantic bureaucratic machines whose processes consume their services and devour their products as quickly and mercilessly as the biological life process itself' (HC: 93).

The second aspect follows on from the first: with the growth of the social realm we not only see the replacement of action by labour, but also the appearance of a new characteristic of public conduct – predictable, normative, oriented towards the compliant reproduction of common values, expectations and beliefs. As already alluded to, Arendt believes this merits the label 'behaviour', contending that 'behaviour has replaced action as the foremost mode of human relationship' (HC: 41).

> It is decisive that society, on all its levels, excludes the possibility of action, which formerly was excluded from the household. Instead, society expects from each of its members a certain kind of behaviour, imposing innumerable and various rules, all of which tend to 'normalise' its members, to make them behave, to exclude spontaneous action or outstanding achievement. (HC: 40)

With the supplanting of action by behaviour comes the rise of the behavioural sciences, in the category of which Arendt implicitly places both economics and sociology. Economics as a scientific discipline could only have arisen once people had become social beings who 'unanimously followed certain patterns of behaviour'. Extending this trend is Marxism, which seems entitled to claim scientific superiority because it posits, as the future realisation of the human essence, a 'socialised man' who 'is even less an acting being than the "economic man" of liberal economics' (HC: 42). Though Arendt clearly describes a human world which is increasingly akin to the 'society' envisaged by social scientists, she is also critical of the social sciences for failing to recognise the historical contingency of modern 'behavioural man', and for neglecting rare instances of action which, precisely by virtue of their exceptional nature, are seen as incomprehensible deviations from statistical norms. She is equally hostile to the attempt to reduce human history to a logical pattern or evolutionary law, which again seems to be symptomatic of the triumph of necessity over freedom, of the life process over the unforeseeable consequences of action, and which therefore fails to recognise that 'history is a story of events and not of forces or ideas with predictable consequences' (HC: 252).

> This is also the reason we know of no historical event which does not depend upon a great number of coincidences or for which we could not imagine one or more alternatives. The necessity which all causal historiography consciously or unconsciously presupposes does not exist in history. What really exists is the irrevocability of the events themselves, whose poignant effectiveness in the field of political action does not mean that certain elements of the past have received their final, definite form, but that something inescapably new was born. From this irrevocability we can escape only through submission to the mechanical sequence of mere time, without events and without meaning. (EU: 326 n14)

In this respect Arendt's approach to the study of history is not dissimilar to Max Weber's contribution to the *Methodenstreit*, or methodological controversy, which engaged German scholars in the last decades of the nineteenth century. Weber, for whose work Arendt, following Jaspers' promptings, had developed a cautious respect,[3] described history as 'an infinite multiplicity of successively and coexistently emerging and disappearing events', a 'vast chaotic stream' whose 'store of possible meanings is inexhaustible', arguing that 'knowledge of the cultural significance of concrete historical events and patterns' – not their causal logic – 'is exclusively and solely the final end' of the social sciences (1949: 72, 111). Though Weber accepted that 'development sequences' might be constructed by the social scientist as heuristic devices or 'ideal types', he warned against confusing this latter concept either with an ethical imperative ('there are ideal types of brothels as well as of religions') or with 'the naturalistic prejudice that the goal of the social sciences must be the reduction of reality to "*laws*"'. Emphasising 'the methodological impossibility of supplanting the historical knowledge of reality by the formulation of laws', Weber stressed the 'perniciousness' of developmental constructs 'as soon as they are thought of as empirically valid or as real (i.e. truly metaphysical) "effective forces", "tendencies", etc.' (1949: 91–2, 99, 101, 87, 103).

A constant point of reference in Arendt's own reflections on the modern concept of history is the attitude of the Greek historians. For the ancients, the deeds and achievements of human beings were never regarded as part of a wider, encompassing movement, force or process. On the contrary, singular actions and events were an interruption of the circular rhythms of daily existence and the endless cycle of biological life. The task of the historian, in this context, was to rescue humans from their futile and perishable deeds and, by converting those deeds into lasting stories, to give them the permanence of remembrance. This emphasis on the shining singularity of the act is apparent in Herodotus's impartial treatment of the Persian Wars, which tells of the heroism of both victors and vanquished, Greeks and barbarians, just as Homer 'undid' the annihilation of Troy by praising the greatness of Hector as well as the triumph of Achilles. For Arendt, the Homeric impartiality of the Greeks shows their awareness of the importance of seeing events from many sides, and their refusal to judge actions as historically significant only if they formed an indispensable link in a great causal chain of happenings (PP: 163–7).[4]

Arendt argues that although the idea of history as a developmental process began to emerge in late antiquity, it became firmly established only in the eighteenth century. This is exemplified in the modern computation of chronological dates, which stretch both backwards and forwards to infinity. This convention dispensed with the idea that history begins with the onset of something altogether new, whether this is the first year in the short-lived French revolutionary calendar, the birth of Christ, or the year of the foundation of Rome. The concept of history as an all-encompassing process instead offered a palliative – a kind of 'earthly immortality' – to what Kant recognised was the true 'melancholy haphazardness' of history, so that what the Greeks accomplished through the remembrance of perishable deeds the modern age achieved by interpreting singular events and happenings as part of an unfolding logic of sequences which, as in the uninterrupted development of Hegel's *Geist*, told a coherent and unambiguous story (PF: 41–90). The casualty of this story, however, was the meaningfulness of action itself:

> the meaningfulness of everyday relationships is disclosed not in everyday life but in rare deeds, just as the significance of a historical period shows itself only in the few events that illuminate it. The application of the law of large numbers and long periods to politics or history signifies nothing less than the wilful obliteration of their very subject matter, and it is a hopeless enterprise to search for meaning in politics or significance in history when everything that is not everyday behaviour or automatic trends has been ruled out as immaterial. (HC: 42–3)

WORLD ALIENATION

Arendt uses another term to describe the displacement of making and acting by *animal laborans* and the 'social' realm. This is 'world alienation', which is clearly a variation on the theme of worldlessness. Arendt traces the origins of our modern world alienation back to the expropriation of the rural population during the late Middle Ages. The sequestration of land and peasantry – which deprived the latter not just of means of subsistence, but of a place in the world that, to the medieval mind, was considered an inalienable condition of existence – created a new labouring class without a stake in the realm of stable things. Arendt also wishes to understand the growth of world alienation in terms of a cultural, if not 'spiritual', transformation. Critical here is the reversal of the old hierarchical supremacy of the *vita contemplativa* over the *vita activa*. The roots of this reversal lie in the birth of Cartesian doubt, which Arendt boldly claims was a consequence of the invention of the telescope. This instrument, and the many comparable inventions that followed in its wake, proved that truth was no longer something that would disclose itself to the patient observer. Galileo's discovery that, contrary to the evidence of the naked senses, it is the earth that circles the sun, proved to the seventeenth-century philosophers that 'only interference with appearance, doing away with appearances, can hold out a hope for true knowledge' (HC: 274).

What Arendt refers to as 'the spiritual consequence of Galileo's discoveries' was the dramatic loss of the conviction that truth will appear of its own accord to people who are well disposed to recognise it. Even the traditional sceptical credo that truth was permanently concealed by a veil of appearance was benign in comparison with this new belief that Being, under the devilish guidance of an evil spirit, actively gives itself a misleading form. The solution to this predicament, according to Arendt, was contained in the event that precipitated it. A movement immediately began away from the pursuit of truth and reality towards the principles of truthfulness and reliability – that is, towards methodical consistency in thinking and doing that rapidly became the hallmark of the new experimental science.

> The point was not that truth and knowledge were no longer important, but that they could be won only by 'action' and not by contemplation. It was an instrument, the telescope, a work of man's hands, which finally forced nature, or rather the universe, to yield its secrets. The reasons for trusting *doing* and for distrusting *contemplation* or *observation* became even more cogent after the results of the first active inquiries. After being and appearance had parted company and truth was no longer supposed to appear, to reveal and disclose itself to the mental eye of a beholder, there arose a veritable necessity to hunt for truth behind deceptive appearances ... In order to be certain one had to *make sure*, and in order to know one had to do. Certainty of knowledge could be reached only under a twofold condition: first, that knowledge concerned only what one had done himself – so that its ideal became mathematical knowledge, where we deal only with self-made entities of the mind – and second, that knowledge was of such a nature that it could be tested only through more doing. (HC: 290)

The upsetting of the ancient hierarchical relationship of contemplation and doing was initially accompanied by the rise to prominence, within the *vita activa*, of the faculties of *homo faber*. Arendt suggests that the elevation of *homo faber* to 'the highest range of human possibilities' is evident in the dominant temper of the early industrial age, from its thoroughgoing utilitarianism, its contempt for thought which yields no material product, and its reduction, by bourgeois philosophers, of political action to making. It is also apparent, as we have seen, in the widespread commitment to a principle of sovereignty which, in the words of Bergson (though Arendt could just as well be citing Heidegger's [1977] account of 'Enframing', the technology-driven attitude which treats reality as 'standing reserve'), 'regards everything given as material and thinks of the whole of nature as of "an immense fabric from which we can cut out whatever we want to resew it however we like"' (HC: 305). The same attitude can be observed in economics, where the superior status of productive activity is such that, in Arendt's view, even Marx was persuaded to deliberately 'misrepresent' the proletariat as fabricators in order to strengthen their claims for economic justice (HC: 306).

The attraction of making over doing, of course, is that unlike action the ends of fabrication can be reliably predicted. But what really needs explaining is not the modern glorification of *homo faber*, but why this enchantment with humanity's fabricating talents was short-lived, being swiftly followed by the ascendance of the *animal laborans*. To address this question Arendt leads us back to the rise of the scientific experiment, where the prerogatives of *homo faber* appear to have been especially at home. By the deliberate 'production' of objects of observation, the new scientists demonstrated the wisdom of their conviction that one can learn about the things that humans have not themselves made only by replicating the natural processes by which they came into being. Inherent in this new mentality, Arendt points out, was a shift in emphasis from questions of 'what' and 'why' to the question of 'how'. This reflected the belief that the objects of knowledge were not things which disclose themselves but rather *processes* which, just like the fabrication process, *disappear in the end product*, and which can therefore be revealed only by *re-enacting* them.

Although it was to the ingenuity of *homo faber*, 'who knew that a production process necessarily precedes the actual existence of every object' (HC: 297), that science therefore looked, a crucial difference still separated the two activities. For while the production process, for the toolmaker, was only the means towards an end, for the scientist the product was a mere by-product – an incidental, though often fortuitously useful, side-effect – of the endeavour to reproduce and fathom the means. So the most significant aspect of this change, in Arendt's view, was not simply the replacement of the contemplator by the maker, but *the introduction of the concept of process into making*.

The introduction of process into making was even more important, according to Arendt, than the ascendance of making over political action. She reminds us that the superiority of political action had always been questioned, and tacitly overruled, in the attitude of the ancient philosophers, for whom contemplation and fabrication had a close affinity that was not mirrored in the oppositional relationship between contemplation and action. This affinity derived from the fact that contemplation could be thought of as an intrinsic component of the fabrication process, for the craftsman was guided by, and evaluated his product in relation to, an idea of perfection. For Plato, this idea or model was not an arbitrary invention of the human mind, but corresponded to the eternal Forms accessible to the intellect. The excellence and permanence of these non-physical Forms could only be spoiled by the comparatively perishable outcome of their material fabrication, however, and this meant that, for Plato, the proper attitude to ideas required the renunciation not just of action, but ultimately of work itself in order to prolong the individual's consciousness of the model for its own sake (HC: 301–4).

This insight marked a subtle but significant departure for the ancient philosophers, who had previously regarded the motionless, speechless wonder at the miracle of Being – which is both the beginning and the end of all philosophical enquiry – as the unintended result of contemplative absorption. Now, however, instead of wonder throwing the individual into a profound but mute revelation of Being, it was through the deliberate cessation of the activity of making, the indefinite prolonging of the beholding of the eternal model with which every act of fabrication began, that the silent apprehension of the truth was achieved.

Arendt's point, therefore, is that the simple reversal of making and beholding was not alone sufficient to destroy the allure of the *vita contemplativa*, for philosophers had already reformulated the latter precisely in order to extend its appeal to the more numerous craftsmen in the ancient world, and thus to the experience of *homo faber*. What was really necessary to force through the expulsion of contemplation, the supremacy of making and, ironically, the latter's eventual defeat by the *animal laborans*, was a change in the understanding of fabrication itself. What the scientific revolution brought about was a shift in emphasis from the product to the process, 'from the question of what a thing is and what kind of thing was to be produced to the question of how and through which means and processes it had come into being and could be reproduced' (HC: 304).

THE GLORIFICATION OF LIFE

The irony is that the growing primacy of process within the work of *homo faber*, the transformation of the means into the end, began to deprive the fabricator of the fixed standards of judgement which had always preceded and outlived the fabrication process. Now the product of the process of creation, the intended usefulness of the fabricated thing, was no longer the motive and end of the productive activity. The product became an incidental by-product of the process itself, and could therefore be freely converted into a *means* of something – into *any* means, not just the use for which the producer intended it. As noted in the previous chapter, Arendt already partly attributes this loss of value in the world of things to the intrinsic logic of *homo faber* which, as soon as it is considered to be the maker of tools rather than the builder of a stable world, finds each of its products greedily consumed by the ever-expanding production process. The increasing primacy of the idea of process undermines the worldly orientation of *homo faber* even further. We can see this, Arendt claims, in the modern revision of two traditional beliefs.

The first of these is David Hume's critique of the causality principle. In Arendt's view, eighteenth-century British empiricism inherited the radical scepticism of Descartes, and with it the world-alienation of modernity, through an attitude of 'extreme subjectivism'. By reducing the sensibly given world to raw sense data which only the repetition of experience could order and render comprehensible, the philosophy of sensation invalidated all confidence in the quality of the sensed object, leaving the individual 'imprisoned in a non-world of meaningless sensations that no reality and no truth can penetrate' (PF: 56). Contrary to the argument, developed by Ralph Fevre in *The Demoralisation of Western Culture*, that the imaginative faculties of faith, trust and sentiment have been undermined, at the cost of society's 'demoralisation', by a modern outlook that 'will only believe what it can see with its own eyes, hear with its own ears and so on' (Fevre 2000: 79), Arendt argues that 'suprasensual truth' lost its validity when the evidence of the five senses was thrown into doubt and the tangible existence of the world was no longer self-evident.

> Reality no longer was disclosed as an outer phenomenon to human sensation, but had withdrawn, so to speak, into the sensing of the sensation itself. It now turned out that without confidence in the senses neither faith in God nor trust in reason could any longer be secure, because revelation of both divine and rational truth had always been implicitly understood to follow the awe-inspiring simplicity of man's relationship with the world: I open my eyes and behold the vision, I listen and hear the sound,

I move my body and touch the tangibility of the world. If we begin to doubt the fundamental truthfulness and reliability of this relationship, which of course does not exclude errors and illusions but, on the contrary, is the condition of their eventual correction, none of the traditional metaphors for suprasensual truth – be it the eyes of the mind which can see the sky of ideas or the voice of conscience listened to by the human heart – can any longer carry its meaning. (PF: 54)

The principle of causality was a natural victim of this radical subjectivism, for as Hume argued the conjunction of two events is only rendered causally connected when, 'after a repetition of similar instances, the mind is carried by habit, upon the appearance of one event, to expect its usual attendant, and to believe that it will exist' (Hume 2000: 59). The abandonment of the idea, familiar to the experience of the fabricator, that everything must have a cause and that this cause must be superior to its effect, paved the way, in Arendt's view, for the science of biological evolution, which traced the origin of higher organisms to the earlier existence of lower forms of life (HC: 312).

The other example given by Arendt of the rise of the concept of process in modern philosophy is the work of Jeremy Bentham, which presents itself as a purely utilitarian-hedonistic approach to human well-being, but which actually supplants the worldly principle of 'utility' with that of 'happiness', which is in turn a euphemism for 'the amount of pain and pleasure experienced in the production or in the consumption of things' (HC: 309). In Arendt's view this doctrine leads inexorably in the direction of a worldless 'life philosophy', that is, a philosophical glorification of the biological process.

True hedonism, as the ancients understood it, was always driven by the avoidance of pain rather than the pursuit of pleasure. This was, Arendt points out, a recognition of the fact that, while 'pleasure' apprehends the qualities of a pleasurable object, only pain contains within it the certainty of its own feeling. Pleasure enjoys 'something beside itself', whereas pain senses nothing but the bodily sensation that it is. According to Arendt, the difference between the ancient philosophies of hedonism and the modern, puritan and utilitarian versions, is that the latter are informed by a profound Cartesian distrust of the senses. Instead of recommending, as the ancients did, an imaginative flight from a painful and troublesome world, instead of enjoying the contemplation of pain from which they were thankfully free or the mental recollection of past pleasures, the modern philosophers, convinced that human nature was altogether corrupt and unreliable, 'needed the calculus of pleasure or the puritan moral bookkeeping of merits and transgressions to arrive at some illusory mathematical certainty of happiness' (HC: 310). Behind this illusory certainty was concealed a deeper and more potent principle, which 'was not happiness at all but the promotion of individual life or a guarantee of the survival of mankind' (HC: 311). Nineteenth-century naturalism thus settled the seventeenth-century conflict between experimental science and rational introspection – the two methods for the pursuit of truth which arose from Galileo's discovery – by opting for the latter, with introspection finally yielding a tangible object: the life process of the organism.

Arendt believes the ultimate proof that hedonism has been replaced by 'life philosophy in its most vulgar and least critical form' (the 'greatest representatives' of which, she claims, are Marx, Nietzsche and Bergson) is that this philosophy lacks a justification for suicide. 'In the last resort, it is always life itself which is the supreme standard to which everything else is referred, and the interests of the individual as well as the interests of mankind are always equated with individual life or the life of the species as though it were a matter of course that life is the highest good' (HC: 311–12). In this respect modern life philosophy has simply built on and consolidated a core tenet of Judeo-Christian thought which has subsequently survived the decline of religious faith. In the ancient world, humans saw themselves as surrounded by the immortality of nature and the gods, and this left them with the heroic, and sometimes life-endangering, task of producing great works, words and deeds which, either through their physical permanence or through the immortal fame they earned, offered their protagonists a place in the eternal cosmos. This perceived division between mortal humans and an immortal world was reflected in the ancients' devaluation of mere life, ranging from their contempt for the burdens of labour and giving birth and their envy over the leisurely life of the gods, to the censure of the physician who prolonged a life with no prospect of health or autonomy (HC: 315).

It was Christianity that transformed this classical understanding of the relationship between life and the cosmos, and this was of course the origin of its tremendous attraction. By promoting mortal human life to the position of potential immortality, Christianity offered hope to those who saw the human world, in political activity as much as in the material artifice, as irredeemably corrupt and perishable. The Christian belief in the sacredness of life thus helped free labouring from the contempt in which it had previously been held, so that one could no longer condemn a person for clinging to a life of enslavement, since 'to stay alive in all circumstances had become a holy duty, and suicide was regarded as worse than murder' (HC: 316).

It was, in summary, the coincidence of the Christian reversal of the relationship between life and world on the one hand, with the later reversal, precipitated by the invention of the telescope, of doing and contemplating on the other, which in Arendt's view formed the intellectual crucible from which the *animal laborans* rose to prominence. Christianity itself certainly failed to yield a positive endorsement of the value of labour, largely because it retained the ancients' commitment to the superiority of the *vita contemplativa* (a commitment challenged, it would seem, by the teachings of Jesus, but only in so far as action – conceived as the capacity to 'perform miracles' – and not labour, was recommended).

With the rise of science and the process of secularisation, Arendt argues, individual life became mortal again, but in a world less stable and permanent than for the early Christians. In the modern scientific age, the only thing left that could rival the immortal status of the body politic in antiquity and the individual in the Christian Middle Ages, was the human species itself. As we shall see in Chapter 4, Arendt believes this glorification of the collective life process found an unlikely ally in Marx who, against the ideological individualism of classical political economy, championed a class whose historic destiny could be impeded only by defying the irresistible dynamic of continually expanding productive forces.

3
From Action to Power:
The Fate of the Political

Given the superior position of political action in Arendt's hierarchy of human activities, and her definition of action as the birth of something new, it is understandable that she turned to the phenomenon of revolution to explore, in the modern historical context, the achievements and the pitfalls of the highest element of the *vita activa*. For revolutions, as Arendt describes them in *On Revolution*, 'are the only political events which confront us directly and inevitably with the problem of beginning' (OR: 21).

Curious, then, is the fact that when the word 'revolution' first entered political discourse it did not refer to novel events and actions, but instead retained an unmistakable echo of its original Latin meaning. An astronomical term, revolution meant the irresistible cyclical motion of the stars, and it is this sense of revolving back to something that has already occurred, of restoring or renovating a previous state of affairs, which is the meaning that was first carried into the political arena. Arendt believes the word was first used as a political term in 1660 in England – not, as the modern concept of revolution would suggest, during Cromwell's rebellion against the crown, but in reporting the defeat of the Rump Parliament that followed it. More famously, it was used in 1688 – the 'Glorious Revolution' – to mark the restoration of the monarchy after James II had fled to France and vacated the English throne.

The eighteenth-century revolutions were also intended as restorations, with the agents of the French and American revolutions initially believing they were recovering ancient liberties that absolute monarchy and colonial power had violated. Though the principle of novelty was paramount in the minds of the philosophers and experimental scientists of the seventeenth century, to the revolutionaries themselves the idea of political action as a new beginning was unfamiliar, and this idea only occurred to them as the events they participated in gathered pace.

Despite these modern events changing the meaning of the word revolution, introducing connotations of novelty and new beginning,

Arendt notes that one aspect of the older meaning of the term has been harder to shake off, particularly on the European stage. This is the idea of 'irresistibility', which originally related to the circular movement of the stars on their preordained path. Arendt claims that we already know when 'revolution' was first used in a political sense to denote an unstoppable process that was *not* considered a return to a previous state of affairs. This was 14 July 1789, when Louis XVI exclaimed, following the fall of the Bastille, that the event was a 'revolt'. He was promptly corrected by the Duke who had delivered the grave news: 'No, Sire, it is a revolution.' Here the act of rebellion, perceived by the King as a revolt against the natural order of the *ancien régime*, was seen by his aid as something so irresistible that even the monarch was powerless to stop it.

Arendt argues that what the fearful Duke had seen on the streets of Paris was the shocking appearance, 'for the first time in broad daylight', of the impoverished and downtrodden multitude, the very people who for centuries had been excluded from the public realm by force of shame and violence. It was the emergence of this desperate majority, onto a stage previously reserved for those who were liberated from the exigencies of survival, which in Arendt's view set the French Revolution on a violent course which all modern theories of revolution as 'historical necessity' have taken as their model. And though the idea of history as process may have other origins, such as the evolutionary paradigm in the natural sciences, the fact that the concept of necessity survived the break with the cyclical worldview proves for Arendt that it was the political events of the eighteenth century, especially the events of the French Revolution as witnessed from the outside, which are decisive in explaining the influence in modern thought of the Hegelian conception of history as an irresistible process. It is because they followed directly in the footsteps of the French Revolution, Arendt suggests, that the protagonists of the Russian Revolution 'saw themselves not merely as successors of the men of the French Revolution but as agents of history and historical necessity, with the obvious yet paradoxical result that instead of freedom necessity became the chief category of political and revolutionary thought' (OR: 53).

THE SOCIAL QUESTION

Arendt claims that the well-documented savagery of the French Revolution was a consequence of the way its leaders were preoccupied with what she calls the 'social question'. This, as

Arendt's association of the 'social' with the necessities of life should already have indicated, is the problem of physical deprivation, a problem that could not be evaded once the poor burst onto the political scene. Driven onto the streets of Paris by the overwhelming urgency of their bodily needs, the massed ranks of the destitute became the biological counterpart of the irresistible motion of heavenly bodies, a surging tide of bottomless misery and want. 'When they appeared on the scene of politics, necessity appeared with them, and the result was that the power of the old regime became impotent and the new republic was stillborn; freedom had to be surrendered to necessity, to the urgency of the life process itself' (OR: 60).

We are already familiar with the connection which Arendt, following the Greeks, makes between necessity and violence. The brute force of physical needs demands an act of primordial violence against what stands in the way of those needs. This violence is, like the nature it must tame and conquer, deaf and mute; it is therefore pre-political in character, being incompatible with communication and disclosure in the space of appearances. According to Arendt, it was the visibility of the impoverished masses during the French Revolution, and the sheer immensity of their needs, which overpowered the political sphere with concerns that could only have been successfully addressed through the 'non-political' processes of technological growth and administrative expertise. When they intruded into the arena of political action, these concerns demanded from political actors a ruthlessness devoid of worldly restraint. The result was the mass executions and purges of *la Grande Terreur*.

Arendt implicitly contrasts the bloody internecine feuding in France during 1793–4 with the civilised debate between the Federalists and Anti-Federalists in the 1780s (though, curiously, she has not a word to say about the deadly civil war this division precipitated eighty years later). The Americans, she remarks, enjoyed an exceptional level of technological development combined with an abundance of natural resources, and this, in her view, had freed most in the colonies from abject poverty. The labouring class in America was poor, but it was not driven by desperate want. The challenge it posed to those who ruled was therefore political rather than social in nature: 'it concerned not the order of society but the form of government' (OR: 68). The principal grievance was not material deprivation but political disenfranchisement and therefore invisibility: the poor in pre-revolutionary America were in revolt because they were 'excluded from the light of the public realm where excellence can shine' (OR: 69).

Arendt's apparent failure to give due attention in this account to the plight of slaves in the American colonies remains a matter of some contention. Although she concedes that 'the absence of the social question from the American scene was … quite deceptive', because 'abject and degrading misery was present everywhere in the form of slavery and Negro labour' (OR: 70), she insists on the contrast between France and America. Those who opposed the 'primordial crime' of slavery, she argues, 'did so because they were convinced of the incompatibility of the institution of slavery with the foundation of freedom, not because they were moved by pity' (OR: 71). Whether poverty and need was actually absent or simply shrouded by obscurity and exclusion, Arendt maintains that the social question in America remained 'non-existent for all practical purposes, and with it, the most powerful and perhaps the most devastating passion motivating revolutionaries' (OR: 72). This passion was the 'passion of compassion', and in France, where the gulf in social conditions between the newly empowered representatives of the people and the people themselves was stark and unavoidable, compassion played a central role. For in order to cross the chasm of inequality and claim both solidarity with the many and legitimacy in representing them, the French revolutionaries needed what Robespierre called 'virtue', which was the capacity to be moved by compassion so as to pity the suffering of the people.

The link Arendt makes between the importance attributed to compassion and the violence of the French revolutionary government is twofold. First of all, Arendt compares compassion to love in the way it refuses to share a 'talkative and argumentative interest in the world' and 'abolishes the distance, the in-between which always exists in human intercourse' (OR: 86). Compassion is worldless, rooted in face-to-face relations, and inherently hostile to political practice, the latter being concerned neither with virtue nor with truth, but rather with the display and exchange of different opinions.

According to Arendt, compassion, being the pain we feel in the presence of another's suffering, is the 'noblest form' of human passion. However, deliberate cultivation of this passion, which Rousseau championed against the selfishness and solitude of rational society,[1] resulted in a more general sentiment or emotion which Arendt characterises as 'pity' (OR: 95, 89). Unlike solidarity, which can, by means of worldly principles and ideals (such as respect, honour and human dignity), unite the strong and the weak in a dispassionate 'community of interest', pity seems to display the same worldless preoccupation with the self and its inner purity that Arendt believes reflects the political deficit in every pursuit of absolute goodness. Parasitic on the existence of misfortune, 'pity can be enjoyed for its own sake, and this will almost automatically lead to a glorification of its cause, which is the suffering of others' (OR: 89). Pity does not share compassion's often speechless concern for the private suffering of particular persons, but is, or at least became under Robespierre's initiative, a kind of public virtue which could no longer attend to specific individuals – hence the immunity of Robespierre to the suffering of the victims of the Reign of Terror is no contradiction – but oriented itself, with boundless emotion, to the immeasurable suffering of *le peuple*.

The objects of pity for the French were the undifferentiated mass of the poor. For the protagonists of the American Revolution this sentiment was inappropriate, Arendt claims, for 'the people' retained a meaning of manyness and variety, whilst the unanimity of the multitude – appearing to them in the guise of crass 'public opinion' – was seen not as a potential source of legitimacy, to be won by reaching out in pity, but as a tyrannical force endangering a public realm whose very existence depended on the exchange of different opinions. For the Americans, the power of united action was rooted in the worldly institutions that a plurality of individuals held in common and sought agreement about (OR: 76). The French revolutionists, on the other hand, had Rousseau's concept of an indivisible and unmediated 'general will' to guide their search for unanimity. This conception of *le peuple* as 'a multiheaded monster, a mass that moves as one body and acts as though possessed by one will', was in Arendt's view a fitting description of the torrent of desperate people who filled the streets of France, 'for what urged them on was the quest for bread, and the cry for bread will always be uttered with one voice' (OR: 94). The apparent oneness of the multitude, and the intensity of its suffering, thus fulfilled the prerequisites for compassionate zeal. The lawless terror that ensued sprang from 'sentiments of the heart whose very boundlessness helped in the unleashing of a stream of boundless violence' (OR: 92).

THE DARKNESS OF THE HUMAN HEART

The second link which Arendt makes between the sentimentalism of the French revolutionaries and the Reign of Terror that followed the Constitution of 1793 concerns the inescapable obscurity of human passions and emotions. According to Arendt, the human heart is always partly shrouded in darkness, so much so that, as social beings whose sense of reality is inseparable from the perceptions of others, our innermost intentions remain unclear and undecipherable even to ourselves. Our awareness of this fact is demonstrated in the way that suspicion always tends to greet the exposure of private passions and motives, however heartfelt they may be. When emotions lay claim to the public realm, they become 'mere appearances', insincere and inauthentic expressions behind which it is assumed darker motives are concealed.

> The same sad logic of the human heart, which has almost automatically caused modern 'motivational research' to develop into an eerie sort of filing cabinet for human vices, into a veritable science of misanthropy, made Robespierre and his followers, once they had equated virtue with the qualities of the heart, see intrigue and calumny, treachery and hypocrisy everywhere. The fateful mood of suspicion, so glaringly omnipresent through the French Revolution even before a Law of Suspects spelled out its frightful implications, and so conspicuously absent from even the most bitter disagreements between the men of the American Revolution, arose directly out of this misplaced emphasis on the heart as the source of political virtue. (OR: 96)

Robespierre's paranoid distrust of both allies and rivals was fuelled by a political doctrine that required him, the self-styled 'Incorruptible', to wilfully display the goodness of his heart. But this doctrine could never dispel his natural suspicion that, since he himself may be a hypocrite concealing murkier, less virtuous motives, the virtue of others must also be in question. All actors were thus transformed into hypocrites by dint of the impossible demand that they display, with perfect transparency, their innermost motives, and it was this war on hypocrisy which turned Robespierre's dictatorship into the murderous unmasking and purging of alleged traitors.

Arendt claims that Robespierre's doctrine was ultimately founded on Rousseau's philosophy of natural goodness, which made society the corruptor of human virtue and those most excluded from society the honest, incorruptible impeachers of the rotten lives of the rich. When the dispossessed masses, the *sans-culottes*, appeared on the streets of Paris, Arendt writes, 'it must have seemed as if Rousseau's "natural man" with his "real wants" in his "original state" had suddenly materialised' (OR: 109). And materialise he did, with an elementary hatred of all 'artificial' laws, rules, identities and roles, seeing 'in the deliberations of the delegates no less a play of make-believe, hypocrisy, and bad faith, than in the cabals of the monarch' (OR: 110), and sparing only those spokesmen who obeyed the naked and authentic force of need.

To the ancients, Arendt reminds us, this elevation of 'natural man' would have made no political sense, and its destructive effects would have been readily foretold. When the Latin term '*persona*' found its way into the legal lexicon of ancient Rome, it referred to the public identity and role which distinguished the citizen from the private person. Somebody deprived of their *persona* would be deprived of legal rights and duties, and this was exactly the consequence of the French revolutionaries' passion for unmasking.

> They believed that they had emancipated nature herself, as it were, liberated the natural man in all men, and given him the Rights of Man to which each was entitled, not by virtue of the body politic to which he belonged but by virtue of being born. In other words, by the unending hunt for hypocrites and through the passion for unmasking society, they had, albeit unknowingly, torn away the mask of the *persona* as well, so that the Reign of Terror eventually spelled the exact opposite of true liberation and true equality; it equalised because it left all inhabitants equally without the protecting mask of a legal personality. (OR: 109)

PUBLIC FREEDOM AND PUBLIC HAPPINESS

On both sides of the Atlantic, of course, the revolutionaries shared a devotion to the idea of freedom. In Europe, this passion had been nourished by *les hommes de lettres*, a term Arendt prefers to 'intellectuals', which she believes should be reserved for the thinkers and writers required by business and government in modern 'mass society'. According to Arendt, intellectuals are indispensable to the administration of modern government, and are therefore an intrinsic part of the 'social'. The 'men of letters', on the other hand, had consciously withdrawn from this kind of service, whether in the royal court or the society of the salon. They were self-educated critics of society who were free from the burden of poverty, but exiled from the political realm where true freedom could flourish. They turned to the study of ancient philosophy not in search of eternal beauty or wisdom, but to understand the political institutions, and political possibilities, of their time (OR: 123).

What is significant, in Arendt's view, is that these men wrote and talked of freedom not as a form of philosophical contemplation or arbitrary choice, but 'with a new, hitherto almost unknown emphasis on *public* freedom'. 'Freedom for them could exist only in public; it was a tangible, worldly reality, something created by men to be enjoyed by men rather than a gift or capacity' (OR: 124). It was not personal liberty and comfort which the men of letters were striving for, as most were already provided with such indulgences as royal compensation for their exclusion from the polity. Instead what they objected to was the fate they shared with the poor: the lack of a public space in which they could engage their passion for action and speech.

What was a mere 'passion' in France, however, was an actual experience in America, and this was reflected, according to Arendt, in the way the Americans spoke not simply of public freedom but of 'public happiness'. The Americans, she claims, already knew that involvement in public affairs was a source of happiness, and the people who attended the various town assemblies that predated the Revolution did so not out of a feeling of duty but because they readily enjoyed decision-making and debate.

When Jefferson described, in 1774, the first European settlers as 'establishing new societies, under such laws and regulations as to them shall seem most likely to promote public happiness', he was, Arendt asserts, defining as the source of happiness not the right to be protected by government against interference in the private pursuit of well-being, but the citizen's right (in Jefferson's own phrase) to be 'a participator in the government of affairs'. 'The very fact that the word "happiness" was chosen in laying claim to a share in public power indicates strongly that there existed in the country, prior to the revolution, such a thing as "public happiness", and that men knew they could not be altogether "happy" if their happiness was located and enjoyed only in private life' (OR: 127). Hence Arendt contends that the passion for constitution-making which subsequently gripped the American states after the end of the war, in which elected conventions drafted documents to be debated and revised in town halls, was not driven, as historians often insist, by fear (among the Anti-Federalists) of an over-central-ised national government, or anxiety (among the Federalists) that without a constitution the country's national security and financial health would remain in jeopardy. Instead it was a direct expression of people's appetite and understanding of the joyful experience of political agency and public dialogue.

THE CONSTITUTION OF POWER

Arendt rejects the idea, popular among the enthusiasts of 'permanent revolution', that the establishment of a constitution by a revolutionary government is necessarily a counter-revolutionary reaction against the original spirit of freedom. The republican ideal, she claims, is 'the foundation of freedom', which means 'constituting a stable worldly structure' to keep intact the freedom of the founders, including the freedom to revise and amend that foundation. Arendt also rejects the conventional definition of constitutional government as simply government limited by law. In this definition, the constitution provides legal safeguards against the abuse of power by government (as framed, for example, in the US Bill of Rights). The political deficiency of these constitutional guarantees, however, is that they are entirely negative in character: 'they claim not a share in government but a safeguard against government' (OR: 143). When constitutions are regarded from this perspective, the 'truly revolutionary element in constitution-making', captured in the words of Thomas Paine which Arendt cites, is inevitably overlooked: 'A constitution is not the act of government,' Paine famously wrote, 'but of a people constituting a government' (OR: 145).

The shortcomings in the theory of constitutional government are matched, Arendt suggests, by the seventeenth-century theories of the social contract. These failed to distinguish clearly between, on the one hand, the 'mutual contract' based on reciprocity and promise-making, whose 'result is indeed "society" or "cosociation" in the old Roman sense of *societas*, which means alliance' (OR: 170), and on the other, the consent to be governed, the contract between ruler and ruled in which power is relinquished to a government in exchange for protection against the violent will of others. In the first case, individual sovereignty is exchanged for the power of combined action; in the second case, power is relinquished in exchange for the government's guarantee of the safety of isolation (OR: 170–1). 'Power for human beings who are not omnipotent can only reside in one of the many forms of human plurality', Arendt writes elsewhere, 'whereas every mode of human singularity is impotent by definition' (RJ: 106).

Comparing the French and American revolutions, Arendt notes how the American revolutionaries were wary of the abuse of power, viewing human nature with much greater suspicion than did the men of the French Enlightenment. But this also meant that the

Americans were equally conscious of the dangers posed to the polity by the unchecked rights and liberties of the citizen. Their primary concern, as a consequence, was with a positive rather than a negative constitution of power: 'not how to limit government but how to found a new one' (OR: 148). In the concept of the separation of powers, which made its way into European thought via Montesquieu, but which originates with Aristotle and Polybius, the American founders appeared to have discovered a solution to the potentially unstable nature of positive freedom. For Montesquieu understood that the only thing capable of arresting power without enfeebling it with laws or destroying it with violence, was power itself. Separate sources of power – executive, legislative, judicial, as well as federal and state – could therefore check the abuse of power with counter-power. Hence 'the true objective of the American Constitution was not to limit power but to create more power' (OR: 154).

THE RIDDLE OF FOUNDATION

Despite their constitutional solution to the problem of power, the Americans faced a second predicament according to Arendt, which was the establishment not of power but of the 'authority' of its constitutional foundation, an authority which was placed in question when the founders severed their ties to King and Parliament. The problem of founding the new body politic was effectively one of legitimacy, which Arendt also refers to as the 'vicious circle in legislating'. This ultimately seems to derive from the 'perplexities inherent in every beginning', whose 'bewildering spontaneity' means that no cause can be found to prove that the founding act of freedom was necessary and therefore justified (LM2: 210).

Without such authority, a new legal constitution is at permanent risk of being undone, as was the French constitution, which was replaced fourteen times between 1789 and 1875. What is interesting about the ancient Greeks and Romans, Arendt notes, is that neither appeared to have been vexed by this problem of the ultimate authority of the law. In the case of the Greek city-states, the process of formulating laws was considered a pre-political enterprise, akin to the physical construction of the city's walls, and it was typically entrusted to someone from outside the city itself. Laws constituted the insurmountable boundaries which protected and enclosed the freedom of the *polis*, holding in check the potentially limitless concatenation of actions and relationships inherent in the conditions of human plurality, and providing a counterweight 'to the transience of the spoken word and to the fleeting moment of the accomplished deed' (PP: 187). Although this separated the process of foundation from the realm of political debate and interrogation, the Greek word for law ('*nomos*') still stressed its artificial, human-made character, and there was no attempt to remove the origin of law from the human world altogether – by protecting it with the disguise of divine authorship, for example. For the Greeks, law was the result of production, not action, and though it produced the space in which citizens met for political exchanges devoid of force, its association with violence and progenitorship made the free citizen of the *polis* 'a "son and slave" his entire life' (PP: 181–2).[2]

For the Romans, by contrast, legislating was a pre-eminently political activity. But the original Latin meaning of the word – '*lex*' meant 'intimate connection' – reflects the fact that for them laws were considered not as mechanisms of control or domination but as the formal ties binding previously hostile parties into a friendship or alliance. While the Greeks saw war, for which command and obedience were indispensable, as inherently non-political, and regarded the strategic negotiations that concluded war as the continuation of war by peaceful means, politics for the Romans 'began as foreign policy'. This is because the political realm appeared and expanded when Rome, showing clemency to the vanquished, made friends of its erstwhile enemies, and opened up a political space for new relationships. It is the opening up of this space between peoples which in Arendt's words 'marks the beginning of the Western world – indeed, it first created the Western world as *world*' (PP: 189).[3]

Even more significant was the fact that the Roman republic derived its authority from a profound veneration of its origins. To the Romans, unlike the Greeks, the founding of their *polis* was the unique and unrepeatable beginning of their history, and the pious Roman was deeply obligated to this legendary beginning and to the preservation of what the ancestors had achieved. Hence 'religion' literally meant '*re-ligare*' – to be tied back – and the most important Roman gods were Janus, the god of beginning, and Minerva, the goddess of remembrance (PF: 120–1). Arendt goes as far as to suggest that the Romans' uncharacteristic acceptance of the cult of the child-saviour peculiar to Asiatic religions reflected an unequalled fascination with and reverence for new beginnings. It was with the Romans, moreover, that the concept of authority, as distinct from power, first appeared, and it is no accident that *auctoritas* derived from the verb *augere* ('to augment'). The Romans saw the role of the Senate, which in the American Constitution is transferred to the Supreme Court, as one of augmenting the authority of the ancestral founders to whom they were connected through an unbroken line of successors. The advice, approval and disapproval provided by the Senate in relation to the actions and decisions of the people were neither commanding nor coercive, but rather carried, with *gravitas*, an authority that derived from the binding weight of the past (PF: 121–4).

So although the founders of the French and American republics searched the archives of antiquity for an answer to the riddle of foundation, Arendt suggests that ultimately they were offered no clear guidance. For it seems that all significant political transformations in Roman history were in fact conceived by their participants as 'reconstitutions', as 'reforms of the old institutions and the retrievance of the original act of foundation', so that even the founding of Rome itself was thought of, thanks to Virgil's epic poetry, as the re-establishment of the legendary city of Troy (OR: 207–8; LM2: 211–3). The protagonists of the American Revolution, however, had seen the ties that bound their actions to the ancient world shattered by the revolt against European colonialism and the founding of a new nation. What had started as an attempt by loyal British subjects to reform the body politic and found 'Rome anew' became, through rebellion against the mother-country, the entirely unexpected task of founding a 'new Rome'.

Despite the outstanding achievement of the separation of powers, Arendt implies that the unique success of the American Revolution – the absence of the violence which in France 'drowned in a "revolutionary torrent"' the beginning as the well as the beginners' (OR: 209), and the stability of the American republic that followed – cannot be fully explained by the theoretical insights of the Founding Fathers, nor by their strategic appeals to eternal and God-given laws. Because they were preoccupied by the absence of an absolute authority capable of legitimising the legal foundations of the new republic, and because they remained perplexed by the 'abyss of nothingness that opens up before any deed that cannot be accounted for by a reliable chain of cause and effect' (LM2: 207), they retained only a faint awareness of a solution to the predicament of action which lies, Arendt argues, in the 'principle' which 'becomes fully manifest only in the performing act itself' (PF: 152).

What saves the act of beginning from its own arbitrariness is that it carries its own principle within itself, or, to be more precise, that beginning and principle, *principium* and principle, are not only related to each other, but are coeval. The absolute from which the beginning is to derive its own validity and which must save it, as it were, from its inherent arbitrariness is the principle which, together with it, makes its appearance in the world. (OR: 212)

Arendt claims support from Montesquieu in treating 'principles' as universal political standards for the judgement of deeds and misdeeds which only become manifest in the course of action, and which constitute the fundamental convictions shared by members of a group when they act together. For Montesquieu, according to Arendt, each principle, 'different in each form of government, would inspire government and citizens alike in their public activity and serve as a criterion, beyond the merely negative yardstick of lawfulness, for judging all action in public affairs' (OT: 467). Arendt argues that different political communities have historically been inspired by different fundamental principles: honour and glory in monarchies ('love of distinction', as Arendt puts it); virtue ('love of equality') in republics; moderation in aristocracies; fear and suspicion in tyrannies (which are ultimately 'antipolitical principles', Arendt claims, because they make 'acting in concert' impossible); fame in the world of Homer; and freedom in classical Athens (PF: 152; LM2: 201; PP: 194–5, 65–9; EU: 329–38).

In Arendt's theory of the unifying role of 'principles', what was most important for the avoidance of violence in the establishment and the survival of the US Constitution was the fact that more than any other principle the one which seemed to inspire its founding citizens was the republican principle of virtue or, as Arendt alternatively defines it, 'the interconnected principle of mutual promise and common deliberation' (OR: 214). It was a 'simple and obvious insight into the elementary structure of joint enterprise as such' which 'caused these men to become obsessed with the notion of compact and prompted them again and again "to promise and bind" themselves to one another' (OR: 173). This simple insight, which was articulated in the closing sentence of the Declaration of Independence ('we mutually pledge to each other our Lives, our Fortunes and our sacred Honor'), was made prevalent because public debate and mutual commitment to a common enterprise were already recognisable elements in the public life of the country. For in contrast to the pre-revolutionary situation in France, the colonial power in America was a limited, not an absolute, monarchy, and the people of the colonies already had widespread experience of 'covenant-making', that is, of binding themselves through mutual promises to keep their collective power – and its inspiring principle – alive.

According to Arendt, this meant that the authority, the 'constituent power', of those who formulated both the state and federal constitutions was never seriously questioned by the people, because the founders' actions enshrined a principle already exercised in the colonisation of the continent: 'the framing of the Constitution, falling back on existing charters and agreements, confirmed and legalised an already existing body politic rather than made it anew' (PF: 140). Arendt concedes that the numerous 'civil bodies politic' formed by the early British settlers were more accurately 'political societies' rather than governments, as their members still saw themselves as royal subjects of the government of England. Yet since their many charters and compacts were made without appeal to royal authority, there was an unbroken line of legitimacy from the Mayflower Compact to the US Constitution: 'it was as though the Revolution liberated the power of covenant and constitution-making as it had shown itself in the earliest days of colonisation' (OR: 168). The Constitution thus received its legitimacy from a principle of action actualised and nourished from below, from already-existing district, county and township bodies who elected the delegates for the various provincial congresses and popular conventions which drafted and ratified the state and federal constitutions.

The legitimacy of the American Constitution also drew strength from another source. We saw that transformative action in the Roman republic derived its authority, according to Arendt, from an attitude of pious reverence towards an original founding act in relation to which all actions were augmentations and reconstitutions. By projecting the original beginning back into the mists of time, where it was shrouded in mystery and legend, the Romans were able to sanctify all human acts of foundation as re-establishments rather than absolute beginnings. Although the radical novelty of the situation facing the American revolutionaries made a Roman understanding of their own actions difficult for them, Arendt notes that ordinary Americans were not so literal-minded. What the American people displayed, she suggests, was an almost religious veneration of the Constitution, and of the act of founding which established it, and it is this, according to Arendt, which helped protect the achievements of the revolution from being radically questioned and undone. This attitude was not religious in the Judaeo-Christian sense of obedience to divine commandments, but rather in the Roman meaning of *religare* – a binding of oneself back to a sacred beginning. For what the people of America exhibited was a kind of imaginative blindness which 'consisted in the extraordinary capacity to look upon yesterday with the eyes of centuries to come' (OR: 198). The act of founding, in other words, though it was the initiation of something new, was immediately regarded as a venerable historical event, clouded in a past too distant to be reversed or overthrown, and whose authority was already guaranteed by the amendments which augmented the act of constitution itself.

THE QUASHED SPIRIT OF REVOLUTION

For all Arendt's admiration for the ideals and achievements of the American Revolution, her view was that American political thought since the eighteenth century had misunderstood the central principles of the Revolution, in the process offering faint resistance to the steady depoliticisation of the country. Though the people themselves retained a formal reverence for the Constitution, they too eventually forgot the origins of their own polity, allowing their government to present itself as an unperfectable model of democracy and, during the Cold War, to oppose revolutionary movements around the world by supporting corrupt regimes that were hated by their own citizens (OR: 217). A republic 'is a living thing' which 'cannot be fabricated', Arendt wrote in 1953. 'If you try to "make America more American" or a model of democracy according to any preconceived idea, you can only destroy it' (EU: 400).

Arendt points out that in pre-modern forms of government the threat against the boundary between the public and private spheres came from the tendency for political power to trespass on people's private freedoms. A bulwark against this threat was the right (albeit for the privileged alone) to private property, and thereby 'privacy'. The danger facing post-revolutionary America, in contrast, was 'the misuse of public power by private individuals', that is, the ceding of the public sphere to people who were encouraged to act in accordance with their private economic and material interests, rather than as citizens of a republic. This danger became a reality as the space for public actions and words was turned into an extension of the private realm, and politics was transformed from action into administration (OR: 252–3). This process became a vicious circle because the disappearance of the space for the formation of opinions through discussion and debate left the public with fickle 'moods' rather than properly tested convictions capable of sustaining robust political dialogue. The end result was a system of government which 'is democratic in that popular welfare and private happiness are its chief goals; but it can be called oligarchic in the sense that public happiness and public freedom have again become the privilege of the few' (OR: 269).

In seeking to explain how the original principles of the revolution became reduced to 'civil liberties, the individual welfare of the greatest number, and public opinion as the greatest force ruling an egalitarian, democratic society' – a transformation which 'corresponds with great precision to the invasion of the public realm by society' (OR: 221) – Arendt returns in *On Revolution* to the wording of the Declaration of Independence. It seems to have been an uncharacteristic error of judgement that led Jefferson to replace the established formula of 'life, liberty and property' with the phrase 'life, liberty and the pursuit of happiness'. Far more significant than the replacement of 'property' with 'happiness', Arendt claims, was the deletion of the standard qualifier 'public'. By virtue of this omission, Jefferson invited a confusion between happiness, which had hitherto been understood as a quality of public life, and private welfare. In doing so he allowed the term 'pursuit of happiness' to 'contribute more than anything else to a specifically American ideology' (OR: 128). This was the ideology that defined exemption from public interference – 'freedom from politics', Arendt willingly concedes, is 'one of the most important negative liberties we have enjoyed since the end of the ancient world' (OR: 280) – as the essential constituent of freedom. It is this ideology which has helped turn politics into a 'profession' whose members are 'chosen according to standards and criteria which are themselves profoundly unpolitical' (OR: 277). And it is this ideology which Jefferson himself seemed to support when, contemplating retirement from public life in a letter to James Madison in 1793, he located his own happiness 'in the lap and love of my family, in the society of my neighbours and my books, in the wholesome occupation of my farms and my affairs' (cited in OR: 128–9).

The original spirit of the American Revolution was also quashed, Arendt argues, by the failure to preserve, and to protect in the Constitution itself, the role of the townships and local meeting halls in providing a space for public debate and decision-making. Once the republic was founded, 'there was no space reserved, no room left for the exercise of precisely those qualities which had been instrumental in building it' (OR: 232). It was, Arendt points out, 'the delegates of the people rather than the people themselves who constituted the public realm', and 'it was the Constitution itself, this greatest achievement of the American people, which eventually cheated them of their proudest possession' (OR: 251, 239).

THE COUNCIL SYSTEM

What, then, is Arendt's answer to the lost spirit of the American Revolution, and to the dwindling space for action she saw in both capitalist democracies and socialist regimes? In her most radical and idealist moments, Arendt's hope was lodged with the council system, which she described as 'the single alternative that has ever appeared in history, and has reappeared time and again' (CR: 231). Ironically, given her withering assessment of the French Revolution, the earliest manifestation of the council system recognised by Arendt was the forty-eight sections of the first Paris Commune. These were originally formed to facilitate the election of delegates to the National Assembly, but they quickly transformed themselves into self-organised bodies from which was constituted a municipal government of Paris. Together with the large number of *sociétés populaires* that had sprung up – which, with the exception of the Jacobin club, were largely non-partisan debating societies rather than pressure groups aimed at seizing state control – the Paris Commune 'contained the germs, the first feeble beginnings, of a new type of political organisation, of a system which would permit the people to become Jefferson's "participators in government"' (OR: 244).

Arendt's somewhat naive admiration – a 'romantic sympathy', in her own words (1979: 327) – for popular councils or communes and their equivalents (*soviets* in Russia, *Räte* in Germany) seems to offer the clearest indication of how she believed political action could establish a permanent home in the modern world, by developing 'a completely different principle of organisation, which begins from below, continues upward, and finally leads to a parliament' (CR: 232). Arendt notes how Marx, commenting on the Paris Commune of 1871, and Lenin, observing the Russian Revolution of 1905, had witnessed the spontaneous emergence of popular organs which were clearly more than mere instruments of revolutionary change, but which were intended to survive the revolution by constituting a lasting space for public freedom. In her analysis, every genuine revolution of the twentieth century produced these political forums independent of, and unanticipated by, revolutionary parties and leaders. In Arendt's account, it was not the card-carrying revolutionaries who liberated the people, but the reverse: 'revolution broke out and liberated, as it were, the professional revolutionists from wherever they happened to be – from jail, or from the coffee house, or from the library' (OR: 259).

Despite the fact that older political forms – such as the medieval townships, Swiss Cantons, and the General Council of Cromwell's army – have been identified by historians as earlier precedents, in Arendt's view no appeal to tradition or ideology can explain the repeated emergence of the council system since the French Revolution. Whether it was the Commune of 1871, the self-governing *soviets* that formed in Russia in 1905, the February Revolution of 1917, the self-constitution of *Arbeiter- und Soldatenräte* in the failed German revolution of 1918–19, and finally the re-emergence of the council system in the Hungarian Revolution of 1956, in each case Arendt insists that the councils appeared and spread without any prompting or planning by trained revolutionaries or party cadres, and in many cases were swiftly able to co-ordinate their functioning with higher regional or provincial councils (OR: 266–7).

Arendt's analysis of the political significance of the council system in the Russian and German revolutions is not wholly uncritical. It was to their detriment, she argues, that the councils often failed to appreciate the need for bureaucratic administration in modern society, assuming that social and economic needs could be seamlessly reconciled with the political principle of public action. With ironic misfortune, the naively optimistic belief of the councils' members that economic production could be efficiently self-managed coincided, Arendt argues, with the efforts of the Party 'to counteract the councils' political aspirations, to drive their members away from the political realm back into the factories' (OR: 274). Economic self-management also failed, sometimes taking with it the public credibility of the councils themselves, because the talents of those who led the take-over of the factories were political not managerial, and their attempts to introduce an element of action into the sphere of necessity and 'the management of things' inevitably led to inefficiencies (OR: 274–5).

Arendt's reflections on the council system are not entirely backward-looking either. Writing in the 1960s, she felt able to identify trends in US political culture that she believed were pointing in a more positive direction. Commenting on the growth of civil disobedience, which she believed was a worldwide phenomenon that is, presumably with the Boston Tea Party in mind, 'primarily American in origin and substance', Arendt praised the civil rights, student and anti-war movement for 'its determination to act, its joy in action, the assurance of being able to change things by one's own efforts'. The political demonstrators and protestors of the late 1960s and early 1970s were the first of a new generation to have 'discovered what the eighteenth century had called "public happiness", which means that when man takes part in public life he opens up for himself a dimension of human experience that otherwise remains closed to him and that in some way constitutes a part of complete "happiness"' (CR: 202, 203). Non-violent blockades and occupations aimed at disrupting the automatic, quasi-natural functioning of society are typical of civil disobedience, and Arendt seemed to commend these when she described as a 'healthy reaction' a 'certain rebellion ... against bigness' in many parts of the world (1979: 327). Had she lived to see the birth of the Solidarity movement in Gdańsk in 1980, the collapse of Communism in 1989, and the popular uprisings that swept across the Arab world in 2011, Arendt's faith in people's appetite for public freedom would almost certainly have been renewed.

THE DOUBLE BETRAYAL OF SOCRATES

The word Arendt uses to describe political action of this kind is 'power', but her use of this term, as may already be apparent, marks an important departure from the mainstream political tradition. Power, to begin with, is to be distinguished from violence, which had itself become a growing temptation to civil disobedients, including pacifists opposed to the war in Vietnam, when their public protests encountered the heavy hand of the state. Against the backdrop of the police and army brutality at the 1968 Chicago Democratic Convention, and with the fatal shooting of student protestors at Kent State, Jackson State College, and Columbia University during the same turbulent period, Arendt was minded to extend her reflections on government to address the growing phenomenon of violence in both domestic political affairs and foreign policy.

The resulting essay, *On Violence* (1970), does not shy away from criticising the romantic glorification of violence among militant elements of the New Left (the Weathermen in the US, the Red Army Faction in West Germany, and the Red Brigades in Italy being the most extreme manifestations of this trend). Arendt was particularly concerned here with the repetition of the original French revolutionaries' failure to distinguish power from violence, a mistake which was abetted by a more general intellectual trend towards relativism and ambiguity in the use of language. Inconsistency in the use of terms such as power, authority, coercion and force, indifference to the etymology of words and the related belief that it is the process of reasoning which we share and 'understand' when we exchange utterances, and not the words themselves, are for Arendt all classic symptoms of our modern worldlessness – our loss of a common linguistic world of stable and lasting meanings.

The conflation of different terms is also interpreted by Arendt as proof of the pernicious influence of functionalist sociology, the methodology of which, she argues, renders identical any phenomena which are deemed to serve the same societal need. In Arendt's representation of this perspective, 'if violence fulfils the same function as authority – namely, makes people obey – then violence is authority' (PF: 95–6, 102–3). The confusion of the distinction between violence and authority is also something that Arendt discerns in the Judaeo-Christian understanding of law as divine commandment. It is further promoted by the modern conception of the individual as driven by the desire to dominate and control others – a conception to which Arendt, referring to the public life of the Athenian slave-owner, takes particular exception, for 'if it were true that nothing is sweeter than to give commands and to rule others, the master would never have left his household' (OV: 40). Its roots, however, go right back to the foundations of Western thought, for it was Plato, in his depiction of a utopian city, who refused to conceive of the authority of law without the necessity of domination. Plato's proposal, in the *Republic*, that 'political power and philosophy be united in the same person' (473b–474a), had its origins in Socrates' failure to persuade the jurors at his trial of the merits of his philosophical teachings. Arendt points out that Socrates did not see himself, as his accusers said he did, as the fount of all wisdom and purveyor of truths (the wisest of all mortals, as the oracle at Delphi had said), but rather as the 'midwife' of truth, as someone who, through reciprocal questioning and dialogue, helped others to be more truthful. Socrates accepted the testimony of the oracle in the belief that he was being honoured for recognising his own ignorance, and Arendt suggests that it was probably the sheer inconclusiveness of Socrates' dialogues with his fellow citizens, his preference for questions over answers, and his failure to produce any definitive insights or opinions, which precipitated the charge that he was a corrupting influence on the practical business of the *polis* (PP: 15–25).

The refusal of Athenians to recognise the wisdom of his mentor led Plato to distinguish the temporary and flawed political opinions of the citizen from the eternal truths beheld by the philosopher. This was, Arendt points out, 'the most anti-Socratic conclusion that Plato drew from Socrates' trial' (PP: 8), for it immunised philosophy from the challenge that Socrates' denial of absolute wisdom had made to it, and broke the delicate link between thought and action which Socrates had promoted through the spoken word. While Socrates believed the public function of the philosopher was to build a common world of friendship, dialogue and exchange, for Plato the *polis* was no safe place for the philosopher, and government should therefore be designed in such a fashion as to guarantee to philosophers their exemption from action and the protection of their freedom to think.

Plato's ideal republic would thus be governed by an intellectual elite whose authentic insights into the truth of things – knowledge of the eternal 'Forms', or 'Ideas', as the concept of *eidos* is usually translated – would yield infallible standards and laws for the government of human action. In the parable of the cave (in Book 7 of the *Republic*), Plato shows that men will understand the wisdom of these rules only if they renounce the realm of human affairs, choose insight over speech, and leave the darkness of the cave in favour of the speechless wonder (*thaumazein*) of philosophical truth.

For the multitude, however, who remain in the cave's worldly realm of appearances and opinions, obedience to the just rules of the city-state could only be elicited with the help of a benevolent lie. The rulers in Plato's *Republic* are therefore advised to propagate the Phoenician fable that humans are moulded in the bowels of the earth and crafted with precious metals whose divine qualities are defiled by the handling of mortal riches. According to whether they are gold, silver, iron or copper, these metals also predispose each individual to a particular station in society which they are obliged to accept. The effect of this deception, according to Plato, would be to make the citizens shun selfish interests, accept the social function allotted to them, and 'feel towards their fellow-citizens as brother children of the soil' (414a–417b). It is with this 'seasonable falsehood' (Plato) in mind that Arendt believes we should read the final pages of the *Republic* (PF: 129, 293 n44). Recounting the mythical tale of Er, son of Armenius, Plato here breaks with his attempt to prove the rational superiority of lawful behaviour without reference to the approval of gods and men, reverting instead to a lengthy evangelical warning of 'the lot that awaits the just and the unjust after death', including 'tenfold retribution' for every crime (613b–621d). As Arendt points out, Plato's account of the graduated bodily punishments metered out on the unjust in the afterlife is clearly a deception aimed at winning the compliance of the multitude, for Plato's own philosophy is premised on the conviction that the soul, but not the feeling, suffering body, was immortal. Since this truth, as with all of Plato's Forms, was invisible to ordinary sense perception, the inhabitants of the cave, amenable to persuasion but not to a truth beyond argument, would have to make do with a necessary fiction (PF: 129–30; EU: 381–3).

Arendt points out that only when the Christian Church began to assume responsibility for secular interests did it face exactly the same predicament of how to impose the absolute standards of the few on the more populated realm of human affairs. And it was the political device of the Platonic hell, which threatened the disobedient not with death at the hands of their masters, but with the far more calamitous fate of eternal suffering, to which it resorted. Thus 'an element of violence was permitted to insinuate itself into both the very structure of Western religious thought and the hierarchy of the Church', a form of 'coercion through fear' which was 'alien to the letter and spirit of teaching of Jesus of Nazareth' (PF: 132–3).

THE SOCIOLOGY OF POWER

The legacy of this conflation of power with violence is also apparent, Arendt stresses, in the work of one of the founding fathers of sociology, and indeed the conception of power as domination remains central to contemporary sociological thought. In 'Politics as a Vocation', Max Weber wrote that 'one can define the modern state sociologically only in terms of the specific *means* peculiar to it, as to every political association, namely, the use of physical force'. In his account, 'the modern state is a compulsory association which organises domination', it is 'a relation of men dominating men, a relation supported by means of legitimate (i.e. considered to be legitimate) violence' (1970a: 77, 82, 78). 'The state', he writes elsewhere, 'is an association that claims the monopoly of the *legitimate use of violence*, and cannot be defined in any other manner' (1970c: 334, his emphasis). From this perspective, Arendt complains, 'violence is nothing more than the most flagrant manifestation of power' (OV: 35).

For Weber, instrumental reasoning ('*Zweckrationalität*') was the unstoppable destiny of the rationalisation process, and politics was no more exempt from this process than the sphere of economic life. Though the political vocation, unlike the value-neutral scientific enterprise, required 'passionate devotion to a "cause"', Weber believed the object of this devotion was ultimately a matter of personal conscience, and between different consciences no form of reason, communication or exchange could mediate. It is because 'ultimate *Weltanschauungen* clash, world views among which in the end one has to make a choice', that politics, for Weber, is always a clash of 'warring Gods' whose believers will yield only in the face of superior force. Weber went as far as to suggest that, once violence becomes the principal means of politics, its legitimacy requires its emancipation from moral passions and 'the complete elimination of ethics from political reasoning'. Though the state also uses war, and the prospect of dying for a greater cause, as a way of consecrating life in a disenchanted world and of creating 'a pathos and a sentiment of community', this ethic of brotherliness is still but a vehicle for the legitimation of force. For Weber, it seems, politics is ultimately a form of making, and to fashion society 'one must be willing to pay the price of using morally dubious means' (1970a: 117–28; 1970b: 153–6; 1970c: 334–5).

It is true that in the writings collected in *Economy and Society* Weber refined his analysis of power, introducing a new distinction between 'power' (*Macht*), which he refers to as the ability of an actor 'to carry out his will despite resistance', and 'domination' (*Herrschaft*), which is 'the probability that a command will be obeyed' (1978: 53). This command is obeyed because it is perceived as 'legitimate'; hence Weber talks here of 'legitimate domination' (*legitime Herrschaft*) or 'authority', as Parsons usually preferred to translate it (1978: 212–6). Though Weber maintained the position that 'legal coercion by violence is the monopoly of the state', he qualified this by denying that physical coercion is the primary means by which legal norms are upheld. 'The motives for obedience may rather be of many different kinds. In the majority of cases, they are predominantly utilitarian or ethical or subjectively conventional, i.e., consisting of the fear of disapproval by the environment' (1978: 314). Weber also divides the 'ultimate principles' on which the legitimacy of domination rests into three types: normative obedience to rational rules (which is characteristic of bureaucracy), personal authority sanctified by tradition (which is characteristic of patriarchalism), and personal authority attributed to the leader's charisma (which is characteristic of tribal, religious and cult communities) (1978: 954; 1970c: 295–9).

So Weber's position is less reductive than Arendt's brief comments on his work suggest, but his analysis of law and the modern state certainly remains trapped within an instrumental interpretation of power. As Weber conceives them, both power and 'legitimate domination' are models of teleological, or goal-directed, action: in the first case, coercion is the means by which a powerful agent realises his or her purposes by overcoming the resistance of others; in the second case, persuasion and agreement are the means by which these self-interests are realised. In neither case, however, is communicative interaction an end in itself, for at best it is a functional vehicle for the achievement of a dominant agent's pre-existing goals. Collective action – which, we shall see in a moment, is Arendt's definition of power – is thus subordinate to, and instrumentalised by, the goal-directed actions of individuals. One could say, in other words, that power – that is, acting in agreement – is reduced by Weber to a means for the legitimisation of domination and violence (see Habermas 1994; 1984: 243–71).

SOME TERMINOLOGICAL DISTINCTIONS

Arendt argues in *On Violence* that we need to distinguish clearly between five terms that are frequently confused in political and sociological thought. These are: force, authority, strength, violence and power. Although in vernacular speech it is normally used as a synonym for violence and coercion, the term 'force' is one that Arendt thinks we should reserve for 'the energy released by physical or social movements' (OV: 45). Her definition of force is cursory and uncharacteristically vague, but in referring to 'force of circumstances' and 'forces of nature' the meaning she conveys is one of anonymous, impersonal movement, a process with an implacable momentum that cannot be slowed or steered by political action and speech. It is, as we have seen, the struggle against the 'force of nature', the often violent endeavour to transcend the forces of necessity, which is for Arendt the pre-political foundation of humans' public freedom. Social movements, like the multitude during the French Revolution, corrupt the meaning of political freedom when they are determined by the same 'force' from which that freedom is meant to deliver them. In Arendt's thinking, this concept of force, as we shall see in Chapter 7, is also applicable to totalitarian movements whose members view themselves as agents of unstoppable historical or biological laws. The same concept seems equally consistent with Arendt's depiction of the anonymous force of bureaucratic domination: 'an intricate system of bureaus in which no men, neither one nor the best, neither the few nor the many, can be held responsible, and which could be properly called rule by Nobody' (OV: 38). Thus, just as Arendt sees an element of violence inherent in humans' struggle against the mute forces of nature, so she also remarks how the attraction of violence grows when public life is bureaucratised and there is nobody left to whom people can address their grievances with a realistic prospect of mutual communication and debate (OV: 81).

We have already seen how important the concept of 'authority' is to Arendt's understanding of the stability of political constitutions, and it is true that she thinks of authority in a way that bears some similarity to Weber's conception of 'legitimate domination'. Authority, she argues, can be vested both in persons (the teacher or the parent) and in offices (like the Roman Senate, the Supreme Court in the American Constitution, or the Holy Orders of the Christian church). The defining characteristic of authority 'is unquestioning recognition by those who are asked to obey; neither coercion nor persuasion is needed' (OV: 45). Authority also appears to be a functional prerequisite for the administration of technology-intensive public spaces, and its breakdown can have chaotic consequences. Arendt gives the example of the reported failure of the transit authorities in New York to convince the passengers in a defective train to evacuate it. The collapse of 'authentic authority in social relations' percolated down to 'its derivative, purely functional form', and the effect was the shutdown of the whole subway network (OV: 46).

'Strength', for Arendt, is 'the property inherent in an object or person and belongs to its character'. The implication is that strength is normally physical, but may also be a psychological attribute (hence we refer to 'strength of character'). Arendt's understanding of strength which, because it is an attribute of the individual, 'can always be overwhelmed by the many' (OV: 44), exhibits a passing resemblance to Weber's definition of 'charisma': 'a highly individual quality' of 'specific gifts of body and mind' (1978: 1111ff).

Phenomenologically speaking, 'violence', according to Arendt, is 'close to strength'. Violence employs instruments which magnify the strength of the individual, 'until, in the last stage of their development, they can substitute for it' (OV: 46). But Arendt points out that no government has ever been able to rule purely by violence, which normally functions as a 'last resort' against rebellious individuals. Violence is an instrument – is instrument*al* – and therefore 'always stands in need of guidance and justification through the end it pursues' (OV: 51). When this guidance and justification is lacking, superior means of violence may be overcome – in revolutions, in colonial uprisings, in Vietnam, in May '68 and the momentous events of 1989 – by the mobilisation of precisely what violence lacks.

What is missing from sheer violence and what it relies on for justification and viability, is 'power'. In contrast to the classical sociological conception of power as a resource for the realisation of predetermined ends – as 'a means of getting things done', to use Giddens's definition (1984: 175) – Arendt sees power as the quality of human plurality which appears when humans, aided by the faculties of communicating and promise-making, act in concert. Hence power 'springs up between men when they act together and vanishes the moment they disperse' (HC: 200). When we speak correctly of someone as being 'in power', Arendt writes, this is not because this person 'possesses' the means for getting their own way, but because we have collectively 'empowered' that person to act on our behalf. For unlike strength, power is not the property of an individual, and unlike authority or violence, relations of domination and obedience are not intrinsic to the existence of power. Power cannot be stored up like the means of violence, and when power is not actualised the public realm of acting and speaking beings disappears. Power is 'dependent upon the unreliable and only temporary agreement of many wills and intentions', and this is why power 'is actualised only when word and deed have not parted company' (HC: 201, 200). The checks and balances of separate wills whose boundless interplay is a natural articulation of human plurality can also generate more power, Arendt suggests. For it is the division and exchange of different perspectives which brings to life the public realm, flooding that realm, through the interspaces between individuals, with a light that illuminates the world as a common concern.

Being instrumental, violence must be justified by its ends, and the further in the future are those ends the more unjustified is violence. As someone who advocated a Jewish army during the Second World War, and who offered her unqualified support to Israel during the Arab-Israeli conflicts of 1967 and 1973, Arendt was clearly not a pacifist. She rejected the assumption that violence was inhuman, noting that when people are truly dehumanised – as they were in the death camps – rage and violence are conspicuous by their absence. Violence is 'anti-political' because it is 'mute by definition', and this is why the voices of politicians during war deserve little public trust: 'here words become "mere talk", they have no acting capacity any longer, everybody knows that action has left the realm of speech' (EU: 376–7). When dissemblance and hypocrisy prevail in public life and language cannot be relied upon as a revelatory medium, rage may be a justifiable reaction to the concealing function of speech: 'To use reason when reason is used as a trap is not "rational"; just as to use a gun in self-defence is not "irrational"' (OV: 66). Using violence in self-defence is acceptable, Arendt argues, because the end which justifies it – the preservation of life – is immediate and uncontroversial.

Power can overcome strength better than violence can, Arendt continues, but violence poses more of a problem to power than it does to strength, because strength is a gift of nature which the individual can preserve by withdrawing from a violent world (HC: 203). Yet while violence can certainly destroy power – 'out of the barrel of the gun grows the most effective command, resulting in the most instant and perfect obedience' (OV: 53) – it cannot create it. Because it depends on what it destroys, violence cannot survive as a stable form of government. Indeed, if all power is destroyed, if all human associations are liquidated and social atomisation reigns, what we have is not violence but terror, which for Arendt is the essence of totalitarianism. 'The decisive difference between totalitarian domination, based on terror, and tyrannies and dictatorships, established by violence, is that the former turns not only against its enemies but against its friends and supporters as well, being afraid of all power, even the power of its friends' (OV: 55).

ARENDT AND FOUCAULT

Arendt's critique of the Platonic-Weberian command-obedience theory of power, and her refusal to equate power with sovereignty, displays interesting similarities with other theoretical approaches to understanding power, including perspectives which arise from very different political and epistemological traditions. Steven Lukes, for example, highlights how Arendt's conception of power as the capacity of combined action shares something with Parsons' conservative description of power 'as a generalised medium of mobilising commitments or obligation for effective collective action', a definition which is enfeebled, according to Lukes, because it 'dissociates it from conflicts of interest and, in particular, from coercion and force' (1974: 28–31). This is also Habermas's chief complaint against Arendt whose 'communicative' theory of power, he argues, though correctly describing power's *emergence*, needs to be complemented by the notion of 'strategic action'. The latter, in his view, offers a more accurate description of the competition for access to *already constituted* power, which is essentially a struggle, normalised by modern legal and political institutions, 'to prevent other individuals or groups from realising their interests' (1994: 222; 1996: 149). One is reminded here of C. W. Mills' Weberian definition of politics: 'All politics is a struggle for power; the ultimate kind of power is violence' (1956: 171).

John Allen, on the other hand, applauds Arendt's attempts to differentiate between the different modalities of what we think of as power. Allen argues that the 'associational' notion of power found in Arendt rightly acknowledges the benefits enjoyed by people when they relate, 'transversally', in the public sphere, instead of competing for strategic resources in a zero-sum game (2003: 54–8). The result, in his view, is a theory well suited to understanding contemporary forms of political mobilisation – such as human rights campaigns, pro-democracy movements, and environmental protests – which are aimed not at elevating, at others' expense, the social position of particular groups, but rather at transcending particular interests in pursuit of an enlarged political sphere. This is similar to Iris Young's argument that the concept of political responsibility must register the routine participation of millions of people in global patterns of social injustice, and that this responsibility can only be positively discharged by social movements empowering themselves to challenge those structural injustices (Young 2003).

One can also detect similarities between Arendt's critique of the instrumental theory of power and Foucault's challenge to what he calls the 'juridico-discursive' model of power. The similarities do not end here, for both thinkers are notable for the doubts they have cast on the idea that the disclosure of the inner self, with its (sexual) desires, motives and emotions, amounts to the liberation of a pre-constituted subjectivity. Arendt and Foucault share a common interest in what Giorgio Agamben (1998) believes is 'the foundational event of modernity'. This is the spread of *animal laborans* into the political sphere – the 'public organisation of the life process' (Arendt), or what Foucault calls the emergence of 'bio-power'. 'For millennia, man remained what he was for Aristotle: a living animal with the additional capacity for a political existence; modern man is an animal whose politics places his existence as a living being in question' (Foucault 1981: 143).

In Agamben's account of this development, Aristotle's fragile distinction (in the *Politics*, 1278b15–30) between mere life and the good life, between *zoē* and *bios*, has been dissolved by 'the entry of *zoē* into the sphere of the *polis*', revealing in the process 'the inner solidarity between democracy and totalitarianism' (1998: 4, 10). Because the political management of life destroys what is distinctively human in politics, the bio-political body becomes naked life, that is, humanity stripped of its political and cultural significance: 'The total humanisation of the animal coincides with a total animalisation of man' (Agamben 2004: 77).

Foucault's theory of bio-politics is famous for rejecting the idea that power is a fixed resource which is wielded in a negative, sometimes murderous, fashion – as something which destroys, subtracts, expropriates, represses, prohibits, conceals and excludes. Instead power is conceived as a dispersed network of relations which mobilise desire, harness bodies and construct individuals as manageable and self-managing subjects.

> The individual is no doubt the fictitious atom of an 'ideological' representation of society; but he is also a reality fabricated by this specific technology of power that I have called 'discipline'. We must cease once and for all to describe the effects of power in negative terms: it 'excludes', it 'represses', it 'censors', it 'abstracts', it 'masks', it 'conceals'. In fact, power produces; it produces reality; it produces domains of objects and rituals of truth. The individual and the knowledge that may be gained of him belong to this production. (Foucault 1991: 194)

Though Foucault speaks of power in 'positive' terms, this is a mathematical rather than normative description; that is, it is a measurement of power's productive output, rather than a judgement of its desirability. This output could be death as much as life; indeed Foucault noted the seemingly paradoxical connection between the political optimisation of life and wholesale slaughters waged in the name of survival: 'If genocide is indeed the dream of modern powers, this is not because of a recent return of the ancient right to kill; it is because power is situated and exercised at the level of life, the species, the race, and the large-scale phenomena of population' (1981: 137).

Bio-power may therefore be deadly, but Foucault was notoriously reluctant to take an explicit normative position on its existence, believing that normative judgements simply perpetuate the disciplinary force of normalisation that is the legacy of Enlightenment humanism. The contradiction in this is clear and well known. On the one hand, Foucault argues that debates over the *legitimacy* of power are caught within the distorting eighteenth-century discourse of liberal right. Instead of theorising unjust power ('oppression') as power which transgresses the rightful limits of contract and consent, Foucault says we should think of power as a permanent, but always unstable and reversible, 'relation of domination' in which 'repression is none other than the realisation, within the continual warfare of this pseudo-peace, of a perpetual relationship of force' (1980a: 92). As Foucault explained of his work in retrospect: 'the question of power needed to be reformulated not so much in terms of justice as in those of technology, of tactics and strategy' (1980d: 184). He therefore stressed that 'relations of power are not something bad in themselves, from which one must free oneself' (1987: 18), claiming that he had moved from a critique of the 'why' to a description of the 'how' – from exploring not the legitimacy of power but rather its method and mode of operation (1980a: 96).

On the other hand, Foucault's determination to evade the disciplinary effects of humanistic discourse, and the critical distance he necessarily assumed between his own ideas and those of the power/ knowledge regimes he studied, itself involves a normative judgement, because it implicitly presents disciplinary power as something to be avoided, subverted and challenged. This presupposition – this 'crypto-normativism', as Habermas (1987a) refers to it – moves to the foreground in Foucault's later work, where he offers the reassurance that his proposition that 'power is everywhere' does not mean that 'there is no liberty', for 'there cannot be relations of power unless the subjects are free', and if the subjects are free then 'there is necessarily the possibility of resistance' (1987: 12). To which one must reply: what good is liberty and what good is resistance to power – indeed, in what sense is resistance to power *any different from power* – unless power itself is normatively 'bad'?

Despite his claims to the contrary, therefore, Foucault's concept of power remains at some level tied to the normatively negative, instrumental sense that is consistent with the Western tradition of political theory. While for Arendt power, unlike violence and authority, is an end in itself, the expression of individuals' highest capacity for combined action, Foucault's conception does not fully break with the idea of power as instrumental control and domination. When questioned about Arendt's attempt to dissociate power from domination, Foucault distanced himself from what he suggested was a purely 'verbal' distinction, pointing out that acting in agreement may itself function as a 'regulatory principle', that is, a mechanism for the reproduction of disciplinary relations. 'The farthest I would go is to say that perhaps one must not be for consensuality, but one must be against nonconsensuality' (1984: 378–9). Power, for Foucault, is thus 'a multiform production of relations of domination', something which is 'utilised in strategies', which functions as the 'means by which individuals try to conduct, to determine the behaviour of others' (1980c: 142; 1987: 18). In fact, by explicitly rejecting Habermas's theory – which, in Foucault's words, 'allows the fundamental operation of power to be thought of as that of a speech-act', whereby a claim to validity is raised and a subject is conceived who 'says yes or no' (1980c: 140) – Foucault comes dangerously close to reducing 'bio-power' to mute and ubiquitous violence, to 'continuous and uninterrupted processes which subject our bodies, govern our gestures, dictate our behaviours etc.' (1980a: 97)

Hence Foucault's claim to have moved beyond the liberal-positivist model of power is not entirely valid, for in practice he combines a constructivist conception of power (power produces subjects, knowledge, desire and norms) with the normative judgement that power is 'subjugation' that precipitates welcome 'resistance'. The incoherence that results from this conflation of perspectives arises because it is impossible to establish in what sense and *for whom* power is something undesirable, something worthy of analysis, condemnation and contestation, when power, in his analysis, functions by producing the individuals it dominates. When Foucault stresses the need 'to dispense with the constituent subject, to get rid of the subject itself' (1980b: 117), one has to ask *who* is empowered to 'dispense with the subject', *who* should mount resistance to power in either its non-consensual or consensual manifestations, and *why*?[4] For whereas power for Arendt is combined action, and action is always the disclosure of an autonomous subject, for Foucault there is no resistance to power which is not already an effect of it.

> [I]t is already one of the prime effects of power that certain bodies, certain gestures, certain discourses, certain desires, come to be identified and constituted as individuals. The individual, that is, is not the *vis-à-vis* of power; it is, I believe, one of its effects.

The individual is an effect of power, and at the same time, or precisely to the extent to which it is that effect, it is the element of its articulation. The individual which power has constituted is at the same time its vehicle. (Foucault 1980a: 98)

If, on the other hand, we adopt a less constructivist interpretation of Foucault's later thinking, and accept his repudiation of the earlier notion of the 'passive subject' (1987: 11), then we are left with a normative vision which Ronald Beiner (1997) argues is really only a form of 'hyper-liberalism'. Reconceptualising the 'care for the self' as an aestheticised practice of liberation, Foucault seemed to give up altogether on the idea of public freedom, proposing instead that the ruse of positive power could be resisted by treating the self as an essentially private 'work of art' whose playful intensity can be sustained 'without any relation with the juridical per se, with an authoritarian system, with a disciplinary structure' (1984: 348; 1987). Freedom can be enjoyed, in other words, whatever the form of government; indeed, the fashioning of the self is now envisaged independently of all historically instituted codes and constraints (Whitebook 2002: 68–9). Only the bleakest possible assessment of the potential for public freedom in the modern world could justify endorsing this privatised theory of resistance. Yet Arendt herself was not immune to such pessimism, nor, as we shall see, to an aestheticised conception of politics. Indeed, as Villa (1992) and Allen (2002) have both argued, it would be wrong to suggest that the differences between these two thinkers are completely unbridgeable.

4
Marxism, Ecology and Culture

In this and the chapter that follows, I want to think more exactingly about Arendt's political philosophy. In the next chapter I will look more closely at Arendt's distinction between the social and the political, using feminist approaches to her work as a starting point for a wider discussion of her political theory. My intention in this present chapter, however, is to examine Arendt's critique of Marx, and then to move on to explore in more detail her understanding of the relationship between nature and culture, and between culture and class, and consider how this relates to her theory of the *vita activa*.

TOTALITARIAN ELEMENTS IN MARXISM

At the outset it should be recognised that Arendt saw Marx as one of the great thinkers of the modern age, though her esteem for his work declined as she began to scrutinise its exact location in the history of Western political thought. Initially she seemed to regard Marx as a Jewish rebel belonging to a noble tradition of 'conscious pariahs', someone who, in his 'fanatical zeal for justice, carried on the Jewish tradition much more efficaciously' than the parvenus who sought assimilation as 'exceptions' (JP: 110). In letters to Jaspers in 1949 and 1950, Arendt complained how, after the Stalinisation of the Soviet Union, 'every little idiot thinks he has the right and duty to look down on Marx'. In his defence she commended Marx for his revolutionary 'passion for justice', and expressed her desire 'to rescue Marx's honour' in the eyes of her mentor and friend (Arendt and Jaspers 1992: 137, 160). Yet Jaspers replied by reiterating his uncompromising opposition to historical materialism, condemning the way Marx 'falls victim to his own hatred and follows, in the name of justice, into an abominable vision', and predicting that Arendt would 'in the end find Marx the intellectually responsible originator of what prepared the way for totalitarianism' (Arendt and Jaspers 1992: 187, 205). By this time Arendt had been awarded a Guggenheim research grant for a study entitled 'Totalitarian

Elements in Marxism', and it was only a few months later, in May 1953, that she rather feebly conceded to her mentor: 'The more I read Marx, the more I see that you were right. He's not interested either in freedom or in justice' (Arendt and Jaspers 1992: 216).

But that certainly wasn't the whole story, for Arendt also saw something valuable in Marx's 'scientific' critique of utopian socialism, with his contempt for bourgeois morality resonating with her own suspicions over the insinuation of moral motives into the realm of public affairs. On this Marx was worthy of praise, for he had 'liberated the socialist movement from its worn-out moralising attitudes, and recognised that the class questions in modern society could no longer be solved by a "passion for justice" or on the basis of slightly modified Christian charity' (Arendt 2002: 309).

Arendt wrote hundreds of pages of notes in preparation for a book on Marx, but the book itself never materialised. Instead she drew on her studies for a Princeton lecture series on 'Karl Marx and the Tradition of Western Political Thought', and incorporated her notes into *The Human Condition*, *On Revolution*, and the essays 'Tradition and the Modern Age' and 'The Concept of History', both of which were republished in *Between Past and Future*. In 2002, excerpts from her manuscripts on Marx were also published in a special issue of the journal *Social Research* (Arendt 2002). It is important to note at this point that the first edition of Arendt's *The Origins of Totalitarianism* had appeared in 1951. This study, which I will review at some length in Chapters 6 and 7, has been criticised for its unbalanced focus on Nazism, and for the obvious discrepancies between Stalinism and Nazism which Arendt's single category of 'totalitarianism' had elided.

Arendt herself appeared to be aware of one important distinction, which was that Nazism was never able to draw ideological sustenance from a genuine intellectual figurehead in the way Bolshevism was able to call on Marx. It is well known that Arendt saw both forms of totalitarian domination as a radical departure from the political history of the Occident, a break which 'could never have been foreseen or forethought, much less predicted or "caused", by any single man' (2002: 281). Arendt had claimed, in *The Origins of Totalitarianism*, that the violent racism of the European imperialists, which laid the practical and ideological foundations for the catastrophes of the following century, displayed an 'utter incompatibility with all Western political and moral standards of the past', and 'led to an almost complete break in the continuous flow of Western history as we had known it for more than two thousand years' (OT: 184, 123). Arendt's insistence on the absolute novelty of totalitarianism has not passed unchallenged, and it has been argued that she was far too eager to exonerate the long and esteemed history of Western intellectual culture from the terrible crimes of twentieth-century Europe, and far too reluctant to acknowledge the significance of earlier instances of race-thinking, Jew-hatred, and colonial atrocities that had preceded the age of imperialism (Bernasconi 2007). Arendt's position is more complex than this, however, as she was equally determined to expose the flawed understanding of the *vita activa*, and the fatal association of power with violence, that Western culture had inherited from the philosophers of antiquity.

So Arendt does not claim that totalitarianism was a direct product of the tradition of Western thought, but that the errors in this tradition made it ill-equipped to recognise and resist the subterranean currents which began to surface in the last decades of the nineteenth century. To put this another way: totalitarianism was a perverted manifestation of humans' unique capacity to break with the past and establish an entirely new form of government; and the philosophical tradition of the West, with its upside-down understanding of the *vita activa*, was incapable of registering the terrible radicalism of this assault on what had gone before.

The fact that Marx was used, or even *mis*used, by a totalitarian movement, therefore suggested two things to Arendt. It implied, on the one hand, that Marx had produced a perceptive analysis of the enormous changes taking place in nineteenth-century Western Europe, since without these insights into the new historical conditions of the time his ideas would have never had the influence they did. On the other hand, it suggested that Marx had failed to break out of the framework of Western philosophy sufficiently to grasp the unprecedented nature of the social transformations he had begun to witness, and thus to fully comprehend the dark future they portended. Though he had overturned the idealism of Hegel and replaced the philosophers' reverence for thinking with a materialist theory of *praxis*, Marx still found himself 'having to deal with new phenomena in terms of an old tradition of thought outside of whose conceptual framework no thinking seemed possible at all' (PF: 25). For Arendt, in fact, 'the line from Aristotle to Marx shows both fewer and far less decisive breaks than the line from Marx to Stalin' (2002: 277). To understand the connection between totalitarianism and Marx, in other words, we must first expose the hidden fault lines in the Occidental philosophical tradition which left its modern heirs unable to foresee the catastrophe that was fast approaching.

According to Arendt, Marx's conscious rebellion against the traditional hierarchy of thought and action, by which he dignified the one activity that philosophers had always despised or deemed irrelevant, was led astray by his inheritance of two tacit assumptions from Western political thought. The first of these two assumptions was the notion that political action is a form of making – that 'history is "made" by men as nature is "made" by God' (HC: 228) – and therefore that violence, as the French and American revolutions had evidently proven, is indispensable to the establishment of a new body politic. The second is the related but seemingly contradictory idea, deeply rooted in Christianity but perpetuated by evolutionary science, Hegel's philosophy of history, and the naturalism of the Romantics, that human life and history is a *process*, analogous to the irresistible imperatives of organic life, whose advancement is destined to outstrip the worldly but never fully permanent accomplishments of individuals.

> To our modern way of thinking nothing is meaningful in and by itself, not even history or nature taken each as a whole, and certainly not particular occurrences in the physical order or specific historical events ... Invisible processes have engulfed every tangible thing, every individual entity that is visible to us, degrading them into functions of an over-all process ... What the concept of process implies is that the concrete and the general, the single thing or event and the universal meaning, have parted company. The process, which alone makes meaningful whatever it happens to carry along, has thus acquired a monopoly of universality and significance. (PF: 63–4)

THE REDUCTION OF ACTION TO MAKING

The first defect in Marx's thinking, then, is what Arendt regards as his failure to grasp the importance of political action. Arendt asserts that the seeds of this failure actually lie in Greek philosophy, the full flourishing of which coincided with the decay of the original conception and experience of the *polis*. For it was the philosophers of antiquity who first gave credence to the view that the public sphere was undeserving of serious concern. Demanding that freedom from the necessities of life be the precondition not of political action, but of the private solitude of the thinker, they took an interest in political affairs only in order to see the *bios theōrētikos* protected.

> Thus our tradition of political philosophy, unhappily and fatefully, and from its very beginning, has deprived political affairs, that is, those activities concerning the common public realm that come into being wherever men live together, of all dignity of their own. In Aristotelian terms, politics is a means to an end; it has no end in and by itself. More than that, the proper end of politics is in a way its opposite, namely, nonparticipation in political affairs, *scholē*, the condition of philosophy, or rather the condition of a life devoted to it. (Arendt 2002: 314)

This turning away from political action was tied up with a revolt against the political faculty of speech. Arendt reserves praise for Aristotle for being, in her words, 'the last for whom freedom is not yet "problematic" but inherent in the faculty of speech', who 'still knew that men, as long as they talk with each other and act together in the *modus* of speech, are free' (2002: 298). But it was Aristotle's teacher, Plato, who did most to prise apart the intimate connection between freedom and speech, responding to the decay of the Greek city-state, epitomised, in his eyes, by the fateful trial of Socrates, by treating the public exchange of opinions as inadequate to the pursuit of truth. The realm of public affairs was now revealed as a confused and transient world of shadowy appearances which could never fulfil humans' need for lasting significance in the imperishable cosmos of nature and the gods. For Plato, the promise of immortality lay in the clear sky of eternal ideas, and this truth could be reached only when the solitary philosopher, in speechless and actionless contemplation, dwelled silently in its neighbourhood.

According to Arendt, the abyss this opened up between speech and action, and between solitude and living together, has never since been closed. Although Marx overturned the Platonic primacy of thought over action, substituting the *animal laborans* for the *animal rationale*, he inherited the philosophers' basic mistrust of speech, combining this with the idea, which had already been voiced in Descartes' suspicion that the truth was concealed by an evil spirit, that the phenomenal forms given to sensory perception are a distortion of the inner reality of things, for 'all science would be superfluous if the form of appearance of things directly coincided with their essence' (Marx 1981: 956). Since appearance had now become essentially mute, and the spoken word, in its various legal, political, spiritual and aesthetic expressions, played the concealing function of ideology, truth for Marx must be revealed through a speechless manipulation of the given. As Habermas puts it: 'Marx declares the will to *make* to be the precondition for the ability to *know*' (1974: 248). This 'will', in Arendt's account, is inherently predisposed to violence:

> Since Plato it had become axiomatic that 'it lies in the nature of *praxis* to partake less of truth than speech'. According to Marx, it is not only *praxis* per se that shows more truth than speech, but the one kind of *praxis* that has severed all bonds with speech. For violence, in distinction to all other kinds of human action, is mute by definition. Speech on the other hand is not only deemed to partake less of truth than action, but is now conceived to be mere 'ideological' talk whose chief function is to conceal the truth. (Arendt 2002: 291)

As most clearly indicated in the 'Theses on Feuerbach', Marx inherited from modern science the view that truth is revealed neither through the exchange of perspectives nor through solitary observation and reflection, but must instead be produced by means of intervening in the structure of the world itself. That this intervention is modelled on the work of the craftsman – on *poiēsis* rather than *praxis*, strictly speaking – is suggested by two elements of Marx's work. First, there is the emphasis on violence as the necessary catalyst for revolutionary transformation. 'Force', Marx wrote, growing impatient with the dialectical laws of history, 'is the midwife of every old society which is pregnant with a new one. It is itself an economic power' (1976: 716). Here we see, in fact, the curious combination in Marx's thinking of the deterministic idea of *process*, which we will consider in a moment, and the seemingly contradictory concept of *making* which, though it always entails an element of violence, embodies the humanistic desire to rise above the forces of compulsion. Since the craft worker must envisage, before setting to work, the form and pattern of the thing to be created, Arendt argues that Marx identified 'the contemplative gaze of the historian with the contemplation of the model (the *eidos* or "shape" from which Plato had derived his "ideas") that guides the craftsmen and precedes all making' (PF: 78). Setting out to unlock the secret process of social change, Marx found in Hegel's philosophy of history a predictive template capable of guiding the dextrous hand of humanity. Armed with this insight into the hidden course of history, proletarians could alter their intentions to make them conform to the inner laws of movement such that freedom and necessity were united. The historical process, in other words, was conceived as a 'pattern', for 'within the limitations of utilitarian thought nothing but patterns can make sense, because only patterns can be "made", whereas meanings cannot be, but, like truth, will only disclose or reveal themselves. Marx was only the first – and still the greatest, among historians – to mistake a pattern for a meaning' (PF: 80–1).

So men could make history, but only by forcing their fellow men to follow the path already prescribed to them:

> the many individual wills active in history for the most part produce results quite other than those they intended – often quite the opposite; their motives therefore in relation to the total result are likewise of only secondary significance ... To ascertain the driving causes which here in the minds of acting masses and their leaders ... are reflected as conscious motives, clearly or unclearly, directly or in ideological, even glorified form – that is the only path which can put us on the track of the laws holding sway both in history as a whole, and at particular periods and in particular lands. (Engels 1934: 59–60)

The reduction of action to making is of course the temptation of all political agents when confronted with the inherent unpredictability of action and with the impossibility of foretelling the consequences of what men and women choose to do. Yet when applied to the realm of human affairs, the utilitarian conviction that 'you can't make an omelette without breaking eggs' not only threatens the essence of political freedom, but also fails to justify its own promethean optimism. Precisely because action, when conducted in conditions of human plurality, is inherently unpredictable, the higher ends aimed at by harmful or heartless means can never be guaranteed. What *is* certain in these situations, however, is the brutality of the means. Hence, where action is concerned, if there is a moral emphasis it must fall on the integrity of the means; which is to say that action defines itself by taking itself as an end. 'Each good action, even for a "bad cause", adds some real goodness to the world', Arendt writes in a rare concession to the idea of moral action; 'each bad action even for the most beautiful of all ideals makes our common world a little worse' (EU: 281). Or as Arendt puts it in her essay on violence: 'The practice of violence, like all action, changes the world, but the most probable change is to a more violent world' (OV: 80).

The second indication that Marx viewed political action as a form of making is that, just as the work of the fabricator comes to an end with the completed product, so Marx seemed to believe that with the abolition of class society 'the public power will lose its political character' and politics, which is associated with violence and domination, will come to an end (Marx and Engels 1967: 105; Marx 1995: 190). Marx's cursory thoughts, mainly in the 'Critique of the Gotha Programme', on a future politics-free government, were expressed more clearly by Engels, and most dogmatically by Lenin in *The State and Revolution*. In *Anti-Dühring* (1969: 333), and then in 'Socialism: Utopian and Scientific' (1951a: 138), Engels looked forward to the 'withering away' or 'dying out' of the state, when 'the government of persons is replaced by the administration of things, and by the conduct of processes of production'. In his note 'On Authority' he continued:

> All Socialists are agreed that the political state, and with it political authority, will disappear as a result of the coming social revolution, that is, that public functions will lose their political character and be transformed into the simple administrative functions of watching over the true interests of society. (Engels 1950: 577)

Though Marx and Engels' vision of communism as the reduction of the sphere of labour and the triumph of freedom over necessity was 'obviously conceived in accordance with Athenian democracy' (HC: 131), Arendt contends that this vision effectively reproduced the outlook of the philosophers instead of capturing the actual experience of the Greek *polis*. For while the citizens of the *polis* enjoyed freedom from labour in the form of participation in public affairs, for Marx and Engels the realm of public decision-making is merely an instrumental adjunct to the realm of necessity, a sphere of administration so simplified that it is of interest only to mediocre minds. Referring to the well-known description of communism in *The German Ideology*, 'where nobody has one exclusive sphere of activity but each can become accomplished in any branch he wishes', and where one can hunt, fish, rear cattle and philosophise 'without ever becoming hunter, fisherman, herdsman or critic' (Marx and Engels 1998: 53), Arendt argues that Marx not only denuded his future society of political action, but also reserved no place for the specialist activity of the worker, whose worldly orientation is dissolved into playful experimentation and entertainment. Having reduced action to work, *praxis* to *poiēsis*, then made this work redundant in a post-capitalist society, the only activities left for the men and women of Marx's communist utopia appear to be worldless forms of leisure.

> Marx predicted correctly, though with an unjustified glee, 'the withering away' of the public realm under conditions of unhampered development of the 'productive forces of society', and he was equally right, that is, consistent with his conception of man as an *animal laborans*, when he foresaw that 'socialised men' would spend their freedom from labouring in those strictly private and essentially worldless activities that we now call 'hobbies'. (HC: 117–18)

THE TRIUMPH OF PROCESS AND THE GLORIFICATION OF LABOUR

When the ancient philosophers turned away from politics, they attributed to political action inferior qualities previously associated only with labouring. The exchange of opinions in the public sphere became a regrettable compulsion, a necessary evil arising out of the fact that people who live together must communicate not just to survive, but also to guarantee the philosopher's precious freedom to think. By the time Marx and Engels were writing, a new reason for doubting the relevance of political action had emerged, which was the hitherto unknown phenomenon of systematic and sustained economic accumulation. As this process, which was now routinely understood in organic terms, was accompanied by an equally unstoppable growth in the industrial proletariat, it was understandable, in Arendt's view, that Marx believed the key to the future of this new world lay in the natural activity of labour.

> The crudest suspicion of the modern age – that 'money begets money' as well as its sharpest political insight – that power generates power – owes its plausibility to the underlying metaphor of the natural fertility of life. Of all human activities, only labour, and neither action nor work, is unending, progressing automatically in accordance with life itself and outside the range of wilful decisions or humanly meaningful purposes. (HC: 105–6)

Witnessing the effects of the industrial revolution and seeking to identify progressive tendencies in the maelstrom of 'everlasting uncertainty and agitation' that characterised the new mode of production, Marx and Engels (1967) presented the productive powers called up from the nether world by the bourgeois sorcerer as irrepressible forces incompatible with the long-term interests of capital, but inseparable from those of the downtrodden proletariat. Hegel, of course, had furnished the philosophical framework enabling Marx and Engels to interpret all manner of accidents, reversals and deprivations in progressive terms, rejecting Feuerbach's 'contemplative materialism' and replacing the worldly stability of things with the irresistible power of the historical *process*.

> The great basic thought that the world is not to be comprehended as a complex of ready-made *things*, but as a complex of *processes*, in which the things apparently stable no less than their mind-images in our heads, the concepts, go through an uninterrupted change of coming into being and passing away, in which, in spite of all seeming accidents and of all temporary retrogression, a progressive development asserts itself in the end – this great fundamental thought has, especially since the time of Hegel, so thoroughly permeated ordinary consciousness that in this generality it is scarcely ever contradicted. (Engels 1934: 54)

Better than anyone else, Arendt believes, Marx and Engels understood the tremendous productivity of labour, strikingly magnified by the development of mechanisation, and they saw in the massed and growing ranks of the labouring class a material force that no amount of philosophical interpretation, idealist speculation or bourgeois political economy could conjure away. But in doing so, Arendt argues, they attributed to the activity of this class a power and dignity which properly belongs not to labour, but to work.

> The modern age in general and Karl Marx in particular, overwhelmed, as it were, by the unprecedented actual productivity of Western mankind, had an almost irresistible tendency to look upon all labour as work and to speak of the *animal laborans* in terms much more fitting for *homo faber*, hoping all the time that only one more step was needed to eliminate labour and necessity altogether. (HC: 87)

Arendt stresses the fact that although labour is bound to necessity and the imperatives of life, the revolution in manufacturing showed that, like nature, the fertility of labour can be increased so that it produces a surplus beyond its immediate needs. But while the modern age 'saw labour elevated to express man's positive freedom, his freedom of productivity' (PF: 32), in reality this activity remained within the constraints of necessity and was not transformed into work, since it was still the reproduction, or multiplication, of life which was its ultimate product. Labour, Arendt stresses, 'can be used for the reproduction of more than one life process, but it never "produces" anything but life' (HC: 88). The surplus produced by labour – 'surplus-value' in Marx's political economy – can of course be accumulated in the form of capital. But the willingness of capitalism to destroy this accumulated surplus, to liquidate it in orgies of war and periodic waves of recession, illustrates how worldless is the output of the labourer. That Marx condemned the contradictions of class society for inhibiting economic growth proved to Arendt that he too was in thrall to the pernicious modern doctrine that the process of life is the highest good: 'the role of revolution was ... to liberate the life process of society from the fetters of scarcity so that it could swell into a stream of abundance. Not freedom but abundance became now the aim of revolution' (OR: 64).

Arendt's complaint in *The Human Condition* that Marx 'describes labour in terms of work' (HC: 313 n76) is slightly misleading, as she spends more time demonstrating how Marx's own descriptions actually fit her own category of labour than she does offering rival accounts of the nineteenth-century labour process in order to prove that it was labour, not work, that Marx should have been examining. What she appears to mean by this is that Marx attributed to labour a degree of esteem that he really should have reserved for the worldly activities of the fabricator. Marx's preoccupation with the generative powers of labour, rather than the world-building faculties of the worker, is certainly suggested by a number of passages in his writings. In *The German Ideology*, for example, Marx and Engels speak of the 'double relationship' inherent in the 'production of life, both of one's own in labour and of fresh life in procreation', implying an intimate correspondence between productive activity and the propagation of life (1998: 48–9). In *Capital* Marx speaks of labour as 'an eternal natural necessity which mediates the metabolism between man and nature, and therefore human life itself', choosing biological terminology which he frequently reused (1976: 133, 198ff, 284, 290). In the third volume of *Capital* the image of a 'human metabolism with nature' appears again, and Marx explains how, in a future communist society, a 'certain quantum of surplus labour is required as insurance against accidents and for the progressive extension of the reproduction process that is needed to keep pace with the development of needs and the progress of population' (1981: 958–9).

Clearly, Marx and Engels recognised the rich productive resources of labour. They understood that labour can facilitate more than the mere reproduction of life, because it can create more of life, both individually and in the plural:

> The first historical act is thus the production of the means to satisfy these needs, the production of material life itself ... The second point is that the satisfaction of the first need (the action of satisfying, and the instrument of satisfaction which has been acquired) leads to new needs; and this production of new needs is the first historical act ... The third circumstance which, from the very outset, enters into historical development, is that men, who daily remake their own life, begin to make other men, to propagate their kind. (Marx and Engels 1998: 47–8)

But what they failed to do, in Arendt's view, was to identify and delineate the higher activities of work and action. Instead labour was made the source of both worldly objects and relations of plurality, and as a consequence of this elision the distinctive attributes of the human condition were reduced to quasi-natural entities, effectively abolishing their higher meaning. Thus Arendt twice cites Marx's statement, from his discussion of productive and unproductive labour in *Theories of Surplus Value*, that 'Milton produced *Paradise Lost* for the same reason that a silk worm produces silk. It was an activity of his nature' (Marx 1969: 401). The self-transcending power of labour is also dramatically expressed, in what can only be described as Lamarckian terms, by Engels in 'The Part Played by Labour in the Transition from Ape to Man':

> Thus the hand is not only the organ of labour, *it is also the product of labour*. Only by labour, by adaptation to ever new operations, by inheritance of the thus acquired special development of muscles, ligaments and, over longer periods of time, bones as well, and by the ever-renewed employment of this inherited finesse in new, more and more complicated operations, has the human hand attained the high degree of perfection that

has enabled it to conjure into being the paintings of a Raphael, the statues of a Thorwaldsen, the music of a Paganini. (Engels 1951b: 75, his emphasis)

What Marx and Engels do for aesthetic accomplishments they also seem to do for what Arendt would regard as political ones. In *The German Ideology*, for example, they emphasise the fact that labour does not simply reproduce the biological existence of individuals, but builds bonds of fraternity (a 'mode of life') which Marx believed would eventually result in a fully 'socialised' humanity, a human nature that is true to its 'species-being' – a being bonded, as only the human animal can be, to the whole collective life of the species. So while claiming to have replaced Feuerbach's purely 'contemplative' materialism with a philosophy of *praxis*, Marx was at the same time defining this practice in terms of an everlasting 'metabolism with nature' through which human nature itself was progressively perfected. In Arendt's terminology, action is replaced by the 'social'. Instead of a worldly materialism, Marx assimilates the human subject to the naturalism of biological, or quasi-biological, processes, to 'the economic law of motion of modern society' or, as Marx happily cited a 'generous' reviewer of *Capital*, to 'a process of natural history, governed by laws not only independent of human will, consciousness and intelligence, but rather, on the contrary, determining that will, consciousness and intelligence' (1976: 92, 101).

So instead of freedom standing against the physical compulsions of the human condition, Marx made this compulsion a force of humanisation and freedom. In Arendt's words: 'when Marx stated that labour is the most important activity of man, he was saying in terms of the tradition that not freedom but necessity is what makes man human' (2002: 290). And to the extent that Marx turned to a natural *process* or historical law of *movement* to seal the breach between thought and action, 'materialism' as much as 'idealism' became a redundant term (PF: 38–9). This is why Marx's theory was primed for totalitarian abuse.

DEFENDING MARX

From Arendt's perspective, then, Marx's glorification of labour paved the way for the 'animalisation of man' which, as André Duarte observes in his discussion of Agamben and Arendt, did not end with the dismantling of the death camps and the gulags, but is today the dominant bio-political discourse that governs political decision-making, and particularly foreign policy, in modern consumer society. Administering to the affluent lives of *animal laborans* and securing the natural growth of the economy, in other words, has now become so vital a need that human rights, and human lives, are increasingly under threat from politics itself:

> whenever politics has mostly to do with the maintenance and increase of the vital metabolism of affluent nation states, *animal laborans* is on the verge of being degraded still further: to the status of *homo sacer*, bare and unprotected life that can be delivered to oblivion and death. Our common sense understanding of politics as the administrative promotion of abundance and the happiness of the human being as *animal laborans* is in fact correlated with economic and political exclusion, racialised prejudice, violence, and even genocide against the naked life of *homo sacer*. (Duarte 2007: 202)

Arendt's indictment of Marx is not without blemish, however, and a number of Marxist scholars have challenged the accuracy of Arendt's analysis. One response has been to contest Arendt's typology of separate activities and to argue, with Marx, that labour and work, in Sean Sayers' words, 'are necessarily and inextricably combined in human productive activity':

> The 'labour' which meets consumption needs also creates a product, it is thus at the same time a form of 'work' in Arendt's sense. For such labour does not simply vanish in consumption: it creates something beyond the satisfaction of material need and the reproduction of 'life'. In its human form at least, it always takes place in a context of social relations; and it produces and reproduces those relations and with them the social world. (Sayers 2003: 116)

Mildred Bakan makes the same point in more sophisticated terms, emphasising the dialectical relationship between labour and nature that both Hegel and Marx described. In contrast to the animal's instinctual relation to nature, where appetites compel the creature to consume nature without reflecting on the object or the subject that desires it, human labour, imposed on the slave by the master, demands the deferral of desire and consequently engenders a consciousness of both external nature and internal desire as objects to which humans are not passively chained. It is through labouring on nature, in other words, that the slave transcends instinctual determination and comes to know both the possibility of human freedom, and the 'sobering reality of things, which ... supplies a context for our senses, without which, indeed, the distinction between dreams and reality disappears' (Bakan 1979: 62). In Bakan's view, Arendt's failure to grasp humans' dialectical relation to nature, and the rootedness of work and action in this relation, leaves her with a purely theatrical conception of action, reduced to a kind of 'unfounded caprice'. 'Taken at its worst, politics in this sense can become the display of idle heroism, "noble deeds" unfounded in anything beyond their own display' (1979: 58–9).

Might it be the case, moreover, that Arendt confuses Marx's theory of labour as nature-driven with his account of *alienated* labour under capitalism (Suchting 1962: 50–4), thus missing the extent to which their separate critiques of capitalist modernity actually coincide, or at least the extent to which 'the criticisms Marx makes of capitalism are substantially similar to those Arendt levels against Marx' (Parekh 1979: 90; see also Ring 1989)? From a psychoanalytic perspective, which views Arendt as possessing a deeply ambivalent relationship to male intellectual authorities like Heidegger and Marx, Pitkin charges Arendt with 'appropriating something very like his fundamental notion of alienation while denying its existence in Marx and fiercely attacking him for having omitted that notion' (1998: 163). As Parekh points out, Marx's distinction between abstract and concrete labour already seems to run parallel to Arendt's division between labour and work.[1] For Marx, in other words, it is precisely under capitalism that work is reduced to labour, such that productive activity, as Parekh puts it, 'loses its individuality, and the labourer becomes an indistinguishable atom in a vast social organism'. 'In an unplanned society geared only to the accumulation of wealth', he continues in his defence of Marx, 'material production becomes, like the processes of nature, autonomous, self-propelling, cyclical, and coercive' (1979: 90). What Marx wished for communism, Jay therefore argues, 'was the overcoming of the reified quality of objectification under capitalism, not [the overcoming of] objectification *per se*'. 'Rather than championing *animal laborans*, Marx was a believer in the power of man as a *homo faber*' (1986: 246).

That Marx understood human labour to be, in its authentic form at least, different from mere animal behaviour, is evident from the famous passage in *Capital* where Marx contrasts the 'first instinctive forms of labour' with 'labour in a form in which it is an exclusively human characteristic', noting that 'what distinguishes the worst architect from the best of bees is that the architect builds the cell in his mind before he constructs it in wax' (1976: 283–4). Arendt treats this passage as an aberration, however, for although it clearly matches her definition of work, not labour, she claims it is inconsistent with the rest of Marx's writings, 'the best proof of this' being 'that the apparently all-important element of "imagination" plays no role whatsoever in his labour theory' (HC: 99 n36). It is true that imagination does not appear explicitly in Marx's labour theory of value, probably because imagination is a subjective and qualitative faculty which cannot be reduced, as all commodities must be under capitalism, to a quantity of labour time 'socially necessary for its production', and perhaps also because Marx, viewing rational human consciousness as grounded in material practices, associated the freedom of the imagination with the ideological flights of fantasy characteristic of religious belief and philosophical idealism. Despite his positivist epistemology, however, Marx certainly stressed the significance of consciousness and purposefulness in distinguishing human from merely animal activity, and it is consistent with this that he wrote of labour, when driven by purely instinctual needs, as a *degradation* of human nature. Thus animals 'produce only when immediate physical need compels them to do so, while man produces even when he is free from physical need and truly produces only in freedom from such need' (Marx 1975a: 328–9). It is precisely this ability to detach itself from its immediate environment and needs which for Marx makes the human animal uniquely a 'species being', that is, a being conscious of the universal category of 'humanity', and aware of the whole of the natural world, not just that which is immediately discernable to the senses, as a potential field of human activity.

Passages like these do indeed suggest a degree of kinship between Arendt's conception of worldlessness and Marx's understanding of alienation. Once 'abstracted from other aspects of human activity and turned into final and exclusive ends', Marx writes of the worker who toils only for the sake of consumption, the 'genuine human functions' of 'eating, drinking and procreating' become the instincts of a mere 'animal' (1975a: 328–9). Both alienation and worldlessness imply an estrangement from the sensible world of objects and a corresponding degradation of human experience. Both recall Aristotle's distinction between natural life and the good life, and thus also Agamben's description of modernity as the reduction of human existence to bare life.

A HUMANIST NATURALISM?

These reflections on the similarities which Arendt's theory of worldliness unwittingly shares with Marx's humanism can be extended, perhaps surprisingly, in a different direction, for what the two thinkers also hold in common is an appreciation of nature that is not typically apparent in conventional treatments of their work. The richest and most descriptive account of alienation in Marx's writings appears in the 'Economic and Philosophical Manuscripts' of 1844, and what is most interesting about this text is how Marx frames his discussion within a kind of humanistic naturalism. Freedom is here conceived not, as it tends to be for Arendt, as an expression of our distance from nature, but rather as the enrichment and fulfilment of the human animal's corporeal essence. With the 'supersession of private property', Marx predicted, the human senses would be free to 'relate to the thing for its own sake'. 'Need or enjoyment have therefore lost their egoistic nature', his description continues, 'and nature has lost its mere utility'. The transcendence of alienation is defined here in terms of the emergence of a 'sensuous consciousness', the cultivation of human sensitivity – 'a musical ear, an eye for the beauty of form, in short, senses capable of human gratification' – and the realisation of the individual who is 'affirmed in the objective world not only in thought but with all the senses' (1975a: 348–55).

If communism is described by Marx in naturalist terms, it is unsurprising that the experience of alienation is formulated in terms of its remoteness from this ideal. When private property estranges people from the products of their labour, the consciousness of the craft worker is stunted, and with it his natural sensibilities and talents. We see this most clearly in Marx's well-known passage on money, which he describes as eroding humans' sensuous relationship to the qualities of things, replacing 'all the physical and intellectual senses' with 'the sense of having', and allowing individuals to purchase objects and services without needing, suffering or appreciating the property they command (1975a: 352, 375–9). Although Marx generally wrote as if the expansion of needs was a progressive process, here he recognises that merely *quantitative* growth in needs is exploitative and dehumanising. 'Lack of moderation and intemperance' become 'the true standard' of money, and instead of the enrichment of needs we have 'bestial degeneration and a complete, crude and abstract simplicity of need', including the 'artificially produced' appetite for 'self-stupefaction'. 'It is not only human needs which man lacks', Marx writes, describing the desperate search for rotten potatoes during the Irish famine, for 'even his animal needs cease to exist' (1975a: 358–63).

Does Marx's appreciation of human nature set him at odds with Arendt's well-trodden distinction between life and world? The apparent elitism in Arendt's attitude to biological needs is challenged by Sayers, who complains that she 'treats with disdain and contempt the labour which meets consumer needs', and that she 'reduces human labour to a sort of animal activity and treats it as something almost sub-human'. Arendt's theory of labour thus leads her, according to Sayers, to depict 'those who perform it as in effect a sub-human species, *animal laborans*' (2003: 117–18).

It was Arendt, to be sure, who wrote that 'man's "nature" is only "human" insofar as it opens up to man the possibility of becoming something highly unnatural' (OT: 455). It is also true that there are passages in Arendt's writings where she implies that the higher faculties of the *vita activa* are not available to all, including her complaint in the 'Prologue' to *The Human Condition* that 'there is no class left, no aristocracy of either a political or spiritual nature from which a restoration of the other capacities of man could start anew' (HC: 5). Yet it is also clear that the categories of *animal laborans*, *homo faber*, and *zoon politikon* do not refer in Arendt's work to different species of the human genus, to different forms of 'human nature', or, as some feminist critics of Arendt have assumed, to different sexes. They refer, rather, to different dimensions of the human condition that each individual must master and hold in balance if those constituting elements, and indeed existence itself, are to be rendered meaningful.

In this respect the similarity between Arendt and Marx extends from their respective accounts of alienation to their understanding of what a truly human life should be. Just as Marx believed that humans' most elementary physical needs – 'eating, drinking and procreating' – become degrading only when 'abstracted' from the higher range of human possibilities, Arendt herself understood the importance of labour to the hierarchy of activities. She writes, for instance, of how labour expresses the fundamental vitality of human life, furnishing an 'elemental happiness' that 'can never be found in work'.

The 'blessing or the joy' of labour is the human way to experience the sheer bliss of being alive which we share with all living creatures, and it is even the only way men, too, can remain and swing contentedly in nature's prescribed cycle, toiling and resting, labouring and consuming, with the same happy and purposeless regularity with which day and night and life and death follow each other. (HC: 106)

The fact that action is founded on the natural condition of natality should also indicate how important humans' rootedness in nature is to the higher activities of work and action, how freedom and necessity are combined in the lives of individual persons, and how freedom is not, therefore, completely unconditioned caprice. Arendt suggests, in fact, that 'an element of action, and therefore of natality, is inherent in all human activities', while at the same time stressing, in words that are reminiscent of Sartre's concept of 'facticity', that 'men, no matter what they do, are always conditioned beings' (HC: 9). Even the highest expressions of the *vita activa* are conditioned, in other words, while even the lowest contain the seeds of human initiative. The experience of physical necessity familiar to the labourer, for example, 'possesses a driving force whose urgency is unmatched by the so-called higher desires and aspirations of man', and this experience can energise the *vita activa* at all levels, acting to 'prevent the apathy and disappearance of initiative which so obviously threatens all overly wealthy communities' (HC: 70–1).

This same insight is implicit in Arendt's statement that the individual 'cannot be free if he does not know that he is subject to necessity, because his freedom is always won in his never wholly successful attempts to liberate himself from necessity', as well as her comment, which surely refutes the charge of class prejudice, that actors must be 'willing to take the burden, the toil and trouble of life, upon themselves' (HC: 121). Referring to the Homeric world in which 'Paris and Odysseus help in the building of their houses' and 'Nausicaä herself washes the linen of her brothers', Arendt points out that 'the selfsame activity' can be a sign either of 'slavishness' and 'subjection to necessity' or of 'sovereignty' and 'greater independence', depending on whether 'sheer survival' (which is the lot of the slave) or 'the self-sufficiency of the Homeric hero' is the motive and goal at stake (HC: 82–3 n7). Providing the labourer also participates in higher activities, in other words, the significance of that labour is far greater than the mere preservation of life:

the perfect elimination of the pain and effort of labour would not only rob biological life of its most natural pleasures but deprive the specifically human life of its very liveliness and vitality ... That the life of the rich loses in vitality, in closeness to the 'good things' of nature, what it gains in refinement, in sensitivity to the beautiful things in the world, has often been noted. The fact is that the human capacity for life in the world always implies an ability to transcend and to be alienated from the process of life itself, while vitality and liveliness can be conserved only to the extent that men are willing to take the burden, the toil and trouble of life, upon themselves. (HC: 120–1)

CONSUMER SOCIETY AND AN UNNATURAL NATURE

A further indication that Arendt does not regard labour with outright contempt is that her description of the alienated character of the modern world does not stop at the reduction of artificial work to natural labour. Just as Marx described how the 'machine accommodates itself to man's weakness in order to turn weak man into a machine' (1975a: 360), Arendt wrote of the way mechanisation has drastically reduced the need for labour – not just quantitatively, but also qualitatively, so that, now devoid of both harshness and vitality, and of the 'individually sensed pain and trouble of living', 'labouring is too lofty, too ambitious a word for what we are doing, or think we are doing, in the world we have come to live in' (HC: 322).

Arendt suggests that if happiness is experienced through labour, then it derives from its comforting rhythmic character, which mimics the metabolism of the body both in its physical movements (HC: 140, 145), and in the cyclical transition from toil to rest, 'where life's processes of exhaustion and regeneration, of pain and release from pain, *strike a perfect balance*' (HC: 134, my emphasis). It is on the basis of this balance, Arendt implies, that the pursuit of higher activities can arise. When this elementary equilibrium is upset, however, and when we are left with 'a labour society which lacks enough labouring to keep it contented' (HC: 134), then the needs of *animal laborans* can find no other outlet than the insatiable practices of *consumption*. The frantic chase for new consumer goods henceforth becomes an irresistible force of compulsion in its own right, a fact that has escaped recognition, according to Arendt, because 'it is more difficult to perceive coercive necessity in the guise of ease than in the harsh brutality of pain and effort' (2002: 311).

Arendt now seems to be describing a kind of pathological disfigurement of nature which is more familiar to contemporary environmentalism than to the classical humanist tradition she is so closely associated with. It is as if the productive movement of labour had been emancipated from the natural ecology of the labouring body, from 'the natural limitation of its own fertility' (HC: 124), and from an awareness, dispelled by modern industry's promise of limitless novelty and change, that life, because it is ultimately futile in its cycle of growth and decay, must be transcended in the direction of worldliness and action. The result of this unfettering of consumer appetites – 'so that consumption is no longer restricted to the necessities but, on the contrary, mainly concentrates on the superfluities of life' – is a situation in which 'our whole economy has become a waste economy, in which things must be almost as quickly devoured and discarded as they have appeared in the world' (HC: 133–4).

> In our need for more and more rapid replacement of the worldly things around us, we can no longer afford to use them, to respect and preserve their inherent durability; we must consume, devour, as it were, our houses and furniture and cars as though they were the 'good things' of nature which spoil uselessly if they are not drawn swiftly into the never-ending cycle of man's metabolism with nature. It is as though we had forced open the distinguishing boundaries which protected the world, the human artifice, from nature, the biological process which goes on in its very midst as well as the natural cyclical processes which surround it, delivering and abandoning to them the always threatened stability of a human world. (HC: 125–6)

The link Arendt makes between the rapacious dynamic of accumulation characteristic of capitalism and the growth of consumer society is self-evident from these passages. Though Arendt shared with Marx a concern for the destructive whirlwind of capital, she did not share Marx's belief that this feverish process of devastation and ruin, the contemporary ideological defence of which Naomi Klein (2007) has felicitously termed the 'shock doctrine' of 'disaster capitalism', was for Marx a necessary stage in a dialectical movement that could advance only by devouring all fixed certainties, needs and worldly attachments. For Marx, the worker had to be dispossessed of the world in order to be in a position to take full command of it, for only those 'who are completely shut off from all self-activity, are in a position to achieve a complete and no longer restricted self-activity' (Marx and Engels 1998: 96). In order to 'give birth to its inner wealth', Marx wrote of the alienation of the senses in the 1844 *Manuscripts*, 'human nature had to be reduced to this absolute poverty' (1975a: 352). Then, having suffered 'the total loss of humanity', the proletariat can 'redeem itself only through the total redemption of humanity', throwing 'into the face of its adversary the defiant words: "*I am nothing and I should be everything*"' (1975b: 254).

Though Arendt acknowledges Marx for recognising 'that capitalism, left to its own devices, has a tendency to raze all laws that are in the way of its cruel progress', she refused to 'share Marx's great enthusiasm about capitalism', describing the transition from capitalism to socialism as merely a continuation of the disastrous logic of expropriation (1979: 334–5). On this matter, one could argue, it is Arendt rather than Marx who shows the greatest sensitivity to the need for the conservation of both natural and human-made environments, with Arendt's proto-ecological critique of capitalist productivism now recognised by a number of commentators (e.g. Whiteside 1994, 1998; Macauley 1996; Szerzynski 2003). This may seem counterintuitive, since Arendt is firmly opposed to sentimental or romantic treatments of nature, and explicitly defines human freedom as the miraculous interruption of the natural processes that surround, condition and outlast us (PF: 168–9). Yet while it is true that protecting the durable human artifice from the imperatives of nature is a primary concern for Arendt, she does not depict the natural environment as an outright menace to human freedom, and she is equally aware that the boundlessness of action must be moderated and contained by laws, promises and agreements. Implicitly at least, Arendt attributes value to the orderly cycles of nature, appearing to recognise that the stability and moderation required by political communities is echoed in the predictable rhythms of living things, in the natural ecology of growth and decay, effort and recuperation, by which organic life, in Arendt's own words, 'is checked and balanced in nature's household'.

We have already noted, for example, how the elemental cycle of toil and rest, of pain and release from pain, which is instantly recognisable to all but the strictest puritan, is central to a consistent doctrine of hedonism, for one can directly enjoy the bodily senses, instead of the worldly objects apprehended by them, only in the limited period during which we are released from physical privation (HC: 112–14).

The intensity of this sensation of being released from pain is beyond doubt; in intensity it is matched only by the sensation of pain itself which is always more intense than any pleasure unrelated to pain could possibly be. No doubt, the pleasure of drinking the most exquisite wine cannot be compared in intensity to the pleasure felt by a desperately thirsty man who gets a drink of water. (RJ: 133–4)

When consumption is liberated from the pain and effort of labour, Arendt seems to suggest, such intense but self-limiting pleasures are lost or devalued. To some extent, and particularly in societies still rich in traditional culture, humans have resisted this tendency by preserving, through abstinence rituals and moral prohibitions on overconsumption, the 'arts' of pleasure by which previous civilisations, better acquainted than our own with the harsh facts of scarcity, had learned to 'make a virtue of necessity'. But as practices of cultural sublimation have been displaced by the economic imperatives of capitalism, the conquering of necessity has resulted in an accelerating supply of instantly disposable goods designed to invalidate the art of moderation and prevent the movement of consumption from stalling. When gratification is no longer checked by want, simple luxuries and familiar pleasures lose their capacity to stir the soul, and only constant growth, novelty and change can satisfy the appetite of the liberated consumer. Expressed in terms of Arendt's more familiar biological metaphors, 'it was as though the growth element inherent in all organic life had completely overcome and overgrown the processes of decay by which organic life is checked and balanced in nature's household' (HC: 47). It is not simply that capitalism has allowed nature to breach the walls of civilisation, in other words, but that a deformed and irrepressible nature – an 'unnatural nature' – has taken its place.

THE 'WORLDLINESS' OF NATURE

So by re-examining Arendt's concept of labour and her references to consumer society, we can see that the threat she identifies is not so much 'nature' as the *deformation* of nature which occurs when labour is unable to take its place as one contributing component in the full hierarchy of human activities. Consistent with this insight is Arendt's suggestion that the natural predictability and balance of the organic world is also jeopardised by humans' most elevated faculty, and here we are again reminded of Arendt's refusal to glorify human freedom at the expense of the other elements of the human condition. Action, Arendt points out, need not be restricted to the realm of human affairs, but can also take place in relation to nature. For Arendt, the splitting of the atom represented a critical stage in the development of the modern world, from which point on humans realised 'that man is as capable of starting natural processes which would not have come about without human interference as he is of starting something new in the field of human affairs' (PF: 58).

> Up to our own age human action with its man-made processes was confined to the human world, whereas man's chief preoccupation with regard to nature was to use its material in fabrication, to build with it the human artifice and defend it against the overwhelming force of the elements. The moment we started natural processes of our own ... we not only increased our power over nature, or became more aggressive in our dealings with the given forces of the earth, but for the first time have taken nature into the human world as such and obliterated the defensive boundaries between natural elements and the human artifice by which all previous civilisations were hedged in. (PF: 60; see also HC: 148)

We have seen that for Arendt unpredictability is a risk inherent in the initiation of something new. When nuclear physicists and molecular biologists initiate natural processes that have never previously existed without human intervention, the lawful orderliness of nature can no longer be guaranteed and the threat posed to the stability and permanence of the human world expands accordingly. Since 'we have manifestly begun to carry our own unpredictability into that realm which we used to think of as ruled by inexorable laws', the result is that 'we are confronted with elemental forces which we shall perhaps never be able to control reliably' (PF: 61–2). The 'unnatural growth of the natural', as Arendt refers to it in *The Human Condition*, is epitomised by this replacement of the stable patterns of natural life and labour with pseudo-natural processes which advance into the future in unforeseen and irreversible ways. In describing 'the situation of radical world alienation' that results from this trend, Arendt suggests that the 'world' is more than just what humans have made, for what we are witnessing is a *'twofold loss of the world – the loss of nature and the loss of human artifice'* (PF: 89, my emphasis).

In the 'Prologue' to *The Human Condition* Arendt introduces the term 'earth alienation' to describe the second dimension of this 'radical world alienation'. 'The earth', she writes, 'is the very quintessence of the human condition', and although human worldliness rescues us from a merely animal existence, 'life itself is outside this artificial world, and through life man remains related to all other living organisms'. Attempts to manipulate the human genome are an expression, according to Arendt, of a hitherto unknown 'wish to escape the human condition' in its most fundamental form, a 'rebellion against the very factuality of the human condition' (OV: 13). Arendt also found this wish encapsulated by the media's response to the launch into space of the world's first satellite, which included the statement that this achievement represented the first 'step toward escape from men's imprisonment to the earth'. 'Christians have spoken of the earth as a vale of tears and philosophers have looked upon their body as a prison of mind or soul', Arendt writes, ruminating on this quote from the front page of a respected US newspaper, but 'nobody in the history of mankind has ever conceived of the earth as a prison for men's bodies or shown such eagerness to go literally from here to the moon' (HC: 2).

While the environmentalist movement began to celebrate the new sense of ecological responsibility that pictures of the planet from space had helped to engender, Arendt saw something more troubling in this development. The exploration of space was the latest stage in the search for an Archimedean point, an attempt to free human consciousness from the shackles of spatiality and the encumbrance of earthly embodiment, and to replace human speech and thought with mathematical signs capable of revealing the secrets of the universe. An awareness of the fragility of the planet may well have been aroused by satellite images of the earth, but they conveyed this fragility from a cosmic standpoint that had already left the earth behind and was therefore no longer bound by it. 'Compared with the earth alienation underlying the whole development of natural science in the modern age', Arendt writes of this pursuit of a universal astrophysical standpoint, 'the world alienation produced in the twofold process of expropriation and wealth accumulation are of minor significance' (HC: 264). For once the earth, the natural world in which humans dwell, is regarded as not just an external object but as *another world* (that is, as one world among many possible, and manufacturable, alternatives), then science can dispose of this world, creating and destroying life with impunity. In doing so it places the stability and longevity of nature – the very qualities, in fact, that the Greeks sought to imitate and rival with their 'immortal words and deeds' – in jeopardy.

So the relationship between worldliness and nature, between taking care of the human artifice and recognising and preserving the stable 'object-ness' of the organic world, is clearly more complex than the simple oppositional relationship implied in Arendt's hierarchy of activities, for neither work nor action provide a direct and cast-iron remedy for the worldlessness of life and labour. It would therefore be wrong, I think, to accept uncritically Simon Swift's assessment that Arendt's 'unpalatable' arguments about the relationship between nature and world 'are difficult claims to square with the ecological consciousness of the twenty-first century' (2009: 38, 136). In addition to her concerns about human action into nature, Arendt repeatedly states that the activity of fabrication contains no guarantee that the fabricated world will be cared for and preserved beyond the lifetime of the maker, since making is devoid of any internal prohibition on the destruction or use of worldly things in the often violent enterprise of production. Work may elevate the creator above the labourer's production of perishable consumer goods, but the survival of even the most durable of things is imperilled by the worker's desire to conquer and use the environment – nature and world alike – as means for the realisation of a preconceived end. Worldliness, in other words, requires not just a world, but *care for the world*.

In her essay, 'The Crisis in Culture', Arendt pointedly reminds us of the Roman origins of that most worldly of human practices, that 'mode of intercourse of man with the things of the world', which we call 'culture':

> The word 'culture' derives from *colere* – to cultivate, to dwell, to take care, to tend and preserve – and it relates primarily to the intercourse of man with nature in the sense of cultivating and tending nature until it becomes fit for human habitation. As such, it indicates an attitude of loving care and stands in sharp contrast to all efforts to subject nature to the domination of man. (PF: 212)

Although it was the Greeks who best understood the threat to worldliness posed by the 'philistine', utilitarian attitude of the artist and creator, Arendt claims that it was the Romans' high regard for agriculture, and their reverence for tradition, which enabled them to look upon the cultural objects inherited from classical civilisation as things to be tended, talked about, cherished and emulated, in the process acquiring the aesthetic discrimination and love of beauty that the Greeks knew could never be gratified by the products of farming. The *cultura animi* – the cultivated mind which Cicero believed was the mark of the philosopher who, as a disinterested spectator, was indifferent to matters of utility and interest – thus had its roots in the 'worldly' Roman attitude towards nature (PF: 212, 215, 296 n5). But the positive influence also passes in the other direction, for this attitude to nature, this perception of nature not as an irresistible, devouring process which humans are at the mercy of, but as a durable and objective structure whose productive potential must be harnessed and tended, *is also an achievement of human worldliness.*

> Only we who have erected the objectivity of a world of our own from what nature gives us, who have built it into the environment of nature so that we are protected from her, can look upon nature as something 'objective'. Without a world between men and nature, there is eternal movement, but no objectivity. (HC: 137)

Drawing on this insight from Arendt, Whiteside argues against those ecologists who call for an ethical relationship to nature that is an extension of our respect for other human beings. Our respect for nature 'arose not from seeing in nature the same moral qualities that we look for in human beings, but rather from seeing in it qualities like those that define our *world*'. Hence 'natural things have "intrinsic validity" because world-like qualities (e.g., stability, beauty) inhere in them. Concern to maintain a much-valued world directs us toward tending, preserving, and caring for things having those qualities' (Whiteside 1998: 34–5). Hence also the conclusion that 'the most fundamental problem of consumer capitalism is not simply that it threatens the "earth" through resource use, pollution and habitat loss, but that it threatens the "world", without which there can be no meaning or value' (Szerszynski 2003: 212). From the perspective of this sympathetic critique of populist environmentalism, Swift's complaint that Arendt's understanding of the relationship between nature and world is 'out of sorts with the consciousness of impending ecological catastrophe that defines our times' is inadvertently accurate (2009: 136). For Arendt, this consciousness is deficient because it lacks appreciation and care for the world.

So both the earth and the human artifice are components of our worldly existence, and our culture – our cultivation of each

– complements and enhances our ability to care for the other. But when modern technoscience acts into nature, unharnessing, from a standpoint outside the world, processes that are alien to earthly life, it carrys human unpredictability, bereft of the remedies that action enjoys in the realm of human affairs, into the organic environment, and this is then followed by the reverberating spread of a kind of artificial nature back into the human world. We have learned this harsh lesson in numerous forms, including climate change, pollution of the air and food chain, the intergenerational effects of nuclear radiation, the creation of antibiotic-resistant superbugs and anthropogenic diseases like Bovine Spongiform Encephalopathy (BSE), and the creation of genetically engineered organisms whose behaviour cannot be controlled or predicted. Not only the human artifice, but nature itself now loses the tangible qualities which humans depend on in order both to model and to build a worldly home, as action 'begins to overpower and destroy not man himself but the conditions under which life was given to him' (HC: 238). Modern science, increasingly distrustful of the natural senses, now discloses through experimental interventions into the natural world possibilities that no mere contemplation, experience, or modelling by *homo faber* could reveal, and in this process the basic 'worldliness' of nature, its essential objective existence, is called into question. The philosopher's primordial wonder at the world then appears obsolete, for in the scientific universe, as Arendt likes to quote Heisenberg, 'man encounters only himself' (HC: 261; PF: 277).

ON MASS CULTURE

If it is wrong to view Arendt as someone who was unsympathetic to environmentalism and ignorant of the conditioning of human actions, it is also misleading to regard her hierarchical model of human activities as elitist. One way to test the accusation of elitism in Arendt's thinking is to explore her critique of 'mass culture'. Arendt suggests that although the tension between 'culture' and 'society' is well recognised by modern critics, it would be a mistake to assume this antagonism first arose with the growth of 'mass society'. The rebellion of the artist at the turn of the eighteenth century, she argues, was not against the society of the masses, which had not yet come into being, but against the 'good and genteel society' of the rising bourgeoisie. It was the latter who were charged with 'philistinism', initially because of their general indifference to what they saw as the 'uselessness' of culture and the arts, and later when they realised that the acquisition of cultural goods could indeed be a useful tool in the struggle for social recognition. The early modern artists were in rebellion against their wealthy patrons, who wanted to acquire their products, names and reputations as a means of self-cultivation and a currency for climbing the status hierarchy. Only because this society was not yet mass society, Arendt claims, could 'the individual' have been fashioned in the crucible of this revolt, escaping into 'non-society strata' and sometimes finding refuge in revolutionary parties containing 'traits of humanity which had become extinct in society' (PF: 200).

Arendt argues that the only 'authentic criterion' for judging cultural products is their degree of permanence. When works of art cease 'to grasp and move the reader or spectator over the centuries', and instead become a vehicle for status rivalry or even a means for self-perfection in the Arnoldian sense (the reader thus missing 'the fact that Shakespeare or Plato might have to tell him more important things than how to educate himself'), the essential quality of cultural objects is compromised. Once converted into a *means*, into a currency or exchange value to be traded for social advancement or self-betterment, the uniqueness of the work of art is lost, and with it disappears 'the faculty of arresting our attention and moving us' (PF: 202–4).

So long as the 'good society' wanted culture for the purpose of social display, status competition and moral improvement, it remained tied to a utilitarian outlook. It 'used and abused' cultural goods, but it did not seek to 'consume' them like objects of the life process. When bourgeois society incorporated the majority of the population and became 'mass society', Arendt argues, a different mindset prevailed. For what mass society desires is 'not culture but entertainment, and the wares offered by the entertainment industry are indeed consumed by society just like any other consumer goods' (PF: 205).

Arendt's analysis of the entertainment industry is interesting for its similarity to the critique of the culture industry advanced by Adorno and Horkheimer. Their 1944 essay, 'The Culture Industry: Enlightenment as Mass Deception', treats the demand for mass produced cultural commodities as a 'manufactured need', a need whose origin lies in the injuries of a 'mechanised work process'. While critics of Adorno and Horkheimer have repeatedly, and rather tiresomely, condemned them for portraying consumers as cultural dopes, indoctrinated by the ideological devices of popular culture, at the heart of their essay is a materialist analysis which understands the need for entertainment as an 'after-image of the work process'.

> Amusement under late capitalism is the prolongation of work. It is sought after as an escape from the mechanised work process, and to recruit strength in order to be able to cope with it again … What happens at work, in the factory, or in the office can only be escaped from by approximation to it in one's leisure time. All amusement suffers from this incurable malady. Pleasure hardens into boredom because, if it is to remain pleasure, it must not demand any and therefore moves rigorously in the worn grooves of association. (Adorno and Horkheimer 1997: 137)

Entertainment, unlike culture, has a function, and the function of entertainment, Arendt argues, is 'to while away time'. This time is not time free from the necessities of the life process, not '*scholē*', the abstention from the demands of everyday wants, which Aristotle regarded as the condition of contemplation. Instead it is, as Arendt puts it, 'left-over time, which still is biological in nature, left over after labour and sleep have received their due'. Such 'vacant time' needs entertainment because entertainment, 'like labour and sleep, is irrevocably part of the biological life process'. Leisure activities were *a-scholē*, according to Aristotle, because, in Arendt's words, 'play and recreation are necessary for the restoration of the human labour force charged with taking care of life's necessities' (LM1: 93). And because the life process is 'a metabolism feeding on things by devouring them', it is inevitable that the commodities produced to meet this need are neither cultural things capable of withstanding the perishability of biological life, nor functional goods capable of being used and exchanged, but are instead 'consumer goods, destined to be used up' (PF: 205–6).

> *Panis et circenses* [bread and games] truly belong together; both are necessary for life, for its preservation and recuperation, and both vanish in the course of the life process – that is, both must constantly be produced anew and offered anew, lest this process cease entirely. The standards by which both should be judged are freshness and novelty, and the extent to which we use these standards today to judge cultural and artistic objects as well, things which are supposed to remain in the world even after we have left it, indicates clearly the extent to which the need for entertainment has begun to threaten the cultural world. (PF: 206)

The modern threat to culture thus comes from two sources, Arendt suggests. As the entertainment industry expands in line with the insatiable appetites of consumers, its designers and producers are impelled to plunder the stock of cultural objects for inspiration, then revise, condense, simplify and simulate those objects to render them suitable for mass distribution. Although we call the result 'mass culture', Arendt argues that when mass society appropriates culture in this way, culture is not spread to the masses but is 'destroyed in order to yield entertainment'. The increasing tendency in contemporary art to prioritise novelty and innovation over permanence and beauty, the deliberate attempt to shock rather than move audiences, could be read as further confirmation of Arendt's argument that culture in mass society bears all the hallmarks of ephemera and disposability that characterise the objects of the life process.

The way is paved for the further destruction of culture whenever we seek to understand cultural objects in functional terms. If the ornate beauty of the cathedral can be explained by the community's spiritual needs, or the sublime work of art by the artist's need for self-expression or the public's need for self-refinement, then the potential discovery of better – quicker, cheaper, more comprehensive – ways of meeting these needs has already rendered the cathedral or the painting redundant. This functional attitude to culture is particularly evident, Arendt writes, in 'the more insidious noises of the cultural snobs in refined society', the 'educated philistines' who treat with contempt 'useless' entertainment but who, in seeking to put culture to good use, fail to grasp its combined qualities of worldliness and transcendence. This is the second threat to culture, according to Arendt, and once again we are reminded of her sensitivity to the integrity of the different hierarchical activities of the human condition, and her contempt for the idea that some people are only fit for one of them. 'The truth is we all stand in need of entertainment and amusement in some form or other, because we are all subject to life's great cycle, and it is sheer hypocrisy or social snobbery to deny that we can be amused and entertained by exactly the same things which amuse and entertain the masses of our fellow men' (PF: 206).

5
Feminism, the Social and the Political

The argument, advanced by some Marxist critics of Arendt, that the categories of labour, work and action imply not just a hierarchy of activities but also an elitist hierarchy of people, has also been shared by some feminist readers of Arendt's work for whom gender is the unspoken premise of her thinking. In this chapter I want to explore the various feminist interpretations of Arendt, and to use this inquiry to open up a broader debate about the division between the political and the social, and the public and the private sphere.

IN THE COMPANY OF WOMEN

Feminist responses to Arendt in the 1970s and '80s were not especially sympathetic. Her defence of the separation of the public and private spheres, her emphasis on the political and existential superiority of public action, and her fascination with an ancient form of politics that was, in practice, predicated on the domestic oppression of women, was never likely to have attracted a host of feminist admirers. To many commentators, Arendt's agonistic conception of politics as a heroic enterprise was an exclusively male formulation, and when combined with her determination, expressed in the language of classical philosophy, to protect the traditionally female private sphere from the disabling, potentially totalitarian spread of the 'social', the result seemed, as Young-Bruehl puts it, like 'a kind of Victorian sexism made out of Aristotelian materials' (1996: 308), and a direct affront to the feminist principle that the personal is also political.

Arendt had never shown an interest in the history of women's exclusion from the public sphere, and she deflected all attempts to highlight the pioneering status of her own achievements as a female intellectual in a male-dominated profession. Amidst a new wave of feminist scholarship in the 1970s, a perspective began to emerge which took to celebrating the traits, attitudes and activities which, whether by nature or by nurture, seemed to have become the sole province of women. Arguing that women were uniquely placed to advance a non-violent, non-instrumental alternative to the politics of conflict, war and conquest, this perspective also regarded Arendt as an adversary, since she appeared to endorse a masculine conception of political agency which disqualified women, as natural beings tied to the imperatives of life, from participation in the sphere of appearances. 'The fact that the modern age emancipated the working classes and women at nearly the same historical moment', Arendt wrote in an incriminating passage in *The Human Condition*, 'must certainly be counted among the characteristics of an age which no longer believes that bodily functions and material concerns should be hidden' (HC: 73).

In a cursory but often-cited comment in an article first published in 1977, Adrienne Rich described Arendt's thinking as that 'of a female mind nourished on male ideologies', calling *The Human Condition* a 'lofty and crippled book' which betrayed women by holding their household labour in contempt (1979: 205, 212). In a more erudite discussion of Arendt's book, Mary O'Brien, taking Arendt to task for 'failing to analyse the significance of reproductive consciousness', interpreted her hierarchy of activities as an endorsement of the sex hierarchy by 'a woman who accepts the normality and even the necessity of male supremacy' (1981: 99–101). In O'Brien's ecofeminist analysis, Arendt's distinction between animality and culture, between biological reproduction on the one hand and 'productive work and political action' on the other, was a male-inspired dualism which was artificial and destructive. This construction of the 'two natures of man', as O'Brien characterised Arendt's thinking, could only be sustained by doing violence to nature and those who tend it.

O'Brien questioned the idea that humans could safely compart-mentalise two rigidly opposed spheres of existence, rising into the public sphere unscarred by the aggressive struggle with necessity that, for Arendt, was the proper burden of the household. It is unclear, O'Brien writes, 'how those who master their first nature by violence will be able to leave that unpolitic [*sic*] characteristic at home', how 'an existential craving for fame and immortality will enable these tyrants to cast off the dark robes of the oppressor, as they cross the mystic gulf between private and public life to don the shining armour of excellence'. If our model of politics is premised on a pre-political act of violence, we should hardly be surprised, O'Brien points out, if violence, 'which in fact permeated Greek public life within the class struggles of the polis itself and in the execution of imperialist ambitions abroad', is routinely carried into the political realm itself (1981: 121, 103).

O'Brien's critique of Arendt appeals to 'a feminist perspective grounded in female experience', which upholds 'integration with the natural world against the "masterful" destruction of that world' (1981: 194, 115). Although I have argued that it is wrong to read Arendt as an enemy of the ecology movement, there are other problems with this feminist critique of Arendt. One serious flaw is identified by Dietz (1995), who notes that it reduces Arendt's tripartite distinction between labour, work and action to a gendered separation of nature and culture, private women and public man, thus missing how the category of action transcends the limiting conditions of both labour and work, and thus, potentially, of gender.

According to Hanna Pitkin (1998), however, this apparent oversight on the part of critics like O'Brien is actually shared by Arendt herself, whose subtle distinctions between three different activities are overshadowed in *The Human Condition* by a gendered conflict between two exaggerated, hypostatized, and ultimately disempowering images: on the one hand, the misogynist, narcissistic machismo of the Greeks; and on the other, the enfeebling maternal embrace of 'the social'.

Pitkin suggests that Arendt displays a long-standing ambivalence in her understanding of the relationship between agency and structure, and that from the 1940s until the early 1960s she was caught between two opposing standpoints, the one emphasising individual responsibility and freedom, the other identifying 'an intentional, active force, composed of humans who have lost their human agency – in short, a Blob' (1998: 93). According to Pitkin, Arendt's 'fantasy of a diabolical Blob' rose to prominence in the final chapter of the first edition of *The Origins of Totalitarianism*, appearing in the form of 'radical evil' and 'total domination', and then became, via the concept of 'mass society', what in *The Human Condition* Arendt theorises using the hypostatised image of 'the social'.

Despite their differences, Pitkin and Dietz agree that Arendt's depictions of labour and work are indeed gendered, although nowhere does Arendt explicitly acknowledge this. The activity of labour is closely associated by Arendt with the pain of giving birth, and her most consistent descriptions of labour refer not to paid employment or agriculture but to imagery which suggests 'the entrapped housewife feeding others in dutiful, repetitive, self-denying monotony' (Pitkin 1998: 166). As Dietz points out, being tied to biological processes has been women's destiny; facing the 'essential worldly futility' of the lifecycle, within the darkness of the private realm, has been women's challenge. The cyclical, endlessly repetitive processes of household labour – cleaning, washing, mending, cooking, feeding, sweeping, rocking, tending – have been time-honoured female ministrations, and also conceived of and justified as appropriate to women. Since the Greeks, the cyclical, biological processes of reproduction and labour have been associated with the female, and replicated in a multitude of historical institutions and practices. It is indeed curious that Arendt never makes this central feature of the human condition an integral part of her political analysis. (Dietz 1991: 240)

Work, by contrast, is depicted by Arendt as an activity of masculine ruthlessness, the violation of nature driven by an instrumental mindset. Just as most labour has historically been performed by women, so work has been largely dominated by men; so much so, in fact, that when women have crossed the threshold of the family sphere in search of paid employment they have historically carried the *animal laborans* with them. For it is women who have borne the brunt of the degradation, bemoaned by Arendt in *The Human Condition*, of work into labour. As Dietz writes:

even when they are in the guise of *homo faber* – in the workplace of the 'artificer' – women have carried out the routinised tasks of stoop labour on assembly lines, and as cleaners, cooks, and clericals. The mechanisms of institutionalised sexism have assigned to women unpaid, devalued, monotonous work, both within the private realm and within the world outside. Nominally *homo faber*, they are really *animal laborans*, transported from life into worldliness. (Dietz 1991: 241)

Although Pitkin and Dietz agree on this much, the consensus ends here. Whereas Dietz, whose arguments I will return to shortly, believes that Arendt's theory of action, because it transcends the gendered categories of labour and work, offers feminists a theory of politics as a 'non-gendered activity', Pitkin believes that the highest activity in Arendt's hierarchy is actually eclipsed, in *The Human Condition*, by the enormous importance Arendt gives to the rise of the social. If, as Pitkin and Dietz concur, labour is a feminine activity, then the social, which is characterised by the transformation of the public sphere into one gigantic, labour-intensive household, is logically feminine too. That 'social' concerns – the sustaining and repairing of relationships, the transmission and enforcement of social norms, the activities of peacemaking, healing, helping and comforting – have for centuries been constructed as almost exclusively 'women's work', is further proof for Pitkin that Arendt saw the social as a female entity.

RETHINKING THE SOCIAL AND THE POLITICAL

Pitkin offers a psychoanalytic explanation for the non-dialectical concept of the social in Arendt's writings, arguing that the childhood trauma of losing, in quick succession, her father, grandfather and uncle, produced in Arendt a weak ego fearful of unrestrained maternal authority. The social, Pitkin argues, should be understood as the intellectual dramatisation of Arendt's unconscious fear of 'an evil, dominating, destructive matriarch constantly seeking to expand her power, to control and infantilise her children', while the 'misogynist machismo' of the Greeks is what promises to keep the overbearing matriarch in check (1998: 175). Given Arendt's well-known hostility to psychoanalysis,[1] her contempt for the indiscretion of the writer who 'aspires to know more than the subject knew about himself or was willing to reveal' (RV: xviii), as well as the self-evident contradiction in attempting to explain the reified concept of 'the social' by reference to the equally irresistible and opaque force of the unconscious, Pitkin's critique of Arendt should be handled with care. Nonetheless, the concept of the social deserves closer scrutiny.

Although, in *The Human Condition*, Arendt theorised the rise of the social in almost wholly negative terms, it is worth pointing out that her subsequent writings show an accommodation with the idea of the social, which she sometimes refers to as the sphere of rationalised production and administration by which the meeting of needs is collectively organised and delivered, and sometimes as the sphere of 'group formation', conformism, and social closure. This latter idea was also implicit in Arendt's earlier study of totalitarianism, where she described social stratification and class identities as bulwarks against the forces of atomisation and loneliness by which totalitarian movements sought to render the masses expendable (OT: 318–23). Arendt later wrote of the sphere of the 'social' in the following terms:

We are driven into this sphere by the need to earn a living or attracted by the desire to follow our vocation or enticed by the pleasure of company, and once we have entered it, we become subject to the old adage of 'like attracts like' which controls the whole realm of society in the innumerable variety of its groups and associations. What matters here is not personal distinction but the differences by which people belong to certain groups whose very identifiability demands that they discriminate against other groups in the same domain ... In any event, discrimination is as indispensable a social right as equality is a political right. The question is not how to abolish discrimination, but how to keep it confined within the social sphere, where it is legitimate, and prevent it trespassing on the political and the personal sphere, where it is destructive. (RJ: 205–6)

Whether it is the rational administration of needs or the sphere of discrimination and group interests, the social, Arendt seems to acknowledge, is a necessary element of modern life. Hence she describes not two but 'three realms of human life – the political, the social, and the private' (RJ: 211). Whichever definition is adhered to, however, the idea that the social and the political can be sharply separated and kept in their rightful place, has some troublesome consequences. Arendt's definition of the social as a sphere of group affiliation and discrimination, for example, led to her misguided argument, in her controversial 1959 essay, 'Reflections on Little Rock', that the compulsory desegregation of black and white school-children in the Southern states of America was an unjustified extension of the political principle of equality into the social sphere, where, in her view, discrimination can neither be legally enforced nor abolished (RJ: 208–9).

On the other hand, Arendt's argument, advanced most explicitly in *On Revolution*, that political action is degraded by the 'social' preoccupation with needs characteristic of the welfare state (OR: 269), and that politics coincides with the highest expression of the *vita activa* only when it is free from the necessities of life, has been interpreted to mean that problems of deprivation, questions of material injustice, and issues relating to bodily health and well-being, are not deserving of political interrogation through public discussion. 'Nothing, we might say, could be more obsolete than to attempt to liberate mankind from poverty by political means', Arendt wrote, 'nothing could be more futile and more dangerous' (OR: 114).

Arendt's arguments are particularly unnerving to those who regard the 'public sector' as the last bastion of civic decency – and, one could also argue, of collective promise-making – against the heartless spirit of free-market capitalism, and who have defined the 'decline of the public' explicitly in terms of neo-liberal anti-statism (e.g. Marquand 2004). By purifying the public sphere of all its 'social' associations with welfare and economic justice, Arendt, according to some critics, arrives at a definition of political action which effectively excludes from the public realm not only *debate* about inequality and deprivation, but also those who are conditioned by its effects (Pitkin 1994: 269).

Arendt did little to disarm her critics when, questioned in 1972 at a conference dedicated to her work, she defined 'social things' as 'things where the right measures can be figured out'. Asserting that political exchange and judgement 'can only deal with things which ... we cannot figure out with certainty', Arendt contrasted these uncertain things with social matters which, being uncontroversial, self-evident, or easily resolvable by appeal to the facts, belong 'in the sphere Engels called the administration of things' where they 'are not then subject to public debate' (1979: 317).

Since women have historically carried the burden of responsibility for acknowledging and administering to people's physical and emotional needs, as well as being beneficiaries of the social-welfare state that formed in the process by which 'housekeeping and all matters pertaining formerly to the private sphere of the family have become a "collective" concern' (HC: 33), Arendt's suggestion that questions of welfare and interpretations of need are not sufficiently controversial to justify their inclusion in public debate is extremely problematic from the perspective of a politics, feminist or otherwise, concerned with inequalities in the distribution of resources and the gratification of needs. Because 'necessity', in Arendt's account, is not a subject fit for public articulation, it is hard not to interpret this position as a defence of the economic status quo, for how else can unmet needs be satisfied except by bringing them to public attention? By making the meeting of needs a purely technocratic, administrative issue, in other words, Arendt's argument implies that social deprivation is a consequence of natural scarcity, productive inefficiency or managerial incompetence. In doing so she effectively *depoliticises* inequalities in health and well-being, whilst remaining curiously silent on the persistence of hunger and want in a world of unprecedented abundance.

If the stark separation of the political and the social serves to legitimise material inequality, it also seems to empty politics of much of its substantive content, leaving in its wake a purely agonal, aristocratic version of political action, conceived as dispassionate competition for recognition and acclaim through memorable words and deeds. Although there are a number of feminists who, as we shall see in a moment, have argued the opposite, this agonal conception does not offer an obvious remedy for the disillusionment with politics in modern Western democracies, since it excludes from the sphere of public debate a whole spectrum of issues – ranging from traditional struggles for workplace autonomy and a living wage, to abortion rights, animal welfare, genetic engineering, nuclear energy, and the new reproductive technologies – which have the potential to arouse large numbers of people in public discussion. Victims of this partition between the social and the political include those 'social' movements which stand in the intermediary space between the public and the private spheres, creating bonds of voluntary association and membership which, as Cohen and Arato point out, are as much an example of the political power formed through covenant and mutual promise-making as they are examples of social discrimination and conformity (1992: 190–1, 198–9).

Arendt's account of political action may also be found wanting for its historical accuracy. Although she has partially rescued the idea of positive freedom from the damaging conviction that only a negative concept of freedom can protect liberal democracies from totalitarianism, Arendt's analysis neglects the role that feelings of social injustice and compassion for those who suffer have played in fomenting political activism and positive forms of solidarity. Can the struggle to be free *from* oppression and injustice not serve as a crucible in which the appetite for positive political freedom is formed? Can necessity not be the mother of invention? Indeed, didn't Arendt convey precisely this sentiment when she stressed the energising role of labour in the *vita activa* of the individual (HC: 121)? If the struggle against necessity is a prerequisite for the assertion of freedom, then deprivation and injustice may equally be, and historically most certainly have been, a stimulus for the political practice of liberation.

Richard Bernstein highlights the paradox that such a determined critic of the social-scientific mindset could envisage the peaceful coexistence of technocracy and democracy, of the social and the political, and thus collude with the 'politically dangerous myth that there is a proper domain of social issues where social knowledge is appropriate – a domain that is better left to experts and social engineers, and is to be excluded from the political sphere'. 'Issues and problems do not simply come labelled "social", "political", or even "private"', he continues. 'Indeed, the question whether a problem is itself properly social (and therefore not worthy of public debate) or political is itself frequently the central *political* issue' (1986a: 252). This, surely, Arendt understood when she wrote publicly – that is, voiced her opinion in anticipation that others would contest it – that freedom from want, this being a precondition for autonomous participation in the realm of public affairs, 'must' be guaranteed for everybody, and that the principle of equality must therefore be imposed on the private, if not the social, sphere:

> if we talk about equality, the question always is: how much have we to change the private lives of the poor? In other words, how much money do we have to give them to make them capable of enjoying public happiness? Education is very nice, but the real thing is money. Only when they can enjoy the public will they be willing and able to make sacrifices for the public good. To ask sacrifices of individuals who are not yet citizens is to ask them for an idealism which they do not have and cannot have in view of the urgency of the life process. Before we ask the poor for idealism, we must first make them citizens: and this involves so changing the circumstances of their private lives that they become capable of enjoying the 'public'. (Arendt 1977: 106–7)

Arendt's assertion, in 'Reflections on Little Rock', that government 'cannot abolish discrimination and force equality upon society' because the validity of the principle of equality 'is clearly restricted to the political realm' (RJ: 204), is self-evidently contradicted by this later claim that we must make citizens of poor people by 'changing the circumstances of their private lives'. One of the paradoxes of Arendt's determination to purify politics of so many human concerns, it seems, is that as these concerns are sifted, categorised and defined through public discourse such as her own, they lose their status as 'things' that belong to the irresistible realm of necessity (of labour), and instead become the focus of political words and deeds in an ongoing process which is continually redrawing the boundaries of the political. Moreover, as modern democratic societies have indeed changed the private lot of the poor and extended access to the public sphere to previously excluded groups, this process of economic and legal equalisation has not yielded the kind of idealised agonistic politics in which materially equal subjects compete amongst their peers for fame and distinction. Instead, as Benhabib argues, there has been a bursting open of the category of the political as different groups, experiences and interests have fought to define the content and meaning of the public good. Only a reactionary anti-modernist, Benhabib suggests, could dismiss this pluralisation of the public sphere in preference for the elitist and exclusionary politics of Greek antiquity.

> With the entry of every new group into the public space of politics after the French and American revolutions, the scope of the public gets extended. The emancipation of workers made property relations into a public political issue; the emancipation of women has meant that the family and the so-called private sphere became political issues; the attainment of rights by non-white and non-Christian peoples has put cultural questions of collective self and other representations on the public agenda ... The distinction between the social and the political makes no sense in the modern world, not because all politics has become administration and because the economy has become the quintessential public ... but primarily because the struggle to make something public is a struggle for justice. (Benhabib 1992: 79)

In Nancy Fraser's view, it is precisely through an engagement in the public interpretation and determination of needs that political actors in modern welfare states are able to *resist*, as Arendt would surely want them to do, bureaucratic disempowerment and the depoliticisation of citizenship which Fraser regards as the direct effect of the 'juridical-administrative-therapeutic state apparatus' when it categorises its recipients as the bearers of technocratically-defined needs. Fraser believes this resistance takes place in 'subaltern counterpublics', which are 'parallel discursive arenas where members of subordinated social groups invent and circulate counterdiscourses to formulate oppositional interpretations of their identities, interests, and needs' (1992: 123). She also borrows Arendt's own term to define the site of political discourse about needs, explaining how her concept of the social departs from Arendt:

> needs are irreducibly interpretive and ... need interpretations are in principle contestable. It follows from my view that the emergence of needs from the 'private' into the social is a generally positive development, since such needs thereby lose their illusory

aura of naturalness as their interpretations become subject to critique and contestation. I, therefore, suppose that this represents the (possible) flourishing of politics, rather than the (necessary) death of politics ... Thus, I would argue for ... an alternative socialist-feminist, dialogical mode of need interpretation and a participatory-democratic institutionalisation of the social. (Fraser 1989b: 160 n32)

It remains to be seen whether this 'interpretivist' conception of needs can yield a progressive politics in which freedom from labour and active participation in public life are themselves rearticulated as 'needs', or whether the discourse of need interpretation will succour the ideological conviction, indispensable to the survival of modern capitalism, that needs are infinitely plastic, idiosyncratic and ultimately insatiable, thus driving people back into the worldless realm of labour and commodity consumption. The deliberate conflation by industry of the necessary with the superfluous, as well as the increasing interdependency of state and private enterprise in the provision of welfare, are now familiar commercial strategies in the battle by capital to perpetuate the wage relationship in the context of growing abundance. Dissolving the boundary defended by Arendt between the social and the political, in other words, carries risks as well as advantages. As the advanced capitalist regimes discovered in the wake of the cultural revolution of the 1960s, the political subversion of established needs, roles and expectations that marked this turbulent period also swept away almost all moral and normative restraints on the accumulation of capital. Whether politics can devote itself to the question of needs without furthering the reduction of citizens to passive consumers, or whether this challenge to Arendt's 'aristocratic' conception of action will put in jeopardy the very idea of politics as freedom and public happiness, is a delicate question with lasting implications for the health of civic life and culture in contemporary capitalist societies.

BENHABIB AND HABERMAS

Seyla Benhabib is one feminist scholar who has shown a constructive sensitivity to the tensions and inconsistencies in Arendt's work. Following d'Entrèves (1994), Benhabib distinguishes between an agonal and what she calls a 'narrative' model of action in Arendt's thinking. Claiming that the former model is 'essentialist' and the latter 'constructivist' – a claim, we shall see in a moment, with which not all feminists agree – Benhabib stresses that the narrative conception, because it places communicative interaction and storytelling ahead of the disclosure of the self and the achievement of individual distinction, is fully compatible with a modern, radicalised understanding of participatory politics.[2] Allied with this definition of action in Arendt's writings, Benhabib argues, is an 'associational' (or 'discursive') rather than institutional conception of the public sphere, which recognises that 'diverse topographical locations become public spaces' when they are used as a site 'of common action coordinated through speech and persuasion' (1992: 78).

For Benhabib, the proof that what Arendt calls the 'space of appearances' is not in fact equivalent to an institutionalised public realm, is the way this space migrates to the private sphere in totalitarian regimes. By redefining action and its space in this way, Benhabib makes narrative action ubiquitous, with 'gossip' being its quintessential everyday form (2003: 124–30). To support this controversial interpretation, Benhabib revisits Arendt's book on Rahel Varnhagen, finding in this study an 'alternative account of modernity' in which the egalitarian and experimental phenomenon of the salon presents us with 'a public sphere radically different from the inegalitarian, exclusive, male, and hierarchical spaces of the Greek polis' (2003: xii). In this new reading of Arendt, Benhabib's analysis owes something to Habermas's historical-philosophical study of the rise (and subsequent decline) of the bourgeois public sphere.

In *The Structural Transformation of the Public Sphere* (1989), Habermas attaches a surprising degree of importance to the process of privatisation and 'solitarisation' experienced by individual family members in bourgeois households from the seventeenth century onwards. This process was reflected in the changing architecture of the home, which involved the replacement of common rooms designed for the whole of the family with specialised spaces for individual family members. These changes gathered pace in the big cities of eighteenth-century Europe, and in Habermas's view they provided the foundations for 'a psychological emancipation that corresponded to the political-economic' emancipation of the bourgeoisie (1989: 46). The private autonomy of property owners, their freedom to pursue their private and commercial interests independent of government controls, was in other words mirrored by a subjectivity set loose from rigid social expectations and roles, and therefore capable of transcending the limited interests of feudal bonds and ranks. In Habermas's view, the intimate sphere of the conjugal family provided the soil in which was planted the seeds of a true universalist outlook, a belief in the possibility of 'purely human' relations undistorted by hierarchy and prejudice.

Bourgeois households did not so much abolish the family room, however, as redefine it as a dedicated space for extra-familial socialising: it became 'a reception room in which private people gather to form a public'. Habermas therefore stresses that the emancipated subjectivity of the early bourgeoisie, nurtured by the expressivism of the Romantics and the birth of the novel, was always oriented to an audience. It took public shape in the narrative form of the letter and the diary, and its 'public sphere' was not in society but in the domestic sphere itself, that is, in the salon, for the divide 'between private and public sphere extended right through the home' (Habermas 1989: 45).

So for Habermas it was the intimate family sphere, not the public realm of the *polis*, which 'was humanity's genuine site'. Combined with the coffee houses and table societies of the early bourgeois towns, this was the location of a new public sphere that was culturally and politically opposed to the aristocratic court on which it was originally modelled. Rooted in the experience of 'interiorised human closeness' as well as in the struggle, by autonomous commodity owners, against absolutist power, the bourgeois family gave birth to a critical public debate that was both universalist, implying 'parity of all cultivated persons', and polemical in its demand for representative government and a civil society free from autocratic rule and censorship. Both these attributes were lacking from the Greek conception, Habermas argues, because the public autonomy of the citizen of the *polis* 'rested on domination without any illusion of freedom evoked by human intimacy'. The Greeks' famed autonomy was more theatrical than real, being 'agonistic merely in the sportive competition with each other that was a mock war against the external enemy and not in dispute with his own government' (1989: 52; see also Wolin 2001: 64–5).

In Benhabib's view, Habermas's wider 'discourse model of public space' is superior to Arendt's because it 'neither restricts access to public space nor sets the agenda for public debate' (1992: 84). Benhabib turns to Arendt's biography of Rahel Varnhagen because Varnhagen's Berlin salon was perhaps the most famous example of the trend described by Habermas. Flourishing in the last two decades of the eighteenth century, its influence on German culture was such that the period from 1780 to the Napoleonic war of 1806 was later known as *die Rahelzeit* (Benhabib 2003: 15). Like the French salons which had developed, earlier in the century, out of the Royal Court of Louis XIV, the Berlin salons, where members of the aristocracy, bourgeoisie and intelligentsia met to exchange intimacies, read letters and poetry, report news and discuss social, literary or political events, were dominated by women. Lacking the ceremonial style of their French predecessors, they were typically run by the daughters or wives of wealthy Jewish patriarchs whose business commitments regularly took them away from the family home.

Viewing the salons 'as transitory but fascinating precursors of a certain transgression of boundaries between the public and the private', Benhabib notes how the Jewish *salonnières* not only emancipated themselves from religious and patriarchal gender prescriptions, but also created an egalitarian, experimental civic space in which men and women from different social backgrounds could cultivate their tastes, subvert traditional roles, and learn new forms of self-presentation. In Arendt's study of Varnhagen, Benhabib claims, an 'alternative genealogy of modernity' is therefore apparent, one which regards the 'rise of the social' in far more promising terms, indicating, in 'a curious space that is in the home yet public', the appearance of 'new forms of sociability, association, intimacy, friendship, speaking and writing habits, tastes in food, manners and arts, as well as pastimes, and leisure activities' (2003: 20, 22). Noting the surviving custom of referring, with apparent indiscretion, to the famous *salonnières* of that period by their first names, Arendt herself commented on how the salons married the personal and the public in such a way that an individual's life could be understood and presented as a coherent narrative, as an objective series of personally meaningful events. 'One could be indiscreet because private life lacked the element of intimacy, because private life itself had acquired a public, objective quality' (EU: 61).

ARENDT AND FEMINIST STANDPOINT THEORY

Benhabib's attempt to locate in Arendt's work a conception of modernity and the public sphere that is more attractive to a feminist politics is innovative, but it is matched, in enthusiasm if not in erudition, by other feminists who have embraced Arendt's political philosophy as uniquely relevant to the experience of women. These 'gynocentric' interpretations of Arendt have often been drawn to her concept of natality. Since natality, the condition of being a new beginning, is what makes possible the miracle of action, Jean Bethke Elshtain and Sara Ruddick have suggested that with this concept

Arendt throws new dignity on the labour of giving birth, and in doing so reconciles the action principles of singularity and self-disclosure with 'maternal concepts of humility, trust, vulnerability, and protection, which characterise the birthing act' (Ruddick 1990: 209). The notion of natality, according to Elshtain, 'stirs recognition of our own vulnerable beginnings and our necessary dependency on others, on mother', and in doing so fosters resistance to the masculine conception of warrior politics by challenging 'the massive denial (of "the female") on which it depends' (1992: 110).

But as Dietz points out, this use of Arendt to develop a feminist discourse is hard to square with a faithful reading of her work (1995: 28). By employing the concept of natality to advance a female politics of nurturance and care, grounded in the physical experience of giving birth and mothering, this perspective inverts Arendt's hierarchy of activities and invalidates the distinctive features of political action, including relations of plurality and the interruption of the rhythmic cycles of nature with the new and unexpected. Moreover, as with some of Arendt's feminist detractors, thinkers like Ruddick and Elshtain imply that the binary gendering of activities and spheres is fixed and unproblematic, thus essentialising women's experience as *animal laborans* and excluding from it novelty and difference, as well as the 'unnatural' contributions of men. As Dietz notes, 'there is nothing intrinsically or essentially masculine about the public realm, just as there is nothing intrinsically or essentially female about labouring in the realm of necessity'. The feminist aim should be 'to undermine the gendering of public and private and move on to a more visionary and liberating conception of human practices' (1991: 247).

Of all the gynocentric readings of Arendt, the positive interpretation advanced by Nancy Hartsock is probably the most compelling, as it remains focused on the nature and prize of politics. Hartsock argues that the combative conception of politics which is hegemonic today, and which was formed and inherited from the exclusively male political community of the ancients, expresses a 'negative' form of *eros*, in which relations with the other are denuded of sensuality and reduced to aggressive competition and the pursuit of control and conquest. 'The gender carried by power in the modern world, as in the ancient, leads to the domination of others, domination of external nature, and domination of one's own nature' (1985: 210).

Hartsock's concern is to identify a 'feminist standpoint', arising out of the particularities of women's experience, which 'not only makes available a privileged vantage point on social relations but also points beyond those relations in more liberatory directions' (1985: 226). In the political theory of Arendt, as in the work of a number of other female thinkers, Hartsock believes the foundations of this standpoint are outlined. Hartsock notes how Arendt viewed the public sphere, even in Greek antiquity, as a realm which does not cancel, invalidate or sacrifice the importance of the private household, and how for her the dualisms of necessity and freedom, body and mind, nature and action, are not oppositional, as they were in the Homeric tradition, but relational and complementary. Arendt, Hartsock writes, 'does not argue for the suppression/repression of the body, but only for the exclusion of bodily concerns from the public realm, whether in the form of labour or in the form of the urge for individual survival' (1985: 214). Hartsock therefore finds in Arendt's work a perspective that may show how women, by combining access to different spheres of life with which men are only cursorily acquainted, are able to 'mute the antagonism' between those spheres and hold their different elements in a more rounded balance. She also recognises that Arendt's concept of action has been shifted 'away from an individual competition for dominance and toward action in connection with others with whom one shares a common life and common concerns' (1985: 217). Arendt's explicit dissociation of power from domination thus suggests a standpoint from which to oppose the masculine construction of '*eros*, and as a result, power, as domination, repression and death' (1985: 226).

A DECONSTRUCTIONIST ARENDT?

Against Hartsock's attempt to derive a feminist standpoint, sensitive to the experience of women, from Arendt's work, a number of other feminists, including Mary Dietz and Bonnie Honig, have leaned towards a deconstructionist interpretation. While 'difference feminism' was offering an undifferentiated conception of womanhood, other feminist thinkers, championing a 'politics of identity', pointed to the diverse articulations of women's identity which became visible when class, ethnicity, sexuality and other social and cultural partitions were given full credence. From this constructivist position it was a modest step further to arrive at a more radical deconstructive feminist politics aimed at disrupting all stable and univocal definitions and rendering the category 'woman' a site for experimentation and transgression. This position reflects Arendt's argument that politics must avoid the worldlessness of those communities who believe their members are united by what lies inside them, and must instead realise that what members of a political community share in common is a world which lies between and outside of them, the reality of which is revealed only when those members exchange different perspectives on it.

In Dietz's view, this 'de-gendering' and de-essentialising version of feminist politics is more faithful to Arendt's thinking because it aims 'to restore the Arendtian who-ness of acting over the what-ness of being' (1995: 35). It is also consistent with Arendt's view that the thinking ego, being a reflective relationship to oneself, can never proclaim a definitive identity: 'Our modern identity crisis could be resolved only by never being alone and never trying to think' (LM1: 187). Or to put this another way, one can escape the fragmentation and division of the self, and attain the status of a distinct and unified subject, only by acting in the presence of others.

Bonnie Honig argues that the real contribution of Arendt to feminist theory lies in her conception of politics as agonistic performance. While theorists like O'Brien have regarded this as an inherently masculine understanding of political action, and sympathetic readers like Benhabib have rejected this conception as restrictive and 'essentialist', Honig believes that the agonal model of action actually constitutes a rejection of identity-based politics, providing a model for contesting binding gender constructions, as well as other normalising identities (such as Jewishness) which Arendt sometimes seemed to treat as indisputable, and therefore essentially private, facts. Honig takes a lead from Arendt's argument in *On Revolution* that political action is self-founding and self-legitimising, partly deriving its authority from its openness to reassessment, revision and augmentation. Action, Honig reiterates, is a 'rebirth', a spontaneous, self-surprising disclosure of a self whose identity cannot be conceived as prior to or independent of the performance. Unlike the irresistible and univocal character of the body, the acting self is 'multiple', the 'site of an agonistic struggle' which is only quieted through performative action, that is, through politics. 'Arendt's actors do not act because of what they already are, their actions do not express a prior, stable identity; they presuppose an unstable, multiple self that seeks its, at best, episodic self-realisation in action and in the identity that is its reward' (1995: 141).

This conception of action does not neatly conform to the 'expressive' model defined by d'Entrèves, or the 'essentialist' conception criticised by Benhabib, because, in Honig's account of Arendt's thinking, 'it resists the attractions of expressivism for the sake of her view of the self as a complex site of multiplicity whose identities are always performatively produced' (1995: 149). The choice between an agonistic and an associational interpretation of Arendt is therefore a false one in Honig's eyes, for Arendt never separated the agonal ideal of action from acting in concert. From Honig's perspective, these misconceptions are equally apparent in the often-heard complaint that Arendt's 'political existentialism', as Martin Jay (1986) originally labelled it, is in the words of Richard Wolin 'antidemocratic' and 'irreconcilable with the values of political solidarity' (2001: 69). This devaluing of the combative, performative character of politics, Honig argues, 'deprives feminism of a much-needed appreciation of the necessary agonistic dimension of all action in concert, in which politically engaged individuals act *and* struggle both with *and* against each other' (1995: 156).

Honig's conviction is that feminists can indeed use the 'agonal passion for distinction', the spirit of contestation and new beginnings which is central to Arendt's thought, to contest the 'violent closures' of identity and to deconstruct the boundary between public and private that Arendt tried to defend, since the distinction is itself a political construction open to amendment, augmentation and critique. Drawing on Judith Butler, Honig believes Arendt's agonistic conception of action allows us to de-naturalise gender identities, especially those rooted in the private sphere (and including those celebrated by 'gynocentric' feminists), by revealing them to be unstable and therefore inherently revisable performances.

The successful result of this approach, according to Dietz, is that it makes possible 'the articulation of an action-coordinating feminism that maintains the category "women" as the critical focus of its politics, *but does not assert it as the political identity of its agents*' (1995: 36). This is also the basis of Moruzzi's sympathetic critique of Arendt, which challenges Arendt's tendency to essentialise womanhood, and her failure to understand that femininity – even a femininity associated with the body – could be a public masquerade by which women knowingly equip themselves for the space of appearances. Referring to Arendt's description, in *On Revolution*, of the Women's March on Versailles as an anti-political 'raging force ... nourished by the necessity of biological life' (OR: 112), Moruzzi argues that the march 'can be reinterpreted as authentic political action' because 'the women may well have known exactly what they were doing in representing themselves as female and wretched before the public gaze' (2000: 46–7).

There is an affinity here between these social constructionist re-workings of Arendt and the version of 'agonistic pluralism' advanced by Chantal Mouffe. Mouffe argues that 'political practice cannot be envisaged as simply representing the interests of preconstituted identities, but as constituting those identities themselves in a precarious and always vulnerable terrain' (2000: 99–100). Mouffe's perspective reflects the influence of Gramsci's concept of ideological hegemony, which in her view supports a theory of political empowerment based on the constitution of 'subject positions traversing classes' (Laclau and Mouffe 2001: 65–71). In this Gramscian spirit she rejects the idea of the 'unitary subject' so central to modernist conceptions of political agency, as well as the Habermasian idea that free, rational debate can produce a frictionless consensus on the true, the beautiful and the good. Seeing the eradication of conflict and antagonism from parliamentary politics as symptomatic of the crisis of modern democracy, Mouffe stresses that 'Arendt was absolutely right to insist that in the political sphere one finds oneself in the realm of opinion, or "doxa", and not in that of truth' (1993: 20, 14; 2000: 102–5).

HABERMAS AND ARENDT

Objections to Habermas's critical employment of Arendt's concept of political action have also been made from similar quarters. Habermas applauds Arendt's conviction that political power should be distinguished from the classical teleological model that renders it synonymous with coercion, viewing this insight as the starting point for his own distinction between instrumental and communicative action. 'The fundamental phenomenon of power', Habermas agrees, 'is not the instrumentalisation of *another's* will, but the formation of a *common* will in a communication directed to reaching agreement' (1994: 212). The power of this 'unimpaired intersubjectivity', since it is an end in itself, cannot be measured in terms of the achievement of practical goals, but only in terms of the rationally motivated recognition of the validity of participants' spoken convictions. It is only with this communicative concept of political action, Habermas concurs with Arendt, that we can properly understand the stability of political institutions, which 'live not from force but from recognition' (1994: 222; 1996: 147–50).

Habermas also criticises Arendt, however, for adhering to what he regards as an overly dogmatic and uncharacteristically reductive definition of politics. The limitations of this definition, he argues, can be surmounted 'only if we extricate it from the clamps of an Aristotelian theory of action' (1994: 220). The flaw Habermas detects in Arendt's thinking derives, he maintains, from her desire to purify political praxis of all the features of instrumental action, reserving the latter for the lower activities of the *vita activa*. We have seen this same desire reflected in some feminist readings of Arendt, and it is also shared by ecological thinkers such as Torgerson (1999), for whom Arendt offers a model for a 'green public sphere' which is no longer tainted with the industrial discourse of instrumental rationality. In Habermas's view, however, this attitude led Arendt to overlook the distinctive characteristics of a type of instrumental action which is not, like labour and work, oriented to the non-human world, but which is instead a form of *social* action aimed at preventing others from pursuing their own interests.

Habermas differentiates this social action type from communicative action by calling it 'strategic action' (1994: 220–2; 1984: 285–6). Physical aggression between states is the most obvious example of strategic action, but it has also been internalised by the *polis*, becoming, in less destructive forms, 'a normal component of the political system' in capitalist-democratic societies. Institutional-ised in economic competition, party politics and the legal struggles of the labour movement, strategic action is the means by which different interest groups vie for and exercise dominance. Although Arendt correctly understood that political groups and leaders cannot *produce* power, but have to 'borrow' it from the people from whose praxis it is generated, Habermas claims that she failed to grasp how power is also 'a good *for* which political groups struggle and *with* which a political leadership manages things' (1994: 224). Without this strategic conception of political action, Habermas argues, Arendt's ideal polity is full of 'absurdities':

> a state which is relieved of the administrative processing of social problems; a politics which is cleansed of socio-economic issues; an institutionalisation of public liberty which is independent of the organisation of public wealth; a radical democracy which inhibits its liberating efficacy just at the boundaries where political oppression ceases and social repression begins – this path is unimaginable for any modern society. (Habermas 1994: 220)

Perhaps most importantly, Habermas questions Arendt's assumption that the public legitimation of political rule is necessarily evidence of the actualisation of liberty. The function of ideology, he points out, is precisely to arm the false views people hold about the world with the power of common convictions, 'thereby communicatively generating a power which, as soon as it is institutionalised, can also be used against them' (1994: 225). Arendt's definition of politics as the realm in which the world is illuminated by the exchange of different opinions, and her quasi-Weberian claim that 'truth', with its 'peculiar opaqueness', is a 'non-violent form of coercion' that belongs outside the political realm (PF: 222–3, 242), thus appears to exclude the kind of rational critique of ideology which is central to Habermas's own attempt to revive the unfinished business of the Enlightenment. In her refusal to recognise the potential for social harmony and consensus which Habermas believes is intrinsic to the rational use of language, Arendt knowingly opened up 'a yawning abyss between knowledge and opinion that cannot be closed with arguments' (1994: 225). To reconcile her concept of plurality with her definition of power as combined action, she was instead forced to revert to what Habermas, Pitkin (1994: 271) and Miller (1979: 192, 202) all argue is merely a reworking of flawed liberal contract theory: 'She has to look for another foundation for the power of opinion, and she finds it in the capability of responsible subjects to make and keep promises' (Habermas 1994: 225).

Habermas's arguments are persuasive in part, but they too are not immune to criticism. We saw in Chapter 3 that Arendt explicitly distinguished the practice of mutual promise-making from the classical tradition of contract theory, a tradition which saw the relinquishment of public freedom as a rational price worth paying in exchange for private security and protection against interference by others. In Arendt's version of the contract, by contrast, it is not the protection of life but the enjoyment of collective action and the enablement of human relatedness which is at stake. And what is traded in exchange for public engagement with others is precisely the safety, predictability and certainty that comes from the solitude of the thinker and the negative liberty of the sovereign holder of private rights. That plurality entails risks and uncertainty, that Arendt's 'contract' does not yield an indivisible unity of opinion and will nor rest on an absolute rational foundation the contravention of which justifies violent retribution, is indicated by the importance Arendt attaches to the role of *forgiveness* in public life. This is explained well by McGowan:

> Unlike violent revenge, forgiveness is also an act in Arendt's terms because it sustains the relationship initially established by

the promise. Forgiveness affirms the effort to keep a space of human relatedness open, whereas vengeance shuts down that space, repudiates the relation to the other. In short, the contract theorists envisioned a wary peace – secured by legal means of redress – between individuals who mostly want to be left alone to pursue their ends. Arendt envisions an excessive, even foolhardy, binding of humans together by acts of promising and forgiving that sacrifice almost everything (including security and property) for the sake of relatedness. The realm created by 'mutual promises' offers no guarantees, beyond its simply existing, that violence will not overwhelm it and the lives of those who are related through it ... Only humans who value this non-violent, political space have the power to keep it open through their continuing acts of promising and forgiving. (McGowan 1997: 285)

Margaret Canovan argues, in a similar vein, that Habermas's modification of Arendt's thinking delivers an inferior theory of political action which reflects a misunderstanding of Arendt's ideas. Habermas accuses Arendt of idealising politics, and yet it is Habermas, not Arendt, who defines the goal of communicative action as 'Agreement [which] rests on common convictions' (1984: 287). Canovan stresses that Arendt never regarded action as the pursuit of 'common convictions', nor collective action as the assertion of a 'common will'. Arendt emphasised the inescapable plurality and heterogeneity of individuals, viewing the preservation of this plurality as a condition of their freedom:

Such men can certainly act together, but not out of anything as stable as a common will based on rational consensus. Instead, human plurality means that action is always a web of intersecting actions with no common goal or definite consummation, always a messy and unpredictable business. This, she points out, is precisely what makes free politics so difficult to achieve, and so fragile when it exists. (Canovan 1983: 110)

The difference between Habermas and Arendt on this point illustrates why some post-modernist and anti-foundationalist thinkers have been attracted to Arendt's political philosophy in recent years. For whereas Habermas champions 'that peculiarly forceless force with which insights assert themselves' (1994: 213), Arendt insisted, as Martin Plot puts it, 'that the persuasive power of action is fundamentally different to any sort of force, even the force of rational or factual truths, and that includes, of course, the force of the "better" argument' (2009: 849). For Arendt, 'the ability of logical reasoning whose premise is the self-evident' was 'the only reliable "truth" human beings can fall back upon once they have lost the mutual guarantee, the common sense, men need in order to experience and live and know their way in a common world' (OT: 477). Truth, in other words, is the certainty that prevails either in private solitude or when people are pressed so closely together that there is no space between them in which a common world can appear. Political understanding, by contrast, is not the establishment of a single shared perspective, but an ability to see the world from different sides, 'to see the same in very different and frequently opposing aspects' (PF: 51).

If, like Arendt, we take 'the self-evident logicality' of mathematical calculation as the purest form of truth-seeking reasoning, then we can draw a useful analogy between agreement on the truth, on the one hand, and the practices of economic exchange in a market economy on the other. In so far as buying and selling is perceived as an exchange of equivalents, economic transactions, like the achievement of a perfect consensus, are the termination of a relationship. Once differences are settled by correct payment, the space across which friendship reaches is closed. Richard Sennett says something similar when he writes that the 'art' of mutual respect, which provides the social bond most appropriate to a society of strangers, 'does not imply justice, truth, or goodness', since its most fundamental premise is not consensus but autonomy. 'Rather than an equality of understanding, autonomy means accepting in others what one does not understand about them' (2003: 177, 226, 262).

Canovan, whose arguments are supported by Disch (1997), thus defends Arendt's account of people acting together on the grounds that it makes recognition of a common world, and recognition of one another's freedom, mutually reinforcing goals:

> They can be united, not because they all think alike in the inner realm of their minds, but because outside in the world they all inhabit the same public space, acknowledge its formal rules, and are therefore committed to achieving a working compromise when they differ. For among people who share a common world of institutions, unanimous conviction is not necessary for practical agreement. Where there is mutual commitment to the continuance of the same public world, differences can be settled through purely political means. (Canovan 1983: 112)

THE PUBLIC AS THEATRE

Reading some of these feminist interpretations of Arendt, one could be forgiven for assuming a direct affinity between Arendt's approach and the 'decisionism' of Max Weber, who at times described politics as a potentially violent conflict between irreconcilable faiths. 'To take a stand, to be passionate – *ira et studium* – is the politician's element.' Politics, wrote Weber, is the place where 'ultimate *Weltan-schauungen* clash, world views among which in the end one has to make a choice' (1970a: 95, 117). Dana Villa is another commentator on Arendt who defends an agonistic conception of political action, viewing it as dramaturgical performance. But in doing so Villa draws attention to Weber's neglected insight that 'mere passion ... does not make a politician', since what is required is 'that firm taming of the soul' which 'is possible only through habituation to detachment in every sense of the word' (Weber 1970a: 115–6). Villa is critical of the way the agonal model of Arendtian politics has been used to deconstruct the boundary between public and private, as in his view this results in the reduction of political action to a form of passionate self-expression, a clashing of 'ultimate *Weltanschauun-gen*' which may put civility itself in jeopardy. Villa's primary concern is to protect Arendt's central notion of 'worldliness', which in his view ranks even higher in Arendt's philosophy than action does (1999a: 135, 244 n26). Villa's point is that not all political action contributes to human worldliness, that is, to the preservation of and commitment to a reality that exceeds the subjective experiences of those who inhabit it. Worldliness requires an exchange rather than mere conflict of perspectives, as it is by seeing the world from different standpoints that its three-dimensional qualities are revealed. Actors who are driven by urgent wants and needs, or by the passionate worldview of their cultural or political tribe, may not be well-disposed 'to appreciate and value the play of perspectives for its own sake' (Villa 1999a: 123).

Arguing, therefore, that 'politicisation as such has no particular connection to the recovery of the public sphere' (1999a: 154), Villa suggests that a boundless definition of political space could endanger rather than strengthen public life, encouraging a fundamentalist politics of authenticity devoid of worldly sociability and friendship. Public life, in his view, should be treated as an impersonal performance, circumscribed by theatrical conventions, accepted codes of self-presentation, and shared political principles. The alternative to this liberal definition of the political, according to Villa, is an aggressive politics of personal self-disclosure whose path, as Arendt suggested in her account of the French Revolution, leads from suspicions of hypocrisy to a worldless violence purified of all artifice and convention.

Villa thus charts a middle course between the communicative model of politics advanced by Habermas and Benhabib and the agonal form advocated by Dietz, Honig and Mouffe. In doing so he draws on Richard Sennett's *The Fall of Public Man* (1977), and I want to summarise Sennett's important book in more detail here.

We have seen that a problematic consequence of Arendt's methodological individualism, which refuses to treat political actors as bearers of structural economic, racial or gender interests, and her Periclean view of politics as memorable public performance rather than as means for the achievement of virtuous ends, is the displacement or exclusion of questions of social justice and need from the public sphere. Sennett's historical analysis of the decline of public life since the eighteenth century is interesting because it regards the erosion of the boundary between the public and private as lamentable precisely because it weakens people's capacity to fight dispersed and globalised structures of class domination and inequality. It does this, Sennett argues, by undermining people's trust in the meaningfulness of the compromises, conventions and public 'masks' which political actors must assume if they are to form bonds of solidarity with strangers.

Sennett was taught by Arendt at the University of Chicago in the early 1960s – 'she flunked me', he later explained in a newspaper interview. 'That's how we became friends' (Honan 1991). Though he has only really acknowledged his intellectual debt to Arendt in more recent work (Sennett 2003: 138–50; 2009: 1–8), Arendt's influence on his thinking is actually most apparent in *The Fall of Public Man*, where strangely she is never mentioned. Sennett begins this book by returning to the notion of 'the public' as it was used in early eighteenth-century Paris and London. There, he argues, it was closely associated with the word 'cosmopolitan', a cosmopolite being somebody who was comfortable amidst diversity, artifice and strangeness. 'Public' came to mean a region outside the natural demands and responsibilities of family life and intimate friends. Sustained by urban parks, coffeehouses, cafes, coaching inns, markets and shops, the public was that unnatural but civilised space where people interacted with unfamiliar members of different social groups. '"Public" behaviour is a matter, first, of action at a distance from the self, from its immediate history, circumstances, and needs; second, this action involves the experiencing of diversity.' The public sphere was therefore 'the forum in which it becomes meaningful to join with other persons without the compulsion to know them as persons' (Sennett 1977: 87, 340).

One sign of a society with a strong public life, Sennett argues, is the existence of a meaningful bridge between stage and street. The ancient tradition of *theatrum mundi* came to life in the rapidly expanding cities of eighteenth-century Western Europe whose residents, living in the midst of a demographic earthquake that made it impossible to ascertain the social origin and rank of their fellow inhabitants, faced the same challenge encountered by actors in relation to their audience, namely, 'how to arouse belief among those who do not know you' (1977: 49).

The public could learn the art of sociability from the stage because, in the eighteenth-century theatre, actor and audience inhabited the same world. In most theatres, the seats of the spectators extended onto the stage itself, and those enjoying this vantage point felt no discomfort at being mixed up with the actors in full view of the audience. With the social status of the actor, like the musical performer, little higher than that of a servant, audiences routinely interfered with plays, calling on actors to repeat memorable lines when they were particularly well-delivered, and raucously unsettling weaker actors, sometimes hounding them off the stage altogether. Sennett points out that, despite the repetition of well-received lines, sometimes up to seven or eight times, and even to audiences already familiar with the play, these performances would provoke extreme emotional responses which would embarrass the typical theatre-goer of today. In Sennett's analysis, this ability to suspend disbelief was rooted in a confidence in the meaningfulness of conventions, codes and ritualised gestures, which could be repeatedly expressed by different individuals without a loss of emotional impact and sense of reality.

This 'anti-symbolic' culture of expression – expression as an immediate sign rather than a symbol of something hidden or absent – extended into the street. There it was understood that acting was the performance of an impersonal role, not the manifestation of an expressive personality. An action could be condemned as morally bad, for example, without rage against the personal character of the wrongdoer, just as an opinion could be challenged without demonising its proponent. The competent actor, whether in the street or on the stage, was someone who had mastered the art of playing roles. But instead of conforming to Goffman's depiction of the passionless manipulator of impressions – a jaundiced analysis, according to Sennett, which is symptomatic of our modern 'inability to imagine social relations which would arouse much passion' (1977: 36) – the actor in eighteenth-century Paris and London, unable to decode people's personalities and background via their appearances, was more than capable of conveying powerful feelings and emotions through stylised gestures and roles.

> Just as the actor touched people's feelings without revealing to them his own character offstage, the same codes of belief he used served his audience to a similar end; they aroused each other's feelings without having to attempt to define themselves to each other, a definition the material conditions of life would have made difficult, frustrating, and probably fruitless. This bridge, in turn, gave men the means to be sociable, on impersonal grounds. (Sennett 1977: 64)

In eighteenth-century Europe the cosmopolitan 'public' was divided from a private realm which was regarded as the domain in which the natural body expressed itself. The family became the seat of nature where adults displayed and gratified their instinctual needs, including a compassionate concern for the needs of vulnerable and dependent others. Yet while the perception of a 'state of nature' shared by all human beings gave rise to both the legal concept of natural rights and a moral interest in moderating the socially induced extremes of pain and distress, to the eighteenth-century imagination only the artificial public world could provide the civility necessary to balance nature's rudeness and turn the human animal into a being worthy of admiration and respect. This 'balance of public and private geography' was clearly reflected in patterns of dress, with loose-fitting garments worn at home by all social classes while in public face-painting and the wearing of masks had become popular fashion, with city inhabitants routinely flouting sumptuary laws, donning the costumes of different trades and professions without provoking charges of inauthenticity. The purpose of public adornment, Sennett writes, was

> to make it possible for other people to act as if they knew who you were. One became a figure in a contrived landscape; the purpose of the clothes was not to be sure of whom you were dealing with, but to be able to behave as if you were sure ... In this sense, then,

clothes had a meaning independent of the wearer and the wearer's body. (Sennett 1977: 67–8)

Much as Arendt views the public world as that 'in-between' which relates and separates people at the same time, Sennett regards social conventions – 'rules for behaviour at a distance from the immediate desires of the self' – as protecting the exposure of the private self in ways which increase sociability and trust between strangers, encouraging people to take risks with unfamiliar situations and to gain that distance from intimate needs and desires which is the mark of the civilised person. 'People are more sociable, the more they have some tangible barriers between them, just as they need specific places in public whose sole purpose is to bring them together' (1977: 15). A culture of impersonal customs and rules is therefore essential to public civility. The 'essence of urbanity', Sennett argues 'is that men can act together, without the compulsion to be the same' (1977: 255).

> I would define civility as follows: it is the activity which protects people from each other and yet allows them to enjoy each other's company. Wearing a mask is the essence of civility. Masks permit pure sociability, detached from the circumstances of power, malaise, and private feeling of those who wear them. Civility has as its aim the shielding of others from being burdened with oneself. (Sennett 1977: 264)

Sennett shares with Arendt a disdain for 'those autobiographies or biographies which compulsively bare every detail of the sexual tastes, money habits, and character weaknesses of their subjects, as though we are supposed to understand the person's life, writings, or actions in the world better by the exposure of his or her secrets' (1977: 265). His critique of our modern culture of intimacy, which equates the impersonal with the meaningless, the stale and the phoney, and sees convention and ritual as an obstacle to the autonomy and authenticity of the individual, is also consistent with Arendt's liberal explanation and defence of the majority's consent to the law in a democratic society. Refusing to give the orders of the policeman the same weight of compulsion as the commands of the gunman, Arendt argues that laws are like the rules of a game which we respect in order to act in concert with others (OV: 97–8). If public life is a form of play, Sennett argues, then we can gain a richer understanding of its logic by looking at the behaviour of children. Play is not spontaneous expression, Sennett points out, but is the mastering and remaking of rules to facilitate human sociability. Although play is always oriented towards an objective, which in Western culture is normally the defeat of an opponent, the actual practices of play are governed by the delay of gratification, and the means by which the goal is deferred – and by which the game kept alive – is the rules. By conforming to the rules – and by revising them when inequalities in talent make competition short-lived – children learn the art of 'self-distancing', sublimating their desire to immediately dominate their adversary by instead engaging in a challenging process of competitive but social interaction. The rejection of play by our adult culture – the rejection of the dramaturgical, agonistic spirit of public life – is in Sennett's view a symptom of narcissism.

THE CULTURE OF NARCISSISM

The roots of this narcissism, according to Sennett, stretch back to the early nineteenth-century, when the equilibrium between public and private spheres began to break down. Private imagery was superimposed on the public in a way which appealed to bourgeois audiences while at the same time promoting political deference and passivity among the working class. The Enlightenment belief in a common humanity gave way to the idea of a distinctive 'personality' which people believed they could read from the minute details of individuals' appearances, habits and dispositions. As the search for clues to people's authentic personalities became ever more obsessive, the reciprocal anxiety about being scrutinised by others became, once repressed, a paranoid fear of involuntary public disclosure which Freud came to classify as the classic aetiology of the hysteric.

Sennett charts the effects of these changes across a number of different institutions and spaces. In music, a new school of thought had arisen which treated the increasing complexity of musical annotation as evidence of music's formless profundity. Since the essence of music transcended the conventions of the text, which could not possibly be an exact representation of how the music was originally conceived and performed by the composer, the performer, in order to bring to life the music's authentic meaning, had to become the composer himself, shocking audiences by making well-known compositions sound completely novel and fresh. The musicians of the 'school of serious egoism' included Niccolò Paganini, whose violent and ingenious improvisations would sometimes end with him playing off a single unbroken violin string. Paganini, Liszt and Berlioz redefined musical performance as a matter of personality rather than technical skill or taste, believing that only by converting the written score into an expression of self could music be wrested from the refractory tools of the manuscript and instrument.

In the theatre itself, Sennett records a similar trend, with the leading actors in the Parisian melodramas of the 1830s lauded for the 'ineffable personalities' they brought to the parts they played. Performances became more natural, with gestures, movements and costumes less exaggerated and ritualised. The public's growing fascination with the private lives, opinions and extraordinary personalities of the actors engendered amongst the audience a passive deference which displaced the control it had previously exercised over performers in the theatres of the eighteenth century. Displays of emotion by audience members were now regarded as a 'primitive' response unbefitting respectable people. Applause no longer interrupted and demanded repetition of outstanding deliveries but was reserved for the end of the performance. Audiences became self-policing, convinced that silence and stillness were required to make contact with the irresistible force of the performer's personality.

This culture of silence and withdrawal passed from the stage into the market, public house and street. In the newly built department stores the ritual and theatre of haggling disappeared as consumers became passive spectators encouraged to browse and window shop. Pubs whose customers engaged in rowdy conversation were branded a threat to respectability and often closed down. Cafés and clubs began to introduce codes of silence 'as a public right of protection against sociability', offering to their customers 'a realm of privatised freedom' (Sennett 1977: 217). The political dimension of this process became apparent in France during the revolution of 1848, when the structural antagonism between proletariat and bourgeoisie, which had remained largely hidden from the working class in the revolution of 1830, aroused workers' suspicions of their bourgeois representatives. Sennett notes the prominent role played by the Romantic poet Alphonse de Lamartine, the best-known political 'personality' during the February days of 1848, who succeeding in silencing the more extreme elements of the working class through his charisma and poetic eloquence. Having rehearsed his speeches in front of a mirror, he pacified the angry masses who repeatedly threatened to storm the Hotel de Ville where the provisional government was meeting, making them feel ashamed for lacking the self-control which he displayed. His personality was 'an anti-ideological force' which invalidated workers' consciousness of their class interests and which persuaded them to judge him not in terms of his actions and achievements but in terms of the quality and sincerity of his emotions. 'In this 19th Century revolutionary upheaval, the leader succeeded in imposing what were middle-class standards of propriety – that is, silence in the face of art – on a working-class audience, outside the theatre and at a moment when the working classes were thoroughly aroused' (Sennett 1977: 230).

Sennett regards Lamartine as the forerunner of the twentieth-century media-savvy politician whose electoral appeal lies in his or her personality and sentiments. Convinced that impersonality is phoney and meaningless, yet fearful of their own involuntary expressions, modern voters lost confidence in judging the 'abstract' implications of the doctrines, policies and actions of individual politicians and their parties, seeking instead public figures gifted with the 'controlled spontaneity' necessary to display, in a kind of 'psychic striptease', their concrete emotions, motivations and beliefs.

Sennett also notes how the thirst for personality in the public realm has resulted in the desire to form communities of shared sentiment, where social bonds are favoured only in so far as they are seen to embody a 'collective personality' forged through mutual disclosure and the unmasking of alienating expectations and roles. Intimate society, Sennett argues, has as its psychological correlative not hysteria but narcissism, and its end result is what he calls 'destructive gemeinschaft': 'a psychological community ... at war with societal complexity' (1977: 311). In the political trend towards localism, the assertion of fixed cultural identities and the psychotherapeutic discourse of authenticity, Sennett sees a fundamentalist pursuit of fraternity which, following the same logic that Arendt detected in Robespierre's merciless war on hypocrisy, almost inevitably leads to fratricide. Often regarding themselves as embattled islands of morality, these communities substitute, for the politics of collective action and engagement with a complex and impersonal world, a vicious circle of purification, whereby genuine members are authenticated by their uncompromising outrage and doubters expelled for their hypocrisy, tainted origins, or lack of conviction.

Arendt argued in her account of the French Revolution (OR: 106–9), and earlier, in her analysis of totalitarianism (OT: 290–302), that the passion for unmasking personalities reaches its most devastating conclusion when people are stripped of their legal 'persona' and reduced to naked specimens of the human animal whose natural rights no 'artificial' body politic can guarantee.

Both Sennett and Arendt show an affinity with the original Greek and Roman understanding of the theatrical mask, as something which covered the actor's countenance whilst facilitating his powers of expression. This understanding was carried into the political terminology of the Roman Republic, the citizen of which was given a legal *persona* 'as though the law had affixed to him the part he was expected to play on the public scene, with the provision, however, that his own voice would be able to sound through' (OR: 107). Trust in the expressive potential of impersonal masks and conventions, Sennett concurs, is essential to the art of public life, for the latter requires a distancing from the self, its physical and psychological needs, in order to test different rhetorical positions, engage in self-criticism, and enjoy the company and opinions of strangers.

CRITICAL THEORY AND THE SOCIOLOGICAL IMAGINATION

Sennett's historical analysis of the rise and fall of the modern public sphere is important because it highlights the risks involved in extending the 'space of appearances' beyond the formalised conventions of public life. In their most radicalised forms, both the agonal and the associational interpretations of Arendt's concept of political action – that is, action as the display and constitution of the self, and action as the spatially pluralized pursuit of consensus – may effectively be courting the same danger, which is that the kind of impersonal sociability required for collective action and a robust public sphere is lost because the medium of politics has ceased to be a common language through which diverse individuals and groups can find a voice.

Sennett's concerns over the depoliticising effects of the culture of intimacy and the public assertion of morally incontestable identities and needs may also have become more pressing in the decades following the publication of his book. Stjepan Meštrović (1997), for example, has linked the rationalisation and disenchantment of social conventions and rituals to the rise of a 'postemotional society', in which the loss of confidence in collective representations of human passions has led to ever more shrill and indignant spectacles of personal grievance. Spurred on by the 'authenticity industry', the result, he argues, is a desiccation of people's expressive powers and the hollowing out of emotions to such an extent that they are increasingly incapable of mobilising people to act.

In a series of books that are too numerous to catalogue, Zygmunt Bauman has also argued that the mass society characteristic of 'heavy', Fordist capitalism has now been replaced by a lighter, 'liquid modernity', in which compulsory individualisation, rather than social normalisation through conformity, is the dominant organising logic. Private problems consequently fill the space vacated by the discussion of public issues, 'chasing away everything which cannot be fully, without residue, expressed in the vernacular of private concerns' (Bauman 2000b: 39).

> The consequence arguably most seminal is the demise of 'politics as we know it' – Politics with a capital P, the activity charged with the task of translating private problems into public issues (and vice versa). It is the effort of such translation which is nowadays grinding to a halt. Private problems do not turn into public issues by dint of being vented in public; even under public gaze they do not cease to be private, and what they seem to be accomplishing by being transferred to the public stage is pushing all other, 'non-private' problems out of the public agenda. What are commonly and ever more often perceived as 'public issues' are *private problems of public figures*. (Bauman 2000b: 70)

Bauman's observations are pertinent to a number of contemporary trends, ranging from the growth of a celebrity culture in which the stellar careers of 'public figures' are manufactured through the spread of gossip and personal revelations, to the proliferation of TV chat shows, internet blogging and social networking websites, where the boundary between public and private is shamelessly dissolved and the bearing of intimate details exchanged for participation in a promiscuous world of fleeting public recognition and friendship. Although the internet is still often condemned for fostering charlatanism and fraud, the power, reach and memory of online information is now such that the demand for authenticity and transparency in internet transactions is almost impossible to deflect. One should also mention the expansion of what some sociologists, following the lead of Arlie Hochschild (1983), have called 'emotional labour', which in its more sophisticated formulations is understood as a logical outcome of the internal contradictions of modern capitalism. As the volume of labour required to meet human needs steadily declines, the preservation of the capital-labour relationship is increasingly dependent on a service industry whose products, presented as embodying the authentic personalities of its workers, are perceived as unique enough to resist the price-reducing (and productivity increasing) effects of market competition (Gorz 2003:

61–3), and authentic enough to substitute for the fast-depleting provision, outside the sphere of economic exchange, of personal care, interest and goodwill (Fevre 2003: 78–9). That the mobilisation and enrolment of workers' subjectivities gives rise to new tensions and conflicts is now a central premise in the sociology of the modern work process (Flecker and Hofbauer 1998).

A less convincing aspect of Bauman's analysis of the contemporary public sphere is his insistence on the distinctive novelty of the trends he describes, and his belief that the new conditions of society have rendered obsolete the theoretical framework of critical theory, developed as it was during the heyday of Fordist mass society. It was in the 1950s, after all, when C. Wright Mills wrote of the need for the sociological imagination to bridge the gap between 'personal troubles' and 'public issues' (1959: 14–20), and even longer ago when he made his memorable analysis of the newly emerging 'personality market', in which 'intimate traits of the employee are drawn into the sphere of exchange' (1951: 182). Thirty years earlier, in 1921, Georg Simmel was reflecting on the historical process by which life, 'owing to its essential restlessness', battles against its inherited forms of objective expression, detecting in the process 'a new phase of the old struggle – no longer a struggle of a contemporary form, filled with life, against an old, lifeless one, but a struggle of life against the form *as such*, against the *principle* of form' (1968: 12). Simmel noted this phenomenon in a variety of cultural trends, including the expressionist painter's conviction 'that the inner emotions of the artist are manifest in his work exactly as he experiences them', a subculture of vitalism (foreshadowing the values of Nazism) among the young, the position of absolute subjectivism adopted in Husserl's phenomenological philosophy, a vocal movement rebelling against the 'legalised cruelty' of the institution of marriage, and a flight from traditional religion towards a mystical belief in 'formless infinity, a mode of expression based only on the powerful longing of the soul' (1968: 230).

Simmel would doubtless have had something similar to say about the revolt against the conventions of punctuation in the electronic messages of the digital generation, and the stout commercial opposition, which is the hallmark of the global fast food industry, to the aesthetics and culture of eating. Writing of the trend he observed towards a rejection of the constraints of sexual morality, Simmel noted the contradictions of this idealistic enterprise, for 'erotic life, as soon as it is expressed in cultural contexts, necessarily requires some form' (1968: 22). A similar observation is made by Sennett, who describes a steady shift 'from eroticism to sexuality'. This involves a rebellion against sexual repression, but one which, by denying that sexuality has a moral, cultural or symbolic dimension, and by rejecting 'the idea that physical love is an action people engage in, and like any other social action might have rules, limits, and necessary fictions which give the action a specific meaning', transforms sexual relations into a 'revelation of self' whose logical outcome is mutual boredom (Sennett 1977: 7). No wonder Sennett asks whether 'this contempt for ritual masks of sociability has not really made us more primitive culturally than the simplest tribe of hunters and gatherers' (1977: 15).

While Bauman (2003) speaks of 'liquid love' and 'pure sex' as contemporary phenomena which mark out today's society from the repressive, homogenising world described in the now outdated work of the Frankfurt School, Sennett's reading of critical theory is more accurate, acknowledging the relevance, for example, of Theodor Adorno's critique, in *The Jargon of Authenticity* (1973), of Heidegger's pastoral subjectivism (Sennett 1977: 29). Bauman is certainly wrong to argue that, because it is now the private that is colonising the public, rather than the other way round, 'the task of critical theory has been reversed' (2000b: 39). Prefiguring Sennett's argument that the preoccupation with the self 'has proved to be a trap rather than a liberation' (1977: 5), it was Herbert Marcuse who in the 1960s coined the term 'repressive desublimation', or 'repressive tolerance', to describe the way the loosening of social taboos had allowed capitalist civilisation to 'extend liberty while intensifying domination'. Marcuse's analysis of the way 'sexuality is liberated (or rather liberalised) in socially constructive forms', also predates Foucault's famous study of the social construction of sexuality in *The History of Sexuality* (1981). There are, Marcuse wrote in *One-Dimensional Man*, 'repressive modes of desublimation, compared to which sublimated drives and objectives contain more deviation, more freedom, and more refusal to heed the social taboos' (1991: 72). Criticising the hippy culture of permissive individualism, Marcuse wrote of the need for 'nonrepressive sublimation', recognising that 'alienation' was 'the constant and essential element of identity, the objective side of the subject', the precondition for a more than immediate fulfilment of the individual's potential. The counter-cultural dogma of self-actualisation and self-expression, on the other hand, 'isolates the individual from the one dimension where he could "find himself": from his political existence, which is at the core of his entire existence. Instead, it encourages non-conformity and letting-go in ways which leave the real engines of repression in the society entirely intact' (Marcuse 1965a: 115).

Habermas himself, whose theory of the 'colonisation of the lifeworld' Bauman caricatures in arguing for the obsolescence of critical theory, included in *The Structural Transformation of the Public Sphere* an analysis of the role played by the mass media in creating 'a secondary realm of intimacy' which cultivates 'sentimentality toward persons and corresponding cynicism toward institutions'. Habermas, whose study was first published in 1962, wrote of how

> the public sphere itself becomes privatised in the consciousness of the consuming public; indeed, the public sphere becomes the sphere for the publicising of private biographies, so that the accidental fate of the so-called man in the street or that of systematically managed stars attain publicity, while publicly relevant developments and decisions are garbed in private dress and through personalisation distorted to the point of unrecognis-ability. (Habermas 1989: 171–2)

It should be noted, nonetheless, that Habermas refuses to dismiss the progressive impact and potential of that culture of intimacy and inwardness that first emerged in the bourgeois homes of the eighteenth century, and which led to the idea of private people gathering to form a public. In Habermas's view, Sennett failed to grasp the novelty of this cultural revolution, falling back instead on a model of the public sphere – which Habermas designates as 'representative publicness' – which is essentially feudal in character, where the king and his court were ceremonially represented 'not for but "before" the people' (1989: 8). Habermas argues that the highly stylised conventions of this representative publicness, whose decline Sennett appears to mourn, 'had already crumbled in the eighteenth century, when bourgeois people formed themselves into a public and therewith became the carriers of a new type of public sphere' (1992: 427).

It would be senseless to dismiss outright the humanising contribution which the romantic movements of the last 250 years have made to political life and culture in the modern world. It would also be foolish to ignore the repressive elements of Western puritanism and the way the ideology of liberalism has made certain political conventions and standards of rationality sacred in order to legitimise the exclusion of disadvantaged groups from participation in and enjoyment of the public sphere. Bauman himself, moreover, thinks a distinction should be made between the cult of authenticity described, and condemned, by Sennett, and the 'communities of occasion' which Bauman believes are more typical of our contemporary 'network society'. The latter, Bauman argues, are fleeting and superficial, with the frantic flow of communication taking precedence over the content of the message, and the constant obligation to speak (text, type, phone) leaving little of the space, and even less of the silence, necessary for contemplative introspection and the thoughtful baring of the soul (2003: 31–5).

Even so, Arendt would have been profoundly uneasy with the argument, advanced by many of the sociologists of 'risk society' and 'reflexive modernity', that the dissolution of previously hallowed categories and divisions has left the Western philosophical tradition marooned. In Giddens's formulation, because 'tradition is no longer traditional, and nature no longer natural', 'politics' and 'life' can no longer be kept apart as separate domains and concerns, but must instead be reunited in the form of a 'life politics' whose central focus is personal experience, questions of lifestyle and self-identity (1994: 90–2). Whether the boundary between private and public, personal and political, nature and culture, can and should be consistently defended, may ultimately depend on where the emphasis lies, that is, whether the most important task for a progressive critique of modern society is the assertion of freedom, the correction of injustice, or the preservation of the 'world' that humans share between them. As the diversity of interpretations of her work bear out, Arendt herself was never entirely clear on which issue should take precedence, and we can be forgiven if our own opinion is not yet settled.

6
Imperialism, Racism and Bureaucracy: The Road to Totalitarianism

No self-respecting intellectual who lived during the middle decades of the twentieth century, let alone a German Jew who narrowly escaped the Holocaust, could have spoken of a crisis in the modern world without reference to the horrors of Nazism and Stalinism. Although Arendt completed *The Origins of Totalitarianism* a decade before *The Human Condition* was published, and despite the fact that she repeatedly stressed the unparalleled novelty of the trends that led to totalitarianism – 'Antisemitism (not merely hatred of Jews), imperialism (not merely conquest), totalitarianism (not merely dictatorship)' (OT: ix) – it is impossible not to read her study as a historical account of what the loss of the public sphere, and the destruction of humans' capacity for action, can ultimately lead to. Totalitarianism, in this sense, is the most extreme known perversion of the human condition and the darkest consequence of the degradation of the *vita activa*. In its sweeping hostility to the stabilising structures of law and constitutional government, totalitarianism devours the space of the political sphere and imposes conditions of worldlessness on victims and perpetrators alike. Describing the modern world as a 'desert of neighbourlessness and loneliness' – the desert, with its featureless open topography, symbolising the loss of the worldly objects and institutions that mark out the spaces and boundaries for forms of political association – Arendt refers to totalitarian movements as 'sandstorms', 'the most adequate political form of desert life' (EU: 344, 348; OT: 466, 478; PP: 202). With their hatred of worldly stability, their nature-like drive towards constant military and territorial expansion, and their ideological insistence that freedom must be sacrificed to a historical or evolutionary process conceived like 'a river flowing freely, in which every attempt to block its flow is an arbitrary impediment' (PP: 120), these movements express the acute world-alienation of modernity.

EXPANSION FOR EXPANSION'S SAKE

Arendt began working on the material for *The Origins of Totalitarianism* in 1944, originally intending to write a study of imperialism which showed how Nazism ('race-imperialism') was the culmination of this historical development. By 1945, in an article first published in *Partisan Review*, she was already challenging the tendency to treat Nazism as a specifically 'German problem', and explaining the vacuum from which Nazism sprung as 'resulting from an almost simultaneous breakdown of Europe's social and political structures' (EU: 111). Arendt's subsequent decision to extend her analysis to Stalinism, and therefore totalitarianism in general, is the cause of some well-known structural discontinuities in the book. It also led Houghton-Mifflin to reject the final manuscript in 1949 for being too lengthy (Tsao 2002: 587).

First published by Harcourt in 1951, *The Origins of Totalitarianism* attempts to draw a link between twentieth-century totalitarianism and the frantic period of imperialist expansion that began with the 1884 Berlin Conference and ended with the First World War. This link is treated by Arendt as conjunctural and non-causal, and not determinate or teleological, because although imperialism foreshadowed totalitarianism and made it conceivable, it did not make it necessary or inevitable. The age of imperialism, which coincided in her view with the modern political ideology of anti-Semitism, is critical to Arendt for the way it succeeded in liberating the use of organised violence from normative, legal and parliamentary constraints, and in doing so facilitated the disintegration of the nation state as a stable and legitimate political system. The outcome of this was that the imperialist domination of indigenous peoples rebounded back to the European metropoles where, armed with pernicious theories of racial superiority, it proceeded to render millions of people expendable.

Arendt's understanding of imperialism acknowledges a large debt to Rosa Luxemburg's argument that 'the accumulation of capital, as an historical process, depends in every respect upon non-capitalist social strata and forms of social organisation', and that 'it proceeds by assimilating the very conditions which alone can ensure its own existence' (Luxemburg 1951: 366). A capitalist economy can manage its internal contradictions, in other words, only by a process of continual expansion through which the natural resources, labour and purchasing power of non-capitalist regions are devoured as temporary remedies for the destructive consequences of exploitation

(OT: 148; see also MD: 39–40). Prior to the last three decades of the nineteenth century, Arendt argues, members of the European bourgeoisie had shown limited interest in the affairs of the state, confident that their economic supremacy would continue without direct control over governments. Their position of dominance was of a peculiar kind, however, for it rested on a dynamic of growth that yielded wealth and impoverishment in similar measures. The depressions of the 1860s and 1870s, which were accompanied by a superabundance of both uninvested capital and unemployed labour, demonstrated to the ruling economic class that there were national limits to the process of accumulation. As European capital began to spread greedily overseas, wild gambling on the stock market led to a series of financial scandals and swindles (including the Panama Affair and the *Gründungsschwindel*[1]) that exposed the need for political protection for exported capital in order to reduce the risks faced by absentee shareholders.

As soon as investors realised the potential value to them of a strong state, Arendt argues, the bourgeoisie re-entered a political community on which they had previously only been parasites. The state could not merely protect their property rights, they realised, but could also help legitimise an economic system which, by creating superfluous labour as fast as superfluous wealth, was stoking dangerous class conflict. Arendt emphasises here how imperialism, involving the expansion overseas of the national instruments of violence, was premised on the geographical detachment of military might from the parliamentary institutions of the nation state, so that ultimately military force was promoted to the position of being the unaccountable representative of the nation abroad. In this process, political action ceased to exercise control over the expansionist dynamic of capital – a dynamic which bears all the hallmarks of the 'forces of nature' against which civilised humans must struggle. Instead it assimilated the principle of expansion for expansion's sake into its own operations. What followed was a process which Arendt suggests would eventually inspire totalitarian leaders to believe that they could conquer the world by riding the waves of history.

Despite initial efforts at empire building, the nationalist aspirations of European political statesmen to incorporate conquered peoples into their own body politic had been defeated by their imperialist compatriots. It was the latter who understood, correctly in Arendt's view, that when the nation appeared as coloniser it would only precipitate a national consciousness and a bitter struggle for independence among the colonised. Far better, then, to expand

political power without exporting the codified rights and responsibilities of national citizenship – to dissociate power, in other words,
from the modern political principle of consent. Imperialism even
offered a lifeblood to nationalism, she suggests, by mobilising
the patriotic conviction that the economic interests of the mother
country were at stake. It allowed state employees to escape the
disintegration of their nation into warring classes, and to instead
become the heroic servants of a fictitiously unified nation by ruling
strange peoples in distant lands. 'Thus the "national state", having
lost its very foundations, leads the life of a walking corpse, whose
spurious existence is artificially prolonged by repeated injections
of imperialistic expansion' (EU: 143).

The irony that the first country to be subject to this policy was
itself becoming superfluous is not missed by Arendt. With the
opening of the Suez Canal in 1869, and the later occupation of Egypt
by the British from 1882 to protect the precious waterway, South
Africa had lost its position as a critical outpost on the maritime
trade route to India. Yet the discovery of diamond and gold in the
1870s and '80s transformed South Africa into a 'culture-bed of
imperialism' at precisely the moment when its functional value to
the Empire had receded.

> Prospectors, adventurers, and the scum of the big cities emigrated
> to the Dark Continent along with capital from industrially
> developed countries. From now on, the mob, begotten by
> the monstrous accumulation of capital, accompanied its new
> possibilities for investment. The owners of superfluous wealth
> were the only men who could use the superfluous men who came
> from the four corners of the earth. Together they established the
> first paradise of parasites whose lifeblood was gold. Imperialism,
> the product of superfluous money and superfluous men, began
> its startling career by producing the most superfluous and unreal
> of goods. (OT: 151)

The significance, in part, of the South Africa gold rush, was that
the substance being pursued was so superfluous to the process of
industrial production, yet so symbolic of pure wealth, that it carried
a pretence of absolute value, and thus offered bourgeois society
'eternal stability and independence of all functional determinants'
(OT: 189). Yet the true source of this stability was not the gold
itself, but the power to appropriate and stamp it with value. Arendt
describes imperialism as a 'movement of expansion for expansion's

sake' because the export of power to foreign countries could only protect the legendary dynamic of economic accumulation – of money that begets money – by assuming that same logic of limitless expansion. No longer would money need to proceed via the tortuous and attritional route of investing in the productive process by which people made things.

> The secret of the new happy fulfilment was precisely that economic laws no longer stood in the way of the greed of the owning classes. Money could finally beget money because power, with complete disregard for all laws – economic as well as ethical – could appropriate wealth. Only when exported money succeeded in stimulating the export of power could it accomplish its owners' designs. Only the unlimited accumulation of power could bring about unlimited accumulation of capital. (OT: 137)

Every political structure or community, whether that of the conquered peoples or that of the conquerors' mother country, constituted a stabilising force against, and therefore ultimately an enemy of, this constant growth of 'power', a term which at this point in *The Origins of Totalitarianism* Arendt employs as a virtual synonym for domination (OT: 135–47), despite introducing her other definition ('acting in concert') in the final chapter of the second edition of the book (OT: 474). This power, being 'power over', can only survive the crushing of its adversaries by continually finding new subjects to command and subdue. Its limitless, self-expanding character is thus profoundly destructive of humans' capacity to rise above the nature-like imperatives of growth and reproduction, since the logic of expansion permits no true mastery. 'The mere export of violence made the servants into masters without giving them the master's prerogative: the possible creation of something new' (OT: 138).

RACISM IN SOUTH AFRICA

Imperialist rule, according to Arendt, required two main 'political devices' to sustain itself. First of all, it required a supporting ideology. When Arendt was writing the 'Imperialism' section of *The Origins of Totalitarianism* she had an underdeveloped theory of ideology. This changed with the addition of the 'Ideology and Terror' chapter to the second edition of the book. There, and elsewhere, Arendt defines ideologies as belief systems that claim to have identified the 'hidden laws' which rule nature and humanity. 'I call all ideologies in this context *isms* that pretend to have found the key explanation for all the mysteries of life and the world' (EU: 349; see also OT: 468–9). The two most dominant ideologies, she writes, are Marxism and racism: respectively, 'the ideology which interprets history as an economic struggle of classes, and the other that interprets history as a natural fight of races' (OT: 159).

Arendt acknowledges that what she calls 'race-thinking' was already prevalent in nineteenth-century Europe. Emerging as an alternative source of collective identity in regions where nationalist sentiments were weak, race-thinking 'sharpened or exploited existing conflicting interests or existing political problems, but it never created new conflicts or produced new categories of political thinking' (OT: 183). Rac*ism*, on the other hand, was the ideological mindset required to inspire and legitimise first imperialism, and later totalitarianism, as a political movement. Without imperialism, Arendt claims, race-thinking would probably 'have disappeared in due time together with other irresponsible opinions of the nineteenth century' (OT: 183).

Again it was South Africa which served as a crucible for the development of racism as a political ideology. Before the 'scramble for Africa', European colonialism had typically followed one of two paths: the formation, as in America and Australia, of settlements which adopted the legal and political institutions of the mother country; and the establishment, as in Asia, of trading posts which were vehicles for profitable economic exchange with foreign countries. With the discovery of the gold mines and diamond fields, South Africa attracted neither colonists nor adventurers and entrepreneurs, but rather 'the mob' – the superfluous victims of an anarchic capitalism who, 'without use or function', 'had not stepped out of society but had been spat out by it' (OT: 189). These were typically men who had refused to fashion a way back into the rapidly disintegrating societies of Western Europe. They shunned the fellowship of the workers' movement, sharing instead the egoism of the bourgeoisie. But they rejected the latter's hypocrisy and sham morality, preferring the unrestrained, unapologetic pursuit of self-interest. Like Kurtz in Conrad's *Heart of Darkness*, these 'armed bohemians' were game for anything but talented at nothing in particular: 'reckless without hardihood, greedy without audacity and cruel without courage' (Conrad), and ultimately capable of casual murder.

Arendt argues that when these superfluous men arrived in South Africa, what they discovered, and swiftly adapted to, was a race society in the making. This was the society of the Boers, descendants of the seventeenth-century Dutch settlers who had originally made a living selling provisions to the European ships that paused at the Cape en route to and from India. As the Cape trading station had expanded, many of the settlers were released from their contracts with Dutch East India Company and allowed to strike out into the interior. The result was a slow abandonment of the village-based organisation of their homeland and the establishment of a clan-like society of isolated, semi-nomadic families, mostly dependent on cattle-rearing due to the poor quality of the soil. (The term 'Boers' comes from 'Trekboers', meaning 'wandering farmers'.) Despite being dispersed over large areas, the separate Boer families were deterred from fighting each other by the common threat of the indigenous black population, whom the Boers ruled by violence and slavery.

Unlike slavery in the ancient world, which was a vehicle for enhancing the political and cultural accomplishments of the slave-owning rulers, and which found justification, in the eyes of those rulers, in the slavish behaviour of their captives who refused to risk their lives to fight for their freedom, Arendt stresses the fact that no human fellowship, no body politic of free citizens, was sustained by the Boers. Each Boer family governed the black population in its vicinity like the native tribal leadership it had liquidated. Having discovered 'the only "raw material" which Africa provided in abundance' (OT: 193), this resource was not used to advance Boer civilisation, but simply to provide the essentials of human existence and to exempt the slave-owners from the necessity of toil. The Boers' hatred of productive activity and their failure to elevate themselves above the primitive level of existence of their slaves, created the need to justify these relations of domination – and to justify a contempt for work that outlasted the institution of slavery – without appealing either to the productive achievements of the rulers, or to the 'slavish' behaviour of the ruled.

The Boers were the first European group to become completely alienated from the pride which Western man felt in living in a world created and fabricated by himself. They treated the natives as raw material and lived on them as one might live on the fruits of wild trees. Lazy and unproductive, they agreed to vegetate on essentially the same level as the black tribes had vegetated for thousands of years ... The Boers lived on their slaves exactly the way natives had lived on an unprepared and unchanged nature. When the Boers, in their fright and misery, decided to use these savages as though they were just another form of animal life, they embarked upon a process which could only end with their own degeneration into a white race living beside and together with black races from whom in the end they would differ only in the colour of their skin. (OT: 194)

Arendt's argument is that the idea of racial supremacy became politically operative when the ruling whites, desperate to distinguish themselves from the 'savages' who seemed to treat nature as their undisputed master, found nothing in their own activities and culture that could justify their superiority. In Arendt's rather narrow-minded and Eurocentric analysis, the native population of South Africa, unlike that of India and China, lacked anything that could be recognised as 'civilisation': 'they behaved like a part of nature', 'they had not created a human world'; at best they 'had developed human institutions only to a very low level' (OT: 192, 177). In passages that have led critics to accuse Arendt herself of racial prejudice (e.g. Presbey 1997; Moruzzi 2000; Gines 2007; Stoetzler 2007), Arendt seemed to show a surprising degree of sympathy for the Boers, who 'were never able to forget their first horrible fright before a species of men whom human pride and the sense of human dignity could not allow them to accept as fellow-men' (OT: 192). But this sympathy ends with the Boers' failure to retain their dignity and rise above a merely 'vegetative' existence. While 'race' first emerged as an 'emergency explanation' for the Europeans' first frightful encounters with the Other, Arendt highlights the way it subsequently became the default justification for their own brutality. With nothing worldly to show for their violent domination over the black population, the Boers could make sense of their own behaviour only by appealing to nature itself. Laying claim to a superior nature the Boer became, like Kurtz in *Heart of Darkness*, the master-savage among savages. If we follow Marx's characterisation of religious ideology as the 'spiritual aroma' of an alienated world (Marx 1975b), then in Arendt's formulation racist ideology is a quintessential pathology of worldlessness.

Following the seizure of the Cape by the British, and the eventual abolition of slavery in 1833, the Boers, whose racial thinking was fused with a claim to be God's chosen people, made further treks into the hinterland. By consolidating their detachment from a territorial homeland and their indifference to a stable, human-fabricated world, the Boers, in Arendt's account, embraced the condition of uprootedness which is the foundation of all race organisations.

When the 'mob' subsequently arrived in South Africa for the gold rush, the abundance of cheap labour in the country convinced the new arrivals that they could, once the means of violence had been deployed to annex the mining areas from their inhabitants, emulate the Boers and share their 'permanent emancipation from work'. The recommended flight of the Boers, this time from a society which, through the anticipated process of industrialisation and the establishment of proper markets for labour and goods, threatened to liquidate the privileges of race, was not justified by the immediate course of events, however. For the gold industry rested on political factors, not rational economic laws. Hence the irony that, although the Boers lost the war with the British, 'they definitely won the consent of all other European elements, including the British government, to the lawlessness of a race society' (OT: 199–200).

Arendt credits Cecil Rhodes, the most powerful figure in the diamond industry of Kimberley, and later the Prime Minister of the Cape Colony, with convincing the British government that expansion of military power was in the national interest, and for introducing a systematic policy of neglecting all forms of industrial enterprise and commodity production which were not directly relevant to the mining industry. It was this policy, according to Arendt, which belatedly convinced the Boers that imperialism was not in fact a threat to race society, and that the imperialists were quite happy to avoid what Arendt refers to as the 'egalitarian tendencies' of normal economic life. Whenever the privileges of race clashed with the imperatives of production, Arendt points out, it was race that won.

> Profit motives were sacrificed time and again to the demands of a race society, frequently at a terrific price. The rentability of the railroads was destroyed overnight when the government dismissed 17,000 Bantu employees and paid whites wages that amounted to 200 per cent more; expenses for municipal government became prohibitive when native municipal employees were replaced with whites; the Colour Bar Bill finally excluded all black workers from mechanical jobs and forced industrial enterprise to a tremendous increase of production costs. The race world of the Boers had nobody to fear any more, least of all white labour, whose trade unions complained bitterly that the Colour Bar Bill did not go far enough. (OT: 204)

The fact that bourgeois society could overrule the profit motive, and continue to reproduce itself on bogus economic principles, was an important lesson for future totalitarian regimes.[2] It is no mere coincidence, moreover, that the Second Boer War saw the first murderous use of mass concentration camps by a European nation, with over 40,000 Boers and black Africans dying in British custody during this period. The South African experience was also telling for the fate of the Jews, for Jewish financiers had played an important role in the first years of gold and diamond speculation. Anti-Semitic racism, in fact, was not simply the European version of white racism in South Africa, for the political and economic conditions of both ideologies were intertwined.

ANTI-SEMITISM AND THE JEWS

It was, according to Arendt, the 'mob elements' among the Jewish financiers who were a third factor in the alliance between mob and capital that shaped the course of European imperialism. This was a 'new caste' of money-lenders and middlemen who 'had become as superfluous in Jewish banking as the wealth they represented had become superfluous in legitimate industrial enterprise and the fortune hunters in the world of legitimate labour' (OT: 201–2). The rootless, worldless, phantom-like existence of these financiers, and the mysterious process by which they turned money into more money without the mediation of matter, inadvertently nourished fantastical rumours of a secret international society of Jews. In South Africa, moreover, the Jews' belief in the chosenness of their people had made them direct rivals to the Boers' claim to racial superiority.

It is important to note here that Arendt does not equate anti-Semitic racism with either religious hatred of Jews or social resentment and discrimination against them. For Arendt, anti-Semitism is a political ideology and movement that emerged in the last third of the nineteenth century, reaching its height of virulence when the Jews had actually lost public influence and were much more interested in cultural, intellectual and professional accomplishments than in the pursuit of wealth and patronage. 'The history of the hatred of Jews was *about* Jews', Arendt writes, contrasting the medieval view of the Jews as the crucifiers of Christ, and the resentment at their success in the commercial fields that were open to them, with a modern ideology of anti-Semitism which 'certainly has no connection whatever with any germinal knowledge about the Jews'. Instead this ideology accuses them 'of being parasites at precisely the point when they have ceased to be parasites', 'weaving fables of a monstrous, diabolic, and secret power at the very point when they are losing power – which was never diabolic or very secret' (JW: 67–70, 75). Arendt therefore rejects what she calls the 'self-deceiving theory' of an 'eternal anti-semitism' which was central to the ideology of Zionism. According to Arendt, this popular viewpoint, premised on a belief in the inveterate hostility and lack of enlightenment of Christians and Gentiles, contends that 'the Jewish people had always been the passive, suffering object' of 'an unbroken continuity of persecutions, expulsions, and massacres from the end of the Roman Empire to the Middle Ages, the modern era, and down to our own time' (OT: 7, xii–xiii).

Arendt's explanation for this account of Jews as eternal victims is that, although the causes of the many calamities in Jewish history were varied, the stateless conditions of the Jewish people and their dependence for protection on non-Jewish authorities, meant that every violent encounter tended to end in conclusive defeat. It was therefore almost inevitable that this long history of persecution and misfortune would be experienced and understood as the repetition of an everlasting fate. Arendt was determined not to portray Jews as the passive victims of centuries of unbroken persecution, and her thoughts on this subject are unflinching in their avoidance of sentimentalism and self-pity – so much so that, for all her complaints against psychologism and the fetishism of interiority, her analysis of the Jewish character, as well as her empathic understanding of racists and imperialists, has been hailed as a near-exemplary form of 'moral psychology' (Kateb 1984: 53–7; 2001: 132–5). Observing the historical coincidence of modern anti-Semitism with Jewish assimilation and secularisation, Arendt notes, for example, how the idea of eternal anti-Semitism was attractive to the Jewish consciousness as a means of salvaging, against the dissolving forces of assimilation, dispersion and physical destruction, an eternal guarantee of Jewish existence.

> This superstition, a secularised travesty of the idea of eternity inherent in a faith in chosenness and a Messianic hope, has been strengthened through the fact that for many centuries the Jews experienced the Christian brand of hostility which was indeed a powerful agent of preservation, spiritually as well as politically. The Jews mistook modern anti-Christian anti-semitism for the old religious Jew-hatred – and this all the more innocently because

their assimilation had by-passed Christianity in its religious and cultural aspect. (OT: 7–8)

Arendt is consistent with this reasoning when she rejects the 'latest myth', the popularity of which she glibly blames on Sartre's *Portrait of the Anti-Semite* (1948), that the Jew is made a Jew by the Gentile's ascription of otherness. In Arendt's account, Jewish dissociation from the Gentile world was a voluntary separation aimed at countering the centrifugal forces of dispersion, and anti-Semitism only contributed to this tendency in the nineteenth and twentieth centuries, when assimilation to non-Jewish society became a popular aspiration. Arendt makes an even bolder challenge to established orthodoxy by arguing that the idea that Jew and Gentile are distinguished by inner nature rather than religious faith was originally a Jewish self-interpretation, dating back to the sixteenth century according to the Jewish historian Jacob Katz, becoming prevalent amongst assimilated secular Jews in the nineteenth century, and only afterwards becoming the cornerstone of anti-Semitic ideology (OT: xii).

It should be noted, of course, that Sartre's own argument was not dissimilar to Arendt's.[3] Sartre offered a lengthy analysis of the 'inauthentic Jew', for example, which matches Arendt's attempt to counter essentialist accounts of the Jewish condition, and both thinkers advanced a theory of Jewish responsibility. 'If one is attacked as a Jew,' Arendt says she realised in the 1930s, 'one must defend oneself as a Jew. Not as a German, not as a world-citizen, not as an upholder of the Rights of Man, or whatever. But: What can I specifically do as a Jew?' (EU: 12; JW: 137–8). This principle – 'that one can resist only in terms of the identity that is under attack' – expresses a refusal of worldlessness and a rejection of the temptation to forsake reality in favour of an abstract humanity (MD: 17–18). Rahel Varnhagen understood this principle when, having spent most of her life trying to 'escape from Jewishness', she realised that 'to negate Jewishness fully and without ambiguity would have had the same effect as an unequivocal affirmation'. 'Rahel had remained a Jew and a pariah', Arendt concludes her study of Varnhagen. 'Only because she clung to both conditions did she find a place in the history of European humanity' (RV: 216, 221, 227).

What for Arendt is our 'worldliness' is for Sartre our 'facticity' – our rootedness in the world of other people and things whose conditioning presence we deny in bad faith, just as we may also flee in the other direction and claim to have an unproblematic place in the world, a social identity, role or purpose, which we coincide with absolutely. Thus for Sartre, 'Jewish authenticity consists in choosing one's self *as a Jew*, in other words, in fulfilling one's Jewish condition'. Inauthentic Jews, by contrast, either deny their Jewishness or essentialise it as constituting everything that they are. On the one hand is the Jew who 'goes so far as to abjure his race, in order to remain no more, on purely individual grounds, than a man without blemish in the midst of other men'; on the other is the one who 'abjures his freedom as a man in order to escape from the sin of being a Jew, and to try and regain the peace and the passivity of the object'. Amongst the latter are those who 'are driven in the end to exalt racial qualities', and who, in so doing, ensure that it is the racism of the anti-Semite which reigns supreme (Sartre 1948: 115, 92, 71).

Sartre also explored the psychological traits which constitute what some psychoanalysts have called the 'Judaic complex', and he explains them as manifestations of inauthenticity typical of assimilated Jews. The obsessive, self-regarding introspection which results from the desperate desire 'to know the Jew *in order to deny him*', is one such characteristic, according to Sartre (1948: 81). Arendt's analysis of the Jewish psyche follows the same path. She notes how, after the legal emancipation of the Jews, social ascension was only achievable by Jews who were identified as 'distinguished exceptions' from the Jewish masses. For nineteenth-century high society, where the Enlightenment ideal of human universalism still offered modest distraction from the growing feelings of ennui plaguing the bourgeoisie, fraternising with exotic Jews – exceptional specimens of an otherwise inferior people – was a way of confirming one's humanitarian credentials whilst simultaneously indulging a titillating fascination with scandal and vice.

The consequences of this, according to Arendt, were twofold. First of all, where social (rather than legal and political) discrimination was the obstacle in their path, Jews were forced to choose between being either a 'conscious pariah' or a conformist 'parvenu'. While many of the first generation of educated Jews elected to be pariahs, the parvenu became the norm for subsequent generations. No matter how much these assimilated Jews wished to repudiate their Jewishness, it was always their Jewishness – albeit their *exceptional* Jewishness – which helped win them entrance into high society. Since this society accepted them because they were Jews, but not common Jews, these parvenus found themselves feeling unusually Jewish among the non-Jews and inadequately Jewish among the

Jews. It was this ambiguous situation, this inability to belong fully to any social group, which according to Arendt helped de-politicise the 'Jewish question', transforming Jewishness 'from a shared social condition, from an impersonal "general woe" into a character trait, a personal defect in character' (RV: 218). The political predicament of the Jews was now a private and emotional problem, but one which ironically continued to mark out the Jew, with his or her tormented inner life, as an object of fascination for bourgeois society (OT: 64–8).

The second consequence of assimilation, according to Arendt, was that Jewishness was dissociated from religious and cultural practices and became a worldless physical or psychological quality which, according to whether you were an assimilated Jew or a Gentile, respectively, could be perceived as either a virtue or a vice. By transforming the 'crime' of Judaism into the fashionable and exotic 'vice' of Jewishness, bourgeois society, with the collusion of Jewish reformers and assimilators, had created a condition which, though a sin less serious than a legal crime, actually made the Jews more vulnerable to extreme persecution. For while the crime of Judaism (the execution of Christ) could be atoned for by punishment and even escaped through conversion, the vice of Jewishness could be neither punished nor escaped, but only exterminated. Unsurprisingly, Arendt interprets this transformation of a criminal act of human will into an innate vice which cannot be repudiated as symptomatic of a society which has 'emancipated itself completely from public concerns', and in which political issues have decomposed into the public display and consumption of private passions, emotional foibles and inner experiences. 'In assimilating crime and transforming it into vice, society denies all responsibility and establishes a world of fatalities in which men find themselves entangled' (OT: 80–1).

THE JEWS AND THE STATE

Arendt claims that it was not high society, however, but rather the mob, 'the residue of all classes', excluded from the public world of parliaments as well as the salons of the intelligentsia, who were first stirred to violent action by the political ideology of anti-Semitism (OT: 106–17). Devoid of both a class status and a class enemy, and unprotected by the nation state, these de-classed individuals saw in the fictional hierarchy of race a new social order which guaranteed them a privileged position. Although Arendt discusses the different social, political and economic conditions which nurtured the various anti-Semitic movements of Europe during the nineteenth century, one common element in early anti-Semitism was the popular identification of the Jews with a corrupt and increasingly dysfunctional nation state. Due to the costs of raising huge armies and the drive to establish a professional bureaucracy independent of both the aristocracy and the bourgeoisie, the absolutist states of the eighteenth century had been saddled with a growing need for credit. This need was beyond the means of the small number of court Jews who, by pooling the resources of the wider Jewish community, had previously handled the financial affairs of princes and nobles, advancing credit, collecting taxes, and dealing in military supplies. Yet it was also beyond the consideration of the rising bourgeoisie, who were not yet prepared to invest in the unproductive activities of state administration and military service. It was therefore in the interests of the major European powers to grant legal rights and protections to prosperous (and largely Western) urban Jews, so much so that, at least in countries where the bourgeoisie was not yet ascendant, assimilated 'Jews were turned into a pillar of the state' (JW: 83).

The association of the Jews with the state was illustrated by the prominent role played by the Rothschild family in directing Jewish wealth into the political enterprises of various European countries, financing the British purchase of the Suez Canal in 1875, for example, and providing sizeable indemnified loans to Germany, France and Russia, among others. As the only non-national people of Europe, the Jews were also invaluable figures in international diplomacy and armistice agreements, as their independence from national causes made them trusted peacemakers and treaty advisors. Standing outside of society, the Jews also helped create the unique social space of the salons, a neutral meeting ground for the aristocracy, actors and 'homeless bourgeois intellectuals' (JW: 88–9).

As the nineteenth-century states publicly toyed with the idea of Jewish emancipation, in countries – such as Germany – where there had been no formal liberation of the bourgeoisie, suspicion over the Jews' seemingly privileged relation to the state was inflamed. The aristocracy, too, was in conflict with the state, opposing the abolition of serfdom and the extension of market forces to landed property. Tying economic liberalisation to Jewish emancipation, the aristocracy began a campaign of anti-Semitic propaganda in which the bourgeoisie were defamed as Jews and usurers, as unpatriotic, lacking a sense of history, enriched by speculation rather than honest work and the stewardship of inherited wealth. The self-doubting bourgeoisie then rid itself of this odium by joining in the chorus of anti-Semitism.

> That the Prussian aristocracy succeeded in drilling these categories and value judgements into the head of the German bourgeois citizen until he was ashamed to be one – that is the real and, as it were, 'ideological' misfortune of German Jewry. For in the end the liberals' truly destructive self-hatred gave rise to a hatred of the Jews, that being the only means liberals had of distancing themselves from themselves, of shifting slander to others who, though they did not think of themselves as the 'bourgeoisie', were forced to be its 100 percent embodiment ... German anti-semitism conquered the world under the banner of the Prussian Junkers. Aristocratic arguments against Jews and the bourgeoisie turned out to be a terrible weapon – not when wielded by the aristocracy itself, but when once placed in the hands of a suppressed and self-doubting bourgeoisie. (JW: 109)

When, under the pressure of the economic crises, financial scandals and political corruptions of the last decades of the nineteenth century, the nation-state system began to break down, the Jews became, as Dreyfus found at great personal cost, an increasingly vulnerable scapegoat for the failings of the modern polity. The turning of each class and national grouping against the state coincided with a new wave of anti-Semitic propaganda, and the more classes and nationalities who were in conflict with the state, the more prevalent was the anti-Semitism. Hence the workers movement, according to Arendt, was largely immunised from anti-Semitism by its conviction that it was another class, not the state, that was the principal enemy (a point which Sartre [1948: 29–30] also makes). In Austria, on the other hand, where at the outbreak of the First World War 'every stratum of society was in opposition to the state', virtually the whole population 'was imbued with active anti-semitism' (OT: 43).

What little government protection that remained for privileged Jews disappeared with the onset of the First World War, for the complete breakdown of European solidarity, and the degeneration of national rivalries into the law of 'victory or death', made the peace-brokering role of the non-national Jew redundant. In fact, Arendt claims, the age of imperialism had already removed governments' interest in the rights of prosperous Jews, as the state and bourgeoisie had now become willing partners in the pursuit of power and wealth overseas. Hence when mining in South Africa became a fully fledged imperialist enterprise, and European governments became the military guardians of national economic interests abroad, the Jewish financiers and middlemen, unprotected by any government, lost their strategic economic position, and might well have been forced to return to Europe had they not astutely turned to precisely those industries and professions, vital to everyday life in a civilised society, which the mining elite had ignored. In doing so, Arendt points out, the Jews in South Africa transformed themselves from shadowy middlemen into model representatives of economic rationality and the only truly productive members of the population. Now the Jews really did endanger the 'phantom world of race' in which the Boers lived, since they threatened to turn South Africa into a 'normal producing part of Western civilisation' (OT: 205).

BUREAUCRACY

If the first political device of imperialism was the ideology of racism, the second, according to Arendt, was bureaucracy. Bureaucracy, which was developed in Algeria, Egypt and India, expressed the racist's disdain for inferior foreign peoples, but converted this into a belief in the benign and protective virtues of secretive and paternalistic administration. Arendt's description of bureaucracy, whose obscure and anonymous functionaries feel no obligation to legal rules because the 'only "law" they obeyed was the "law" of expansion' (OT: 215), appears to owe more to Franz Kafka than to Max Weber's classic sociological study of the phenomenon. Bureaucratic management, for Weber, 'is based upon written documents'; it 'follows *general rules*, which are more or less stable, more or less exhaustive, and which can be learned'; and it presupposes 'a system of rationally debatable "reasons" [which] stands behind every act of bureaucratic administration'. Bureaucracy is in Weber's view the purest institutional manifestation of 'rational legal authority', which replaces personal discretion, favouritism and arbitrariness with 'rule-bound and cool "matter-of-factness"' exercised 'according to calculable rules and "without regard for persons"' (Weber 1978: 956ff, 217–26).

Weber saw bureaucracy as indispensable to the administration of complex societies ruled by constitutional government. He disputed the idea that bureaucracy is essential to imperial expansion, writing that the Roman and British empires 'rested upon bureaucratic foundations only to the smallest extent during their most expansive periods' (1978: 970). Somewhat paradoxically, and more consistent with Arendt's analysis, he also recognised that the bureaucratic organisation was possessed by a 'striving for power', and 'bureaucracy's own interests' were routinely served by keeping external parties ignorant of its internal processes, accumulated knowledge and expertise (1978: 225). The tension Weber detected between bureaucracy and representative government is well known: 'Bureaucracy naturally prefers a poorly informed, and hence powerless, parliament – at least insofar as this ignorance is compatible with the bureaucracy's own interests' (1978: 992–3).

In matters of foreign policy, certainly, Weber's description of bureaucracy is much closer to Arendt's. Having begun his academic career as a fervent nationalist, Weber effectively condoned the principle of 'functionally motivated secrecy', viewing it as entirely in keeping with the national interest. He was mortified at the way this principle had been repeatedly violated by the German government, causing huge diplomatic embarrassment and helping stoke the hostile coalition against German interests which culminated in the First World War. One example given by Weber is the Krüger telegram of January 1896. In this dispatch from Kaiser Wilhelm II, personal congratulations were offered to the President of the Transvaal Republic for the Boers' success in repelling the Jameson Raid from the Cape Colony, an incursion which Cecil Rhodes had originally planned as a way of precipitating an uprising of the British settlers in the Boer region. The telegram, which was naively published by the proud German press, implied that Germany would have provided assistance against the British if it had been requested, despite the fact that Germany lacked the military resources to honour that pledge. Weber seems to attribute the series of diplomatic blunders by the German government in the decades leading up to the First World War to a breakdown in 'the crown jewel of civil service duty' – the 'service secret' that was so common to the functioning of domestic administration, but which seemed so much more valuable in matters of foreign affairs (1978: 1439).

When Weber's description of bureaucracy is set beside Arendt's, an immediate point of contrast is that Arendt regards bureaucracy not as rule by law but rather as 'rule by decree'. Rule by decree is hampered neither by the entanglement of the legislator in matters of principle, nor by the executors' ponderous interpretation of the law, for the decree 'does not exist at all except if and when it is applied'. 'In governments by bureaucracy decrees appear in their naked purity as though they were no longer issued by powerful men, but were the incarnation of power itself and the administrator only its accidental agent' (OT: 243–4). Rule by decree is inherently secretive, since it derives not from codified principles but from ever-changing circumstances whose intricacies are known only to the expert functionary. The only complete picture of government by bureaucracy was the Russian Empire, according to Arendt, where an atmosphere of arbitrariness, inconsistency and accident so permeated the process of administration – a characteristic superbly depicted in Kafka's fiction – that the world acquired a pseudo-mystical aura of divine enigma, profundity and depth.

But in Arendt's view it was overseas imperialism which pioneered the use of bureaucracy and rule by decree as a mechanism for imposing the process of expansion on subject peoples and cementing the division between ruler and ruled. Given Arendt's theory of the 'boomerang effect', which captures the way overseas experiments in lawlessness ended up deranging the domestic polities from which they originated, it is perhaps surprising that she didn't pay more attention to Germany in this context, with only brief references to Carl Peters, the Commissioner of German East Africa whose cruel treatment of indigenous Africans made him a historical hero in Hitler's eyes (OT: 134, 185, 189, 206). But the reverberations of imperialism, for Arendt, were international in scope, spreading across Europe an infectious disrespect for the institutional framework of all Western states. Still, it is worth noting that it is Britain, a country whose imperialist policies did *not* result in a totalitarian state, which gets the lengthiest treatment in this section of Arendt's book. She thus draws heavily on the writings of Lord Cromer, the British Consul-General in Egypt, who confessed an aversion to every 'written instrument, or, indeed, anything which is tangible', as well as on two biographies of Cecil Rhodes who, in his constantly re-written will, pledged money for the founding of a 'secret society' whose members, drawn exclusively from the 'Nordic Race', would dedicate their roving lives to expanding the British Empire according to 'the dream of the Founder' (OT: 214–6). According to Arendt, Cromer 'recognised that "personal influence" without a legal or written political treaty could be enough for "sufficiently effective supervision over public affairs" in foreign countries', a policy he favoured because, in Arendt's words, 'it could be altered at a moment's notice and did not necessarily involve the home government in case of difficulties' (OT: 213).

Arendt's account of imperialist rule thus has more in common with Weber's description of pre-bureaucratic patriarchal domination:

'The master wields his power without restraint, at his own discretion and, above all, unencumbered by rules', whereas the power of the 'bureaucratic official goes in principle only as far as his special "competence" permits, and this in turn is established by a rule' (Weber 1978: 1006–7). Yet for Arendt, what seems to unite the principle of domination by personal decree, the passion for secrecy, and the seemingly incompatible idea of the bureaucrat as functionary, is the tendency of overseas administrators to imagine themselves to be the faithful servants of an impersonal purpose, thus substituting a duty to written laws with the 'superstition of a possible and magic identification of man with the forces of history' (OT: 216). Devoting himself to the 'law' of indefinite expansion, the imperialist bureaucrat could renounce all human-made treaties, with their stabilising and constraining effects, making himself the cipher and conduit of a force so powerful it transforms those it touches into gods.

> No matter what individual qualities or defects a man may have, once he has entered the maelstrom of an unending process of expansion, he will, as it were, cease to be what he was and obey the laws of the process, identify himself with anonymous forces that he is supposed to serve in order to keep the whole process in motion; he will think of himself as mere function, and eventually consider such functionality, such an incarnation of the dynamic trend, his highest possible achievement. Then, as Rhodes was insane enough to say, he could indeed 'do nothing wrong, what he did became right. It was his duty to do what he wanted. He felt himself a god – nothing less.' (OT: 215)

THE PAN-MOVEMENTS

Overseas imperialism, as Arendt describes it, had constitutional government at home, and government by bureaucratic decree abroad. Continental imperialism, on the other hand, originated in countries which had never known constitutional government and which were already governed by bureaucracies. The success of Western European imperialism had captured the imagination of the Central and Eastern European powers, yet for these land-locked countries only Europe itself was a realistic target for expansionism. Here, however, the limited geographical distance between home nation and prospective colony militated against the separation of administrative regimes that was characteristic of overseas imperialism. It also offered limited investment opportunities for superfluous money, and thus attracted the support of race-thinking intellectuals more than the support of profit-hungry capital. Continental imperialism instead aspired towards an 'enlarged tribal consciousness' along the lines of the Boers, and this, according to Arendt, gave it a 'much closer affinity to race concepts' (OT: 223–4).

The two most significant movements in this context were pan-Germanism, which aimed to unite the German-speaking peoples of Central Europe, and pan-Slavism, which had the same goal for the peoples speaking the Slavic languages. Amongst the oppressed populations of Czarist Russia, Austria-Hungary and the Balkans, the envious desire for national emancipation had been frustrated by the unsettling effects of centuries of changing frontiers and forced migrations. It was precisely the rootless conditions of these populations which in Arendt's view fostered, as an alternative to the modern nationalism pioneered by the French a century earlier, a tribal consciousness that promised to transcend the narrow and artificial character of state boundaries by uniting its dispersed people in a mythical folk community, a 'completely uprooted, racially indoctrinated horde' (OT: 242). 'Rootlessness was the true source of that "enlarged tribal consciousness" which actually meant that members of these peoples had no definite home but felt at home wherever other members of their "tribe" happened to live' (OT: 232).

Breaking with the Judaeo-Christian belief in the divine origin of human beings, the pan-movements now began to preach the chosenness of their own people. Differences, conflicts and divisions within those chosen people were ignored, while national unity was now made immune to the dispersive social and political forces of war, conquest and flight. The affinity between the pan-movements' nationalist philosophy and racism was a logical one, for the difference separating the 'divine people' from other peoples was akin to the separation of species, species whose respective destinies could only be determined by the harsh rules of the animal kingdom.

The growth of tribal nationalism also solidified the anti-Semitic currents in the pan-movements' theories. Once again, the Jews appeared to represent the most intractable obstacle to the assertion of tribal supremacy. One obvious reason for this was the rootless condition of the Jewish people, which was the consequence of centuries of persecution, social exclusion and political disenfranchisement. The Jews were a people without a territorial home who had succeeded in retaining their collective identity – and therefore their nationhood – for two thousand years without the visible institutions of a state. The oppressed ethnic groups of Central and Eastern Europe, combined with the 'uprooted masses of the big cities', shared something of the Jews' experience of living beyond the pale of society and of the protective embrace of the nation state, and naturally found in the consciousness of the Jewish people both an answer, and a rival, to their own predicament.

Perhaps more important was the already mentioned fact that the Jews shared a claim to divine election. It mattered little that the original Jewish idea of chosenness granted the elect neither exclusive divine origin nor the right to dominate other peoples, but was properly understood as a religious mission, a covenant of special obligations and duties to redeem the whole fallen world of humankind, all of whose members had been made in the image of God. The anti-Semites' hateful fear that God may have chosen the Jews, not themselves, to rule the earth, was also untroubled by the factual conditions and activities of the Jews, which were hardly conducive to, or indicative of, a plan for global domination. But since the national pride of the pan-movements was, like the racism of the Boers, independent of any practical conditions or achievements, their hatred of Jews could be equally indifferent to Jewish deeds and misdeeds (OT: 241).

Amongst a growing number of secularised Jews, moreover, the belief in divine election had survived the abandonment of the specific cultural and religious practices of Judaism, thus contributing to an essentialist, quasi-biological interpretation of the Jewish concept of chosenness. Later, when Arendt was in Jerusalem covering the Eichmann trial, she was alarmed to discover this sentiment expressed by Israel's foreign minister, Golda Meir. When, in response to the publication of Arendt's *Eichmann in Jerusalem*, she was accused by her former friend, the Jewish philosopher Gershom Scholem, of lacking 'love of the Jewish people', Arendt replied by recalling her conversation with Meir.

> Let me tell you of a conversation I had in Israel with a prominent political personality who was defending the – in my opinion disastrous – non-separation of religion and the state in Israel. What he said – I am not sure of the exact words any more – ran something like this: 'You will understand that, as a Socialist, I, of course, do not believe in God; I believe in the Jewish people.' I found this a shocking statement, and, being too shocked I did not reply at the time. But I could have answered: the greatness

of this people was once that it believed in God, and believed in Him in such a way that its trust and love towards Him was greater than its fear. And now this people believes only in itself? What good can come of that? – Well, in this sense I do not 'love' the Jews, nor do I 'believe' in them; I merely belong to them as a matter of course, beyond dispute and argument. (Arendt and Scholem 1964: 54)[4]

In *The Origins of Totalitarianism* Arendt records the historical emergence of this form of 'Jewish chauvinism', which was typical of 'exception Jews' like the imperialist politician and British prime minister, Benjamin Disraeli, who came to 'believe in his own chosenness without believing in Him who chooses and rejects' (OT: 73–4). Competing with the claims to noble birth of his aristocratic peers, Disraeli flaunted, and indeed fabricated, his Jewish pedigree, which he believed bound him to an ethnic elite of Jewish European financiers. But he knew so little about Jewish religion and customs (he was baptised into the Anglican church when he was thirteen) that he saw the Jew in much the same way as the Gentile did – as a strange and exotic Sartrean 'Other' whose qualities he could innocently cultivate and accentuate unhindered by the demands of authenticity. Assimilated Jews like Disraeli were too 'enlightened' to believe in God, yet too successful to give up a belief in their own aristocratic destiny. In turning the idea of chosenness from a religious vocation into a quality of birth and nature, they had transformed its meaning from the essence of Judaism to the essence of 'Jewishness'.

If tribal nationalities pointed to themselves as the centre of their national pride, regardless of historical achievements and partnership in recorded events, if they believed that some mysterious inherent psychological or physical quality made them the incarnation not of Germany but Germanism, not of Russia but the Russian soul, they somehow knew, even if they did not know how to express it, that the Jewishness of assimilated Jews was exactly the same kind of personal individual embodiment of Judaism and that the peculiar pride of secularised Jews, who had not given up the claim to chosenness, really meant that they believed they were different and better simply because they happened to be born as Jews, regardless of Jewish achievements and tradition. (OT: 240)

In Nazism, the idea of chosenness combined with the deluded belief in the existence of a world conspiracy of Jews to provide the German masses with a ready made model for their own 'Germanic world empire' (Himmler). Small wonder, then, that Hitler, according to Himmler, had 'learned by heart' the *Protocols of the Elders of Zion*,[5] and made it a compulsory part of the German school curriculum (Whitfield 1980: 64). As Arendt quotes Goebbels, 'the nations that have been the first to see through the Jew and have been the first to fight him are going to take his place in the domination of the world' (OT: 360).

That even Franco had the *Protocols* translated in the 1930s, in a country which had virtually no Jews until it began receiving refugees from Germany during the war, was proof to Arendt that modern anti-Semitism was never merely a form of extremist nationalism. As we shall see in the next chapter, it was their internationalist ambitions which also explains the willingness of the Nazis, despite the patriotic propaganda of 'love of the Fatherland', to ravage and destroy their own country. 'Only when fascism is understood as an anti-national international movement does it become intelligible why the Nazis, with unparalleled coolness, not distracted by national sentimentality or humane scruples as to the welfare of their people, allowed their land to be transformed into a shambles' (EU: 144).

7
Totalitarianism

Arendt suggests that the historical significance of the pan-movements should be measured not so much in terms of territorial expansion but in view of the challenge these forerunners of totalitarian movements began to pose to the new nation states. The strength of this challenge derived from their self-characterisation as 'movements' outside a party system whose reputation was in serious decline. It was in the new multiparty systems of continental Europe in particular that the movements were most popular, for they appealed directly to those disillusioned with the factional strife and inefficiency that was associated with multiparty politics.

The claim to be a 'party above parties', however, was not an honest reflection of the motives and goals of either totalitarianism or its predecessor, the pan-movements. Although the term 'totalitarianism' was first used by Italian Fascists in the 1920s, Arendt repeatedly warns against confusing totalitarianism with single-party dictatorships. Italian Fascism, it is true, sought to appeal to the masses by calling itself a 'movement', and in this respect its propaganda was totalitarian in flavour. But in practice the movement was simply a vehicle for the party to take over the state machinery and fill all the government positions with its own members.

In identifying the ruling party with the state, Arendt argues, Fascism was effectively tying itself to the stable structures of the machinery of government. But while the Fascists pretended to be a movement while remaining a party, the Nazis were doing the opposite – pretending to be a 'party above parties' while remaining a movement. According to Arendt, this was one reason why Hitler was successful in winning the support of the economic elite, as its members wrongly believed he would place the machinery of the state in the service of their own class interests.

What the German bourgeoisie, along with everyone else, had failed to see was that the transformation of parties into movements, which was the most important legacy of the pan-movements, had produced social and ideological tendencies which were dangerously hostile to the authority of the state as a lawful institution. Consistent with her description of the spread of nature-like imperatives into the public sphere, Arendt characterises these 'movements' in quite literal terms as having no determinate end other than preserving their onward momentum. Formal goals and programmes were therefore a hindrance to the movements' motion and, like the stable rules and procedures of the state itself, were obstacles that could and would be swept aside. In this sense, the concept of 'totalitarian state' is actually a contradiction in terms, for in Arendt's account totalitarian movements 'can remain in power only so long as they keep moving and set everything around them in motion' (OT: 306).[1]

Although it was certainly Mussolini who pioneered leadership as the political mobiliser in place of formal proposals and a definite programme of rule, Mussolini's aim, Arendt argues, was still the seizure of state power. Hitler and Stalin, by contrast, were not content to rule by external means, since these means set brakes and limits on the process of domination.

> Their idea of domination was something that no state and no mere apparatus of violence can ever achieve, but only a movement that is constantly kept in motion: namely, the permanent domination of each single individual in each and every sphere of life. The seizure of power in any given country is only a welcome transitory stage but never the end of the movement. The practical goal of the movement is to organise as many people as possible within its framework and to set and keep them in motion; a political goal that would constitute the end of the movement simply does not exist. (OT: 326)

FROM STATELESSNESS TO WORLDLESSNESS

Arendt argues that it was the dissolution of Austria-Hungary and the Russian and Ottoman Empires following the First World War, and the celebration of nationhood by the most numerous ethnic groups in the highly heterogeneous populations of the new states, which finally exposed the tension between nation and state which the centralised bureaucracies of eastern Europe and the Baltics had previously managed to contain. A nation, Arendt agreed with J. T. Delos in her 1946 review of his book on the subject, is a people with a historical consciousness of itself; it is therefore 'a closed society to which one belongs by right of birth'. The state, by contrast, 'is an open society' which 'knows only citizens no matter what nationality: its legal order is open to all who happen to live on its territory'

(EU: 208). International recognition of 'national minorities', thanks to the Minority Treaties by which the newly formed League of Nations granted those minority groups within the successor states of the defeated powers an external but unenforceable guarantee of basic rights, ironically nourished governments' belief that the state, already infected by the secrecy and lawlessness practised in overseas territories, was justified in limiting the rights of citizenship according to ethnicity rather than geographical residency. When the minorities gained formal protection *as minorities*, their second-class status was sealed. The result was the steady 'perversion of the state into an instrument of the nation and the identification of the citizen with the member of the nation' (OT: 231). 'The state conquered by the nation became the supreme individual before which all other individuals had to bow' (EU: 209).

The large-scale migrations of persecuted minorities and stateless refugees that followed the triumph of the nation over the state created further conditions suitable for totalitarian rule. The predicament of the stateless persons, whose numbers were swelled by the various inter-war decrees with which the new nation states had denationalised individuals with affiliations – familial, geographical, political – to groups and nationalities perceived as enemies of the newly founded states, was indeed a warning of the dark fate awaiting the victims of the Third Reich. Increasingly regarded by the receiving countries in the same hostile terms as the aggressor that had expelled them, the plight of stateless peoples during the 1930s was a practical demonstration of the Nazis' claim that there is no such thing as natural or inalienable human rights.

The denial of natural rights was of course fundamental to totalitarian rule, as illustrated by the treatment in Nazi Germany of foundlings as stateless until their racial characteristics were determined. The deprivation of legal rights was the second stage (the first, according to Arendt, being the loss of a home) in the process by which people were to be made expendable (OT: 475). Yet Nazism also exposed the deep contradiction at the heart of the 'Rights of Man', which had defined human rights as 'inalienable', as irreducible to any special law or power higher than Man himself, while simultaneously founding them on membership of a nation whose government was willing to recognise, protect and enforce them. Arendt's anti-foundationalist stance therefore acknowledges the 'pragmatic soundness' of Edmund Burke's otherwise reactionary opposition to the French Revolution's Declaration of the Rights of Man, for Burke understood that rights were of neither divine nor natural origin, but rather were the 'entailed inheritance' of a national community (OT: 299). Declarations of human rights were always something less than the rights of nationals, and 'were invoked only as a last resort by those who had lost their normal rights as citizens' (OR: 149).

It is because there is no permanent or transcendent foundation for the existence of universal rights that Arendt believed the imperialists' experiments in lawless violence posed such a threat to the constitutional framework of the 'civilised' world. The hostile reception given to many stateless refugees not only demonstrated the flexibility of Western standards of justice, but also proved beyond doubt that there was no sacred dignity in the sheer nakedness of being human and that, when the protective embrace of law and government was withdrawn, all that was left of the Rights of Man were idealistic declarations which 'showed an uncanny similarity in language and composition to that of societies for the prevention of cruelty to animals' (OT: 292). And it was an awareness of precisely this fact – the fact that the 'right to have rights' depends on membership of an organised political community – which encouraged the increasingly fierce assertion of separate national identities among stateless peoples threatened with permanent displacement. 'Their distrust of natural, their preference for national, rights comes precisely from their realisation that natural rights are granted even to savages' (OT: 300).

MASSIFICATION, ATOMISATION AND LONELINESS

The predicament of stateless peoples during the 1930s was in some respects echoed, Arendt argues, in the experiences of the urban masses. Arendt regards the masses as the principal raw material for totalitarianism, and in those countries – Italy, Portugal, Spain, Hungary, Rumania – where a class or party dictatorship fell short of outright totalitarian domination, this may have been because this raw material was not sufficiently abundant, so that 'the tyrants in these small countries were forced into a certain old-fashioned moderation lest they lose whatever people they had to rule' (OT: 310).

The 'masses', in Arendt's account, lack an appetite for political organisation and a consciousness of their specific economic location and class interests. *Inter-est* means, Arendt reiterates, what lies between people, a 'common ground' or a 'common purpose' which both links and separates individuals in an articulate way (EU:

406). Indifferent to the appeal of political parties, trade unions or professional groups, the masses stood outside the networks of social and political affiliation. Because of this they became supremely receptive to the unconditional loyalty demanded by totalitarian movements, and thankful for the sense of identity and self-respect which demonstrations of racial or ideological purity appeared to offer. The movements' racist or politically eschatological 'language of prophetic scientificality' was perfectly primed for those 'who had lost their home in the world and now were prepared to be reintegrated into eternal, all-dominating forces which by themselves would bear man, the swimmer on the waves of adversity, to the shores of safety' (OT: 350).

Arendt herself is dismissive of the elitist argument that the malleability of the masses is a product of the democratisation of education and the spread of popular culture, pointing to the attraction which the totalitarian movements and their predecessors had to highly cultured people and members of the 'mob' (in contrast to the masses, the mob are 'the *déclassés* of all classes', including the failed adventurers and privileged misfits who make up what Arendt refers to as the 'underworld of the bourgeoisie'). In her view, 'mass society' was largely a result of the collapse of the party system which had previously fostered the rational articulation of class interests and held in check the atomising tendencies of bourgeois society. As class solidarities themselves began to decompose, 'the psychology of the European mass man developed', a mentality characterised by a 'self-centred bitterness' which, despite its ubiquity, failed to develop into a sense of common interest capable of immunising people from the lonely thought that they were expendable (OT: 315).

While the harsh economic circumstances of Germany in the 1920s and 1930s had already created the masses for Hitler, Stalin had to contend with the relatively stable class structure of Lenin's Russia. Arendt's interpretation of the logic behind the New Economic Policy, initiated in Russia in 1921, is that Lenin had understood how the stability of the revolution depended on the identification and enhancement of various social, national and economic strati- fications. It was for this reason that he legalised the expropriation of land by the peasantry, encouraged independent trade unions in the cities and, by permitting the partial existence of free markets, allowed for the appearance of wholesalers and a limited middle class. It was Lenin's talent for statesmanship, rather than his Marxist convictions, which in Arendt's view led him to introduce further cultural and structural differentiations in order to promote 'national consciousness and awareness of historical and cultural differences even among the most primitive tribes in the Soviet Union' (OT: 319).

In this context, the challenge faced by a ruler with totalitarian ambitions was clearly to liquidate these very differentiations, for they were a far cry from the atomised, structureless mass that was required for totalitarian rule. Stalin thus removed the threat of an independent working class by marginalising the workers' councils or Soviets and imposing alongside them a more powerful hierarchy of Bolshevik Party functionaries. The Stakhanov movement, which introduced ferocious labour competitions within factories and plants alongside a new aristocracy of trained managers, also eroded class solidarity among the workers. The independent peasantry were liquidated by means of deportations, artificial famines and the forced collectivisation of farming, and the middle classes disappeared when all remaining market freedoms were replaced by centralised planning. Even the party bureaucracy, which had facilitated previous liquidation policies, was repeatedly purged by Stalin, despite it showing not the slightest hint of hostility towards the regime.

Unlike previous tyrannies, totalitarianism aimed to dominate and control more than just the political sphere. By using the permanent threat of betrayal to create an atmosphere of paranoid distrust between family members, colleagues and friends, totalitarian regimes sought to destroy all non-political bonds which might have formed a bulwark against the demands of the movement. The fomenting of mutual suspicion and paranoia was designed to isolate individuals from their neighbours in order to disempower them, for 'power' – and here Arendt uses the concept in a way that is consistent with its later meaning – 'always comes from men acting together' (OT: 474). Although isolation has always been a weapon of tyrannical governments, such systems have generally permitted the survival of private bonds and have left unmolested 'the capacities for experience, fabrication and thought' which totalitarianism, by contrast, sought to destroy. Arendt's arguments here are enriched by the distinctions she makes between isolation, loneliness and solitude. Isolation is destructive of the power to act, but is, as we saw in discussing *The Human Condition*, a necessary element of the productive activity of *homo faber*. In the activity of fabrication the individual, though removed from the world of common concerns, 'remains in contact with the world as the human artifice'. It is only when the capacity for *poiēsis* is also destroyed, Arendt continues, so that individuals are as 'deserted by the world of things' as from the condition of human plurality, that isolation turns into loneliness and becomes unbearable. This, she suggests, is common in a society which has transformed all creative human activity into labouring, where only 'the effort to keep alive is left and the relationship with the world as human artifice is broken'. It is also typical of totalitarianism, which 'bases itself on loneliness, on the experience of not belonging to the world at all' (OT: 474–5). Loneliness is ubiquitous in societies whose members have been transformed into masses, where people are pressed together so tightly that no common world can emerge between them.

Yet loneliness is not equivalent to solitude, according to Arendt, though the latter can certainly lead to the former. While loneliness is suffered most keenly in the presence of others whom I cannot address and trust as my equal, in solitude I can be 'by myself' in a constructive relation of inner dialogue. Solitude is to the thinker what isolation is to *homo faber*: while isolation sustains the capacity of the individual to create, solitude nourishes the individual's capacity to think. And no matter how exemplary one's behaviour, 'the human capacity to think is also a capacity to change one's mind' (OT: 430). Hence this capacity totalitarianism must also suppress, replacing it, under threat of abandonment in a sea of terrifying events and incomprehensible happenings, with ideological premises whose consequences can be deduced with the absolute certainty of a natural law. In this way 'even the slim chances that loneliness may be transformed into solitude and logic into thought are obliterated' (OT: 478).

THE TOTALITARIAN SYSTEM

I noted earlier that Arendt believed the intellectual power of ideological propaganda was not at the core of the totalitarian movement as a regime of domination. Arendt saw propaganda as primarily an appeal to the non-totalitarian world, though it also played an important recruiting role in the early stages of the movement. When a movement achieves control, however, its efforts are directed not at changing people's beliefs to fit the ideology of the movement, but on changing reality to make all contrary beliefs, including common sense, seem as ludicrous as faulty arithmetic. 'Totalitarian propaganda can outrageously insult common sense', Arendt explains, 'only where common sense has lost its validity' (OT: 352). With plurality all but extinguished, it was now the condition of 'narrativity' – the ability to bear witness to and make sense of the events that were unfolding – which was under gravest threat.

Subversive writings and ideas were thus not simply 'wrong' according to Stalin; they were, along with their murdered authors, thinkers and readers, unreal and non-existent. Questioning the validity of anti-Semitism when access to food, jobs, marital partners and friendship was determined by racial ancestry, was to all intents and purposes 'like questioning the existence of the world' (OT: 363). Challenging the murderous paranoia of the totalitarian leader was meaningless once he had given everyone good reason to fear him, and therefore given himself credible justification for pre-emptive aggression in self-defence. The Nazis' claim that Germany was fighting for its very existence was rendered unquestionable by the deliberate ravaging of their own country. In the extermination camps themselves, which in Himmler's own words existed for the sake of 'better demonstration of the laws of inheritance and race' (OT: 386), there was no ideological indoctrination save the practical education of racially organised power, humiliation and death. The ability to exterminate Jews like bedbugs ultimately made it 'no longer necessary to propagate that Jews are bedbugs' (OT: 413). The terrible fate of the millions who disappeared in the death camps and the gulags was not used as a warning to deter potential opponents, nor justified by aggressive propagandising. These people were effectively dead before they were murdered, for all traces and memories of their lives were made to disappear with them.

The ruthlessness of totalitarian rule also helps illustrate the difference, mentioned earlier, which Arendt draws between totalitarianism and other more familiar forms of tyranny, such as Spanish and Italian Fascism. In the classic party dictatorship, the aim is to unify the party with the state, after which the party plays the propaganda role of selling the achievements of the government to the nation. The absolute political power enjoyed by the one-party state is primarily negative – it prohibits all opposition to its rule. Its positive powers, on the other hand, are restrained by the established structure of government: 'the government and the army exercise the same power as before, and the "revolution" consists only in the fact that all government positions are now occupied by party members' (OT: 419). The limits of its positive power also mean that dictatorships tend to leave private life and non-political activities untouched. This stands in stark contrast to totalitarian domination, which attempts to reach into every corner of social, cultural and domestic life in order to implicate everyone in the criminal deeds of the regime.

Arendt argues that totalitarian rule has to retain the separation of state and movement in order to prevent the latter from being absorbed and burdened by the apparatuses of government and the military. When in power, the two paramount dangers that faced the totalitarian movements were a tendency to ossify into a form of absolute government, on the one hand, and a tendency to revert to a position of defensive nationalism, on the other. Both dangers, by introducing stability and normalisation into the movement, would have spelled the end of the 'total' character of totalitarianism. In the first case, domination would have settled into recognisable institutions and legal processes. Terror might well have persisted as a weapon of state violence, but it would have been aimed at genuine opponents of the regime rather than arbitrarily threatening 'harmless citizens without political opinions' (OT: 322). In the second case, the end of the movements' external expansion would have forced the totalitarian government to 'take its place among the widely differing and profoundly contrasting ways of life of the nations of the earth' (OT: 391). In other words, it would have had to succumb to the 'law' of nations, to the pluralistic principles of statesmanship and diplomacy and the reciprocal recognition of territorial sovereignty.

As with imperialism before it, the survival of totalitarianism depended on the expansion of power, which meant that any insurmountable obstacles to the total domination of the earth's peoples were a threat to its continued existence. Totalitarian rule perpetuates itself by creating a situation of permanent instability which Arendt describes, borrowing Trotsky's term, as a 'permanent revolution'. In Russia, Stalin continually revolutionised society by means of deadly purges, while in Germany the process of racial selection and extermination of the unfit was continually broadened to enable new victims to be found – from the insane to the incurably sick and then to the families of the sick and insane; from Jews to half-Jews and then to quarter Jews; from the Jews to the Poles (who in Germany during the war were already marked with a distinguishing badge). The lack of legal documents and definitions, as Lord Cromer had found in Egypt in the 1880s, made this organised instability much easier to sustain – hence Himmler's recorded request, cited by Arendt, 'not to issue any decree concerning the definition of the term "Jew"' because 'with all these foolish commitments we will only be tying our hands' (OT: 365).[2]

The avoidance of worldly stability was also reflected, Arendt argues, in the command structure of totalitarian rule. Though this structure was not unique, borrowing elements from military dictatorship and authoritarianism, what was distinct was the absence of the clear hierarchy of offices and responsibilities that are conventionally associated with bureaucratic organisations. The reason for this, according to Arendt, is that hierarchical systems, no matter how dictatorial, inhibit the power of a totalitarian leader by making him dependent on the chain of command and the filtering of orders through the various layers of the organisation. With a hierarchical system comes authority, and 'the principle of authority', according to Arendt, 'is diametrically opposed to that of totalitarian domination'. For while authority aims to constrain or limit freedom, totalitarianism sought to destroy it by 'eliminating human spontaneity in general' (OT: 405).

If the totalitarian regimes appeared to casual observers to function like authoritarian states, this is precisely the façade they projected to the non-totalitarian world. In practice the totalitarian leader claims total responsibility for every official action, successful or otherwise, carried out by every functionary of the regime, and he is therefore the only representative of the movement who can give an explanation for what he is doing. His total power is illustrated by the remarkable absence of internal revolts and attempted *coups* against Hitler and Stalin, despite the resources available to the police in both countries. Again Arendt stresses that this monopoly of responsibility is not shared by the ordinary despot, who would happily use his subordinates as scapegoats for his misdeeds, but would never identify with them (his subordinates either obey or disobey his orders, but they do not exercise his will). For the totalitarian ruler, on the other hand, the mistakes of a subordinate are so grave in potential consequence that they must be punished by charging the offender with a heinous type of fraud: not disobeying the leader, but *impersonating* him (OT: 406, 374–5).

The threat which structural stability posed to the totalitarian regimes of Hitler and Stalin was also combated by the duplication of offices. In Arendt's unique account, totalitarian government is not a monolithic structure, but is characterised by a peculiar amorphousness that results from the construction of overlapping jurisdictions, parallel authorities and duplicated functions. Instead of the archetypical image of the bureaucratic machine as a hierarchical pyramid, Arendt compares the structure of the totalitarian movement to that of an onion (OT: 430; PF: 99–100). Each layer of the onion functions as a front organisation designed to conceal, or render respectable, the radicalism of the next, more militant, formation.

The latter, faced on the one side by the milder ideology of the outer layer, and on the other by the greater fanaticism of the next rank in the hierarchy, is protected from encounters with the outside world that would reveal its own outlook and beliefs – ostensibly 'moderate' when seen in the context of the movement's hierarchy – to be entirely fictitious, if not insane (OT: 366–7).

In its most basic form, this layering of offices involved the transformation of the state (or Soviets, in the case of Russia) into a façade of 'sympathising bureaucrats' whose job was to spread confidence amongst citizens and outside observers, but whose offices were secretly replicated by members of the party. Because simple duplication might encourage a settled and transparent relationship between the party and the state as its external façade, the true totalitarian tendency, Arendt claims, is towards the *multiplication* of offices, which in the case of Nazi Germany allowed responsibilities and powers to be replicated across members of the civil service, the party, the SA, the SS and the Security Service. Neither citizens nor functionaries knew whose authority was the superior one, and this uncertainty was not helped by the way directives were frequently issued in vague or insinuating terms, underpinned by the principal obligation not to *obey* formal commands but simply to 'execute the will of the leadership'. In Russia, Stalin continually created new administrative positions to either conceal, or be concealed by, former sources of power, whilst periodically curbing the inexorable process of bureaucratic growth by means of ruthless purges. In both regimes the only certainty was that 'the more visible government agencies are, the less power they carry, and the less is known of the existence of an institution, the more powerfully it will ultimately turn out to be' (OT: 403).

Arendt suggests that the multiplication of offices in the totalitarian system is partly intended to guarantee that all commands – even those that are vague, contradictory, or swiftly revised – will be executed, thus giving the totalitarian leader unprecedented independence from his subordinates and making the regime 'shock-proof because of its shapelessness' (OT: 409). It enables the will of the leader to be embodied everywhere and anywhere, reducing the intervening levels of hierarchy to 'an ostensible, spurious imitation of an authoritarian state' (OT: 405). But the deliberate shapelessness of the totalitarian state is hugely inefficient from a practical point of view, wasting precious labour time and leading to confusion and delay in the implementation of orders. It is important to note how Arendt remarks again and again on the perversely anti-utilitarian logic of totalitarian rule, which is bewildering to anyone who has confused it with despotic government or a centrally planned economy. For a productivist mentality was unsustainable in a context where personal performance had little bearing on one's fate, where the accumulation of experience and relations of co-operation were rendered impossible by constant personnel changes, and where the reason for one's actions was never fully visible. Utilitarian logic and the dominance of 'instrumental rationality' cannot explain the liquidation of thousands of Red Army officers on the eve of the Second World War, nor the massive expansion of the gulag system in which millions of people, many with priceless technical skills, were condemned to deadly slave labour. The Nazis equally failed to utilise in any rational way the surplus stocks of labour power gathered in the concentration camps, or to use the threat of violence, or the potential for indoctrination, to produce economically or militarily useful behaviour. The construction of extermination facilities and the transporting of their victims was an insane waste of precious building materials and rolling stock in the midst of war, and the prisoners themselves were only put to genuinely productive work during the last years of the war when Germany was beset by an acute labour shortage.[3]

Arendt therefore demands that social scientists use the evidence of totalitarianism to rethink the axiomatic assumptions of their discipline, particularly the 'functional' interpretation of social conduct. Although she repeatedly talks of 'administrative massacres', the mechanisation of execution and the mass production of corpses, what Arendt believes is definitive of totalitarian domination is not, as Bauman (2000a) argues, the demoralising consequences of instrumental rationality and bureaucratic organisation writ large, but precisely the non-instrumental, anti-utilitarian logic of a regime which demoralised humans by making rational thought and conduct superfluous.

> Our common sense, trained in utilitarian thinking for which the good as well as the evil makes sense, is offended by nothing so much as by the complete senselessness of a world where punishment persecutes the innocent more than the criminal, where labour does not result and is not intended to result in products, where crimes do not benefit and are not even calculated to benefit their authors. For a benefit expected to be realised in centuries can hardly be called an incentive, especially not in a situation of great military emergency. (EU: 241)

Totalitarian 'terror' differs from the terror of both revolution and tyranny in that it dispenses with the category of means and ends. Totalitarian terror truly begins, in fact, when the other forms of terror have achieved their ends. It is precisely when the last traces of opposition have been liquidated that totalitarianism can begin to terrorise a population by making conscious the fact that nobody is protected from arbitrary imprisonment, torture or death, and it is this ultimate superfluity of everyone which distinguishes totalitarianism from earlier forms of genocidal aggression. Since innocence, conformity or obedience are no guarantee of safety, the threat of these terrible fates has no 'functional' rationale – nothing people think or do can rescue them from their fear.

It is Arendt's argument that this merciless disregard for both the individual and the national interest, combined with totalitarianism's shocking neglect of the immediate consequences of the regime's actions, can only be comprehended from the perspective of a movement which considers the country over which it rules to be 'only the temporary headquarters of the international movement on the road to world conquest', a movement which measures 'victories and defeats in terms of centuries or millennia' (OT: 411). Arendt thus notes how the Nazis did not believe that the Germans were a 'master race' – Hitler in fact prohibited the use of the term 'German race' because it would encourage, as he put it, the 'sacrifice of the racial idea as such in favour of a mere nationality principle' – but rather that they would be led by a master race that had not yet been born (OT: 412).

TOTAL DOMINATION

In the early stages of totalitarian rule, the role of the secret police in hunting down, provoking and removing internal opponents is not dissimilar to their actions in a typical dictatorship. Once the internal 'suspects' have been liquidated, however, the pursuit of 'objective enemies' begins, and it is here, Arendt argues, that totalitarianism reveals its 'total' character. The objective enemy, Arendt writes, 'is defined by the policy of the government and not by his own desire to overthrow it. He is never an individual whose dangerous thoughts must be provoked or whose past justifies suspicion, but a "carrier of tendencies" like the carrier of a disease' (OT: 423–4). Arendt suggests that the concept of 'objective enemy' – which made Stalin's victims, in their owns words, 'criminals without a crime' (OT: xxxiii) – is more important to understanding totalitarian rule than the racial or economic characteristics of its victims, for if hatred of specific groups were definitive of totalitarianism then the liquidation of those groups would spell the restoration of normal government. When put into practice, the notion of 'objective opponents', which referred to deviant racial types in Hitler's Germany and members of 'dying classes' in Stalin's Russia, allowed new foes to be continually identified, thus enabling both regimes to survive in the form of a movement which continually recalibrated its advance by finding new obstacles to conquer.

The concept of objective enemy was also accompanied by the idea of the 'possible crime'. In contrast to the 'suspect', whose profile the authorities believe to be the subjective match for an unsolved offence, the 'possible crime' is the foreseeable result of future objective developments. And because the central assumption of totalitarianism is that 'everything is possible', a limitless multiplicity of possible crimes – obstacles to and deviations from the movement's remorseless march – were conceived of as having likely agents who had to be hunted down and punished. In practice this also meant that a clear legal categorisation of crimes could be avoided, for it was impossible to predict exactly what might endanger the regime in the future.

In the last stage of totalitarian rule, Arendt points out, the notions of objective enemy and possible crime were abandoned. Victims were then chosen with complete randomness, even without charges, thus eliminating the challenge of free consent, which 'is as much an obstacle to total domination as free opposition' (OT: 541).

> This consistent arbitrariness negates human freedom more efficiently than any tyranny ever could. One had at least to be an enemy of tyranny in order to be punished by it. Freedom of opinion was not abolished for those who were brave enough to risk their necks. Theoretically, the choice of opposition remains in totalitarian regimes too; but such freedom is almost invalidated if committing a voluntary act only assures a 'punishment' that everyone else may have to bear anyway. Freedom in this system has not only dwindled down to its last and apparently still indestructible guarantee, the possibility of suicide, but has lost its distinctive mark because the consequences of its exercise are shared with completely innocent people. (OT: 433)

The surprising infrequency of suicide among prisoners in the concentration camps demonstrates to Arendt the terrible effectiveness of totalitarianism which, having first killed the juridical person by making arrest and punishment an arbitrary occurrence, then succeeded in murdering 'the moral person in man ... by making martyrdom, for the first time in history, impossible' (OT: 451). Unlike the victims of previous pogroms, the Jewish inmates of Nazi extermination camps could not have died for their faith, as conversion or renunciation would not have stayed the hands of their executioners. The process of moral degradation produced countless victims of extermination who, despite sufficient knowledge of their impending destruction, felt so lacking in human life – Arendt refers to them as 'living corpses' – that there was nothing left to risk, and therefore no dignity to gain, by attempting to resist or escape their murderers. This, for Giorgio Agamben, is the ultimate form of biopolitics, where life is profaned to the point where it can no longer be sacrificed:

> The Jew living under Nazism is the privileged negative referent of the new biopolitical sovereignty and is, as such, a flagrant case of a *homo sacer* in the sense of a life that may be killed but not sacrificed. His killing therefore constitutes ... neither capital punishment nor a sacrifice, but simply the actualisation of a mere 'capacity to be killed'... The truth ... is that the Jews were exterminated not in a mad and giant holocaust but exactly as Hitler had announced, 'as lice', which is to say, as bare life. The dimension in which the extermination took place is neither religion nor law, but biopolitics. (Agamben 1998: 114)

Arendt describes the camps, which were for her 'the true central institution of totalitarian organisational power', as 'laboratories in the experiment of total domination' (OT: 438, 436). By this she means that the ultimate goal of the camps was not simply genocide, but the transformation of human beings into 'specimens of the human animal' – *homo sacer* in Agamben's account – who have lost the distinctly human capacity for spontaneity. Having perfected the techniques of dehumanisation, having seemingly eliminated the human condition of natality, totalitarian rule would then extend these devices to the population at large. 'Totalitarianism strives not toward despotic rule over men, but toward a system in which men are superfluous. Total power can be achieved and safeguarded only in a world of conditioned reflexes, of marionettes without slightest trace of spontaneity' (OT: 438, 455, 457).

Arendt refers to the return to the intelligible human world of those 'inanimate men' who survived the death camps as akin to the 'resurrection of Lazarus', pointing out that the bestial horrors of their experiences were so without parallel in the ordinary living universe that even those who survived often shared with disbelieving observers an uncertainty as to whether what they had experienced and witnessed had actually taken place. As Hitler knew too well, the victims of the most enormous, most improbable crimes will always be the last to be believed (OT: 439–41). Arendt suggests, in fact, that this incredulity over the enormity of the crimes of Hitler and Stalin is insuperable, for it refers to a form of 'radical evil' which, 'because it can no longer be deduced from humanly comprehensible motives' (OT: ix), defies all collective standards of human sinfulness and atonement.

> When the impossible was made possible it became the unpunishable, unforgivable absolute evil which could no longer be understood and explained by the evil motives of self-interest, greed, covetousness, resentment, lust for power, and cowardice; and which therefore anger could not revenge, love could not endure, friendship could not forgive. (OT: 459)

It is the destruction of spontaneity, then, which is the ultimate aim of totalitarian rule. Its purpose is to destroy the existence of purpose, to destroy the possibility of beginning something new, to eliminate the unnatural in humans, their distance from nature and the artificial practices by which they set limits to nature and provide a stable home for the exercise of freedom. However, since the capacity for initiative, arising with the fact of natality, can never be wholly extinguished, the totalitarian project must have the same lifespan as the human species. In fact, so long as it serves evolutionary laws, totalitarianism must continue to find 'new categories of parasitic and unfit lives' or else declare that nature itself has come to an end (EU: 306; OT: 464). Although Arendt traced the origins of totalitarianism to bourgeois society and imperialism, she eventually argues that it is not lust for power or profit which ultimately drives totalitarianism forward, but rather an ideology of natural or historical laws, fidelity to which is incompatible with the contingency of human affairs, and with 'the unpredictability which springs from the fact that men are creative, that they can bring forward something so new that nobody ever foresaw it' (OT: 458).

THE DEGRADATION OF ACTION TO MOTION

It is ironic that, for all the apparent arbitrariness of totalitarian domination, its rulers claimed to be more obedient to ultimate sources of legitimacy than those of any previous polity. 'The totalitarian dictator, in sharp distinction from the tyrant, does not believe that he is a free agent with the power to execute his arbitrary will, but, instead, the executioner of laws higher than himself' (EU: 346). It has been suggested, by George Kateb for example, that Arendt's admiration for political action – action which repeatedly rises up from and surpasses the mundane concerns of physical survival and mere usefulness – bears a worrying resemblance to the Nazis' own promethean 'rebellion against the human condition, an assertion of the unnatural and artificial against the natural or the everyday' which also constituted a radical, if not 'revolutionary', break with all known forms of government (Kateb 1977: 165; 1984: 29–30). Arendt's insistence on the unprecedented nature of this calamitous system, however, does not invalidate her understanding of totalitarianism as the extreme manifestation of the development she called 'the unnatural growth of the natural', a development which combines determinism with nihilism by associating absolute power with the abdication of freedom to inhuman forces. The 'higher laws' of racial selection and class conflict do not *transcend* human nature, in other words, so much as precede and shape it with a force that no action can resist.

Arendt stresses that although totalitarianism conceives of the forces of nature or history as 'laws', these do not perform the function of the positive laws of constitutional government. The latter work to provide a stabilising legal and normative structure within which individuals can act and start things anew. In totalitarianism, by contrast, the relationship between laws and individuals has been reversed, so that 'laws' are conceived as rules of relentless *movement* in the face of whose suprahuman force all mortals have become inert, thing-like and superfluous. Arendt herself thus comments on the 'seemingly contradictory insistence on both the primacy of sheer action and the overwhelming force of sheer necessity' (OT: 331). But she shows how this contradiction is effectively resolved by the degradation of action to 'motion', that is, by a political programme designed 'not only to liberate the historical and natural forces, but to accelerate them to a speed they never would reach if left to themselves' (OT: 466). Hence the essential device of totalitarian government, according to Arendt, is neither lawfulness, the democratic ideal of which is to provide a stable home for human freedom, nor lawlessness, which is typical of tyranny, but rather 'terror', the function of which is 'to "stabilise" men in order to liberate the forces of nature or history' (OT: 464–5).

Arendt traces this idea that 'law' is a principle of motion rather than a stable framework for human action, back to the nineteenth-century belief, strengthened by Darwin's theory of evolution, that the appearance of things is only a temporary manifestation of a long-term process of development. Totalitarian terror does not serve living human beings, but exists in order to accelerate the movement of nature or history, making individuals either the executioners or the victims of its irresistible laws, but rendering them all ultimately superfluous. Unlike fear, terror does not function as one of Montesquieu's guiding principles of action, because human action has been dispensed with altogether. Instead it 'substitutes for the very desire and will to action a craving and need for insight into the laws of movement according to which the terror functions' (EU: 348–9). In the final chapter of *The Origins of Totalitarianism*, which was added to the enlarged 1958 edition of the book, Arendt suggested that this need is met by 'ideology'.

Arendt defines ideologies etymologically as deductive systems of logic which, starting from the premise of a particular 'idea', proceed 'with a consistency that exists nowhere in the realm of reality'. While the function of terror is the prevention of humans' capacity to begin something new, the goal of ideology is to prevent human thought from recognising this capacity, essentially by reducing truth to a matter of deductive consistency and by replacing the judgement of the senses with the 'tyranny of logicality'. This is why, Arendt suggests, the content of ideologies is to a large extent irrelevant; the superfluousness of the person is demanded by iron rules of reasoning which impose their sterile logicality, as a substitute for thought and as a remedy for loneliness, 'without regard for facts and experience'. In a sense, it is the shallowness of ideologies – which treat 'the course of events as though it followed the same "law" as the logical exposition of its "idea"' – which explains their power to inspire people with 'the murderous network of pure logical operations' (EU: 356–8; OT: 469). 'What makes conviction and opinion of any sort so ridiculous and dangerous under totalitarian conditions is that totalitarian regimes take the greatest pride in having no need of them, or of any human help of any kind' (OT: 456–7).

Ideology thus extends the experience of superflousness from the outer world of doing to the inner world of thinking, from the *vita activa* to the *vita contemplativa*, such that, as André Gorz writes of the ultimate triumph of economic rationality, thinking becomes a technique 'whose operations function without the involvement of the subject and whose absent subjects are unable to account for themselves' (1989: 124). As Gorz indicates, such a degradation of thought is clearly not confined to totalitarian regimes, and Arendt herself noted how the same faculty that enables the political actor in a republic to withdraw from the world as it really is in order to imagine it being otherwise can also be turned to the service of lies that are so internally consistent they protect the self-deceiving experts from any contact with reality. Reflecting on what the Pentagon Papers had revealed about the formulation of US military and political policy in Vietnam after the Second World War, Arendt recalled her 'impression that a computer, rather than "decision-makers", had been let loose in Southeast Asia', with the result that judgement was replaced by mechanical calculation and 'the evidence of mathematical, purely rational truth' (CR: 37). The link between the mathematisation of thought and the machine age had of course already been made by Adorno and Horkheimer in *Dialectic of Enlightenment*: 'Thinking objectifies itself to become an automatic, self-activating process; an impersonation of the machine that it produces itself so that ultimately the machine can replace it' (1997: 25).

Arendt ends *The Origins of Totalitarianism* with a sober warning. Although we are inclined to think of intellectuals as the champions of free thought and individual freedom, philosophers from Plato to Heidegger have shown an alarming attraction to tyrants and führers. What attracts the philosopher to the steely embrace of ideological thinking, Arendt suggests, is that the solitude of the intellectual, which is so fundamental to his or her vocation, is always in danger of slipping into loneliness, where the thinker is deserted by the self as a dependable companion. Having voluntarily withdrawn from the realm of public affairs, the philosopher may be as susceptible to loneliness as the atomised masses. Attuned to the rigours of thinking, greater may be the obedience of the intellectual to that 'inner coercion whose only content is the strict avoidance of contradictions that seems to confirm a man's identity outside all relationships with others' (OT: 478).[4]

TENSIONS, OMISSIONS, CONTRADICTIONS

Arendt's study of totalitarianism can be read as an attempt to understand the potential for limitless violence that arises when the worldly artifice of human affairs is annulled and inhuman laws take the place of fallible human conversation and agreements. These inhuman laws include the laws of logic, and Arendt's condemnation of the 'coercive force of logicality', which 'springs from our fear of contradicting ourselves' (OT: 472–3), conveys a sentiment that is also perhaps reflected in the dense and uneven composition of *The Origins of Totalitarianism*, whose various digressions, historical subplots and surprising cameos combine to make a 'totalising' summary of the book a difficult task. In responding to the criticism that her study 'was lacking in unity', Arendt emphasised that her intention was always to explore the history of totalitarianism in a non-causal fashion, mindful of the fact that even the darkest, most degrading of human events belong to the future as well as the past, in the sense that they mark a new beginning which 'is caused invariably by some factor which lies in the realm of human freedom'. The phenomenon of totalitarianism thus 'illuminates its own past' but 'can never be deduced from it' (EU: 319, 402–3, 325–6 n11–18).

Among the complaints made of Arendt's book was the claim, advanced by Whitfield (1980) among others, that she had conflated the distinctive characteristics of Nazism and Stalinism. Arendt had in fact only decided to extend her analysis from Nazism to the Soviet Union once she had all but completed the first and second parts of the book, and this certainly helps explain its unbalanced structure. Arendt neglected the different functions of the concentration camps, for instance, which for the Nazis were a means for the mass production of death, whereas the Russian gulag system was principally conceived as a means of accelerating the process of industrial development, and death was a by-product of deprivation and overwork rather than its *raison d'être*. The warmongering belligerence of the Nazis was not exactly shared by the Bolsheviks either, whose ideological motif, decorated with humanism rather than unapologetic anti-Semitism, was the worker rather than the warrior, and whose leader placed the national interest – the preservation of the socialist state – ahead of world domination, avoiding Hitler's reckless policy of military expansionism.

While some commentators believed the conflation of Soviet Communism with German Fascism did a historical disservice to the Bolshevik project – Martin Jay, for instance, described *The Origins of Totalitarianism* as 'a monument of the Cold War' (1986: 238) – it has also been argued that Arendt's analysis failed to register the way Hitler's destructive rule was far more selective, and far less arbitrary, than that of Stalin. Part of the peculiarity of the analysis of totalitarianism which makes up the third part of Arendt's book is that in a number of respects the descriptions of 'total domination' offer a more accurate account of Stalin's Soviet Union than of Hitler's Reich. Arendt's sparse references to Nazi genocide and the planned extermination of European Jewry, and her focus on the regime's constant purging of its own members – which was not typical of Nazi Germany, where the systematic terrorising of acquiescent and 'racially pure' citizens was avoided – suggest that her understanding of totalitarian domination was primarily based on Stalin's gulag and on conditions in the German concentration camps before the occupation of Poland (Tsao 2002).

Some of these omissions in Arendt's analysis contributed to the perception that she had failed to recognise the magnitude of the destruction visited on European Jewry. Historians have also argued that her insistence on the novelty of twentieth-century totalitarianism caused her to overlook instances of genocidal tyranny, which met many of the criteria for Arendt's definition of totalitarianism, in the ancient world, among native Africans, and in the earlier system of European colonialism (Stanley 1994, Gines 2007). Arendt's belief, which diverged from the original theme she proposed for *The Origins*, in the absolute novelty of totalitarian domination, and her refusal to consider it as the extreme end of a long-established political continuum, also provoked the criticism that her analysis effectively normalised non-totalitarian dictatorships, as is most apparent in her almost admiring discussion of Lenin (Arato 2002).

Given the scale of Arendt's project, it is perhaps not surprising that there are also theoretical tensions and inconsistencies in the book. One of the more perplexing of these is the way she combines the imagery of industrial gigantism – bureaucracy, administrative massacres, a 'mechanised system' for the 'cold and systematic destruction of human bodies' – with descriptions of totalitarianism as radically hostile to order, predictability, stable hierarchies and the rule of law. Arendt's analysis of the organisation of the totalitarian movement as constituted by multiple overlapping layers of responsibility, her Kafkaesque account of bureaucracy as characterised by secrecy and arbitrary decree, and her depiction of totalitarianism, in contrast to more familiar forms of tyranny and dictatorship, as a movement inimical to the fixed constitutional structures and rule-bound offices of the state, therefore seems at odds with another image of totalitarianism as a functionally rationalised and impersonally routinised industrial mega-machine. This more recognisable picture of 'totalitarian bureaucracy' –

'rule by nobody', as Arendt frequently calls it, or the definitive form of 'the social' in *The Human Condition* – is consistent with Zygmunt Bauman's influential sociological study of the Holocaust, which treats the administration of the Final Solution as a model of Weberian bureaucracy inseparable from the rationalisation of modernity (Bauman 2000a).

One reason to be sceptical of attempts to enlist Weber to help explain the role of bureaucracy in totalitarianism is that Arendt's understanding of bureaucracy, as noted in the previous chapter, departs in significant ways from Weber's. In any case, Paul du Gay has noted that Weber never argued, as Bauman suggests he did, that rational bureaucratic institutions created a morally bankrupt universe devoid of normative commitments. Weber believed bureaucratic administration to be ruled by a distinctive ethos of professionalism and disinterestedness – a refusal to be corrupted by the influence of status or prestige, lured by the familiar bonds of class or kinship, or tempted by the passion of moral absolutes – which was intended to uphold the principle of 'formal equality of treatment' and 'the "democratic" sentiment of the governed which demands that domination be minimised' (Weber 1978: 225, 1000–1).

> In other words, while the ethos associated with formal rationality is certainly premised upon the cultivation of indifference to certain moral ends, that very indifference is predicated upon an awareness of the irreducible plurality of and frequent incommensurability between passionately held moral ends and thus of the possible costs of pursuing any one of them at the expense of the others. Viewed thus, formal rationality is not consequent with the development of an attitude of amoral instrumentalism, but on the cultivation of a liberal-pluralist ethics of responsibility which does take account of the consequences of attempting to realise essentially contextable values that frequently come into conflict with other values. (Du Gay 2000: 76)

According to du Gay, Bauman's failure to recognise the close connection, apparently understood by Weber, between bureaucratisation and democratisation, is compounded in Bauman's study of the Holocaust by a historically inaccurate account of the role of the civil service in Nazi Germany. Drawing on Jane Caplan's study, *Government without Administration* (1988), du Gay describes a process of *de-bureaucratisation* under the Third Reich, where civil servants were encouraged to see themselves as the Führer's vassals, and the institutional framework of government was dissolved in order to sustain the fictional image of 'an organic community of co-operation' (du Gay 2000: 50). Nazi ideology made Weberian bureaucracy, with its dispassionate and professional spirit, the sworn enemy of the *Volk* and its ancient virtues, and eventually it paid the price: 'by seeking to operationalise a fantasy of government without modern administration, the regime proved incapable of generating the conditions of its own stabilisation and reproduction' (du Gay 2000: 51).

In a similar vein, Arendt, citing from *Mein Kampf*, notes how in Nazi doctrine 'the "living organisation" of the movement is contrasted with the "dead mechanism" of a bureaucratic party' (OT: 361, n56). But she still held that this movement was 'bureaucratic' in character, distinguishing, for example, 'between the old-fashioned rule by bureaucracy and the up-to-date totalitarian brand', arguing that while the former 'left the whole inner life of the soul intact', the latter has a far more radical reach (OT: 245). As Arendt described it in her analysis of imperialism, bureaucracy is not rigidly codified administration but rather a shapeless form of government 'whose very essence is aimless process' and whose functionaries preferred to serve the secret yet eternal movement of world history instead of the positive laws of their country (OT: 216–21). Adolf Eichmann, Transportation Administrator for the Final Solution, was the perfect incarnation of the bureaucrat in this distinctive sense. Scrupulously devoted to fulfilling the Führer's unwritten command to destroy the Jews of Europe, Eichmann saw this process of annihilation as a higher law, in the face of which the written orders of his superior, Heinrich Himmler, to cease the transportation of Hungarian Jews, trade Jews for trucks, and close the extermination facilities, were devoid of authority (EJ: 146–7).

If there is a final discrepancy in Arendt's study which is worth mentioning here, then it is the tension between her condemnation of ideology as a substitute for thinking and her more equivocal attitude towards storytelling, religious belief, myths and philosophical systems of thought. George Kateb has argued that while Arendt's critical analysis of the role of ideology in totalitarianism is 'essentially correct', her own lack of what he calls 'a cultivated ability to endure meaninglessness' meant that she herself was drawn to exalt the role of the storyteller, forgetting that all stories can induce aesthetic intoxication and the fanaticism of sworn believers.

All this means that there are significant affinities between what Arendt admires and what she deplores ... This is the case not only with stories ... and ideologies, but also with such pairs of concepts as action and lying; genuine political actors and totalitarian elites; warrior heroes and sinister secret agents; those who bind themselves by promises for authentic political action and conspirators; the homelessness of philosophical thinking and that of the masses in modern life; the abstraction from reality and the senses that is shared by thinking and ideology; contingency and meaninglessness; meaning and untruth. (Kateb 2002: 352)

Kateb's argument that 'the quest for meaning can turn inhuman' (2002: 326) is one with which Arendt would not disagree, as her critique of the tendency among philosophers to build metaphysical systems designed to make further thinking unnecessary bears witness (LM1: 15–16, 89–91). The overall validity of Kateb's interpretation of Arendt depends on whether she regarded storytelling or thinking as the real vehicle for meaning. Arendt's admiration for Socrates, who understood that an unexamined life was a meaningless one, and who never attempted to construct a philosophical doctrine from his thinking activity, might suggest the latter. And as we shall see in Chapter 9, it is precisely the purging effect of thinking, its shattering of idols and the way it loosens the rigid convictions of fanatics and dogmatists, which protects the thinker from conforming to inhuman imperatives.

IS *THE ORIGINS* STILL RELEVANT?

For all the criticisms that have made been made of Arendt's analysis, *The Origins of Totalitarianism* remains one of the most powerful and respected studies of the catastrophe of the twentieth century. There is, moreover, no shortage of scholars convinced as to the relevance of the book to the post-totalitarian world. Some commentators, for example, have focused on more recent instances of tribal nationalism and so-called ethnic cleansing, such as the 1993 massacre of Muslim refugees by Bosnian Serb troops in Srebrenica during the war in former Yugoslavia (Jalušič 2007), and the 1994 genocide in Rwanda (Stone 2007). After the 2001 attacks on the World Trade Centre and the Pentagon, Arendt's epistemological sensitivity to the unique and unprecedented was also embraced as a model for grasping the new kind of threat facing Western democracies, with the supranationalist aspirations of radical Islamism described as a 'novel form of totalitarianism' (Benhabib 2002: 541; Young-Bruehl 2002: 573). Focusing on the final 'Ideology and Terror' chapter added to the 1958 edition of *The Origins of Totalitarianism*, some observers have credited Arendt with a prescient description of modern Islamic fundamentalism, with its intolerance of diversity and dissent, its strict religious regulation of everyday life, and its ability to produce zealous militants eager to die for a higher cause. 'Arendt wrote of German and Soviet selfless devotion to the idealised collective,' Samantha Power notes in her introduction to Schocken's latest edition of Arendt's book, 'but what greater testament to such selflessness can there be but martyrdom of the kind that thousands of young Muslim men and women are queuing up to undertake today?' (2004: xxii)

Arendt actually claimed that people in totalitarian movements 'will not follow the example of religious fanatics and die the death of martyrs', suggesting that once the movement itself stalled or was destroyed, its members would cease to subscribe to a redundant dogma (OT: 363). Moreover, this particular use of Arendt does not do full justice to the political grievances of the Muslim world, nor to the history of terrorism as the preferred weapon of underdeveloped societies and non-state actors against militarily dominant occupiers. It also sits awkwardly alongside Arendt's own fear that it was Zionism – arguably the most critical factor in the worldwide radicalisation of Muslims – which had, certainly in the vision of its founder Theodor Herzl, most in common with racist ideology. 'Zionism can be included among the many "isms" of that period,' Arendt wrote of the politicisation of the Jewish question in the late nineteenth century, 'each of which claimed to explain reality and predict the future in terms of irresistible laws and forces' (JP: 168).

After the Holocaust, Arendt noted, it was understandable that Herzl's earlier argument that anti-Semitism was the natural reaction of all Gentiles to the existence of the Jews became common currency among the Diaspora. The problem was that this belief swiftly hardened into a 'crazy isolationism' modelled on the ideology of European nationalism and an ethnic understanding of statehood which, at least where the Arabs of Palestine were concerned, was premised on 'plain racist chauvinism' (JP: 183). 'It is nothing else than the uncritical acceptance of German-inspired nationalism', Arendt wrote of Herzl's vision of a Jewish state. 'This holds a nation to be an eternal organic body, the product of inevitable natural growth of inherent qualities; and it explains peoples, not in terms of political organisations, but in terms of biological superhuman personalities' (JP: 156). Arendt also vociferously opposed the campaigning visit to the US in December 1948 of Menachem Begin, erstwhile leader of the Jewish terrorist organisation the Irgun, then founder of its political offspring the Herut ('Freedom') Party, and a future Prime Minister of Israel. Arendt described Herut as 'a political party closely akin in its organisation, methods, political philosophy, and social appeal to the Nazi and Fascist parties' (JW: 417), referring to the Deir Yassin massacre by the Irgun as evidence of its extremist character.

Redolent of this older Jewish chauvinism are the condescending assessments, which have become commonplace in political discourse over the last few decades, of the ability of Arab peoples to govern their own societies without intervention from Western states, as well as the public equivocation of Western leaders in the face of Israel's strategy of collectively punishing the population of the Palestinian territories by disabling the public infrastructure and launching disproportionate reprisals for attacks by Islamic militants on Israeli soil. It is therefore not surprising that more searching use of Arendt has been made closer to home, exploring, for example, the proto-totalitarian components of the 'war on terror' that was launched by the US in the aftermath of the 2001 attacks – a war whose enemy is so dehumanised and impersonal that 'the door is open to limitless war outside of all rules of war' (Young-Bruehl 2006: 62). It was of course this supposed war, and the putative threat to 'national security' against which it claimed to be engaged, which became the sacred justification for pre-emptive military action and the curtailment of civil liberties, for Guantanamo Bay, Abu Ghraib, extraordinary renditions, torture, detention without trial, and the 'collateral' killing of innocent civilians, both abroad and at home.

Perhaps it is, then, the second part of Arendt's book which offers most to the contemporary reader of *The Origins of Totalitarianism*, for her analysis of imperialism looks particularly applicable to the political and military presence of the US, supported primarily by the UK, in Afghanistan and the Middle East, and her theory of the 'boomerang effect' seems ever more relevant to the abuse of civil rights in the Western metropoles where the overseas 'war on terror' has already undermined the rule of law at home. In her 1967 preface to Part Two of the book, Arendt was already considering whether the competition between Cold War superpowers meant 'we are back, on an enormously enlarged scale, where we started from, that is, in the imperialist era and on the collision course that led to World War I'. She noted how 'American foreign policy feels committed to wage war in one country for the sake of the integrity of others that are not even its neighbours', with nations treated as pawns in the pursuit of 'rule over a third country, which in turn became a mere stepping stone in the unending process of power expansion and accumulation' (OT: xviii).

Since lifelong Republican Alan Greenspan, who as Chairman of the US central bank from 1987 to 2006 was one of the most powerful champions of American capitalism, acknowledged in his autobiography the 'politically inconvenient' fact that 'the Iraq war is largely about oil' (Greenspan 2007: 462), the link between US foreign policy and the logic of economic accumulation never seemed as close or as clear. Naomi Klein, describing the tens of billions of dollars that flowed in to help 'reconstruct' Iraq following the second Gulf War, only to flow out again, along with $20 billion of Iraq's oil money, to the Western companies who were gifted the lucrative contracts, argues that the 'shock doctrine' that was imposed on Iraq was delivered with such open contempt for the rights of its people that its imperialist provenance was without any pretence or disguise. 'Elsewhere, there would still be free trade lite, with its hothouse negotiations, but now there would also be free trade heavy, without proxies or puppets, seizing new markets directly for Western multinationals on the battlefields of preemptive wars' (Klein 2007: 343).

In David Harvey's analysis of the 'new imperialism', it is the export of superfluous Western capital – the social investment of which is prohibited by the anti-state ideology of neo-liberalism – which has driven the US military to the far reaches of the globe. In the post-Cold War ideological battle Communism has been replaced by Islamism, but the continuing support provided by Western governments to authoritarian Arab regimes that are hated by their citizens proves that it is access to trade and resources, and not the civil and political rights of foreign peoples, which is the prize to be protected from radical Islam. Quoting with approval Arendt's 'acute observation' that the limitless accumulation of capital requires a correspondingly unlimited accumulation of power, Harvey argues that Arendt understood how 'bourgeois history must be a history of hegemonies expressive of ever larger and continuously more expansive power' (2005: 34).

Even so, it is worth remembering here that Arendt saw the imperialist principle of ever-expanding power as capable of paving the way for totalitarianism because of its increasing indifference to economic rationality. For Arendt, as Robin reminds us, capitalist expansion 'provides a model, not a motive, for the imperialist, who patterns the acquisition of power on the accumulation of capital' (2007: 19). It was Nobel Prize winning economist Joseph Stiglitz who stunned readers in February 2008 with the calculation that the war in Iraq had already cost US tax payers more than the twelve-year war in Vietnam, with the conservative estimate that its final cost to the US treasury would be over $3 trillion – more than half the cost borne by US citizens (when adjusted for inflation) for the Second World War (Stiglitz and Bilmes 2008). If this was an economically rational war, it was only in the Marxist sense that capitalism, in order to manage its internal contradictions, has to periodically destroy surplus wealth in order to create the conditions for more profitable investment.

To these contemporary analyses one must also add a brief commentary on the startling numbers of people in the world today who have been displaced from their homes by poverty, conflict and, increasingly, natural disasters. When Germany surrendered to the Allies in 1945, an estimated 40 million people had been displaced in Europe, at least 10 million of whom were, like Arendt herself, not recognised as nationals by any state. In 2009, the number of people in the world forcibly displaced by conflict and persecution was counted by the UN at 43.3 million, including 4.8 million Palestinian refugees, and 27 million internally displaced persons (more than half of whom were receiving UN humanitarian aid). This figure also includes only a verifiable half of the 12 million people whom the UNHCR (2010) estimates are *de facto* stateless, and it excludes the tens of millions (36 million in 2008) who have been displaced by natural disasters. These figures are global totals, of course, and they reflect multiple, often heterogeneous conflicts, tensions and disasters in different parts of the world. Yet if Arendt was right to describe homelessness as the first stage of a process by which humans are subsequently made rightless and then rendered expendable, then the economic, military and environmental dislocations sweeping the earth, the second-class treatment of immigrants, refugees and guest workers by the wealthy nation states, and the disregard for basic rights that is increasingly shared by both democratically elected governments and their unflinching enemies, are cause for serious concern.

Commenting on the burgeoning networks of transit camps, detention centres and military holding facilities that are used to contain, interrogate and repatriate de-territorialised 'aliens' who are often denied the most basic of human rights, Patrick Hayden argues that these new 'spaces of superfluousness' reflect a crisis of statelessness 'that has grown more rather than less acute since the time of Arendt's intervention'. Describing a 'virulent system of global apartheid which establishes a permanent underclass of superfluous human beings', Hayden reminds us of the continuing relevance of Arendt's critique of the nation-state system, and her insistence that the political integrity of the state depends on its legal protection of 'all who happen to live on its territory' (EU: 208). 'To guarantee the right to have rights', Hayden avers, 'we must begin to sever citizenship from nationality and rearticulate the state as an institution of legality rather than sovereignty.' Our failure to remedy the ongoing calamity of statelessness is nothing short of 'political evil' (Hayden 2009: 90, 86, 91; see also Krause 2008).

8
In Search of the Subject

If the perils of modernity identified by Arendt remain with us, then questions of responsibility and judgement must be paramount in the minds of those who want to learn lessons from the darkest chapter in recent human history. Of the many interesting issues which Arendt began to raise in *The Origins of Totalitarianism*, perhaps the most complex and challenging concerns the role of moral agency in politically oppressive societies, and whether the Holocaust obliges us to re-evaluate long-established notions about the nature of good and evil. In the remainder of this book I want to explore Arendt's philosophy of moral responsibility, beginning here with a discussion of her observations on the 1961 trial of the Nazi war criminal, Adolf Eichmann, and then considering in the next chapter her incomplete writings on thinking, willing and judging, which were posthumously published in *The Life of the Mind* (1978), the *Lectures on Kant's Political Philosophy* (1982), and *Responsibility and Judgement* (2003). In the process I want to show how Arendt resisted the allure of sociological systems theory, and how her attempt to link the rise of the bureaucratic sphere of the 'social' with the phenomenon of thoughtlessness, and thoughtlessness with evil, expressed her determination to establish a human explanation for the inhuman deeds of totalitarianism.

EICHMANN

Eichmann in Jerusalem was published in 1963, having appeared earlier in the same year as a series of five articles in the *New Yorker*. The book is sometimes read as the diminutive and better-known offspring of Arendt's monumental study of totalitarianism. It commanded a larger readership because of its dramatic courtroom content, its starkly factual subject matter, and its relative brevity. It also caused a storm of controversy amongst the Diaspora, as many prominent Jewish intellectuals, religious and Zionist organisations, and even a number of Arendt's erstwhile friends, took angry exception to her criticisms of the *Judenräte* (the Jewish councils), whose members, Arendt implied, co-operated too readily with the Nazis. What to many people made those criticisms especially unpalatable was Arendt's accompanying depiction of Eichmann not as an evil monster but as a petty-minded functionary. For there is no doubt that what captured the attention most about this book was the moral and sociological ramifications of its eye-catching subtitle: *A Report on the Banality of Evil*.

According to Young-Bruehl, when Arendt first saw Eichmann in the court in Jerusalem she was startled by his ordinariness (2004: 329, 374). Her realisation that Eichmann was 'not even sinister' functioned like a '*cura posterior*' – a remedy for the state of speechless incomprehension with which she had faced the 'absolute evil' of totalitarianism since the war. In *Eichmann in Jerusalem*, the portrait she drew of the war criminal opposes at every point the remorseless efforts of the prosecution to depict him as a 'perverted sadist' and a 'monster'. In Arendt's view Eichmann was more a clown than a tyrant, and his chief moral defect was not a malevolent will but an 'inability to think'. This was reflected in his self-acknowledged preference for speaking in 'officialese', his dependence on which was so ingrained that 'even when he did succeed in constructing a sentence of his own, he repeated it until it became a cliché' (EJ: 49). Even at his execution, Eichmann regurgitated the stock phrases of a funeral oratory, declaring, despite his renunciation of Christianity and the belief in life after death, that 'we shall all meet again', and promising not to forget the mortal world he was leaving. As Arendt comments on the last seconds of his life, Eichmann's infamously poor memory 'played him the last trick ... and he forgot that this was his own funeral' (EJ: 252). His decline of the offer of a hood for his execution was fully in keeping with his attitude of evasion and self denial: he had no need of a blindfold because he was already wearing his own (Terada 2008: 99).

That Eichmann played a central role in the implementation of the Final Solution has never been in doubt. Only this absence of doubt, in fact, could have justified in the eyes of the world the illegal kidnapping of Eichmann in Buenos Aires by Israeli agents in May 1960. But Arendt also stresses that his role was something less than what the prosecution, and unfortunately the judges as well, believed it to be. Born in Solingen in the Rhineland in 1906 and raised in Austria, Eichmann was 'the déclassé son of a solid middle-class family', whose characterless background destined him for a life of anonymous mediocrity. In a bid to escape a series of mundane sales jobs, he had successfully applied for a job in the Security

Service of the SS in 1934. The following year he was moved to a new department concerned with Jewish affairs, where he diligently educated himself with Zionist literature, convincing himself that the solution to the Jewish question was, in his own words, to 'get some firm ground under the feet of the Jews'.

After Germany annexed Austria in March 1938, Eichmann was sent to Vienna for his first major assignment, the forced emigration of 150,000 Jews. Eichmann developed and then finely tuned the strategy of using the influence of prominent and wealthy Jews to make this process more efficient. In the beginning these included Zionist emissaries who, viewing Britain, not Germany, as their primary adversary, negotiated with Eichmann to facilitate the clandestine immigration of Jews into British-ruled Palestine.

When Hitler invaded Czechoslovakia the following Spring, Eichmann was appointed to set up another emigration centre for Jews in Prague. Then, after war broke out later in the year, he was recalled to Germany to head the Reich Centre for Jewish Emigration. By this time the Nazis had abandoned their pro-Zionist stance, the Reich had acquired over two million more Jews through the conquest of Polish territories, and the channels for overseas emigration had become severely congested. Eichmann briefly flirted with a number of alternative, but ultimately abortive, plans, such as the establishment of a Jewish territory in the Nisko region of Poland (where he probably believed he would be appointed Protector), and the ludicrous idea, proposed by the German Foreign Office but already entertained by the Polish government in 1937 and the French Foreign Minister Georges Bonnet in 1938, to ship four million Jews to the French colony of Madagascar. According to Arendt, Eichmann was one of only a handful of officials to take the Madagascar project seriously, for its real purpose was to provide 'a cloak under which the preparations for the physical extermination of all the Jews of Western Europe could be carried forward', ensuring that 'everybody was psychologically, or rather logically, prepared for the next step: since there existed no territory to which one could "evacuate", the only "solution" was extermination' (EJ: 77).

Architectural plans for Auschwitz, gas chambers included, have now been dated from as early as May 1941 (Connolly 2008), but Hitler was still publicly talking about resettling the Jews in 1942, by which time more than 300,000 Jews had already been murdered by the *Einsatzgruppen* in Russia, where mobile gas chambers were also in operation (EU: 287). For all her interest in the bureaucratic character of Eichmann and the 'banality' of evil, it is worth pointing out here that Arendt's account of the Final Solution, which traces its origins to the euthanasia programme initiated by Hitler in September 1939, departs from the now dominant 'functionalist' understanding of the Holocaust. This perspective, which originated with Karl Schleunes' claim that the road to Auschwitz was 'twisted' rather than 'straight' (Schleunes 1970), and which was developed by German historians such as Hans Mommsen (1986), was also adopted by Zygmunt Bauman (2000a) in his sociological study of Nazism. All these scholars share the view that there was no preconceived plan to destroy the Jews of Europe, but instead a 'crooked', inconsistent pattern of often contradictory policies and initiatives targeted at addressing the Jewish question, with mass extermination becoming the default option, selected by Nazi bureaucrats on purely technical grounds, only after other enterprises had failed and the war situation had narrowed the range of alternatives.

Eichmann's first deportation from Germany involved the shipment of 1,300 German Jews from Stettin to Poland in February 1940. In the Autumn he deported more than 7,000 Jews from Baden and Saarpfalz to France, where they were sent by the Vichy government to the same concentration camp at Gurs from which Arendt herself had escaped earlier in the year. Eichmann was first informed of the plan for 'the physical extermination of the Jews' by his boss, Reinhardt Heydrich, in the Summer of 1941. In November 1941, Heydrich penned a letter to the High Command of the Army declaring that he had been 'entrusted for years with the task of preparing the final solution of the Jewish problem', confirming Arendt's belief that the killing of the Jews was conceived far earlier than January 1942, when senior Nazis met at the Wannsee Conference to discuss how to co-ordinate the elimination of European Jewry. This belief is in many respects consistent with what has been called the 'intentionalist' interpretation of the Final Solution (e.g. Breitman 2004: 62–3), which typically dates Hitler's genocidal ambitions at least as far back as the infamous 'Prophesy Speech' made before the Reichstag on 30 January 1939.

As for Eichmann, by the time of the Wannsee Conference he had already seen the half-built gas chambers in Treblinka, and had visited Kulm, where the use of gas vans was well established. In Russia and Poland he had also witnessed the results of the mass shootings by the *Einsatzgruppen*, the mobile killing units which operated at the rear of the advancing Germany army in the East, and which by the end of the war had murdered nearly one-and-a-half million Jews.

THE TRIAL

Arendt saw the kidnapping that made possible Eichmann's trial as an ignominious start to the legal process, though given Argentina's poor record on the extradition of Nazi war criminals she concedes there was probably no realistic alternative. The ideal, she suggests, would have been to follow the precedents set by Soghomon Tehlirian and Shalom Schwartzbard in the 1920s. Tehlirian was a survivor of the Ottoman pogrom of 1915, in which over a million Armenians were driven from their homes by the Turkish military and slaughtered or starved to death in concentration camps. In 1921 in Berlin, Tehlirian shot dead Mehmet Talaat Pasha (also known as Talaat Bey), who as the Minister of Interior had planned and directed the Armenian genocide. Schwartzbard was a Ukrainian anarchist whose family were among the thousands killed during the anti-Jewish pogroms of 1919. In 1926 he tracked down Simon Petlyura, chairman of the Ukrainian National Republic between 1918 and 1920, and shot him dead in broad daylight in a Paris street. Both assassins gave themselves up to the authorities, then used their trials, and the media attention they received, to publicise to the wider world the crimes committed against their people. Both men were acquitted.

But Tehlirian and Schwartzbard, whose actions seem to be exemplary cases for the just and meaningful use of violence, were members of persecuted ethnic groups without a nation state or legal system. Since the Jews now had their state, the assassination of Eichmann would have been unjustified, Arendt argues, and bringing him to trial in Israel the only legitimate option.

The trial itself proved beyond any measure of doubt that Eichmann knowingly shipped hundreds of thousands of Jews to their death. It also found him guilty – incorrectly in Arendt's view – of 'participating' in the programme of mass slaughters by the *Einsatzgruppen*, of deporting the Jews from the Polish ghettos (whose running and eventual liquidation he was also found guilty of), and also of being responsible for what happened in the extermination camps themselves. As Arendt complained: 'The prosecution, unable to understand a mass murderer who had never killed (and who in this particular instance probably did not even have the guts to kill), was constantly trying to prove individual murder' (EJ: 215).

Eichmann was finally convicted on fifteen counts, the first four of which constituted crimes 'against the Jewish people'. Counts five through to twelve dealt with 'crimes against humanity' – which in Israeli law ranged from the mass murder of non-Jewish peoples to

the displacement or persecution or murder of Jews and non-Jews –
while the last three counts charged him with membership of criminal
organisations. By the order of the counts, and given the range of
severity in offences constituting 'crimes against humanity' in Israeli
law, the clear implication was that Eichmann's most serious crimes
were those actions intended to destroy the Jewish people. Arendt's
discomfort with this verdict was exacerbated by the subsequent
judgement of the Court of Appeal, which implicitly revised the
decision of the lower court by describing Eichmann as 'his own
superior' who, in the absence of higher orders, implemented the
Final Solution with 'fanatical zeal' and 'unquenchable blood thirst'
(cited in EJ: 249).

Arendt's unease over the trial partly derived from what she
believes was the court's failure to recognise the unprecedented
nature of the crimes Eichmann committed. This may seem an
unlikely deficiency given the lengths the Israeli state had gone to
capture Eichmann, and the dedication of half the court sessions
in the trial to the hearing of prosecution witness statements. (In
spending seven weeks recounting their tales of horror, the witnesses,
who were mostly from Poland and Lithuania where Eichmann's
authority was practically non-existent, were exercising what Arendt
says was a moral 'right to be irrelevant'.) Yet for Arendt this was no
contradiction, for it provided the context for interpreting Eichmann's
crimes as anti-Semitic atrocities, and for the prosecution's efforts to
impress on the judges the need of the victims for vengeance. The
root of this shortcoming, in Arendt's view, was the Jewish self-
understanding which saw the Holocaust as the most terrible pogrom
in a long history of anti-Semitic persecution. What was consequently
ignored was the way Hitler's totalitarian movement was not inclined
to stop – and indeed did not stop – at the slaughter of the Jews.
What needed to be considered was whether the extermination of
whole peoples, whether these be Jews, Poles, Gypsies, or some other
targeted sector of the population, constituted more than a crime
against those particular groups, and whether 'the international
order, and mankind in its entirety, might have been grievously hurt
and endangered' (EJ: 276).

Against the argument of the prosecution, who claimed to be in the
righteous company of 'six million prosecutors', that justice would
be pursued in the name of the victims, Arendt draws attention to
the distinction between penal (or criminal) law and civil law. 'The
wrongdoer is brought to justice because his act has disturbed and
gravely endangered the community as a whole, and not because, as

in civil suits, damage has been done to individuals who are entitled to reparation' (EJ: 261). What was seriously damaged by the Nazis and most in need of urgent repair, according to Arendt, was not the interests of the plaintiffs but the 'body politic' itself. The 'public order' that had been violated, moreover, not only transcended the community of Jews, but also exceeded the jurisdiction of the Jewish state. Justice therefore required that Eichmann be tried in an international court capable of reasserting the order of humankind:

> just as a murderer is prosecuted because he has violated the law of the community, and not because he deprived the Smith family of its husband, father, and breadwinner, so the modern, state-employed mass murderers must be prosecuted because they violated the order of mankind, and not because they killed millions of people. Nothing is more pernicious to an understanding of these new crimes, or stands more in the way of the emergence of an international penal code that could take care of them, than the common illusion that the crime of murder and the crime of genocide are essentially the same, and that the latter therefore is 'no new crime properly speaking'. The point of the latter is that an altogether different order is broken and an altogether different community is violated. (EJ: 272)

The extermination of the Jews, as Arendt puts it, 'was a crime against humanity, perpetrated upon the body of the Jewish people', and the nature of the crime could not be understood, nor justice brought to bear on its perpetrators, by interpreting it exclusively as an act of extreme anti-Semitism. 'Insofar as the victims were Jews, it was right and proper that a Jewish court should sit in judgement; but insofar as the crime was a crime against humanity, it needed an international tribunal to do justice to it' (EJ: 269). Although international courts have, since the Nuremberg trials, been convened as *ad hoc* responses to genocidal atrocities, it would be another forty years, with the formation of the International Criminal Court in The Hague, before such a tribunal was permanently established.

RADICAL EVIL

Arendt's suggestion that the Holocaust was a crime of a different kind, and not just of a different magnitude, to the anti-Jewish pogroms of the past, invites us to return to the concept of 'evil' as it was addressed in *The Origins of Totalitarianism* and *The Human*

Condition. There Arendt had written of an absolute form of evil which 'can no longer be deduced from humanly comprehensible motives', and which cannot be revenged, endured, punished or forgiven (OT: ix, 459; HC: 241). By defining this evil as 'absolute' and 'radical', Arendt implied a violation of moral norms which was so extreme, and so devoid of comprehensible intent, that it placed the criminal outside the legal community which seeks to understand the crime, to calibrate its seriousness and to arrive at a just and proportionate punishment of the offender. By rendering impotent our moral vocabulary and legal norms – by forcing us to call 'criminal' what 'no such category was ever intended to cover' (OT: 441) – this crime, Arendt implied, cannot be expiated, defying the community's efforts to repair itself by passing final judgement. Hence the damage it inflicts on the body politic is permanent and irrevocable.

In *Eichmann in Jerusalem*, on the other hand, evil now seems to have a human face: its 'banality' means it can be held in contempt, scorned, perhaps even laughed at. Eichmann was a small-minded careerist and conformist rule-follower who was so confident that his professional conduct was blemish-free that, in his trial, he was more perturbed by the allegation (which was rejected by the court) that he had beaten a Jewish boy to death, than he had ever been by the charge of assisting in the slaughter of millions. Eichmann was clearly not an indoctrinated anti-Semite, and was 'normal' enough to feel repulsed by what he had seen in the killing centres of the East. When his principal excuse – that he was a meticulous rule-follower – was challenged by the prosecution, who presented him with the evidence that in September 1941 he had *defied* orders and sent a shipment of Rhineland Jews and Gypsies not to Russia, where they would have been swiftly shot by the *Einsatzgruppen*, but to the Lódz ghetto where extermination plans were not yet in place, Eichmann forswore a fortuitous opportunity to demonstrate a limited concern for the welfare of his victims. Instead he insisted that he had not disobeyed his superiors and in fact was given a choice (EJ: 94–5). Proving his obedience to his superiors, in other words, was more important to him than demonstrating the flickering of a moral conscience. Virtue, for Eichmann, was following the orders of the Führer.[1]

This, then, is the conventional reading of Arendt's changing understanding of culpability and justice in the crimes of totalitarianism. But is it the correct one? This may seem a spurious question to ask, given that Arendt herself, in a famous exchange with the Jewish philosopher Gershom Scholem, agreed that, terminologically at least, 'I changed my mind and do no longer speak of "radical evil"' (Arendt and Scholem 1964: 56). But it can be argued, first by looking again at how Arendt understood the crimes of the Nazis in her writings of the 1940s and 1950s, and then by exploring in more depth the later concept of the banality of evil, that Arendt's 'change of mind' is not as striking as it first appears.

CONTINUITIES IN THE CONCEPT OF EVIL

The common assumption, particularly in the light of the angry accusations by Jewish commentators that Arendt had trivialised the culpability of Eichmann in her coverage of his trial, has always been that Arendt previously saw the senior members of the SS as demonic monsters driven by a primitive and irrational passion to do harm. Thus when Arendt speaks of evil in *The Origins of Totalitarianism* she actually indicates that Kant's conception of 'radical evil', which he presents in *Religion Within the Limits of Reason Alone*, is inadequate for the unprecedented horrors of totalitarianism (OT: 459). Evil, for Kant, is not willed for its own sake, but is the temptation to exempt oneself from a law which one expects others to legitimately follow (even murderers, for example, want moral standards and laws to keep themselves safe from harm). This view that radical evil presupposes what it rejects is an insight that Western philosophy, religion and literature, by portraying the evildoer as a 'fallen angel', moved by envy or hatred of the good, and haunted, sometimes nobly so, by a disquiet or despair that always points a way towards redemption, has almost universally promoted.[2]

Arendt, however, was clearly not satisfied with the idea that evil is always the corruption of a prior and more fundamental acquaintance with virtue. But when we recall the arguments of *The Origins of Totalitarianism*, and scrutinise the lecture notes, essays and letters written by Arendt between 1945 and 1954, we can also see that neither was she happy with the idea that Nazi war criminals were incorrigible sadists intent on 'evil for evil's sake'. Two months after commenting, in a letter to Jaspers written in August 1946, on how the 'monstrousness' of the Nazi crimes resided in the way they shattered the legal conception of criminal guilt (which is, she adds, precisely 'why the Nazis in Nuremberg are so smug'), Arendt received a reply from her mentor warning her against mythologising this evil. Jaspers recommended that she avoid ascribing to the Nazis a streak of demonic greatness, and proposed instead that she 'see those things in their total banality, in their prosaic triviality, because that's what truly characterises them'. In her response Arendt wrote that she found Jaspers' advice 'half convincing', recognising she had 'come dangerously close to that "satanic greatness" that I, like you, totally reject'. But while stressing the need 'to combat all impulses to mythologise the horrible', Arendt suggested that what constituted the unprecedented evil of the Holocaust was not wicked motives but rather a system which aimed to make all human motives obsolete: 'an organised attempt ... to eradicate the concept of the human being' (Arendt and Jaspers 1992: 54, 62, 69).

Equipped with Jasper's insight into the 'total banality' of the Nazis' motivations,[3] Arendt then characterised the essence of totalitarian domination, in *The Origins of Totalitarianism*, as the rendering of humans superfluous in the face of the movement of history or nature, reducing them all to the 'executioners or victims of its inherent law' (OT: 468). In an essay published a year before her book, she emphasised the 'completely normal' character of the SS guards who policed the camps (EU: 238–9), and around the same period she reflected on how it was not the *content* of the particular ideology of the totalitarian regime which mobilised the executioners of its crimes – witness 'the disconcerting ease with which so many changed from a red shirt into a brown, and if that did not work out, into a red shirt again' – but rather the irresistible appeal of abstract reasoning which promised logical consistency without the need to consult reality or experience (EU: 355–8; OT: 473). Totalitarianism thus aimed at 'the abolition of convictions as a too unreliable support for the system; and the demonstration that this system, in distinction from all others, has made man, insofar as he is a being of spontaneous thought and action, superfluous' (EU: 354; OT: 468).

The 'radical evil' referred to in *The Origins of Totalitarianism* thus 'emerged in connection with a system in which all men have become equally superfluous' (OT: 459). What this implies is a troubling continuity between the extreme evil perpetrated on the victims of the Holocaust, who were morally and juridically destroyed – transformed into 'living corpses' – before they were murdered, and the 'banal evil' of those who perpetrated genocide by means of their own transformation into the disposable instruments of totalitarianism. In her 1945 essay, 'Organised Guilt and Universal Responsibility', Arendt had already written of 'that vast machine of administrative mass murder, in whose service not only thousands of persons, not even scores of thousands of selected murderers, but a whole people could be and was employed'. In the same essay she recounts the report of an American eyewitness at the liberated Maidanek death camp in Poland. When the camp paymaster confirmed to the correspondent the atrocities that had been perpetrated there, the journalist informed him that the Russians would probably hang him. Bursting into tears, the officer's reply demonstrated the sharpness of Jaspers' insight into the 'total banality' of the Nazi functionary: 'Why should they? *What have I done?*' (EU: 126–7).

Asking what caused people to behave 'as cogs in the mass-murder machine', Arendt suggests it was Himmler, the most 'normal' of all the Nazi leaders, who understood that effective organisation 'relies not on fanatics, nor on congenital murderers, nor on sadists; it relies entirely upon the normality of jobholders and family men'. It was, Arendt continues, not the pathological bigot but rather the ordinary bourgeois family man who became 'the great criminal of the century' (EU: 128–9). More precisely, it was the *breakdown* of the bourgeoisie as a social class, and the abandonment of those publicly paraded virtues 'which it not only did not possess in private and business life, but actually held in contempt' (OT: 334), which set loose its philistine instincts and in doing so provided ample justification for a growing nihilistic disgust among wider society of the moral hypocrisy and the sham civic virtues of the respectable classes. 'The mass man whom Himmler organised for the greatest mass crimes ever committed in history bore the features of the philistine rather than of the mob man, and was the bourgeois who in the midst of the ruins of his world worried about nothing so much as his private security, was ready to sacrifice everything – belief, honour, dignity – on the slightest provocation' (OT: 338).

Dedicated to the economic security of his wife and children, to his pension and his life insurance, this 'new type of functionary' was all too willing to sacrifice whatever interest he had previously held in the realm of public affairs and the exercise of civic virtues, in order to safeguard his private existence. The exact opposite of the Greek citizen, his commitment to the public sphere was purely opportunistic and instrumental. 'When his occupation forces him to murder people he does not regard himself as a murderer because he has not done it out of inclination but in his professional capacity. Out of sheer passion he would never do harm to a fly' (EU: 130).

THE 'SOCIAL SYSTEM'?

So the concept of evil, as it was employed by Arendt in the 1940s and 1950s, does not support a picture of Nazi war criminals as zealous anti-Semites and sadistic murderers who, taking pleasure in causing and contemplating the suffering of others, want evil for evil's sake. Despite abundant references to the role of ideology, Arendt is continually grappling during this period with the possibility that the specifics of political dogma and prejudice are less essential to the existence of totalitarianism than a system of thought and organisation that functions independently of people's direct psychological impulses and ideological convictions. Though the Nazis 'acted consistently with a racist or anti-semitic, or at any rate a demographic ideology,' she later wrote, 'the murderers and their direct accomplices more often than not did not believe in these ideological justifications' (RJ: 43). Looking back from the vantage point of her study of Eichmann, Arendt wrote to her friend Mary McCarthy in September 1963:

If one reads the book carefully, one sees that Eichmann was much less influenced by ideology than I assumed in the book on totalitarianism. The impact of ideology upon the individual may have been overrated by me. Even in the totalitarian book, in the chapter on ideology and terror, I mentioned the curious loss of ideological content that occurs among the elite of the movement. The movement itself becomes all important, the content of anti-semitism for instance gets lost in the extermination policy, for extermination would not have come to an end when no Jew was left to be killed. (Arendt and McCarthy 1995: 147–8)

Arendt's questioning of the role of ideological beliefs and prejudices in the administration of domination is not devoid of sociological pedigree, and it is tempting to draw parallels between Arendt's analysis of the quasi-natural forces set loose by bureaucratic, and later totalitarian, organisations, and both functionalist and Marxist perspectives in sociology. It was the founder of Europe's first university department of sociology, Émile Durkheim, who believed the sociologist should ignore 'questions of intention' because they are 'too subjective to be dealt with scientifically' (1982: 123), and who eventually conceded that societies could reproduce themselves not only through the transmission of shared values and beliefs, but also by means of purely functional interdependencies (1964: 4, 399).

Durkheim's well-known concern over the neglect of morality in both utilitarian individualism and Marx's materialism was therefore balanced by an awareness that Auguste Comte had equally exaggerated the role of moral consensus in maintaining social stability (Gouldner 1962). Implicit in Durkheim, as Habermas (1987b: 113–8) has argued, was an awareness that modernity involved a process of structural differentiation, a process better grasped by Herbert Spencer, Durkheim's primary foil. Spencer understood that the market economy was a mechanism that co-ordinated human interactions by releasing individual behaviour from the grip of collective belief systems and inserting it into functional networks, the latter winning the compliance of actors by appealing not to their value-commitment to common goals, but to their desire to protect their rationally calculated self-interest. Both market forces and stratified forms of power – the 'forced division of labour' in Durkheim's account – can generate relatively stable social relationships which bypass the need for strong shared convictions. Though du Gay (2000), as noted in the previous chapter, offers a contrary interpretation, something similar can be read into Max Weber's account of the growth of rational bureaucracy, a structure which 'develops the more perfectly, the more it is "dehumanised", the more completely it succeeds in eliminating from official business love, hatred, and all purely personal, irrational, and emotional elements which escape calculation' (Weber 1978: 975). As the British sociologist David Lockwood later complained of Parsons' 'normative functionalism', sociology must now distinguish 'system integration' from 'social integration' (Lockwood 1956; 1964). Or as Habermas put it, reflecting on the unresolved tension in Durkheim's work: 'This distinction between a social integration of society, which takes effect in action orientations, and a systemic integration, which reaches through and beyond action orientations, calls for a corresponding differentiation in the concept of society itself' (1987b: 117).

Arendt's description of the superfluity of individuals in the face of their functional organisation, and her later concept of the 'social', thus run parallel to both mainstream and critical sociological traditions. A certain kinship might also be identified between Arendt's approach and the materialist critique of the 'dominant ideology thesis' by British sociologists Nicholas Abercombie, Stephen Hill and Bryan Turner. Drawing on Durkheim, Weber and Marx, Abercrombie and his colleagues challenged the belief, common among leftist intellectuals who trade in ideas, that ideology is the primary vehicle for the reproduction of modern class society, focusing instead on the persuasive force of state violence and the 'dull compulsion of the economic' (Abercrombie, Hill and Turner 1980; Marx 1976: 896–9). Perhaps more pertinently, Arendt's work has had a significant influence on Zygmunt Bauman, whose acclaimed sociological study of the Holocaust emphasised how the technical and organisational separation of the consequences of people's actions from their personal beliefs, emotions and intentions has brought with it an unparalleled capacity for economic production which can be readily converted to the most monstrous of deeds: 'the setting which in modern society renders mass or regular killing possible is indistinguishable from that which makes mass production and unstoppable technological rationalisation possible' (Bauman 2000a: 237).

But despite these interesting similarities, Arendt's early thoughts on the nature of human wickedness, and its relationship to the conditions of totalitarian domination, were not informed by the work of sociologists, and it is questionable whether the parallels really do justice to the originality of her thinking. She was of course familiar with the German classics – not just Marx and Weber,[4] but also Simmel, whose essay on 'secret societies' she drew on to explicate the totalitarianism movement (OT: 376ff) – and she maintained friendships and correspondence with a number of figures in the discipline, including Raymond Aron, Daniel Bell and David Riesman.[5] But still Arendt had a generally low opinion of the post-war sociological mindset, the chief defect of which she believed was a congenital blindness towards the unique and the unprecedented – whether this was the unpredictable novelty of human action, or the radically new regime, which in the case of Nazism seemed to mark a decisive break with the whole philosophical and political tradition of the West, that was totalitarianism. The banal generalisations of the positivist sociologist had too much in common, from Arendt's viewpoint, with the banality of thought characteristic of the bureaucrat. Both served to normalise the unprecedented and the unacceptable, while their fetishising of disinterestedness – both the bureaucrat and the scientist were loyal to the principle of *sine ira ac studio* – ignored the 'methodological necessity' of bearing testimony to the appalling nature of dehumanising conditions, no matter how routinised or familiar. Whether this is the condition of poverty in the midst of plenty, or the sheer hell of the concentration camp, the task, according to Arendt, should be to describe such phenomena 'as occurring, not on the moon, but in the midst of human society'.

> The natural human reaction to such conditions is one of anger and indignation because these conditions are against the dignity of man. If I describe these conditions without permitting my

indignation to interfere, I have lifted this particular phenomenon out of its context in human society and have thereby robbed it of part of its nature, deprived it of one of its important inherent qualities. For to arouse indignation is one of the qualities of excessive poverty insofar as poverty occurs among human beings ... To describe the concentration camps *sine ira* is not to be 'objective', but to condone them; and such condoning cannot be changed by a condemnation which the author may feel duty bound to add but which remains unrelated to the description itself. When I used the image of Hell, I did not mean this allegorically but literally. (EU: 403–4)

Habitualised to thinking in terms of established concepts and functional classifications, the social scientist is taught to regard factual singularities as merely 'phenomenal variations' of unvarying structural essences or 'ideal types'. 'This kind of confusion – where everything distinct disappears and everything that is new and shocking is (not explained but) explained away either through drawing some analogies or reducing it to a previously known chain of causes and influences – seems to me to be the hallmark of the modern historical and political sciences' (EU: 407). The lack of imagination Arendt detected in this analogical mindset was particularly telling in the analysis of the gulag and the death camp, which so gravely insulted established categories of thought that Bruno Bettelheim's study of human behaviour, based on his internment in Dachau and Buchenwald before the outbreak of the Second World War, was repeatedly rejected by disbelieving journal editors who complained about lack of documentary evidence and the non-replicable nature of its findings (Bettelheim 1979: 15–6). A similar fate befell Alexander Werth's report from the liberated Maidanek death camp, which the BBC refused to use, believing it was a piece of Russian propaganda (Werth 2000: 890).

Peter Baehr has helpfully documented the contrasting fortunes of some of those sociologists who chose, in contrast to Bettelheim and Werth, a more conventional academic tack (2010: 10–34). The *American Journal of Sociology* did indeed publish articles on the Nazi concentration camps which displayed the kind of mechanical thinking that Arendt was so dismissive of. Herbert A. Bloch, for example, suggested that the camps were worthy of disinterested analysis because, by depriving prisoners of 'the usual social framework', they revealed the primal nature of humans' ability to relate to one another – the 'untrammelled socius' – and in doing so

provided 'a heuristic prototype for comparative study with institutionalised and more normal patterns of groupings' (Bloch 1947:
335). H. G. Adler also underplayed the unprecedented horror of
totalitarianism by claiming that, despite their most original and
appalling features, 'the concentration camps [can] still be categorised
under the system of slavery' (Adler 1958: 515). Hans Gerth (1940)
had argued, in the same journal, that the National Socialist Party in
Germany could best be understood using a fusion of Weber's concepts
of charismatic and bureaucratic domination – an interpretation
explicitly rejected by Arendt because it failed to grasp how the
totalitarian leader was no less a functionary than his subordinates,
and how the spirit that animated the totalitarian movement was one
of restless motion rather than bureaucratic rigidity (OT: 361–2, n57;
Baehr 2010: 24–6). Weber's methodological device of the 'ideal type'
was invented to delineate the essential features of unique historical
phenomena – not, as Talcott Parsons seemed to think when he
agreed with Gerth's account of the 'charismatic elements' prominent
among the Nazi leadership, to produce a filing cabinet capable
of accommodating every unfamiliar action, organisation or event
(Parsons 1942: 163). Even Erving Goffman, a sociologist hardly
sympathetic to the functionalist mindset, was happy to classify
civic organisations as diverse as monasteries, boarding schools,
poor houses and mental hospitals under the common category of
'total institutions', and to casually lump concentration camps into a
subgroup that included jails and penitentiaries (Goffman 1961: 16).

THE BANALITY OF EVIL

The functionalist paradigm that she believed was representative
of the social sciences therefore had little appeal to Arendt, and the
concept of the 'social system' was of no obvious use to her. Arendt
wanted to retain an intellectual grasp of the dynamic interplay
of freedom and determinism, action and process, the initiation of
something new and the force of necessity. In Habermas's critical
view, in fact, Arendt was so resistant to 'leaving her action-theoretic
framework in order to inject a functionalist analysis into it' that she
'would not draw any distinction even between Hegel and Parsons;
both investigate historical and social processes that pass over
the heads of those involved' (Habermas 1994: 222). Yet Arendt
remained determined to shed light on the peculiar way that humans,
tempted by the promise that 'anything is possible', appeared so
willing to exchange their freedom for the absolute omnipotence of

inhuman forces. This, for Arendt, was a test of her own powers of political judgement, which in her definition must refuse to subsume the distinctive features of a historical event under pre-existing classifications, trends or laws.

Arendt's response to this challenge gained momentum with her coverage of the Eichmann trial. What she witnessed in Jerusalem, Arendt later admitted, forced her to re-evaluate the importance of the interior domain of the thinker. This unworldly realm had assumed such exaggerated significance in Western philosophy, Arendt had previously complained, that the shadow it cast 'blurred the distinctions and articulations within the *vita activa* itself' (HC: 17; LM1: 7). It was the lofty and undiscriminating outlook on the *vita activa* of the classical Athenian philosophers – for whom 'even political activity was levelled to the rank of necessity, which henceforth became the common denominator of all articulations within the *vita activa*' (HC: 85) – that had encouraged Arendt to ignore the charms of the *vita contemplativa*. What she saw in Eichmann, however, compelled her to revisit the importance of the life of the mind:

> Some years ago, reporting the trial of Eichmann in Jerusalem, I spoke of 'the banality of evil' and meant with this no theory or doctrine but something quite factual, the phenomenon of evil deeds, committed on a gigantic scale, which could not be traced to any particularity of wickedness, pathology, or ideological conviction in the doer, whose only personal distinction was a perhaps extraordinary shallowness. However monstrous the deeds were, the doer was neither monstrous nor demonic, and the only specific characteristic one could detect in his past as well as in his behaviour during the trial and the preceding police examination was something entirely negative: it was not stupidity but a curious, quite authentic inability to think. (RJ: 159)

Arendt recognised that there were men among the elite formations of the Nazi movement who were guilty of terrible personal atrocities, particularly in the early period of the camps when the SA were the commanding authority and a regulated death rate had not yet been introduced (EU: 238). The 1963 Frankfurt trial of Auschwitz officers, for example, revealed to Arendt a kind of 'naked criminal guilt' which she had not seen in the Jerusalem trial. The random killings, arbitrary torture and rape, suggested a darker and more menacing wickedness than can be captured by the concept of 'banality'. At the same time, however, Arendt saw in the 'sheer moodiness' of these camp guards further testimony to the insubstantial nature of this phenomenon.

> What changes more often and swifter than moods, and what is left of the humanity of a man who has completely yielded up to them? ... [T]hose who lived up to the Nazi ideal of 'toughness', and are still proud of it ... were in fact like jelly. It was as though their ever-changing moods had eaten up all substance – the firm surface of personal identity, of being either good or bad, tender or brutal, an 'idealistic' idiot or a cynical sex pervert. The same man who rightly received one of the most severe sentences – life plus eight years – could on occasion distribute sausages to children; Bednarek, after performing his speciality of trampling prisoners to death, went into his room and prayed, for he was then in the right mood; the same medical officer who handed tens of thousands over to death could also save a woman who had studied at his old alma mater and therefore reminded him of his youth; flowers and chocolates might be sent to a mother who had given birth, although she was to be gassed the next morning...
>
> It is certainly true that there was 'almost no SS man who could not claim to have saved someone's life' if he was in the right mood for it; and most of the survivors – about 1 percent of the selected labour force – owed their lives to these 'saviours'. (RJ: 253–5)

Here we see what Arendt meant when she rejected the notion of 'radical' evil, describing evil instead as 'a surface phenomenon' that we resist 'by not being swept away by the surface of things, by stopping ourselves and beginning to think' (JW: 479).

> It is indeed my opinion now that evil is never 'radical', that it is only extreme, and that it possesses neither depth nor any demonic dimension. It can overgrow and lay waste the entire world precisely because it spreads like a fungus on the surface. It is 'thought-defying', as I said, because thought tries to reach some depth, to go to the roots, and the moment it concerns itself with evil, it is frustrated because there is nothing. That is its 'banality'. Only the good has depth and can be radical. (Arendt and Scholem 1964: 56)

CO-OPERATION AND COMPLICITY

Arendt's explanation of the banality of evil as a kind of thoughtless adaptation to a bureaucratised society might easily lend itself to a picture of diminished responsibility and, as her harshest critics claimed, a trivialising of the crimes of the Third Reich. If we follow Arendt's argument with consistency, Beatty argues, 'Eichmann cannot be considered morally or legally responsible since he was unable to think and, hence, his moral judgement was blinded' (1994: 70). Yet Arendt was determined to challenge the idea, which had been close to her own previous outlook, that because of the magnitude of destruction involved, and because of the dispersal of responsibility by a social system that implicated every sector of the German population in thoughtless complicity, the Holocaust had made moral and legal judgement impossible. Thus she came to praise the 'undeniable greatness of the judiciary' for its implacable focus on the responsibility of the individual, and for creating a temporary public space whose participants can be addressed, and must account for themselves, through the mask of a juridical persona. For although bureaucracy, 'the rule of nobody', displaces responsibility as 'a matter of daily routine', in the presence of the court 'these definitions are of no avail' and 'this whole cog business made no sense'. 'The speechless horror, which I mentioned before as an adequate reaction to the system as a whole, dissolves in the courtroom where we deal with persons in the ordered discourse of accusation, defence, and judgement' (RJ: 30–2, 57–8). The system of administration then becomes the mitigating context which, like the conditions of hardship influencing the crimes of the poor, cannot take the place of the individual who stands trial. To think otherwise would be equivalent to allowing a criminal to cite high crime rates as proof that the crime 'was statistically expected' and 'that it was mere accident that he did it and not someone else' (EJ: 289). Hence the Eichmann trial was of moral interest precisely because it 'transformed the cog or "referent" of Section IV B4 in the Reich Security Head Office into a man' (RJ: 31–2).

In shifting our attention from the guilt of the ardent murderer to that of the passionless cog, it was perhaps inevitable that Arendt's analysis also raised difficult questions about the 'non-criminal participants' in the Nazi regime. The outcry that greeted *Eichmann in Jerusalem* focused heavily on her unsympathetic treatment of the Jewish functionaries and members of the Councils of Jewish Elders – the *Judenräte* that were set up by Eichmann and his colleagues to help manage the transportation and extermination programme in an orderly way – and her related observations on the varying levels of native opposition encountered by the Nazis in different countries under German occupation. The terrible fate of the Jews in Holland, for example, where the Dutch Jewish Council, Jewish police and the Dutch police all co-operated with the Nazis, stood in stark contrast to what happened in Denmark, where non-violent resistance from all layers of society bred doubt among the occupiers, who in turn began to question the orders received from Berlin. The subsequent failure of the German authorities in Denmark to properly execute the deportation order of 1 October 1943, revealed that they 'possessed neither the manpower nor the will power to remain "tough" when they met determined opposition' (EJ: 165).

In an often-quoted passage from *Eichmann in Jerusalem*, Arendt had carelessly described the 'role of the Jewish leaders in the destruction of their own people' as 'undoubtedly the darkest chapter of the whole dark story' (EJ: 117). The *Judenräte* were responsible for cataloguing the personal details and property of Jewish residents. It was their job to select the victims to fill the transportation quotas, to secure funds from individuals as payment to the Nazis for the cost of their 'resettlement', and, with the help of the Jewish police, to maintain law and order in the ghettos and to create a semblance of respectable governance in the midst of appalling hardship and the permanent spectre of death. Without the co-operation of the *Judenräte*, as Eichmann himself testified, the policy of extermination would have run into serious difficulties. Had they been forced to hunt down each individual Jew, the Nazis' brutality would have been on constant public display, and the indifference of the civilian population to the fate of the Jews would have been severely tested. 'Active resistance arouses admiration; watching violent subjugation of the victim evokes revulsion; while passive compliance permits most of us to put it all out of our minds fairly soon' (Bettelheim 1979: 269). A refusal of such compliance, according to Arendt, would have resulted in 'either complete chaos or an impossibly severe drain on German manpower' (EJ: 117).

Though Arendt denied using her commentary on the Eichmann trial to 'reproach the Jewish people with nonresistance' (EU: 15), it is clear from her writings that the more she thought about the issue of responsibility the more it was the everyday co-operation with the 'legal crimes' of the Nazi regime, including 'the matter-of-course collaboration from all strata of German society', and not the bestial cruelty of individual Nazis, which struck her as the real moral challenge (RJ: 53). 'The problem, the personal problem, was not what our enemies did but what our friends did', she said in an interview in 1964 (EU: 10–11; see also Arendt and Scholem 1964: 54). Arendt describes how she was raised in a time and place where personal insistence on moral virtues would have been roundly dismissed as a philistine trait, since morality, like character, was assumed to be a matter of course, such that, when morality and legality came into conflict – a conflict Arendt recognises as 'the calamity of citizenship even in the best body politic' (EU: 334) – it was the moral voice of the conscience which was naturally regarded as the higher law. After the speechless horror of the death camps themselves, what disturbed Arendt most about the events that led to the Holocaust was the 'overnight change of opinion that befell a great majority of public figures in all walks of life and all ramifications of culture, accompanied, as it was, by an incredible ease with which lifelong friendships were broken and discarded' (RJ: 24). This moral disintegration of respectable society – the refusal of educated and liberal Germans to raise their voices against measures which, as darker portents gathered pace, expelled their Jewish friends and colleagues from public life, and the speed with which coveted moral principles were abandoned by such people in order to preserve their own jobs – was for Arendt a 'dress rehearsal' for the total moral breakdown of German society.

FEAR OF JUDGING

Arendt's refusal to allow the idea of evil's 'banality' to excuse evildoers of responsibility for their acts is also apparent in her critical comments on what she believes is a widespread fear of passing moral judgement (EJ: 295–6). She gives a number of different examples of this. One is the apparent guilt experienced by young Germans on behalf of their parents' sins, an emotion that Arendt derides as 'cheap sentimentality' designed to excuse themselves from challenging the moral authority of a whole generation of Nazi sympathisers now ensconced in the German establishment (EJ: 251). Another is the argument that nobody can judge who was not there – a claim made by Gershom Scholem against Arendt's criticism of the *Judenräte* (Arendt and Scholem 1964: 52), but one that was also used in court by lawyers defending Nazi war criminals. A third aversion to the task of judging is detected by Arendt in the argument that acceptance of a lesser evil, and 'getting one's hands dirty', was justified by the accompanying opportunity to do some good, and that, for the most unfortunate victims of the totalitarian regime, the only alternative to complicity with evil was potentially deadly punishment.[6] The notion of the 'lesser evil', which, given the magnitude of the evil in question, arguably does not deserve the term 'lesser' at all, was of course part of the rational mechanism of totalitarian domination, which induced predictable and controllable behaviour in its victims by convincing them that lives could be saved by participating in murder (Bauman 2000a: 129–34). Prominent in this respect was the introduction by German bureaucrats of 'privileged categories' – German Jews over Polish Jews, for example, or German Jewish veterans of the Great War over civilian German Jews – which the *Judenräte* accepted and then used to help 'save lives', seemingly oblivious to the fact that the dividing lines between the saved and the condemned were purely contingent and revisable, but surely aware that by accepting the exceptions they were justifying the rule (EJ: 132–3).

Were the Jewish leaders, the German soldiers, the civil servants and administrators who helped organise and orchestrate the *Endlösung* 'forced' to participate in or co-operate with genocide? Arendt is unwavering on this point, insisting that, even if commanded to kill with a gun pointed at one's head, acting in obedience to this command is a legally pardonable temptation, but not an irresistible compulsion. Thus, 'while a temptation where one's life is at stake may be a legal excuse for a crime, it certainly is not a moral justification' (RJ: 18). There were, of course, many prominent Jews who refused to surrender to this temptation. Some examples are given by Bauman:

> Before committing suicide, the *Präses* of the Równe *Judenräte*, Dr. Bergman, told the Germans that he could deliver for 'resettlement' only himself and his family. Motel Chajkin of Kosów Poleski scornfully rejected the *Stadtkommissar's* offer to save him. David Liberman of Luków threw in the face of the German supervisor money collected for an unsuccessful bribe – which he had first torn into shreds, shouting 'Here is your payment for our trip, you bloody tyrant!' He was shot on the spot. Faced with the Nazi demand to select a contingent of Jews for the 'work in Russia', the entire Jewish Council of Bereza Kartuska committed suicide at the meeting of 1 September 1942. (Bauman 2000a: 141)

In *Eichmann in Jerusalem* Arendt refers to the memoir of a German army physician who witnessed the use of the gas vans on the Russian front. Explaining his and others' failure to challenge what obviously repulsed them, the doctor wrote of the way totalitarianism, by letting 'its opponents disappear in silent anonymity', destroyed the opportunity to die a heroic death in defence of one's moral beliefs, and in the process invalidated all possibility of meaningful defiance. As Arendt's cites from his book: 'None of us had a conviction so deeply rooted that we could have taken upon ourselves a practically useless sacrifice for the sake of a higher moral meaning' (EJ: 232).

Arendt responds to this argument, which rests on the apparent separation of functionally useful actions from those with purely symbolic value, by recalling the scene in the Jerusalem court when the story was told of a German sergeant, Anton Schmidt, who had helped a group of Jewish partisans while on patrol in Poland, supplying them, over a period of several months, with forged papers and military trucks. As the tale of the soldier's bravery, and his subsequent execution, was recounted at Eichmann's trial, a stillness descended on the courtroom 'as though the crowd had spontaneously decided to observe the usual two minutes of silence in honour of the man named Anton Schmidt', and the sense prevailed of 'a sudden burst of light in the midst of impenetrable, unfathomable darkness'. For Arendt, what the telling of the story proved – as with the stories re-told by Bauman – is that the totalitarian 'holes of oblivion' into which, as she had described in *The Origins of Totalitarianism*, all possibility of human action was designed to disappear, do not in fact exist.

> Nothing human is that perfect, and there are simply too many people in the world to make oblivion possible. One man will always be left alive to tell the story. Hence, nothing can ever be 'practically useless', at least, not in the long run ... For the lesson of such stories is simple and within everybody's grasp. Politically speaking, it is that under conditions of terror most people will comply but *some people will not*, just as the lesson of the countries to which the Final Solution was proposed is that 'it could happen' in most places but *it did not happen everywhere*. Humanly speaking, no more is required, and no more can reasonably be asked, for this planet to remain a place fit for human habitation. (EJ: 232–3)

ARENDT AND BAUMAN

The sociology of Zygmunt Bauman has been mentioned frequently in this book, and readers of Bauman will know that he makes generous reference to Arendt in his own work. One source of their intellectual affinity is their shared distrust of sociogenic theories of morality, with Durkheim being Bauman's principal opponent. Durkheim viewed human nature as *homo duplex*, divided between the potentially insatiable and anti-social appetites of the body on the one hand, and the internalised moral rules of society on the other. 'It is from society and not from the individual that morality derives', Durkheim had written in 1906, defining morality as 'a collection of maxims, of rules of conduct', distinguishable from others by the sense of 'duty' we feel to abide by them and the 'charm' or 'pleasure' that accompanies their fulfilment (Durkheim 1974). Claiming as self-evident the observation that moral agents cannot have themselves as their objects of concern, Durkheim had deduced from this that neither could *other individuals* be the intended beneficiary of our moral action. If others, being equal to ourselves, were to enjoy this privilege, this could only be the indirect result of our mutual respect for common values. Hence it is the sacredness of the collective which leads us, unwittingly, to care for the individual:

> When one loves one's country or humanity one cannot see one's fellows suffer without suffering oneself and without feeling a desire to help them. But what binds us morally to others is nothing intrinsic in their empirical individuality; it is the superior end of which they are the servants and instruments. (Durkheim 1974: 53)

Immorality, for Durkheim, was therefore the consequence of a deficit in social rules, a failure of socialising forces to contain the ego-centric drives of the pre-social organism. Yet what the collapse of 'respectable society' in Germany had revealed to Arendt was that the people who expressed the greatest reverence for established moral norms were the most unreliable. It was they, not the moral sceptics, who were the first to yield to the Nazis, and they did so not because they lacked traditional standards of right and wrong but because they were so eager to conform to social rules that when the rules changed they were more than content to replace the old system of values with a new one. Morality was therefore revealed as nothing more than a set of customs, usages and habits 'which could be exchanged for another set with no more trouble than it would take to change the table manners of a whole people' (RJ: 43). Indeed, this collapse of the moral order occurred not once, but twice, as the 'old' moral rules were immediately restored, and 'normality' resumed, following Germany's defeat.

Bauman's critique of Durkheim draws on Arendt's insights, noting that society may itself act as a 'morality-silencing' force, procuring obedience to immoral rules, and quashing authentic moral sentiments that are, in Bauman's opinion, 'rooted in existential factors unaffected by contingent rules of cohabitation' (2000a: 174). Thus Bauman refers to Nechama Tec's *When Light Pierced the Darkness* (1986), a study of Nazi-occupied Poland which set out to identify the social factors that explained the altruism of those Christian Poles who helped their Jewish compatriots, but which found such a diversity of social, cultural and political backgrounds (including anti-Semitism), that the very notion of a socially produced morality had to be rejected. Tec's study showed, in Bauman's view, that the 'ability to tell right from wrong' is intrinsic to the human person, although every society attempts to shape, suppress or manipulate this ability in different ways. Bauman's argument is that 'the Holocaust was as much a product, as it was a failure, of modern civilisation', because 'the civilisation process has succeeded in substituting artificial and flexible patterns of human conduct for natural drives, and hence made possible a scale of inhumanity and destruction which had remained inconceivable as long as natural predispositions guided human action' (2000a: 88–9, 95).

According to Bauman, humans' natural moral faculty is revealed in its naked purity through the condition of 'being with others', the existential analysis of which he develops by drawing on the philosophy of Emmanuel Levinas. From Levinas Bauman takes the idea that the primary mode of being in the proximity of the other is the mode of 'responsibility', a selfless care for the other's well-being which is an innate impulse rather than a rational insight or orientation to a social rule. Bauman describes this primordial response as an unconditional and disinterested attentiveness, a pre-social 'being *for* the Other before one can be *with* the Other'. Proximity is therefore not only 'the birthplace of the moral self', but is constitutive of the most fundamental structure of subjectivity. It is 'the first reality of the self, a starting point rather than a product of society' (Bauman 2000a: 182–3; 1993: 13, 89).

[M]orality is endemically and irredeemably *non-rational* – in the sense of not being calculable, hence not being presentable as following impersonal rules, hence not being describable as following rules that are in principle universalisable. The moral

call is thoroughly personal; it appeals to my responsibility ...
As a moral person, I am alone, though as a social person I am
always *with* others ... 'Being *with* others' can be regulated by
codifiable rules. 'Being *for* the Other' conspicuously cannot. In
Durkheim's terms, though in defiance of Durkheim's intuitions,
we could say that morality is the condition of perpetual and
irreparable *anomie*. Being moral means being abandoned to my
own freedom. (Bauman 1993: 60)

Bauman's account of morality and modernity, which explores the
way technological and administrative systems suppress the moral
impulse by introducing mediation and distance into our relationship
to others, bears some resemblance to Arendt's thinking. Though
she repeatedly stresses the 'unpolitical' nature of moral virtues
like compassion and goodness, on a number of occasions Arendt
cites Rousseau's belief that humans possess an 'innate repugnance
to see others suffer' (RJ: 81; MD: 12; EJ: 93, 106; OR: 79–81).
Bauman refers directly to Arendt in this context, noting how 'the
well-nigh instinctual human aversion to the affliction of physical
suffering' constituted a serious obstacle to the prosecution of the
Final Solution (Bauman 2000a: 20). Thus while Bauman explains
the Nazi death factories as the final logical step in the depersonali-
sation of murder, Arendt notes how the Nazis, unable to suppress
this empathic instinct altogether, instead directed it inward, towards
a sentimental concern for those who carried the burden of killing.

> The trick used by Himmler – who apparently was rather strongly
> afflicted with these instinctive reactions himself – was very
> simple and probably very effective; it consisted in turning these
> instincts around, as it were, in directing them toward the self.
> So that instead of saying: What horrible things I did to people!,
> the murderers would be able to say: What horrible things I had
> to watch in the pursuance of my duties, how heavily the task
> weighed upon my shoulders! (EJ: 106)

Something similar appears to occur in run-of-the-mill
bureaucracies, which function with predetermined categories,
codified types and formal divisions into which people must
be pressed if they are to be recognised and processed by the
administrative system. What is dehumanising for the human client
of the bureaucracy – namely, the insensitivity of the organisation
to the specific qualities and needs of the person – is rationalised by

the functionary of the bureaucracy as the 'nuisance factor', that is, the awkward and unpredictable subjectivity of the person which the organisation must overcome, no matter how persuasive or determined the protests. The functionaries are then morally united by mutual sympathy for the difficulty of their jobs and loyalty to the enterprise at hand. 'It is not the objects of bureaucratic action, but its subjects who suffer and deserve compassion and moral praise' (Bauman 2000a: 104; see also Bauman 1993: 9–10). Responsibility *for* is thus converted into responsibility *to*. This may be responsibility to oneself – an attitude which Bauman believes is more typical of the self-obsessed consumer (2008: 107–8). Or it may be responsibility to the organisation which exploits the individual's sense of duty. In May's sociological reading, Arendt's writings on bureaucracy illustrate what Habermas meant by the 'colonisation of the lifeworld', as organisations trade the functional disposability of their employees for the promise of a new moral community, and in doing so '"socialise" their members to be more loyal to the institution than to city, nation, or humanity' (May 1996: 84).

In her essay on Lessing, 'On Humanity in Dark Times', which was originally delivered as a public address in German in 1959, Arendt reiterated her belief that 'compassion is unquestionably a natural, creature affect which involuntarily touches every normal person at the sight of suffering' (MD: 14). Yet Arendt also makes clear, both in this essay and in *On Revolution*, that the humanitarian ethic of compassion is of limited moral, and certainly of no political, significance. Compassion, like fear, is a 'passive' emotion which 'makes action impossible'. And even if compassion could indeed move us to act for the good of others, such action would be tainted by the force of nature: 'should human beings be so shabby', she asks, 'that they are incapable of acting humanly unless spurred and as it were compelled by their own pain when they see others suffer?' (MD: 15) The worldless quality of compassion which, thanks to Rousseau's political philosophy, misled the leaders of the French Revolution into believing it could produce a natural bond between men capable of sustaining national unity, is described by Arendt in *On Revolution*:

> Because compassion abolishes the distance, the worldly space between men where political matters, the whole realm of human affairs, are located, it remains, politically speaking, irrelevant and without consequence. In the words of Melville, it is incapable of establishing 'lasting institutions'. Jesus's silence in 'The Grand

Inquisitor' and Billy Budd's stammer indicate the same, namely their incapacity (or unwillingness) for all kinds of predicative or argumentative speech, in which someone talks *to* somebody *about* something that is of interest to both because it *inter-est*, it is between them. Such talkative and argumentative interest in the world is entirely alien to compassion, which is directed solely, and with passionate intensity, towards suffering man himself. (OR: 86)

Though Arendt acknowledges that sympathy for the other 'makes insult and injury endurable', her analysis does not really support Bauman's argument that care for the other is the foundation of the moral agent, and that society arises from, rather than produces, the moral impulse ('we live in society, we *are* society, thanks to being moral' [Bauman 1993: 61]). For while Bauman shifts the object of moral consciousness away from the abstraction 'society', as it was for Durkheim, towards the concrete 'other', Arendt actually goes a step further, questioning the philosophical orthodoxy that equates morality with selflessness. As Himmler had demonstrated, a moral conscience founded on self-denial can be turned to all manner of atrocities – it was with the assistance of a peculiar notion of selflessness, after all, that the Nazis were able to bear the burden of their duty to murder. Instead Arendt searches for the roots of moral awareness by looking inward, towards 'the intercourse of man with himself'. 'In the centre of moral considerations of human conduct stands the self', Arendt writes, while 'in the centre of political considerations of conduct stands the world' (RJ: 153). We shall examine what this means in the next chapter.

9
The *Vita Contemplativa*

Arendt's claim that morality is ultimately founded not on one's relationship to the other, but on a relationship with oneself, clearly has a Kantian flavour to it. For evil, in Kant's account, was to be in contradiction with oneself, to want to be protected by a general rule while simultaneously exempting oneself from its regulatory force. Moral behaviour, it follows, 'certainly is not a matter of concern with the other but with the self, not of meekness but of human dignity and even human pride. The standard is neither the love of some neighbour nor self-love, but self-respect' (RJ: 67).

But the real champion of the moral conscience, in Arendt's view, is not Kant but Socrates. That Arendt reaches back to antiquity here is somewhat surprising, as it is well established that Greek society was a 'shame culture' rather than a 'guilt culture', where the primary consideration was not the quality of one's own judgement or intentions, but rather the appraisal and opinion of others (Gouldner 1967: 81–90). That she chooses Socrates as her model is also unexpected, for although Plato seemed to attribute to Socrates a belief that sensitivity to moral truths is a matter of the kind of 'soul' one possessed, Socrates did not evidently think that there were transcendent standards of right and wrong, and he certainly did not see himself as in the possession of great knowledge or insight.

In the *Gorgias*, as in all Plato's Socratic dialogues, the conversations revolve around the nature of the ethical life, and why one should act justly rather than unjustly. Although the dialogue is always aporetic, leading to no absolute certainties or agreements, Arendt claims that in this text Socrates does appear to arrive at one definitive moral insight. Declaring that 'the man who does wrong is more miserable than the man who is wronged', he asserts: 'I would rather suffer wrong than do wrong' (479e, 469b). The clue to the meaning of this statement, according to Arendt (LM1: 181), is contained in Socrates' later reply to Callicles: 'it would be better for me to have a lyre or a chorus which I was directing in discord and out of tune, better that the mass of mankind should disagree with me and contradict me, than that I, a single individual, should be out of harmony with myself and contradict myself' (482b–c).

Arendt suggests that the 'harmony' Socrates is aspiring to here is the two-in-one process of *thinking*, the silent and unending conversation with oneself which makes each of us our own companion, and which consequently demands from us that we act in ways that we can account for to our own internal witness. Socrates, who never claimed to know the answers to the questions he asked, engaged in thinking not for the sake of knowledge, but because he believed that an unexamined live would not be worth living, that is, would not be a *meaningful* life. Crediting Kant with the distinction between knowing and thinking (LM1: 13–16), Arendt stresses how knowing seeks 'truth', which 'compels with the force of necessity' what we are driven 'to admit by the nature either of our senses or of our brain' (LM1: 60–1). The knowledge that arises from cognition and the intellect, as opposed to the restless activity of thinking, has a worldly dimension to it: 'The activity of knowing is no less a world-building activity than the building of houses' (RJ: 163). Although the desire to know is never quenched, for its achievements always establish new horizons of knowable things, 'the activity itself leaves behind a growing treasure of knowledge that is retained and kept in store by every civilisation as part and parcel of its world' (LM1: 62).

Thinking, by contrast, yields no tangible product, being a search for meaning 'which subjects everything it gets hold of to doubt' (LM1: 52). Unlike knowing, thinking 'does not ask what something is or whether it exists at all – its existence is always taken for granted – *but what it means for it to be*' (LM1: 57). Thinking, as Plato understood the origins of philosophy, begins with an admiring wonder (hence to 'think' and to 'thank' are, according to Heidegger, essentially the same), leads to perplexity, and then returns to the wonder with which it began (LM1: 142, 150, 166). Being most at home in the asking of unanswerable questions, thinking cannot therefore be stilled by the gifts of the wise and knowledgeable, who may themselves, incidentally, display a limited ability to think. Instead the need to think can only be satisfied by the activity itself, an activity which, like the natality of action, must perpetually begin afresh. Like Penelope with her shroud, thinking 'undoes every morning what it had finished the night before' (RJ: 166).

Though knowing and thinking are distinguishable, they are also connected, Arendt argues, at least inasmuch as thinking is the ultimate precondition for all our mental operations. Only a thinking being, Arendt suggests, could find *meaning* in the accumulation of knowledge: 'men, if they were ever to lose the appetite for meaning we call thinking and cease to ask unanswerable questions, would lose not only the ability to produce those thought-things that we call works of art but also the capacity to ask all the answerable questions upon which every civilisation is founded' (LM1: 62).

Against all the obvious intellectual prejudices, Arendt does not regard thinking as the prerogative of academics and philosophers, insisting that 'you find it present in all walks of life and may find it entirely absent in what we call intellectuals' (RJ: 94). By the same token, thoughtlessness is by no means the monopoly of the stupid, for thoughtless obedience to customs and rules is a basic requirement for the social organisation of the life process.

> Absence of thought is indeed a powerful factor in human affairs, statistically speaking the most powerful, not just in the conduct of the many but in the conduct of all. The very urgency, the *a-scholia*, of human affairs demands provisional judgements, the reliance on custom and habit, that is, on prejudices. (LM1: 71).

THE MORAL SIGNIFICANCE OF THINKING

If thinking, unlike knowing, is an essentially worldless activity, and one which typically requires a retreat from the domain of plurality in order to enjoy the pleasure of one's own company, how can thinking have moral significance? Arendt repeatedly describes thinking as an invisible activity which 'takes place only in solitude, in a withdrawal from the world of appearances' (LM2: 64). She also notes the ancient affinity between thinking and death (LM1: 79–85). For the Romans in particular, the mental activity of the philosopher was meant to provide guidance on, if not a remedy for, the predicament of mortality, while philosophers themselves, especially during their periods of contemplative detachment from worldly concerns, were often perceived as being in love with death. Since death was to cease to be amongst other people, so thinking was a death-like retreat from plurality.

But perhaps it would be wrong to interpret too rigidly the solitude evidently required for the activity for thinking, as Arendt's choice of Socrates as the exemplary thinker should indicate. Socrates, it appears, did most of his thinking out loud, in the company of other citizens in the Athenian *agora*. 'What he actually did was to make *public*, in discourse, the thinking process – that dialogue that soundlessly goes on within me, between me and myself; he *performed* in the marketplace the way the flute-player performed at a banquet' (LK: 37). And yet, even Socrates was guilty of deserting the realm of appearances, and it is tempting to conclude that what Socrates really did is share the provisional *results* of his thinking with his interlocutors, while in the activity of thinking itself he was always absent from their company. For thinking is not identical with speech so much as dependent on it for proof of its communicability, which is why Arendt claims that when there is no one with whom one can share one's thoughts, then the faculty of thinking atrophies. As Arendt cites Kant: 'the external power which deprives man of the freedom to communicate his thoughts *publicly* also takes away his freedom to *think*' (LK: 41).

If Arendt's phenomenology of thinking is accurate, then, Socrates' dialogue with the citizens of Athens was not a 'thinking in plural', not a two-in-one of the self and its interlocutor, but rather a thinking *made public*, a thinking performed in the space of appearances. If this is correct, conversations with Socrates would have been perpetually interrupted by moments of contemplation in which the philosopher would have been blind and deaf to all but his own thoughts. Thinking 'is withdrawal not so much from the world', Arendt stresses, 'as from the world's being *present* to the senses' (LM1: 75), implying that thinking may take place in public, but only by making the world absent. One might say, in fact, that it is *absent-mindedness*, rather than physical solitude, which is the necessary condition of thinking. This is evident from Arendt's other portrait of Socrates:

> thinking is always out of order, interrupts all ordinary activities and is interrupted by them. The best illustration of this may still be – as the story goes – Socrates' habit of suddenly 'turning his mind to himself', breaking off all company, and taking up his position wherever he happened to be, 'deaf to all entreaties' to continue with whatever he had been doing before. Once, we are told by Xenophon, he remained in complete immobility for twenty-four hours in a military camp, deep in thought, as we would say. (LM1: 197)

Arendt also describes thinking as a kind of remembrance, a reflection on what has been done, what is absent and as yet unexamined, and this is critical to her attempt to draw moral implications from the activity of thinking. Remembrance, of course, is a precondition for guilt and repentance, and its real moral significance, according to Arendt, consists in the way it constrains the doer from absolute recklessness. Though thinking is retrospective, people who are accustomed to thinking know that, as thinking beings, they will have to account for themselves, *to themselves*, after they have acted. Although sociologists since Mead have tended to view social interaction as the source of people's ethical self-consciousness, Arendt follows Aristotle's observation in the *Nicomachean Ethics* (1166b4) that wicked people seek social contact in order to forget themselves and avoid the scrutiny of their own company. It was the chief aim of Socrates, then, to lead people back to themselves, extracting and clarifying the implications of their conduct and opinions, and obliging them to account for what they thought, said, and did. And though the two-in-one of thinking is conducted in the mode of questioning and doubt, Arendt implies that this is not the same as becoming an adversary to oneself, which is what happens when doubt admits no reply and the friendly dialogue of thinking hardens into mutual enmity. It is the fear of making an enemy of oneself – the fear, which is unique to the thinker, that even actions hidden from the eyes of others will still be seen by a witness 'condemned to live together with a wrongdoer in an unbearable intimacy' (RJ: 90) – which Arendt believes functions as a moral brake on people's behaviour.

> To Socrates, the duality of the two-in-one meant no more than that if you want to think, you must see to it that the two who carry on the dialogue be in good shape, that the partners be *friends*. The partner who comes to life when you are alert and alone is the only one from whom you can never get away – except by ceasing to think. It is better to suffer wrong than to do wrong, because you can remain the friend of the sufferer; who would want to be the friend of or have to live together with a murderer? Not even another murderer. (LM1: 188)

'Conscience', as Arendt defines it, is therefore 'the anticipation of the fellow who awaits you if and when you come home' (LM1: 191). The rootedness of the moral conscience in the activity of thinking is evident, Arendt claims, in the characters of those who refused to co-operate with the Nazis. Arendt suggests that these people were never plagued by moral doubts and did not attempt to weigh up the costs and benefits of co-operation. They were not guided by a sense of 'obligation', nor by the pressure to conform to a moral rule. They were not 'tempted' by evil, nor persuaded by the fear of an avenging God. 'They simply said, I can't, I'd rather die, for life would not be worthwhile when I had done it' (RJ: 278 n10). Instead of asking what they *ought* to do or not do,

> they asked themselves to what extent they would still be able to live in peace with themselves after having committed certain deeds; and they decided that it would be better to do nothing, not because the world would then be changed for the better, but simply because only on this condition could they go on living with themselves at all. Hence, they also chose to die when they were forced to participate. To put it crudely, they refused to murder, not so much because they still held fast to the command 'Thou shalt not kill', but because they were unwilling to live together with a murderer – themselves.
>
> The precondition for this kind of judging is not a highly developed intelligence or sophistication in moral matters, but rather the disposition to live together explicitly with oneself, to have intercourse with oneself, that is, to be engaged in that silent dialogue between me and myself which, since Socrates and Plato, we usually call thinking. (RJ: 44–5)

Thinking and remembering are therefore for Arendt the means by which, stabilising ourselves with roots into the past, we constitute ourselves as persons. This is why the great moral challenge posed by people like Eichmann was that, by refusing to think what they were doing and had done, and by insisting that they had never acted with initiative but only on their superiors' commands, 'they renounced voluntarily all personal qualities, as if nobody were left to be either punished or forgiven'. Thus 'the greatest evil perpetrated is the evil committed by nobodies, that is, by human beings who refuse to be persons' (RJ: 111). 'Unthinking men', Arendt writes, 'are like sleepwalkers' (LM1: 191).

> The greatest evildoers are those who don't remember because they have never given thought to the matter, and, without remembrance, nothing can hold them back. For human beings, thinking of past matters means moving in the dimension of depth, striking roots and thus stabilising ourselves, so as not to be swept away by whatever may occur – the Zeitgeist or History or simple temptation. The greatest evil is not radical, it has no

roots, and because it has no roots it has no limitations, it can go to unthinkable extremes and sweep over the whole world. (RJ: 95)

We can see here why Arendt says that the 'moral' in 'moral personality' is a redundant adjective. We can also see that Arendt, though she rejected the earlier term 'radical evil', did not abandon the idea that even the 'banal' evil which is the distinctive capability of 'the nonwicked everybody who has no special motives', can be an extreme, if not 'infinite', evil (RJ: 188). It is because this thoughtless evil is rootless and devoid of personality that it carries with it a capacity for limitless destruction, and it is for the same reason that the protagonist of this destruction cannot be forgiven. For 'in granting pardon, it is the person and not the crime that is forgiven; in rootless evil there is no person left whom one could ever forgive' (RJ: 95).

If one moral implication of thinking is that it gives substance and integrity to the self, a second is, paradoxically, that thinking dissolves common prejudices and beliefs. Because of the inconclusive and elusive character of thinking, and the purgative effect it has on people's established opinions and values, thinking is in principle anti-authoritarian and anti-ideological. In Plato's *Meno*, Socrates conveys the unproductive, if not destructive, spirit of thinking when, reminded by Meno of his reputation 'that you are always in a state of perplexity and that you bring others to the same state', he agrees that 'I myself do not have the answer' and 'am more perplexed than anyone' (80a–d; LM1: 172). Socrates did not teach others moral certainties, so much as infect them with an appetite for self-reflection which had a radical liquefying effect, defrosting all dogmas, customs and rules, and preventing all beliefs from hardening into unquestionable convictions.

Of course there is no guarantee that thinking will not give rise to its opposite, as Socrates discovered when he found himself accused of sponsoring nihilism. His fellow citizens, including Alcibiades and Critias, thus 'changed the non-results of the Socratic thinking examination into negative results: If we cannot define what piety is, let us be impious' (LM1: 175–6). Though nihilism is 'an ever-present danger of thinking', Arendt stresses that this 'danger does not arise out of the Socratic conviction that an unexamined life is not worth living, but, on the contrary, out of the desire to find results that make further thinking unnecessary' (LM1: 176). It was with a similar vulgar cynicism that the 'mob' rebelled against the pious and hypocritical banalities of the bourgeoisie in 1930s Europe, where 'it seemed revolutionary to admit cruelty, disregard of human values, and general amorality, because this at least destroyed the duplicity upon which the existing society seemed to rest' (OT: 334). And we find the same temptation to put an end to thinking, Arendt points out, whenever philosophers have become intoxicated by their own cleverness, believing, like Hegel, that they had discovered the methodological structure of reason. Included by Arendt in this category, perhaps surprisingly, is Kant, who 'could not part altogether with the conviction that the final aim of thinking, as of knowledge, is truth and cognition', and who 'announced publicly that he had laid the foundation of all future metaphysical systems' (LM1: 63, 89).

Arendt argues that although thinking does not therefore yield positive guidelines for behaviour, in 'boundary situations', such as totalitarian rule, where 'everybody is swept away unthinkingly by what everybody else does and believes in', the refusal of the thinker to endorse the values and rules of the thoughtless majority – the refusal to act – becomes an invaluable form of moral defiance. How thinking survives in totalitarian conditions where it cannot enjoy, as Kant believed it must, the test of public exposure, is a contradiction which Arendt fails to register here. Under these exceptionally oppressive circumstances, Arendt contends, the thinker's 'refusal to join in is conspicuous and thereby becomes a kind of action' which, presumably by setting a visible example, becomes 'political by implication' (LM1: 192). Hence: 'The marginal situation in which moral propositions become absolutely valid in the realm of politics is impotence' (RJ: 156).

In Rei Terada's slightly different interpretation of Arendt, thinking is the means by which people, denied the opportunity for public speech and action, are able to register a horrible and oppressive reality without either accepting it or reverting to fictitious alternatives. Though Arendt writes that thinking 'withdraws from the sensorily given and hence also from the feeling of realness' (LM1: 52), Terada reads Arendt's comment, in the 1967 Preface to *The Origins of Totalitarianism*, that 'comprehension' is 'the unpremeditated, attentive facing up to, and resisting of, reality' (OT: xiv), as evidence that thinking, for all its worldlessness, is for Arendt essentially a form of 'reality testing' similar to that experienced in the first clash between the pleasure principle and the reality principle. Just as the infant, in Freud's analysis, takes note of reality in order to safeguard a longer and more assured pleasure, so the adult, refusing to adapt to a terrible reality like a survival-driven animal, registers repugnant facts and feelings that it does not accept:

> love of reality testing has the general function of being something, anything, more fundamental than the desire to survive. The realism that belongs to this kind of realisation is thus not the cynical 'realism' of getting on the winning side. It is even the opposite of that, if getting on the winning side means overlooking one's realisation. Arendt insists that thinking holds on to the thread of self-interest, and at the same time that self-interest can differ from self-survival whenever survival comes into disastrous conflict with the desire for autonomy. The self that learned to look at and object to its conditions did so without the assistance of the self that decided to adapt. This primordial self may say 'Fuck you' to a man holding a gun to its head, even if no one benefits. (Terada 2008: 102)

Thinking may have moral significance, then, but Arendt freely concedes that this significance is limited to 'political emergencies', and is for the most part negative in character, with the thinker refusing to do wrong but choosing to suffer rather than act. Because thinking is, moreover, incompatible with other activities, because 'in our world there is no clearer or more radical opposition than that between thinking and doing' (LM1: 71), then the moral injunction, recommended by Arendt in the Prologue to *The Human Condition*, that we should 'think what we are doing', is not entirely adequate. Better is the idiomatic precept, '*stop* and think' (RJ: 105; LM1: 78).

Though Socrates himself certainly fulfilled his responsibilities as a citizen, serving as a member of the *boule* as well as a soldier in several military campaigns, Socratic morality clearly does not speak with the political voice of the citizen, who unlike the thinker is 'more concerned with the world than with his self'. From the perspective of the world, and therefore of politics and action, what is most important 'is that a wrong has been done; and for this, it is irrelevant who is better off, the wrong-doer or the wrong-sufferer. As citizens, we must prevent wrong-doing because the world in which we all live, wrong-doer, wrong-sufferer, and spectator, is at stake' (LM1: 182). Arendt makes a similar point in her discussion of the conscientious objector, like the abolitionist Henry Thoreau who 'spent one night in jail for refusing to pay his poll tax to a government that permitted slavery, but ... let his aunt pay it for him the next morning' (CR: 59–60).

THE PHENOMENON OF THE WILL

Arendt's ruminations on the faculty of thinking both tantalise and frustrate. Thinking is the precondition for resistance to injustice and evil; yet thinking is essentially unworldly, and therefore cannot alone rouse men and women to action. When Arendt started *The Life of the Mind*, she intended it to be a three-part study devoted to what she believed were the three essential activities of the *vita contemplativa*: thinking, willing and judging. Given her hierarchical account of the *vita activa*, it would be reasonable to assume that Arendt was trying to do something similar for the mental life. That willing and judging may be 'higher' faculties of the mind is indicated by the fact that neither involve the radical withdrawal from the world that is characteristic of thinking. Whereas thinking 'deals with the invisibles in all experience and always tends to generalise', willing and judging 'deal with particulars and in this respect are much closer to the world of appearances'. These particulars have 'an established home in the appearing world, from which the willing or judging mind removes itself only temporarily and with the intention of a later return' (LM1: 213, 92). The suggestion here is that willing, and especially judging, may be the mental companions of the highest element of the *vita activa*, public action, and may therefore provide a bridge between the life of the mind and the love of the world that is Arendt's remedy for our modern alienation.

Arendt's comments on this possible interpretation are hardly encouraging, however. 'It would be wrong, I believe, to try to establish a hierarchical order among the mind's activities, but I also believe that it is hardly deniable that an order of priorities exists' (LM1: 76). The surprise is that this 'order' grants sequential priority to *thinking*, for it is thinking which, by removing objects from the senses, and by re-representing what is absent, allows the mind to will and to judge:

> Only because of the mind's capacity for making present what is absent can we say 'no more' and constitute a past for ourselves, or say 'not yet' and get ready for a future ... Thus, in order to will, the mind must withdraw from the immediacy of desire, which, without reflecting and without reflexivity, stretches out its hand to get hold of the desired object; for the will is not concerned with objects but with projects, for instance, with the future availability of an object that it may or may not desire in the present. The will transforms the desire into an intention. (LM1: 76)

Arendt initially describes the phenomenon of the will as 'identical with the power of beginning something new' (LM2: 29), but subsequently distinguishes between the 'I-will' and the 'I-can', the latter being a political rather than merely philosophical freedom which 'is possible only in the sphere of human plurality' (LM2: 200). She points out that the notion of the will was foreign to the ancients, who understood the conflict, won by whichever proved stronger, between desire and reason, but who had no conception of a third faculty able to say yes or no to the demands of either. Though Aristotle's concept of '*proairesis*' allowed a small space for the operation of free choice (LM2: 61–2), it was early Christian thought which really gave rise to the notion of the will, and with it the idea of a freedom governed neither by the desires of the flesh nor the universal voice of reason. The concept of freedom played no role in classical philosophy, Arendt claims, because freedom in the ancient world was a political practice which philosophy, founded in opposition to the *polis*, could never embrace. 'Only when the early Christians, and especially Paul, discovered a kind of freedom which had no relation to politics, could the concept of freedom enter the history of philosophy' (PF: 158).

Discovered by theologians and experienced in solitude, freedom appeared as a mental capacity – that of the 'will' – arising from the thinker's inner conversation with himself. But simultaneous with this discovery of the will was the suspicion that in fact humans might not be free, because the faculty of the will was found to be self-contradictory. For while 'the predominant mood of the thinking ego is *serenity*, the mere enjoyment of an activity that never has to overcome the resistance of matter' (LM2: 38), the will reaches towards a future which it has no guarantee of realising.

> Every volition, although a mental activity, relates to the world of appearances in which its project is to be realised; in flagrant contrast to thinking, no willing is ever done for its own sake or finds its fulfilment in the act itself. Every volition not only concerns particulars but – and this is of great importance – looks forward to its own end, when willing-something will have changed into doing-it. In other words, the normal mood of the willing ego is impatience, disquiet, and worry (*Sorge*), not merely because of the soul's reacting to the future in fear and hope, but also because the will's project presupposes an I-can that is by no means guaranteed. (LM2: 37)

Standing in the way of the will's contentment is not just the resistance of matter, but the resistance of the will itself. Although it was the apostle Paul who first established the importance of freedom in Christian philosophy, Arendt highlights the significance of Augustine for grasping most clearly the divided nature of the will. For willing is not the same as acting. Real freedom is not the 'I-will' but the 'I-can'; it 'is not an attribute of the will but an accessory of doing and acting' (PF: 165). Because the will is not action, but rather the *command* to act, Augustine understood that the will is eternally riven, not peacefully like the two-in-one of the thinking self, but in a paralysing stand-off, 'a merciless struggle which lasts unto death' (RJ: 119). Inherent in the will is the capacity to resist itself; the will wills – speaks to itself in imperatives – and in doing so finds its freedom under threat from the demand that it *obey*. The will cannot command, in other words, without arousing a counter-will. This brokenness of the will is not the familiar division between the mind and the body which first preoccupied Paul, but rather a purely mental contest between the will and itself. The worst fear of the thinking ego – the fear of being 'at variance with oneself' – now appears, where the will is concerned, to be inescapable. Being independent of the particular content of the will, this conflict is 'part and parcel of the human condition' (LM2: 83).

Augustine's insight that 'to will and to be able are not the same', and that it is 'not monstrous therefore partly to will and partly to nill' (LM2: 87, 94), was then perfectly expressed by Nietzsche in *Beyond Good and Evil*:

> We are in every given case at the same time those who issue the orders and those who obey them; insofar as we obey, we experience the feelings of coercion, urging, pressing, resisting, which usually begin to manifest themselves immediately after the act of willing; insofar however ... as we are in command ... we experience a sensation of pleasure, and this all the more strongly as we are used to overcoming the dichotomy through the notion of the I, the Ego, and this in such a way that we take the obedience in ourselves for granted and therefore identify willing and performing, willing and acting. (Cited in LM2: 161; RJ: 132)[1]

The dividedness of the will suggests that freedom is always exercised at a price, as it must overpower that part of the will which wills not, which resists and refuses to obey. Another way of putting this is to say that the condition of the will is *contingency*, for the will to act is the will to overcome, and thus to give up, the possibility of acting otherwise. According to Arendt it was the medieval Franciscan theologian, Duns Scotus, who first understood the contingency of human freedom, and who resolved the paradox of the will by showing how the openness of the will to its contrary only persisted in the forming of volitions, but disappeared in the moment of *action*.

Before Scotus, it was Thomas Aquinas who had equated the will with desire, believing that the will attained perfection when it arrived at possession of the desired object. For Arendt, as for Augustine and for Scotus, this was an error, for the moment of possession marks not the perfection but rather the destruction of the will. Defined as desire, the aim of the will is to not will (to will the completion of a book, for example, in order to be rid of the will to write). The question of how the will can will rather than nill, how it can affirm itself without pursuing its own negation, is answered by Augustine and Scotus in similar terms. Both believed that the will must be transformed into *love*, for love does not, like desire, pursue the creation or possession of an object – a journey that is necessarily transient, since its goal is to extinguish itself with what it lacks – but instead achieves 'the stillness of an act resting in its end' by simply willing that which exists: 'love's abiding power is felt not as the arrest of motion – as the end of the fury of war is felt as the quiet of peace – but as the serenity of a self-contained, self-fulfilling, everlasting movement' (LM2: 145).

Noting, along with the rise of science and the philosophical faith in progress, the modern resurgence of interest in the will as the spring from which humans are to master the future, Arendt also considers Nietzsche's answer to the dividedness of the will. Nietzsche's 'trick' was to propose that the will 'escape the conflict by identifying itself with the commanding part and to overlook, as it were, the unpleasant, paralysing sentiments of being coerced and hence always on the point of resisting' (LM2: 161–2). Building on the ancient insight that the intensity of pleasure varies in proportion to the degree of discomfort it overcomes, Nietzsche associated the pleasure of the will with the surmounting of resistance to it, thus making the feeling of being coerced a prerequisite for the more delectable joy of power.

For Nietzsche, the goal of the will-to-power is not domination and control – again, external accomplishments which signal the will's imminent termination – but rather the will itself, for will and power are the same in Nietzsche's thinking: 'the Will generates power by willing', Arendt explains, 'hence the will whose objective is humility is no less powerful than the will to rule over others' (LM2: 168). *What* the will should will therefore remains unresolved in Nietzsche as in other philosophers. Arendt suggests that Heidegger was wrong to interpret Nietzsche's concept of power in promethean terms – a view 'of which he found himself guilty when he tried to come to terms with his brief past in the Nazi movement' (LM2: 173). But she is also critical of Heidegger's subsequent repudiation of the will as a destructive force inherent in modern technology, the purposive character of which he believed could be resisted only by a 'will-not-to-will', a 'letting go', the essential mode of which was thinking. Heidegger, displaying the traditional prejudice of the philosopher, thus called for a withdrawal from the raucous froth and chatter of public life towards a serene but essentially solipsistic attentiveness to Being (LM2: 178–87).

In Nietzsche, by contrast, the will is grasped as a gratuitous force of transcendence which, in Arendt's words, 'corresponds to the overwhelming superabundance of Life' – the surplus of vitality by which the *Übermensch* is able to 'overcome' himself and his irresistible biological needs (LM2: 168–9; RJ: 134–5). This 'lavishness of the will', as Arendt puts it, is a kind of 'extravagant generosity', an 'overflowing strength' which mirrors Scotus's depiction of the mental faculty of the will as a light which 'is permanently renewed from its source' (LM2: 142).

Arendt's reflections on the theologians and philosophers of the will suggest she believed Kant was wrong to speak of a morally rational and 'lawful' will, that is, a will made good and non-contradictory by the categorical imperative of 'practical reason'. For Arendt, Duns Scotus stands out because he alone was 'ready to pay the price of contingency' for the spontaneity and 'ineluctable randomness' of the will – of the freedom 'to do what could also be left undone' (LM2: 195, 198). In curiously Sartrean language, Arendt concludes that her examination of the will reveals 'no more than that we are *doomed* to be free by virtue of being born, no matter whether we like freedom or abhor its arbitrariness'. But to this she adds the suggestion that a solution to the arbitrariness of freedom may lie with a third mental faculty, 'the faculty of Judgement' (LM2: 217).

JUDGING

When Arendt died, less than a week after completing her discussion of the will, she left behind on her typewriter only the first page of the third and final part of her study, with 'Judging' as the title but nothing more than two epigraphs, from Cato and Goethe, to indicate what was to follow. Scholars of Arendt have instead tried to anticipate and reconstruct her intellectual intentions, drawing on lectures she delivered on moral philosophy at the New School for Social Research in 1965, at the University of Chicago in 1966, and back at the New School, this time with Kant as the primary subject, in 1970.

When Arendt originally planned *The Life of the Mind*, she saw it as a two-volume work, with 'Thinking' comprising the first volume, and 'Willing' and 'Judging' making up the second one. That Arendt may have seen judgement as a faculty close to the will is also suggested by earlier statements where she toyed with the idea that judgement represented the 'arbitrating function' of the will. This is not the same will which spontaneously prompts us to act, but the will as '*liberum arbitrium*', as that impartial judge which 'arbitrates between reasons without being subject to them' (RJ: 131, 136–7). 'Hence, freedom of will as *liberum arbitrium* never starts something new, it is always confronted with things as they are ... And in this respect, there is indeed an element of willing in all judgements. I can say yes or no to what is' (RJ: 283 n21).

Though Arendt was tempted to treat judgement as a second faculty of the will, she was also convinced that, in contrast to the will's absolute spontaneity, the capacity for judgement, 'which one may call with some reason the most political of man's mental abilities', was liberated by, and therefore closely related to, thinking (LM1: 192–3). In exploring the relationship between thinking and judging, it seems that Arendt was drawn to Kant for help with this enterprise for two reasons. First of all, Kant offered a theory of judgement – 'thinking the particular', as he referred to it – which was not premised on the application of general rules, and which therefore incorporated an element of what Arendt regards as the thinking ego's fundamental autonomy. Second, Kant understood judgement as a public faculty by which the self was freed from vital needs and acquisitive interests and inserted into the world of appearances.

Arendt's original reading of Kant begins with the surprising claim that of Kant's three critiques – the *Critique of Pure Reason* (which examined the basis of knowledge and truth), the *Critique of Practical Reason* (which studied the foundations of moral autonomy), and the *Critique of Judgement* (whose subject is aesthetic taste) – it is the third, not the second, critique which offers the greatest insight into the faculty of moral judgement. That morality is a question of judgement, or 'taste', and not, as Kant claimed in the second *Critique*, a matter of the will, is in Arendt's view already indicated by the fact that Kant's later book, the *Metaphysics of Morals*, was started with the working title 'Critique of Moral Taste'.

In the *Critique of Judgement*, Kant distinguished between 'determinant' and 'reflective' judgements.[2] Determinant judgements evaluate the particular from the standpoint of a general rule, and for Kant this is how moral-practical reason operates, demanding that we act on the basis of maxims that we will to be a universal law. The deduction of the particular from the general is also apparent in Kant's account of cognition, for we can know and talk about the infinite variety of existing things only in so far as we recognise each uniquely existing thing as a particular instance of an abstract specie or schema, the latter existing nowhere except in the eyes of the mind, assuming a tangible form only by becoming another particular instance of it. Without the general concept of, say, 'table', we would not recognise particular tables as tables, and would only be able to refer to 'that table' as 'that'.

We shall see in a moment that Arendt does not claim that judgement must proceed without any standards or guidance. But she had good reason to doubt that conformity to rules was a solid foundation for moral action, just as she had good reason to be suspicious of the sociological reliance on functional generalisations which rendered the novelty of human enterprise – including the enterprise of totalitarianism – undetectable. In his police interrogation, Eichmann himself had disingenuously claimed to have been loyal to Kant's categorical imperative (EJ: 135–7), although it was ultimately his sense of duty to the Führer's will (not to the 'superior orders' of Himmler, and certainly not the victims of his actions) which guided his conduct. But Arendt does not need Eichmann's self-deception to make her point, for it was precisely the thoughtless disposition to follow general rules which had led innumerable 'paragons of virtue in respectable society' – '*les salauds*', in Sartre's account of bad faith – to pledge themselves to a regime of mass murder.

What people then get used to is less the content of the rules, a close examination of which would always lead them into perplexity, than the *possession* of rules under which to subsume particulars. If somebody appears who, for whatever purposes, wishes to abolish the old 'values' or virtues, he will find that easy enough, provided he offers a new code, and he will need relatively little force and no persuasion ... to impose it. The more firmly men hold to the old code, the more eager will they be to assimilate themselves to the new one, which in practice means that the readiest to obey will be those who were the most respectable pillars of society. (LM1: 177)

Noting how the perversion of ethical standards and rules during the Holocaust has left us, with regard to moral matters, 'in the same situation in which the eighteenth century found itself with respect to mere judgements of taste', Arendt suggests that it is the concept of 'reflective' judgement, which Kant applied exclusively to aesthetic taste, which should now be extended to the moral domain (RJ: 139). Reflective judgement is Kant's description of our ability to take contemplative pleasure in the appearance of a particular object, without treating that object as merely the manifestation of a general category or rule. When we see beauty in a rose, for example, we do not reason: 'All roses are beautiful, this flower is a rose, hence this rose is beautiful' (LK: 13). Reflective judgement, on the contrary, reaches out to the thing itself and says '*this* is beautiful', '*this* is wrong', '*this* is good', and only subsequently seeks a generalised description of the qualities encountered in order to communicate and expose them to the judgement of others. Judgement in this sense is the ability to see the particular in its own right, to *attend to the thing itself* instead of treating it as an instance of a pre-existing concept, category or trend. 'The beautiful is, in Kantian terms, an end in itself because all its possible meaning is contained within itself, without reference to others – without linkage, as it were, to other beautiful things' (LK: 77).

Arendt's account of reflective judgement depends on another distinction, which is the division of the human senses into the 'subjective' and the 'objective'. In the former category, which phenomenologists sometimes call the 'proximity senses', Arendt places the sense of smell and, quintessentially, the sense of *taste*. These senses are 'subjective' because they dissolve the objective existence of things into *sensations* which cannot be communicated or proven to be compelling to the appraisal of others. They are rightly described as 'inner' senses, 'because the food we taste is inside ourselves, and so, in a way, is the smell of the rose' (LK: 66).

As Freud describes them in *Civilisation and its Discontents*, the proximity senses are the lowest, most animal of the human senses (2002: 41–4). Their original prominence was displaced (and their lowly significance established) when our distant ancestors assumed an upright posture so that our mouths and noses were no longer in easy reach of the ground. But the real significance of the proximity senses, according to Arendt, is that they are *discriminatory*, by which she means that they respond, in a manner not unlike reflective judgement, to the absolute individuality, the sheer 'this-ness' of things, instead of to the classifiable and communicable qualities that they share with other objects. The sensations of taste and smell are experienced as 'it pleases' or 'it displeases', and according to Arendt this is precisely the meaning of Kant's assertion that the opposite of the Beautiful is not that which appears ugly, pointless or unjust – for war, disease and destruction can always be depicted in a beautiful way – but rather 'that which excites *disgust*' (Kant 1914: 116; LK: 68).

Using Kant's theory of aesthetics in *Critique of Judgement* as her guide, Arendt wants to argue, then, that moral judgement is a matter of *taste*, a question of that which arouses pleasure or displeasure. Yet taste is also the most private and incommunicable of senses, and it is therefore difficult to see how judgements of taste can be anything other than idiosyncratic. If, on the other hand, we take the 'objective' senses, of which sight is the most definitive, though Arendt also includes hearing and touch in this category,[3] then the opposite is the case. The objects of these senses can be held at a distance, they do not irresistibly affect us, and judgement on them can be withheld if required. As Hans Jonas described it in his phenomenological account of the 'nobility of sight': 'in seeing, the percipient remains entirely free from causal involvement in the things to be perceived. Thus vision secures that standing back from the aggressiveness of the world which frees for observation and opens a horizon for elective attention' (2001: 148). At the same time, unlike olfactory sensations which cannot be accurately recalled when the original tastes and smells are absent, the objects of sight, hearing and (less obviously) touch, can be re-presented to consciousness – and therefore talked about in disinterested fashion to others – even when they are no longer present. Hence 'the image is handed over to the imagination, which can deal with it in complete detachment from the actual presence of the original object: the detachability of the image, i.e., of "form" from its "matter", of "essence" from "existence", is at the bottom of abstraction and therefore of all free thought' (Jonas 2001: 147).

This is how Arendt summarises the resulting paradox:

> The most surprising aspect of this business is that ... the faculty of judgement and of discriminating between right and wrong,

should be based on the sense of taste. Of our five senses, three clearly give us objects of the external world and therefore are easily communicable ... Smell and taste give inner sensations that are entirely private and incommunicable; what I taste and what I smell cannot be expressed in words at all. They seem to be private senses by definition. Moreover, the three objective senses have this in common: they are capable of *re*presentation, of making present something that is absent. I can, for example, recall a building, a melody, the touch of velvet. This faculty – which in Kant is called Imagination – is possessed by neither taste nor smell. On the other hand, [taste and smell] are quite clearly the discriminatory senses: one can withhold judgement from what one sees and, though less easily, one can withhold judgement from what one hears or touches. But in matters of taste or smell, the it-pleases-or-displeases-me is immediate and overwhelming. (LK: 64)

Arendt believes the answer to this puzzle lies in the role Kant attributed to the faculty of the imagination. For in Arendt's interpretation the imagination is not only able to make present what is absent, but also 'transforms the objects of the objective senses into "sensed" objects, as though they were objects of an inner sense' (LK: 65). This act of the imagination, which 'closes' the objective senses, prepares the object for the 'operation of reflection' which Arendt argues 'is the actual activity of judging something'. In reflective judgement, in other words, what is reflected on is not an object but its representation, and this representation is both communicable *and* exposed to the inner sense of pleasure or displeasure, and therefore to judgements of beauty and goodness. The imagination re-presents objects which are no longer given directly and objectively to the senses, thereby freeing judgement from the force of instinct, inclination and interest, and instead allowing impartiality and 'disinterested delight' to combine with the subjective capacity for discrimination. Arendt refers to the figure of Homer, the 'blind poet', to make her point here: 'By closing one's eyes one becomes an impartial, not a directly affected, spectator of visible things' (LK: 68):

One then speaks of judgement and no longer of taste because, though it still affects one like a matter of taste, one now has, by means of representation, established the proper distance, the remoteness or uninvolvedness or disinterestedness, that is requisite for approbation and disapprobation, for evaluating something at its proper worth. By removing the object, one has established the conditions for impartiality. (LK: 66)

Imagination may be, as Arendt claims, the primary vehicle for judgement, but what standards do we use when we judge? Arendt says that the ultimate criterion for judgement is its *communicability*, for judgements cannot tolerate the worldlessness of the thinking ego, and though you may require solitude in order to think, there is always an element of intersubjectivity involved in judgement: 'you need company to enjoy a meal' (LK: 67). And what is communicable, Arendt continues, is determined by the 'sixth' and least private sense. Kant called this the *sensus communis* in order to distinguish it from the idea of a 'common sense' that is universal but essentially private. According to Kant, a man with this 'communal sense', as he also called it, is 'a man of enlarged thought', the 'world citizen' who 'disregards the subjective private conditions of his own judgement ... and reflects upon it from a general standpoint (which he can only determine by placing himself at the standpoint of others)' (Kant 1914: 101–3; LK: 71). Reflective judgement thus tests its communicability by taking into account the judgements of others whose agreement must be courted or 'wooed' through a real or imaginary exchange. Lest this revives the idea of a Habermasian consensus, we should note that Arendt stresses how the impartiality of judgement 'is not the result of some higher standpoint that would then actually settle the dispute by being altogether above the melée' (LK: 42). Impartial or representative judgement is not the abdication of a personal standpoint, for 'in cutting ties to our own interests, we run the danger of losing our ties to the world and our attachment to its objects and the affairs that take place in it'. Hence: 'The ability to see the same thing from various standpoints stays in the human world; it is simply the exchange of the standpoint given us by nature for that of someone else, with whom we share the same world' (PP: 168). This is captured more clearly in Arendt's definition of 'representative thinking', which she had earlier described as the key faculty of political judgement:

> Political thought is representative. I form an opinion by considering a given issue from different viewpoints, by making present to my mind the standpoints of those who are absent; that is, I represent them ... The more people's standpoints I have present in my mind while I am pondering a given issue, and the better I can imagine how I would feel and think if I were in their

place, the stronger will be my capacity for representative thinking and the more valid my final conclusions, my opinion. (PF: 241)

So judgement – aesthetic, moral and, it would seem, political – is, in Arendt's formulation, attuned by reflection and the inner sense of taste to grasp the distinctiveness of things, testing and weighing its results through a real or imaginary dialogue with the judgements of others. For judgement the imagination must be trained to 'go visiting' (LK: 43), an aptitude that Eichmann, in his inability to imagine the suffering of his victims, had clearly not acquired, and which Arendt also suggested was missing from the judgement of the Jerusalem court, which was determined to subsume Eichmann under the familiar criminal category of a fanatical killer. In Bilsky's interesting analysis, Arendt herself was deficient in this regard, showing remarkable insight into the new type of criminal produced by totalitarianism, but failing 'to practice enlarged mentality in relation to her own spectators, in particular, the Jewish victims' (Bilsky 2001: 272).

Though judgement seeks corroboration from other members of the judging community, it does not do this by applying, as in Habermas's theory of communicative action, generalisable rules or the rational force of cognitive reason, and nor does it aim at a definitive closure of the dialogue itself. Judgement is as much a contribution to human plurality as a product of it. As Bilsky puts it: 'judgement is an act of narration that sets a process in motion; an act of participation in the public realm, informed by a sense of individual responsibility to the community. A sign of good judgement is the way that it binds together actors and spectators in a human community' (2001: 273). And where judgement on the particular requires guidance, it derives this guidance, Arendt claims, from other particulars that previous acts (or failures) of judgement have turned into *examples*, that is, into standards set by and embodied in exemplary individuals, objects and events which persuade by force of inspiration rather than by reason or evidence. These exemplary instances of virtues and vices, once purified into 'ideal types', serve as 'the guideposts of all moral thought' (RJ: 169–70, 144). In Arendt's own thinking, for example, Bernard Lazare (the 'conscious pariah'), Jesus ('forgiveness'), Eichmann (the 'banality of evil') and Socrates (the 'good citizen'), are all constructed as exemplary typifications of human actions and traits (see Parvikko 1999). Thus Socrates' moral edict that 'it is better to suffer wrong than to do wrong' has retained its persuasiveness in

Western civilisation, Arendt argues, because Socrates gave his life to exemplify this belief.

> We judge and tell right from wrong by having present in our mind some incident and some person, absent in time or space, that have become examples. There are many such examples. They can lie far back in the past or they can be among the living. They need not be historically real; as Jefferson once remarked: 'the fictitious murder of Duncan by Macbeth' excites in us 'as great a horror of villainy, as the real one of Henri IV' and a 'lively and lasting sense of filial duty is more effectually impressed on a son or daughter by reading *King Lear*, than by all the dry volumes of ethics and divinity that ever were written.' (RJ: 145)

This is how Arendt believes the particular can be judged without surrendering to absolute moral rules, and how moral standards can make a worldly appearance that persuades in the form of 'opinions', rather than coercing with the force of an irresistible truth. Indeed, this is also how exemplary individuals succeed in stabilising the consequences of their own exceptional actions, establishing standards to be admired and followed by their successors, thereby resolving the tension between genesis and normativity that, as Cascardi (1997) emphasises, is at the heart of Arendt's political thought. Arendt thus defines the 'example' as 'the particular that contains in itself, or is supposed to contain, a concept or a general rule'. 'This exemplar is and remains a particular that in its very particularity reveals the generality that otherwise could not be defined' (LK: 84, 77).

To illustrate her point that moral judgement does not answer to objective rules, but instead follows the concrete examples set by exceptional individuals, Arendt refers to a passage in the *Tusculan Disputations* where Cicero rejects the possibility of objective truth and, contemplating a choice between Plato and his Pythagorean opponents, chooses to 'go astray with Plato'. Cicero's bold statement against privileging the truth is interpreted by Arendt as a shining model of humanism: we humanise the world by refusing to be coerced by absolutes, and by choosing not principles, facts or ideas, but the people we want to be like and to be with. 'Cicero says: In what concerns my association with men and things, I refuse to be coerced even by truth, even by beauty' (PF: 225). And, of course, even by goodness.

This sentiment – which is curiously echoed in Foucault's later attempt to identify a Greco-Roman conception of morality that was oriented to autonomous 'practices of the self' rather than to formally codified rules (Foucault 1992) – is also conveyed by Arendt with a historical anecdote supposedly involving the medieval theologian Meister Eckhart. On meeting the happiest of beggars, Eckhart asked if the beggar would still be happy if he found himself in hell. The beggar, who believed his love of God guaranteed His divine company, replied: 'I'd much rather be in hell with God than in heaven without him.' Both accounts demonstrate for Arendt how 'there comes a point where all objective standards – truth, rewards and punishments in a hereafter, etc. – yield precedence to the "subjective" criterion of the kind of person I wish to be and live together with' (RJ: 110–11, 125, 145–6).

Conclusion: Going Astray with Arendt

Given her tendency to describe judgement as 'the most political of man's mental abilities' (RJ: 188; LM1: 192; PF: 221), one might logically conclude that judgement is for Arendt the reconciliation and transcendence of the division between the solitary life of the mind and the active life of the citizen, and the means by which the political realm of opinion or *doxa*, held in contempt by science and philosophy since Plato, is finally dignified and redeemed. In Habermas's view, Arendt regarded judgement 'as the core of rational orientations in the *Vita Activa*' and the last connecting piece in 'an ethics of communication which connects practical reason to the idea of a universal discourse' (1980: 130–1). Judgement, as Habermas sees it, is practical reasoning aimed at establishing a free and uncoerced consensus.

The same interpretation of Arendt is implicit in Ronald Beiner's reading of her early work, though Beiner argues that Arendt, to her discredit, retreated from this neo-Aristotelian position in her later writings on Kant, eventually 'excluding any reference to the *vita activa* within the revised concept of judgement', and in the process transforming political deliberation over practical ends into an 'unwarranted aestheticisation of politics' (1992: 134–9). When Arendt first introduced the notion of 'representative thinking' in the essays published in *Between Past and Future*, judgements of taste were treated as an essential component of political life, with culture and politics, judgement and opinion, 'belonging together' because both seek to take care of the world by sharing a plurality of perspectives on it (PF: 220–6). In her later lectures on Kant and in *The Life of the Mind*, on the other hand, Arendt appears to attribute the exercise of judgement to the impartial perspective of the non-acting spectator, emphasising that the meaning of the whole is never revealed to the engaged actor but only to those disinterested witnesses of the spectacle of human affairs. This was also where she located her own standpoint as an intellectual who 'understood something of action precisely because I looked at it from the outside', describing herself as able to 'live without doing anything', but unable to 'live without trying at least to understand whatever happens' (Arendt 1979: 303).

Echoing the apparent contradiction of the Greeks, whose love of beauty did not protect the artist from the reproach of philistinism, Kant seemed to recognise the superior position of the non-acting judge when he subordinated the 'lawless freedom' and 'genius' of the creator to the disciplined taste of the spectator, and when he praised the historical achievement of the French Revolution while simultaneously condemning the actions of its rebellious participants (LK: 62, 44–8). Where the spectator, rather than the actor, is concerned, the public context of judgement appears to be potential and imaginative rather than actual. Judgement, Arendt writes, 'still goes on in isolation, but by the force of imagination it makes the others present and thus moves in a space that is potentially public, open to all sides' (LK: 43). In Beiner's view, this is Arendt's solution to the conundrum of temporality and proof that her overriding concern was not action but worldliness. While the practical outlook of the actor looks forward to what should be done, it is the backward glance of the spectator which lends permanence, durability, and narrative coherence to the world. 'Judging, or the saving power of remembrance, helps us to preserve what would otherwise be lost to time; it lets endure what is essentially perishable. In other words, the ultimate function of judgement is to reconcile time and worldliness' (Beiner 1992: 155).

In Beiner's account of Arendt's later work, judgement is clearly much closer to thinking than it is to action. This interpretation is endorsed by Wellmer, who believes Arendt eschewed Aristotle's theory of prudently reasoned action because she was fixated on the idea that truth and rationality were ultimately enemies of political autonomy. By drawing idiosyncratically on Kant's writings on aesthetics, Wellmer argues, Arendt gave credence to the anti-modernist idea that judgements 'are not based on definite concepts, are not open to argument but only to "contention"'. In doing so she was led 'to dissociate judgement from action as well as from argumentation', thus abandoning the idea of a public sphere modelled on the rational pursuit of consensus (Wellmer 1996: 38, 33).

The claim that Arendt's reflections on the *vita contemplativa* signal a philosophical disengagement from the world of political debate and action, even exposing, as Wellmer suggests, flaws in the original concept of action that Arendt began with, is an uncomfortable challenge to those wishing to gain political inspiration and insight from Arendt's writings. This critical reading of Arendt can be disputed, however, for there are ambiguities in her thinking which invite more productive interpretations of her work. It is notable, for instance, that earlier in *The Life of the Mind* Arendt had distinguished 'the withdrawal of judgement' from 'the withdrawal of the philosopher', stressing the fact that 'spectators are members of an audience' and therefore 'are not solitary'. The judgement of the spectator, Arendt followed Kant's reasoning, is therefore political rather than merely philosophical in character, because it does not abandon the realm of plurality. 'The spectator, not the actor, holds the clue to the meaning of human affairs – only, and this is decisive, Kant's spectators exist in the plural, and this is why he could arrive at a political philosophy' (LM1: 94, 96).

Even if we concede that judgement may in some cases be a solitary activity, it is still one which thrives on real public conversation with other spectators whose perspectives must be constantly re-presented in a process of imaginary dialogue. To judge autonomously one must escape, by subjecting to self-scrutiny, one's personal experiences, private interests and inclinations, and it is only by adopting different standpoints – there is, in reality, no 'view from nowhere' that is suspended above particular locations – that such a self-critical perspective can be achieved. Here the difference between the soundless dialogue of the thinker and the intercourse with the other that facilitates judgement does indeed look slender, but this signals a public dimension to thinking rather than suggesting a withdrawal from the domain of plurality altogether. As Arendt had written of the notion of 'representative thinking' in her earlier work:

> this enlarged way of thinking, which as judgement knows how to transcend its individual limitations, cannot function in strict isolation or solitude; it needs the presence of others 'in whose place' it must think, whose perspective it must take into consideration, and without whom it never has the opportunity to operate at all. (PF: 220–1)

Challenging Arendt's tendency to view *moral* judgement as an essentially worldless inner dialogue aimed at agreement with oneself, Benhabib (2001) has argued that this very understanding of political judgement should really be extended to the moral province of the thinker as well. For morality is always context-dependent, and moral decisions must be informed both by our own personal stories and by the real and anticipated interpretations of others. The more narrative perspectives we can bring to bear on our moral understanding of situations, Benhabib argues, the more able we are to 'judge the particular' without surrendering to the false universals that have blighted moral philosophy since the Enlightenment.

Jennifer Nedelsky (2001) has also defended Arendt's theory of judgement, arguing that it provides logical support for the widening of diversity and inclusiveness in the membership of decision-making bodies such as the judiciary (though this may be equally applicable to parliament and the boardroom). Critics have complained that pro-diversity policies, such as quotas for women and minorities, legitimise the pernicious idea that the role of public decision-makers is to fight for the specific interests of the groups they represent, thereby absolving them of the requirement to be autonomous judges. Drawing on Arendt's Kantian notion of the 'enlarged mentality', however, Nedelsky emphasises that diversity is a requirement not for a better 'representation of interests', but for increasing the range of available perspectives in public life so as to enhance the possibility of genuinely autonomous and impartial judgement. As standpoint feminism has long argued, true objectivity does not float imperiously above the fray, but is instead strengthened through an educated acquaintance with different experiences and opinions.

There are, moreover, some obvious problems with the Habermasian critiques of Arendt. As Villa (1999b) points out, when judgement is reduced to rational public debate and collective decision-making, the purgative operation of critical thinking from which judgement arises is discarded, and with it is lost the ability to think and judge 'without banisters' which becomes so crucial when public standards have become empty clichés and political action has broken down. That Arendt, like Socrates, was willing to risk public resentment and the indictment of 'common sense' in order to exercise her capacity for autonomous discrimination – prompting vilification by the Jewish community, for example, by criticising the behaviour of the *Judenräte* while describing Eichmann's wickedness as 'banal' – is proof for Villa that judgement may often find itself at odds with the political demand for solidarity and consensus.

Is the link between critical thinking and politics a tenuous one, hanging precariously on Arendt's suggestion that thinking becomes politically relevant during historically rare times of crisis, when the refusal to follow the prefabricated opinions and behaviour of the majority becomes an exemplary act? Taylor (2002) is right to remind us that Arendt believed politics in the modern world was in a lasting state of crisis, with violence, deception and double-speak eclipsing the light of the public realm with the near-permanent shadow of 'dark times'. Villa's defence of Arendt is even more forceful in this respect. With politics subservient to the imperatives of capitalist growth and the preservation of a national security state, the opportunities for genuine public deliberation are fugitive at best. What we are witnessing, Villa claims, is a 'de-worlding of the public world' combined with a 'relentless subjectification of the real'. Both of these trends require, if they are to be resisted, a 'worldly form of estrangement' from an increasingly privatised and administered public sphere.

> Modern world alienation dissolves the *sensus communis*, with the result that the only things 'seen and heard by all' are the false appearances (Heidegger's 'semblances') offered up under the single aspect of mass culture ... The mistake of the Habermasians, the communitarians, and the participatory democrats is to assume that there may be a late modern substitute for this feeling for the world...
>
> It is not a question, therefore, of pretending that we can resurrect the agora or some approximation thereof by appealing to deliberation, intersubjectivity or 'acting in concert'. What matters is our ability to resist the demand for 'functionalised behaviour' and to preserve, as far as possible, our capacity for initiatory, agonistic action and spontaneous, independent judgement. (Villa 2001: 304–5)

When read against her theory of modern worldlessness, Arendt's account of the thinking ego thus acquires clearer significance. Although thinking is a means of defrosting rigid certainties, and in this sense seems peculiarly in harmony with a world of constant uncertainty and compulsory change, the disengagement from activity implied in the moral injunction to 'stop and think' may have growing salience when both stopping and thinking are highly unfavourable to those 'functionalised behaviours' required for the rapid circulation and exchange of commodities in the organised chaos that is contemporary capitalism. Stopping and thinking may also place the thinker out of the ever more intrusive reach of modern corporations, whose mastery of the art of manipulation enrols almost every willing participant in the communications revolution into an asymmetrical dialogue of seduction and submission. Of course, political mobilisation requires action, not inertia; but exit and refusal is the first prerequisite for breaking with the status quo, and claiming 'time to think', to reflect on and wonder at the world, is both an act of resistance to the global economic juggernaut and a means of cultivating a deep and lasting care for the human artifice and the natural environment – both of which Arendt believed were gravely endangered by trends in twentieth-century modernity.

That the fragmentation and parcelling of everyday consciousness is a critical barrier to progressive political engagement in the modern world is perhaps a truism today. Arendt's writings on thinking and judging are refreshing because they remind us that it is the imaginative ability to see this world from different perspectives – including the perspectives of figures too absent or marginalised to be recognisable members of our ailing polity, yet whose actions and sufferings are now inextricable from our own – which is the starting point for making political judgements about social justice and responsibility in a globalised society. This may be the standpoint of the illegal immigrant, the Asian sweatshop worker, the radicalised Muslim, the wretchedly impoverished inhabitants of war-torn or hyper-exploited states, or even the future generations who will inherit this damaged and depleted planet. If a dialogue with these figures proves impossible, then it is our ability to think from the standpoint of absent others, to make those others the company we keep when we are alone and conversing with ourselves, which keeps alive the possibility of a common world amidst the yawning chasm of global inequality and radically dissimilar life-chances. For global poverty, as Patrick Hayden (2009) has argued, must surely qualify as an extreme 'evil' in Arendt's sense of the term. Reducing to 'bare life' nearly a sixth of the world's population – 925 million people were estimated by the UN to be undernourished in 2010, with food deprivation causing a third of the 8.8 million annual child deaths worldwide (UNFAO 2010: 45, 33) – global poverty has been called a 'crime against humanity' the daily reproduction of which is normalised, Hayden points out, by our routine adjustment to the perfidy and charms of the affluent society. It is the 'preponderance of banal thoughtlessness', protected by the ideology of neo-liberalism, which Hayden argues has desensitised us to the ongoing political evil of extreme economic rights violations.

I have noted in this book how Arendt's fierce defence of the primacy of political action is tempered and inflected by a concern for stability and worldliness, and how her reflections on these matters offer social theorists new ways of engaging with environmental politics, with the critique of capitalism, with the changing nature of work, and with the need for a public sphere that respects people as citizens without demanding their affection, sincerity or love. What

Arendt offers, above all, however, is a lesson in the art of judgement. For there are few better examples of a truly original thinker, of someone who was determined to 'think the particular' in all its vivid and exceptional detail, to see the extraordinary amidst the ordinary, to make the normal look strange – sometimes shining with splendour and excellence, sometimes displayed in thought-defying horror – and in doing so to disrupt our complacent acquiescence to a world we have forgotten not just to question, but also to claim and to cherish as our own. For the trained social scientist, Arendt's originality may be unnerving, and her arguments may at times lead us astray. But the company, in my view, is unrivalled, and the conversation always enlivening. If, in the course of this book, I have pointed a few new readers in her direction, then writing it will have been a worthwhile public exercise and my interest in Arendt a more than private pleasure.

Notes

INTRODUCTION: TIME FOR ACTION

1. A few sections of text from Chapters 8 and 9 have been taken from my article 'Comparing Bauman and Arendt: Three Important Differences', published in *Sociology*, vol. 25, no. 1 (2011). I thank the publisher for allowing me to reproduce them here.

1 THE *VITA ACTIVA*

1. The *agora*, or marketplace, was the political and legal centre of the Greek city-state (the *polis*). Containing municipal offices and law courts, as well as shops and stalls, it was where people met to gossip and socialise. In Athens, formal debate between citizens took place in the assembly, or *ekklesia*, which was originally part of the *agora*, but which was later moved to an auditorium, called the Pnyx, constructed on the outskirts of the city. A minimum of 6,000 citizens were necessary for a session to begin, and the assembly met on average every nine days. A council, or *boulē*, of 500 members was also elected annually by the assembly, meeting daily in order to run the administrative and judicial affairs of the city. The *agora* is sometimes thought of (e.g. by Bauman 1999: 87ff) as a sphere of mediation between the formal site of politics (*ekklesia*) and the private household (*oikos*). Whether Arendt is referring to the *agora* in general or the assembly in particular is never clear in her account of the *polis*, for ultimately the *polis* is the space created by people in public interaction. 'The *polis*, properly speaking, is not the city-state in its physical location; it is the organisation of the people as it arises out of acting and speaking together ... "Wherever you go, you will be a *polis*": these famous words [of Pericles] became not merely the watchword of Greek colonisation, they expressed the conviction that action and speech create a space between the participants which can find its proper location almost any time and anywhere' (HC: 198).
2. 'The point is that genuine kings do not actually *do* things themselves; they *govern* people whose domain is doing, and they know when to embark on and initiate courses of action which are particularly important to a state, and when it's better to hold back. They delegate action to others' (Plato, *Republic*: 305c–d, emphasis in text).

2 CRITIQUE OF MODERNITY

1. For the vice of clinging servilely to life the Greeks had their own word: *philopsychia*, or love of life (PP: 122; Arendt 2002: 287).
2. The fact that Arendt always lived in rented accommodation suggests that she did not believe that the shelter and security of a stable private realm could only be

delivered through economic ownership of one's home. Given the extraordinary boom in the housing markets of Europe and the US following the deregulation of the finance industry in the 1980s, the effect of which was to transform people's homes into commercial investments, Arendt's conceptualisation of 'private property' needs to be handled carefully to avoid confusing it with the bourgeois concept of 'wealth'. What she had in mind when she spoke of private property was the exclusive right to stay in one's home – to make it a permanent place to live – not the right to trade one's home as a commodity. Hence: 'What is necessary for freedom is not wealth. What is necessary is security and a place of one's own shielded from the claims of the public' (Arendt 1977: 108). From Arendt's perspective, the apparently common fear, during a downturn in the housing market, of being 'trapped' in negative equity, only makes sense in a worldless society which treats housing as a liquid asset rather than a place to live in.

3. Jaspers, who was a friend of Max Weber, told Arendt of a dream he had just had in which Arendt was 'warmly welcomed' to Weber's apartment. She wrote back to Jaspers in the summer of 1950: 'Prompted by your dream I've read a lot of Max Weber. I felt so idiotically flattered by it that I was ashamed of myself. Weber's intellectual sobriety is impossible to match, at least for me' (Arendt and Jaspers 1992: 148–50). Arendt was nonetheless opposed to Weber's nationalism, and her theory of political action differed markedly from Weber's sociological treatment of power (see Baehr 2001).

4. A contrasting interpretation of Homer's impartiality is offered by Simone Weil, who attributed 'the extraordinary sense of equity which breaths through the *Iliad*' to Homer's understanding of the indiscriminate destructiveness of war. In the interpretation given by Weil, whose essay on the *Iliad* – which she describes as 'the purest and loveliest of mirrors' – was written at the beginning of the Second World War, Homer does not admire the greatness of the warriors, victors and vanquished alike, but instead depicts 'the human spirit as modified by its relations with force, as swept away, blinded, by the very force it imagined it could handle, as deformed by the weight of the force it submits to'. Homer's impartiality, for Weil, is a manifestation of his understanding that there are no heroes in war, that force 'turns anybody who is subjected to it into a *thing* ... Somebody was here, and the next minute there is nobody here at all.' 'The true hero, the true subject, the centre of the *Iliad* is force' (Weil 2005: 3, 32–3).

3   FROM ACTION TO POWER: THE FATE OF THE POLITICAL

1. 'Compassion must, in fact, be the stronger, the more the animal beholding any kind of distress identifies himself with the animal that suffers. Now, it is plain that such identification must have been much more perfect in a state of nature than it is in a state of reason ... It is then certain that compassion is a natural feeling, which, by moderating the activity of love of self in each individual, contributes to the preservation of the whole species' (Rousseau 1973: 68).

2. This was Socrates' explanation for refusing the offer of escape from his friend Crito. In preference to exile from the city that gave him his freedom, Socrates chose to die a citizen, respecting the laws under which he had been condemned (*Crito* 50a–51c).

3. Hence Rome's law of the Twelve Tables, which settled the conflict between the patricians and the plebes, created a common world not by unifying the opposing parties, but by linking them with a permanent tie. The Greek conception of law as boundary undoubtedly carried a price, which was the failure to develop an empire, as the city-states 'could never join together and unite in a permanent alliance'. The price of the Roman conception of law as connection, on the other hand, was a process of relentless expansion that could only end in eventual collapse, as well as the loss of the Greek and Homeric promotion of excellence and celebration of greatness (PP: 187–8).

4. In an interview conducted in the last year of his life, Foucault offered a revised understanding of power, distinguishing 'power as strategic games' from power as 'states of domination', suggesting that the normative ideal is to 'allow these games of power to be played with a minimum of domination'. Despite his explicit rejection here of the concept of 'bad power', what appears to distinguish normatively acceptable power from 'states of domination' is that the former involves strategic attempts to 'determine the behaviour of others' which are fluid, not static, and are therefore reversible. 'To exercise power over another, in a sort of open strategic game, where things could be reversed, that is not evil' (1987: 18–9). But the question remains: *who* should 'reverse' this operation of power, and *why*, if there is no subject and there is no 'evil' state of domination to be opposed? For a fuller discussion of Foucault's 'normatively confused' concept of power, see Fraser (1989a), Dews (1987, 1989) and Habermas (1987a).

4   MARXISM, ECOLOGY AND CULTURE

1. In the opening chapter of *Capital*, Marx distinguishes between abstract and concrete labour, describing them as two dimensions of the same activity. Thus all labour is concrete, in the sense of being a unique activity aimed at the production of specific use-values; but under capitalism, where labour is a commodity which must be exchanged in the form of equivalents, concrete labour is treated as the expression of a given magnitude of identical units of abstract labour – labour in the most elementary and generic form of a simple expenditure of physical energy. Skilled labour, therefore, is measured in terms of the equivalent units of unskilled labour expended in the production and reproduction of that labour, 'so that a smaller quantity of complex labour is considered equal to a larger quantity of simple labour' (Marx 1976: 135). Hence Arendt's claim that 'unskilled work is a contradiction in terms' (HC: 90) is a faint echo of Engels' remark, added as a footnote to Marx's text: 'The English language has the advantage of possessing two separate words for these two different aspects of labour. Labour which creates use-values and is qualitatively determined is called "work" as opposed to "labour"; labour which creates value and is only measured quantitatively is called "labour", as opposed to "work"' (Marx 1976: 138 n16). In the *Grundrisse*, Marx describes how, in the most advanced capitalist societies, abstract labour is transformed from an aspect of labour's commodification to a form of practice in itself. 'Indifference towards specific labours corresponds to a society in which ... labour ... has ceased to be organically linked with particular individuals in any specific form ... Here ... the point of departure of modern economics, namely the abstraction of the category "labour", "labour as such", labour pure and simple, becomes true in practice' (1973: 104–5).

5   FEMINISM, THE SOCIAL AND THE POLITICAL

1. In a rare gesture of generosity towards the social sciences, Arendt described sociology as superior to psychoanalysis because the former displays a historical sensitivity to 'what still is or once was within the realm of human freedom', whereas the investigations of the latter always end with the 'ahistorical' realm of the unconscious 'over which human beings do not have, and never have had, control' (EU: 33).
2. Benhabib claims that there are three conditions of human action according to Arendt: natality, plurality and what Benhabib calls 'narrativity' (2001: 187–9). What Arendt referred to as the 'web of human relationships' (HC: 183) is for Benhabib best understood as a web of discourses and stories rather than the concatenation of deeds and events.

6   IMPERIALISM, RACISM AND BUREAUCRACY: THE ROAD TO TOTALITARIANISM

1. The company responsible for building the Panama Canal ruined half a million French middle-class investors when it was declared bankrupt in 1889. Over 22,000 labourers had by this time lost their lives working on the project. Ferdinand de Lesseps, the entrepreneur and diplomat who led the Panama enterprise following his success in building the Suez Canal, was found to have bribed members of the press, parliament and civil servants to maintain support for the failing venture. The *Gründungsschwindel* was the German stock-market crash of 1873, which was the result of an unregulated speculative boom in which newly created joint stock companies unscrupulously mismanaged their creditors' investments. In the third volume of *Capital*, Engels adds a parenthetical editor's note to Marx's exposure of the central contradiction of the joint-stock company, which uses *social* capital (i.e. the combined savings of society) to exert private command over *social* labour (i.e. the combined contributions of co-operating workers), thus announcing 'the abolition of capital as private property within the confines of the capitalist mode of production itself'. Referring to Marx's withering assessment, Engels adds: 'The whole Panama swindle is exactly described here, a full twenty years before it took place' (Marx 1981: 566–70).
2. Marcel Stoetzler has challenged Arendt's apparent attempt to defend, against the parasitical greed and laziness of the bourgeois philistine and mob, a 'normal', egalitarian form of capitalism that is respectful of rights and committed to economic rationality and civilising work. In Stoetzler's view Arendt's position is not dissimilar to liberal anti-Semitism, and it helps explain 'her notorious racist comments on African "savages"'. 'She did not recognise that the bourgeois contempt for people who do not share the bourgeois concepts of time, labour, and history could also be racist' (Stoetzler 2007: 142–3).
3. Arendt was on the whole sympathetic to French existentialism for attempting to reverse the philosopher's retreat from the public realm. Thus she praised Sartre, Merleau-Ponty, Malraux and Camus for having 'taken seriously the rejection of academic philosophy and the abandonment of the contemplative position', and for standing 'apart from other trends in modern philosophy in that they are the only ones whose concern with politics is at the very centre of their work' (EU: 437–9, 188–93).

4. The exchange of letters between Scholem and Arendt was first published in Israel in the Summer of 1963, then in two German newspapers later in the year, and finally in *Encounter* in the US in January 1964. At Scholem's request, Arendt disguised the identity of Golda Meir by using the male pronoun. See Young-Bruehl (2004: 332–3) for a fuller account.

5. The *Protocols* was a document purporting to be the minutes of a fictitious meeting by scheming Jewish leaders in Basel in 1897. It was forged by a Russian agent with the aim of discrediting, by linking them to a wider Jewish plot, the economic reforms of the liberal minister of finance, Sergei Witte.

7   TOTALITARIANISM

1. In *Eichmann in Jerusalem*, Arendt refers to Eichmann's description of his own work – 'everything was always in a state of continuous flux, a steady stream' – as 'plausible to the student of totalitarianism, who knows that the monolithic quality of this form of government is a myth' (EJ: 152).

2. Of course the order had to be disobeyed by the legal experts charged with identifying the Reich's next victims. Bauman also argues that clarity of definition was necessary to appease those who were spared this fate: 'Precise definition of the Jew was necessary for reassuring the witnesses to the victimisation that what they saw or suspected would not happen to them, and hence that their interests were not under threat' (2000a: 125). I shall return to the discrepancy between the analyses of Arendt and Bauman – which to some extent echo the ambiguities in Weber's own account of bureaucracy – in this and the following chapter.

3. Whitfield also points out that the Nazis were so committed to the myth of female domesticity that they refused to allow women to work in the armaments factories (1980: 36).

4. Hence Arendt's phenomenological critique of logical positivism: 'truth is always supposed to reveal something, whereas consistency is only a mode of fitting statements together, and as such lacks the power of revelation. The new logical movement in philosophy, which grew out of pragmatism, has a frightening affinity with the totalitarian transformation of the pragmatic elements inherent in all ideologies into logicality, which severs its ties to reality and experience altogether' (EU: 317).

8   IN SEARCH OF THE SUBJECT

1. There is an interesting parallel here with the behaviour of Robert Oppenheimer at the McCarthy-inspired Atomic Energy Commission (AEC) hearing of April–May 1954, after which his security clearance for the Los Alamos laboratories was withdrawn. The lawyer representing the AEC aimed to prove that Oppenheimer had voiced no moral scruples about the development and use of the atom bomb, and that, in the light of his ethically neutral position on the A-bomb, the well-known reservations which the scientist now had about the hydrogen bomb could only be motivated by political, not ethical, considerations – it was proof, in other words, that he was a communist sympathiser. Not realising the trap that had been laid for him, Oppenheimer chose to demonstrate his professional obedience, and thus to inadvertently prove the lawyer's point: 'I did my job which was the job I was supposed to do. I was not in a policymaking position at Los

Alamos. I would have done anything that I was asked to do, including making the bombs in a different shape, if I had thought it was technically feasible' (see Polenberg 2003). On this theme it is also significant that *Eichmann in Jerusalem* intensified the growing divide between the Old and the New Left in the US, as members of the anti-war movement drew comparisons between Eichmann's lack of ideological convictions and the liberal politicians and state functionaries who administered the war in Vietnam (see Young-Bruehl 2004: 361).

2. Hence Sartre's description of the paradox faced by Jean Genet in his attempt to be evil: 'the greatest evil is to have an intimate knowledge of Good, to be *born good* like every human creature, and to reject that blinding light, to plunge deliberately into darkness' (Sartre 1964: 172–3).

3. Jaspers later congratulated Arendt for the phrase 'banality of evil' which, forgetting his own earlier use of the term, he was led to believe came from Arendt's husband, Heinrich Blücher (Arendt and Jaspers 1992: 542).

4. Arendt's familiarity with Weber stems from the influence of Jaspers, who was a close member of Weber's circle in Heidelberg, and who published studies on his work in 1932 and 1958. Jaspers' efforts to impress on Arendt the importance of Weber's thinking are recorded in his letters to her, beginning in April 1950 (Arendt and Jaspers 1992: 148). Parvikko (1999) argues, unconvincingly in my view, that Arendt was indebted to Weber, particularly for his methodological concept of ideal types, and that their conceptions of political responsibility and judgement were similar.

5. Arendt and Riesman shared a fertile period of correspondence, mainly on the subject of totalitarianism and the conformist nature of modern behaviour, in the four years leading up to the publication of their respective books, *The Origins of Totalitarianism* (1951), and *The Lonely Crowd* (1950), drafts of which they exchanged and commented on. Riesman was more effusive in his praise for Arendt's work than she was of his, though Baehr (2004), who challenges Arendt's monolithic depiction of totalitarian domination, argues that it was ironically Riesman, the classical social scientist, who was most conscious of the singular and the heterogeneous, and who understood the nuanced forms of resistance and fake compliance by which the 'total' character of the regime was undone.

6. A contemporary example of this moral relativism, which shows clearly the legacy of the Holocaust, is John Gray's *Straw Dogs* (2002). Arendt also refers to the more mundane case of Charles Van Doren, the US game-show contestant who in 1959 admitted to conspiring with the producers of *Twenty-One* to ensure a two-month winning streak which brought him considerable fame and fortune. Arendt was startled by the lack of public condemnation of his or the producers' behaviour. This did not express a rebellion against sanctimonious respectability and a championing of the fun of cheating over the tedium of piety and good will. Public opinion, rather, was that the temptation to cheat was irresistible and therefore could not be criticised (RJ: 60). There is an obvious parallel here with the American public's sympathy with President Clinton following the exposure of his adulterous affair with the White House intern Monica Lewinksy. As Fevre points out, 'Clinton was saved from judgement by common-sense views about the imperfectability of human nature' (2000: 67). Sexual indiscretion was an irresistible temptation which the public identified with and therefore refused to judge.

9   THE *VITA CONTEMPLATIVA*

1. Since this quote is not the same as the relevant passage in both the original (1907) Helen Zimmern translation and the later (1966) Walter Kaufmann translation, it must be Arendt's own translation from the German.
2. 'If the universal (the rule, the principle, the law) be given, the Judgement which subsumes the particular under it ... is *determinant*. But if only the particular be given for which the universal has to be found, the Judgement is merely *reflective*' (Kant 1914: 11–12).
3. In Hans Jonas's more persuasive account, touch is perhaps the least objective sense, as to touch the world is always to enter into intercourse with it, to encounter and be moved by its practical resistance. This contrasts with the effortlessness of sight, which beholds 'the thing as it is in itself as distinct from the thing as it affects me' (2001: 147).

References

Abercrombie, N., S. Hill and B. S. Turner (1980) *The Dominant Ideology Thesis*. London: George Allen and Unwin.

Adler, H. G. (1958) 'Ideas Toward a Sociology of the Concentration Camp', *American Journal of Sociology*, vol. 63, no. 5.

Adorno, T. (1973) *The Jargon of Authenticity*. London: Routledge.

Adorno, T. (1978) *Minima Moralia*. London: Verso.

Adorno, T. and M. Horkheimer (1997) 'The Culture Industry: Enlightenment as Mass Deception', in *Dialectic of Enlightenment*. London: Verso.

Agamben, G. (1998) *Homo Sacer: Sovereign Power and Bare Life*. Stanford, CA: Stanford University Press.

Agamben, G. (2004) *The Open: Man and Animal*. Stanford, CA: Stanford University Press.

Allen, A. (2002) 'Power, Subjectivity, and Agency: Between Arendt and Foucault', *International Journal of Philosophical Studies*, vol. 10, no. 2.

Allen, J. (2003) *Lost Geographies of Power*. Oxford: Blackwell.

Arato, A. (2002) 'Dictatorship Before and After Totalitarianism', *Social Research*, vol. 69, no. 2.

Arendt, H. (1971) 'Martin Heidegger at Eighty', *New York Review of Books*, vol. 17, no. 6, October 21.

Arendt, H. (1977) 'Public Rights and Private Interests', in M. Mooney and F. Stuber (eds.), *Small Comforts for Hard Times: Humanists on Public Policy*. New York: Columbia University Press.

Arendt, H. (1979) 'On Hannah Arendt', in M. A. Hill (ed.), *Hannah Arendt: The Recovery of the Public World*. New York: St. Martin's Press.

Arendt, H. (2002) 'Karl Marx and the Tradition of Western Political Thought', *Social Research*, vol. 69, no. 2.

Arendt, H. and G. Scholem (1964) '"Eichmann in Jerusalem": An Exchange of Letters Between Gershom Scholem and Hannah Arendt', *Encounter*, vol. 22, no. 1, January.

Arendt, H. and K. Jaspers (1992) *Correspondence, 1926–1969*, eds. L. Kohler and H. Saner. New York: Harcourt Brace Jovanovich.

Arendt, H. and M. McCarthy (1995) *Between Friends: The Correspondence of Hannah Arendt and Mary McCarthy 1949–1975*, ed. C. Brightman. New York: Harcourt Brace.

Aristotle (1976) *Nicomachean Ethics*. Trans. J. A. K. Thomson. Harmondsworth: Penguin. Revised edition.

Aristotle (1981) *The Politics*. Trans. T. A. Sinclair. Harmondsworth: Penguin. Revised edition.

Baehr, P. (2001) 'The Grammar of Prudence: Arendt, Jaspers, and the Appraisal of Max Weber', in S. E. Aschheim (ed.), *Hannah Arendt in Jerusalem*. Berkeley: University of California Press.

Baehr, P. (2002) 'Identifying the Unprecedented: Hannah Arendt, Totalitarianism, and the Critique of Sociology', *American Sociological Review*, vol. 67, no. 6.

Baehr, P. (2004) 'Of Politics and Social Science: "Totalitarianism" in the Dialogue of David Riesman and Hannah Arendt', *European Journal of Political Theory*, vol. 3, no. 2.

Baehr, P. (2010) *Hannah Arendt, Totalitarianism, and the Social Sciences*. Stanford: Stanford University Press.

Bakan, M. (1979) 'Hannah Arendt's Concepts of Labor and Work', in M. A. Hill (ed.), *Hannah Arendt: The Recovery of the Public World*. New York: St. Martin's Press.

Bauman, Z. (1993) *Postmodern Ethics*. Oxford: Blackwell.

Bauman, Z. (1994) *Alone Again: Ethics After Certainty*. London: Demos.

Bauman, Z. (1999) *In Search of Politics*. Cambridge: Polity.

Bauman, Z. (2000a) *Modernity and the Holocaust*. Cambridge: Polity.

Bauman, Z. (2000b) *Liquid Modernity*. Cambridge: Polity.

Bauman, Z. (2001) 'Consuming Life', *Journal of Consumer Culture*, vol. 1, no. 1.

Bauman, Z. (2003) *Liquid Love*. Cambridge: Polity.

Bauman, Z. (2008) *The Art of Life*. Cambridge: Polity.

Beatty, J. (1994) 'Thinking and Moral Considerations: Socrates and Arendt's Eichmann', in L. P. Hinchman and S. K. Hinchman (eds.), *Hannah Arendt: Critical Essays*. New York: State University of New York Press.

Beiner, R. (1984) 'Action, Natality and Citizenship: Hannah Arendt's Concept of Freedom', in Z. Pelczynski and J. Gray (eds.), *Conceptions of Liberty in Political Thought*. London: Athlone Press.

Beiner, R. S. (1990) 'Hannah Arendt on Capitalism and Socialism', *Government and Politics*, vol. 25, no. 3.

Beiner, R. (1992) 'Hannah Arendt on Judging', in H. Arendt, *Lectures on Kant's Political Philosophy*. Chicago: University of Chicago Press.

Beiner, R. (1997) 'Foucault's Hyper-Liberalism', in *Philosophy in a Time of Lost Spirit: Essays on Contemporary Theory*. Toronto: Toronto University Press.

Benhabib, S. (1992) 'Models of Public Space: Hannah Arendt, the Liberal Tradition, and Jürgen Habermas', in C. Calhoun (ed.), *Habermas and the Public Sphere*. Cambridge, MA: MIT Press.

Benhabib, S. (2001) 'Judgement and Politics in Arendt's Thought', in R. Beiner and J. Nedelsky (eds.), *Judgement, Imagination, and Politics: Themes from Kant and Arendt*. Lanham, MD: Rowman and Littlefield.

Benhabib, S. (2002) 'Political Geographies in a Global World: Arendtian Reflections', *Social Research*, vol. 69, no. 2.

Benhabib, S. (2003) *The Reluctant Modernism of Hannah Arendt*. Lanham, MD: Rowman and Littlefield.

Benjamin, W. (1973) *Illuminations*. London: Fontana.

Berger, P. and T. Luckmann (1967) *The Social Construction of Reality*. Harmondsworth: Penguin.

Berlin, I. (1969) 'Two Concepts of Liberty', in I. Berlin, *Four Concepts of Liberty*. Oxford: New York.

Bernasconi, R. (2007) 'When the Real Crime Began: Hannah Arendt's *The Origins of Totalitarianism* and the Dignity of the Western Philosophical Tradition', in R. H. King and D. Stone (eds.), *Hannah Arendt and the Uses of History: Imperialism, Nation, Race and Genocide*. New York: Berghahn.

Bernstein, R. J. (1986a) 'Rethinking the Social and the Political', in *Philosophical Profiles: Essays in a Pragmatic Mode*. Cambridge: Polity.

Bernstein, R. J. (1986b) 'Judging – the Actor and the Spectator', in *Philosophical Profiles: Essays in a Pragmatic Mode*. Cambridge: Polity.

Bettelheim, B. (1979) *Surviving and Other Essays*. London: Thames and Hudson.

Bilsky, L. Y. (2001) 'When Actor and Spectator Meet in the Courtroom: Reflections on Hannah Arendt's Concept of Judgement', in R. Beiner and J. Nedelsky (eds.), *Judgement, Imagination, and Politics: Themes from Kant and Arendt*. Lanham, MD: Rowman and Littlefield.

Bloch, H. A. (1947) 'The Personality of Inmates of Concentration Camps', *American Journal of Sociology*, vol. 52, no. 4.

Bowring, F. (2003) *Science, Seeds and Cyborgs: Biotechnology and the Appropriation of Life*. London: Verso.

Brand, A. (1986) 'The "Colonization of the Lifeworld" and the Disappearance of Politics – Arendt and Habermas', *Thesis Eleven*, no. 13.

Breitman, R. (2004) *The Architect of Genocide: Himmler and the Final Solution*. London: Pimlico.

Butler, J. (2007) '"I Merely Belong to Them"', *London Review of Books*, vol. 29, no. 9, May.

Canovan, M. (1983) 'A Case of Distorted Communication: A Note on Habermas and Arendt', *Political Theory*, vol. 11, no. 1.

Caplan, J. (1988) *Government Without Administration: State and Civil Service in Weimar and Nazi Germany*. Oxford: Oxford University Press.

Cascardi, A. J. (1997) 'Communication and Transformation: Aesthetics and Politics in Kant and Arendt', in C. Calhoun and J. McGowan (eds.), *Hannah Arendt and the Meaning of Politics*. Minneapolis: University of Minnesota Press.

Cicourel, A. V. (1974) *Cognitive Sociology*. New York: Free Press.

Cohen, J. L. and A. Arato (1992) *Civil Society and Political Theory*. Cambridge, MA: MIT Press.

Connolly, K. (2008) 'Auschwitz Blueprints Emerge on 70th Anniversary of Kristallnacht', *The Guardian*, 10 November.

d'Entrèves, M. P. (1994) *The Political Philosophy of Hannah Arendt*. London: Routledge.

Dews, P. (1987) *Logics of Disintegration: Post-Structuralist Thought and the Claims of Critical Theory*. London: Verso.

Dews, P. (1989) 'The Return of the Subject in Late Foucault', *Radical Philosophy*, no. 51, Spring.

Dietz, M. G. (1991) 'Hannah Arendt and Feminist Politics', in M. L. Shanley and C. Pateman (eds.), *Feminist Interpretations and Political Theory*. Cambridge: Polity.

Dietz, M. G. (1995) 'Feminist Receptions of Hannah Arendt', in B. Honig (ed.), *Feminist Interpretations of Hannah Arendt*. University Park, PA: Pennsylvania State University Press.

Dietz, M. G. (2002) *Turning Operations: Feminism, Arendt, and Politics*. London: Routledge.

Disch, L. (1997) '"Please Sit Down, but Don't Make Yourself at Home": Arendtian "Visiting" and the Prefigurative Politics of Consciousness-Raising', in C. Calhoun and J. McGowan (eds.), *Hannah Arendt and the Meaning of Politics*. Minneapolis: University of Minnesota Press.

Du Gay, P. (2000) *In Praise of Bureaucracy*. London: Sage.

Duarte, A. (2007) 'Hannah Arendt, Biopolitics, and the Problem of Violence: From *animal laborans* to *homo sacer*', in R. H. King and D. Stone (eds.), *Hannah*

Arendt and the Uses of History: Imperialism, Nation, Race and Genocide. New York: Berghahn.

Durkheim, E. (1951) *Suicide: A Study in Sociology*. New York: Free Press.

Durkheim, E. (1964) *The Division of Labour in Society*. New York: Free Press.

Durkheim, E. (1973a) 'Individualism and the Intellectuals', in *On Morality and Society*, ed. R. N. Bellah. Chicago: University of Chicago Press.

Durkheim, E. (1973b) 'The Dualism of Human Nature and its Social Conditions', in *On Morality and Society*, ed. R. N. Bellah. Chicago: University of Chicago Press.

Durkheim, E. (1974) 'The Determination of Moral Facts', in *Sociology and Philosophy*. New York: Free Press.

Durkheim, E. (1982) *The Rules of Sociological Method and Selected Texts on Sociology and its Method*. London: Macmillan.

Elias, N. (2000) *The Civilizing Process*. Revised edition. Oxford: Blackwell.

Elshtain, J. B. (1992) *Meditations of Modern Political Thought: Masculine/Feminine Themes from Luther to Arendt*. University Park, PA: Pennsylvania State University Press.

Engels, F. (1934) *Ludwig Feuerbach and the Outcome of Classical German Philosophy*. London: Martin Lawrence.

Engels, F. (1950) 'On Authority', in K. Marx and F. Engels, *Selected Works. Volume 1*. Moscow: Foreign Languages Publishing House.

Engels, F. (1951a) 'Socialism: Utopian and Scientific', in K. Marx and F. Engels, *Selected Works. Volume 2*. Moscow: Foreign Languages Publishing House.

Engels, F. (1951b) 'The Part Played By Labour in the Transition from Ape to Man', in K. Marx and F. Engels, *Selected Works. Volume 2*. Moscow: Foreign Languages Publishing House.

Engels, F. (1969) *Anti-Dühring*. London: Lawrence and Wishart.

Fevre, R. (2000) *The Demoralization of Western Culture*. London: Continuum.

Fevre, R. (2003) *The New Sociology of Economic Behaviour*. London: Sage.

Flecker, J. and J. Hofbauer (1998) 'Capitalising on Subjectivity: The "New Model Worker" and the Importance of Being Useful', in P. Thompson and C. Warhurst (eds.), *Workplaces of the Future*. London: Macmillan.

Foucault, M. (1980a) 'Two Lectures', in *Power/Knowledge: Selected Interviews and Other Writings*. New York: Pantheon.

Foucault, M. (1980b) 'Truth and Power', in *Power/Knowledge: Selected Interviews and Other Writings*. New York: Pantheon.

Foucault, M. (1980c) 'Power and Strategies', in *Power/Knowledge: Selected Interviews and Other Writings*. New York: Pantheon.

Foucault, M. (1980d) 'The History of Sexuality', in *Power/Knowledge: Selected Interviews and Other Writings*. New York: Pantheon.

Foucault, M. (1981) *The History of Sexuality. Volume 1: An Introduction*. London: Penguin.

Foucault, M. (1984) 'On the Genealogy of Ethics: An Overview of Work in Progress', in P. Rabinow (ed.), *The Foucault Reader: An Introduction to Foucault's Thought*. Harmondsworth: Penguin.

Foucault, M. (1987) 'The Ethic of Care for the Self as a Practice of Freedom: An Interview with Michel Foucault', in J. Bernauer and D. Rasmussen (eds.), *The Final Foucault*. Cambridge, MA: MIT Press.

Foucault, M. (1991) *Discipline and Punish*. London: Penguin.

Foucault, M. (1992) *The History of Sexuality. Volume 2: The Use of Pleasure*. London: Penguin.

Fraser, N. (1989a) 'Foucault on Power: Empirical Insights and Normative Confusions', in *Unruly Practices: Power, Discourse and Gender in Contemporary Social Theory*. Cambridge: Polity.

Fraser, N. (1989b) 'Women, Welfare, and the Politics of Need Interpretation', in *Unruly Practices: Power, Discourse and Gender in Contemporary Social Theory*. Cambridge: Polity.

Fraser, N. (1992) 'Rethinking the Public Sphere: A Contribution to the Critique of Actually Existing Democracy', in C. Calhoun (ed.), *Habermas and the Public Sphere*. Cambridge, MA: MIT Press.

Freud, S. (2002) *Civilization and its Discontents*. London: Penguin.

Fromm, E. (1956) *The Sane Society*. Routledge and Kegan Paul.

Gerth, H. (1940) 'The Nazi Party: Its Leadership and Composition', *American Journal of Sociology*, vol. 45, no. 4.

Giddens, A. (1984) *The Constitution of Society: Outline of the Theory of Structuration*. Cambridge: Polity.

Giddens, A. (1994) *Beyond Left and Right: The Future of Radical Politics*. Cambridge: Polity.

Gines, K. T. (2007) 'Race Thinking and Racism in Hannah Arendt's *The Origins of Totalitarianism*', in R. H. King and D. Stone (eds.), *Hannah Arendt and the Uses of History: Imperialism, Nation, Race and Genocide*. New York: Berghahn.

Goffman, E. (1961) *Asylums*. Harmondsworth: Penguin.

Gorz, A. (1989) *Critique of Economic Reason*. London: Verso.

Gorz, A. (2003) *L'immatériel. Connaissance, valeur et capital*. Paris: Galilée.

Gouldner, A. W. (1962) 'Introduction', in E. Durkheim, *Socialism*. New York: Collier.

Gouldner, A. W. (1967) *Enter Plato: Classical Greece and the Origins of Social Theory*. London: Routledge and Kegan Paul.

Gray, J. (2002) *Straw Dogs: Thoughts on Humans and Other Animals*. London: Granta.

Greenspan, A. (2007) *The Age of Turbulence*. London: Allen Lane.

Habermas, J. (1972) *Knowledge and Human Interests*. London: Heinemann.

Habermas, J. (1974) 'Between Philosophy and Science: Marxism as Critique', in *Theory and Practice*. London: Heinemann.

Habermas, J. (1980) 'On the German-Jewish Heritage', *Telos*, no. 44.

Habermas, J. (1983) 'Hannah Arendt: On the Concept of Power', in *Philosophical-Political Profiles*. London: Heinemann.

Habermas, J. (1984) *The Theory of Communicative Action. Volume 1: Reason and the Rationalisation of Society*. Cambridge: Polity.

Habermas, J. (1987a) 'Some Questions Concerning the Theory of Power: Foucault Again', in *The Philosophical Discourse of Modernity*. Cambridge: Polity.

Habermas, J. (1987b) *The Theory of Communicative Action. Volume 2: The Critique of Functionalist Reason*. Cambridge: Polity.

Habermas, J. (1989) *The Structural Transformation of the Public Sphere*. Cambridge: Polity.

Habermas, J. (1992) 'Further Reflections on the Public Sphere', in C. Calhoun (ed.), *Habermas and the Public Sphere*. Cambridge, MA: MIT Press.

Habermas, J. (1994) 'Hannah Arendt's Communications Concept of Power', in L. P. Hinchman and L. K. Hinchman (eds.), *Hannah Arendt: Critical Essays*. New York: State University of New York Press.

Habermas, J. (1996) *Between Facts and Norms*. Cambridge: Polity.

Habermas, J. (2003) *The Future of Human Nature*. Cambridge: Polity.

Hartsock, N. C. (1985) *Money, Sex, and Power: Toward a Feminist Historical Materialism*. Boston: Northeastern University Press.

Harvey, D. (2005) *The New Imperialism*. Oxford: Oxford University Press.

Hayden, P. (2009) *Political Evil in a Global Age: Hannah Arendt and International Theory*. London: Routledge.

Heidegger, M. (1962) *Being and Time*. Oxford: Blackwell.

Heidegger, M. (1977) 'The Question Concerning Technology', in *The Question Concerning Technology and Other Essays*. New York: Harper and Row.

Hobbes (1968) *Leviathan*. Harmondsworth: Penguin.

Hochschild, A. R. (1983) *The Managed Heart: The Commercialization of Human Feeling*. Berkeley: University of California Press.

Honan, W. H. (1991) 'Helping Hostile Cultures Touch', *New York Times*, 4 February.

Honig, B. (1995) 'Toward an Agonistic Feminism: Hannah Arendt and the Politics of Identity', in B. Honig (ed.), *Feminist Interpretations of Hannah Arendt*. University Park, Pennsylvania: Pennsylvania State University Press.

Horkheimer, M. (1974) 'The Concept of Man', in *Critique of Instrumental Reason*. New York: Seabury.

Horkheimer, M. (1982) 'Authority and the Family', in *Critical Theory: Selected Essays*. New York: Continuum.

Hume, D. (2000) *An Enquiry Concerning Human Understanding*, ed. Tom L. Beauchamp. Oxford: Clarendon Press.

Jalušič, V. (2007) 'Post-Totalitarian Elements and Eichmann's Mentality in the Yugoslav War and Mass Killings', in R. H. King and D. Stone (eds.), *Hannah Arendt and the Uses of History: Imperialism, Nation, Race and Genocide*. New York: Berghahn.

Jay, M. (1986) 'The Political Existentialism of Hannah Arendt', in *Permanent Exiles: Essays on the Intellectual Migration from Germany to America*. New York: Columbia University Press.

Jonas, H. (2001) 'The Nobility of Sight: A Study in the Phenomenology of the Senses', in *The Phenomenon of Life: Toward a Philosophical Biology*. Evanston, IL: Northwestern University Press.

Kant, I. (1914) *Critique of Judgement*. London: Macmillan.

Kateb, G. (1977) 'Freedom and Worldliness in the Thought of Hannah Arendt', *Political Theory*, vol. 5, no. 2.

Kateb, G. (1984) *Hannah Arendt: Politics, Conscience, Evil*. Totowa, NJ: Rowman and Allanheld.

Kateb, G. (2001) 'The Judgement of Arendt', in R. Beiner and J. Nedelsky (eds.), *Judgement, Imagination, and Politics: Themes from Kant and Arendt*. Lanham, MD: Rowman and Littlefield.

Kateb, G. (2002) 'Ideology and Storytelling', *Social Research*, vol. 69, no. 2.

Klein, N. (2007) *The Shock Doctrine: The Rise of Disaster Capitalism*. London: Allen Lane.

Krause, M. (2008) 'Undocumented Migrants: An Arendtian Perspective', *European Journal of Political Theory*, vol. 7, no. 3.

Laclau, E. and C. Mouffe (2001) *Hegemony and Socialist Strategy: Towards a Radical Democratic Politics*. Second edition. London: Verso.

Lenin, V. I. (1976) *The State and Revolution*. Second edition. Peking: Foreign Languages Press.

Lockwood, D. (1956) 'Some Remarks on "The Social System"', *British Journal of Sociology*, vol. 7, no. 2.

Lockwood, D. (1964) 'Social Integration and System Integration', in G. K. Zollschan and W. Hirsch (eds.), *Explorations in Social Change*. London: Routledge and Kegan Paul.

Lukes, S. (1974) *Power: A Radical View*. London: Macmillan.

Luxemburg, R. (1951) *The Accumulation of Capital*. London: Routledge and Kegan Paul.

Macauley, D. (1996) 'Hannah Arendt and the Politics of Place: From Earth Alienation to *Oikos*', in *Minding Nature: The Philosophers of Ecology*. New York: Guilford.

McGowan, J. (1997) 'Must Politics Be Violent: Arendt's Utopian Vision', in C. Calhoun and J. McGowan (eds.), *Hannah Arendt and the Meaning of Politics*. Minneapolis: University of Minnesota Press.

Marcuse, H. (1965a) 'Repressive Tolerance', in R. P. Wolff, B. Moore and H. Marcuse, *A Critique of Pure Tolerance*. Boston: Beacon Press.

Marcuse, H. (1965b) 'Socialism in the Developed Countries', *International Socialist Journal*, year 2, no. 8.

Marcuse, H. (1970) 'The Obsolescence of the Freudian Concept of Man', in *Five Lectures*. London: Allen Lane.

Marcuse, H. (1991) *One Dimensional Man*. Second edition. London: Routledge.

Marquand, D. (2004) *Decline of the Public*. Cambridge: Polity.

Marx, K. (1951) 'Critique of the Gotha Programme', in K. Marx and F. Engels, *Selected Works. Volume 2*. Moscow: Foreign Languages Publishing House.

Marx, K. (1969) *Theories of Surplus Value. Part 1*. London: Lawrence and Wishart.

Marx, K. (1973) *Grundrisse*. Harmondsworth: Penguin.

Marx, K. (1975a) 'Economic and Philosophical Manuscripts', in *Early Writings*. Harmondsworth: Penguin.

Marx, K. (1975b) 'A Contribution to the Critique of Hegel's Philosophy of Right. Introduction', in *Early Writings*. Harmondsworth: Penguin.

Marx, K. (1976) *Capital: A Critique of Political Economy. Volume 1*. Harmondsworth: Penguin.

Marx, K. (1981) *Capital. Volume 3*. Harmondsworth: Penguin.

Marx, K. (1995) *The Poverty of Philosophy*. New York: Prometheus.

Marx, K. and F. Engels (1967) *The Communist Manifesto*. Harmondsworth: Penguin.

Marx, K. and F. Engels (1998) *The German Ideology*. New York: Prometheus.

May, L. (1996) 'Socialisation and Institutional Evil', L. May and J. Kohn (eds.), *Hannah Arendt: Twenty Years Later*. Cambridge, MA: MIT Press.

Meštrović, S. G. (1997) *Postemotional Society*. London: Sage.

Miller, J. (1979) 'The Pathos of Novelty: Hannah Arendt's Image of Freedom in the Modern World', in M. A. Hill (ed.), *Hannah Arendt: The Recovery of the Public World*. New York: St. Martin's Press.

Mills, C. W. (1951) *White Collar*. Oxford: Oxford University Press.

Mills, C. W. (1956) *The Power Elite*. New York: Oxford University Press.

Mills, C. W. (1959) *The Sociological Imagination*. Oxford: Oxford University Press.

Mommsen, H. (1986) 'The Realisation of the Unthinkable: "The Final Solution of the Jewish Question" in the Third Reich', in G. Hirschfeld (ed.), *The Policies of Genocide: Jews and the Soviet Prisoners of War in Nazi Germany*. London: Allen and Unwin.

Moruzzi, N. C. (2000) *Speaking Through the Mask: Hannah Arendt and the Politics of Social Identity*. Ithaca: Cornell University Press.

Mouffe, C. (1993) *The Return of the Political*. London: Verso.

Mouffe, C. (2000) *The Democratic Paradox*. London: Verso.

Nedelsky, J. (2001) 'Judgement, Diversity, and Relational Autonomy', in R. Beiner and J. Nedelsky (eds.), *Judgement, Imagination, and Politics: Themes from Kant and Arendt*. Lanham, MD: Rowman and Littlefield.

Nietzsche, F. W. (1907) *Beyond Good and Evil*. Trans. Helen Zimmern. Edinburgh: Foulis.

Nietzsche, F. W. (1966) *Beyond Good and Evil*. Trans. Walter Kaufmann. New York: Random House.

O'Brien, M. (1981) *The Politics of Reproduction*. London: Routledge and Kegan Paul.

Parekh, B. (1979) 'Hannah Arendt's Critique of Marx', in M. A. Hill (ed.), *Hannah Arendt: The Recovery of the Public World*. New York: St. Martin's Press.

Parsons, T. (1942) 'Max Weber and the Contemporary Political Crisis', *The Review of Politics*, vol. 4, no. 2.

Parvikko, T. (1999) 'Committed to Think, Judge and Act: Hannah Arendt's Ideal-typical Approach to Human Faculties', in J. J. Hermsen and D. R. Villa (eds.), *The Judge and the Spectator: Hannah Arendt's Political Philosophy*. Leuven: Peeters.

Pitkin, H. F. (1994) 'Justice: On Relating Private and Public', in L. P. Hichman and L. K. Hinchman (eds.), *Hannah Arendt: Critical Essays*. New York: State University of New York Press.

Pitkin, H. F. (1995) 'Conformism, Housekeeping, and the Attack of the Blob: The Origins of Hannah Arendt's Concept of the Social', in B. Honig (ed.), *Feminist Interpretations of Hannah Arendt*. University Park, PA: Pennsylvania State University Press.

Pitkin, H. F. (1998) *Attack of the Blob: Hannah Arendt's Concept of the Social*. Chicago: University of Chicago Press.

Plato (1995) *Statesman*. Trans. R. Waterfield. Cambridge: Cambridge University Press.

Plato (1997) *Republic*. Trans. J. L. Davies and D. J. Vaughan. Ware: Wordsworth.

Plato (2002) *Five Dialogues: Euthyphro, Apology, Crito, Meno, Phaedo*. Trans. G. M. A. Grube. Second edition. Indianapolis: Hackett.

Plato (2004) *Gorgias*. Trans. W. Hamilton and C. Emlyn-Jones. London: Penguin. Revised edition.

Plot, M. (2009) 'Communicative Action's Democratic Deficit: A Critique of Habermas's Contribution to Democratic Theory', *International Journal of Communication*, vol. 3.

Polanyi, K. (1957) *The Great Transformation*. Boston. Beacon Press.

Polenberg, R. (2003) 'The Ethical Responsibilities of the Scientist: The Case of J. Robert Oppenheimer', in W. H. Chafe (ed.), *The Achievement of American Liberalism: The New Deal and its Legacies*. New York: Columbia University Press.

Power, S. (2004) 'Introduction', in H. Arendt, *The Origins of Totalitarianism*. New York: Schocken.

Presbey, G. (1997) 'Critique of Boers or Africans', in E. C. Eze (ed.), *Postcolonial African Philosophy: A Critical Reader*. Oxford: Blackwell.

Rich, A. (1979) *On Lies, Secrets, and Silence: Selected Prose*. New York: W.W. Norton.

Riesman, D. (1961) *The Lonely Crowd*. Abridged edition. New Haven: Yale University Press.

Ring, J. (1989) 'On Needing Both Marx and Arendt: Alienation and the Flight from Inwardness', *Political Theory*, vol. 17, no. 3.

Robin, C. (2007) 'Dragon-Slayers', *London Review of Books*, vol. 29, no. 1, 4 January.

Rousseau, J.-J. (1973) *The Social Contract and Discourses*. London: Dent.

Ruddick, S. (1990) *Maternal Thinking: Towards a Politics of Peace*. London: Women's Press.

Sartre, J.-P. (1948) *Portrait of the Anti-Semite*. London: Secker and Warburg.

Sartre, J.-P. (1964) *Saint Genet*. New York: Mentor.

Sayers, S. (2003) 'Creative Activity and Alienation in Hegel and Marx', *Historical Materialism*, vol. 11, no. 1.

Schleunes, K. A. (1970) *The Twisted Road to Auschwitz: Nazi Policy Toward German Jews 1933–1939*. Urbana, IL: University of Illinois Press.

Schraube, E. 'Anders, Günter', in C. Mitcham (ed.), *Encyclopedia of Science, Technology, and Ethics*. New York: Macmillan.

Seale, C. (1999) 'Quality in Qualitative Research', *Qualitative Inquiry*, vol. 5, no. 4.

Sennett, R. (1977) *The Fall of Public Man*. London: Penguin.

Sennett, R. (1998) *The Corrosion of Character: The Personal Consequences of Work in the New Capitalism*. New York: W. W. Norton.

Sennett, R. (2003) *Respect: The Formation of Character in an Age of Inequality*. London: Penguin.

Sennett, R. (2009) *The Craftsman*. London: Penguin.

Simmel, G. (1968) 'The Conflict in Modern Culture', in *The Conflict in Modern Culture and Other Essays*. New York: Teachers College Press.

Simmel, G. (2004) *The Philosophy of Money*. Third edition. London: Routledge.

Simon, W. and John H. Gagnon (1976) 'The Anomie of Affluence: A Post-Mertonian Conception', *American Journal of Sociology*, vol. 82, no. 2.

Solzhenitsyn, A. (1974) *The Gulag Archipelago, 1918–1956: An Experiment in Literary Investigation*. London: Harvill Press.

Stanley, J. L. (1994) 'Is Totalitarianism a New Phenomenon? Reflections on Hannah Arendt's Origins of Totalitarianism', in L. P. Hinchman and S. K. Hinchman (eds.), *Hannah Arendt: Critical Essays*. New York: State University of New York Press.

Stiglitz, J. and L. Bilmes (2008) 'The Three Trillion Dollar War', *The Times*, 23 February.

Stoetzler, M. (2007) 'Anti-Semitism, the Bourgeoisie, and the Self-Destruction of the Nation-State', in R. H. King and D. Stone (eds.), *Hannah Arendt and the Uses of History: Imperialism, Nation, Race and Genocide*. New York: Berghahn.

Stone, D. (2007) 'The Holocaust and "The Human"', in R. H. King and D. Stone (eds.), *Hannah Arendt and the Uses of History: Imperialism, Nation, Race and Genocide*. New York: Berghahn.

Suchting, W. A. (1962) 'Marx and Hannah Arendt's *The Human Condition*', *Ethics*, vol. 73, no. 1.

Swift, S. (2009) *Hannah Arendt*. London: Routledge.

Szerszynski, B. (2003) 'Technology, Performance and Life Itself: Hannah Arendt and the Fate of Nature', *Sociological Review*, vol. 51, no. s2.

Taylor, D. (2002) 'Hannah Arendt on Judgement: Thinking for Politics', *International Journal of Philosophical Studies*, vol. 10, no. 2.

Tec, N. (1986) *When Light Pierced the Darkness: Christian Rescue of Jews in Nazi-Occupied Poland*. New York: Oxford University Press.

Terada, R. (2008) 'Thinking for Oneself: Realism and Defiance in Arendt', *Textual Practice*, vol. 22, no. 1.

Torgerson, D. (1999) *The Promise of Green Politics: Environmentalism and the Public Sphere*. Durham, NC: Duke University Press.

Tsao, R. T. (2002) 'The Three Phases of Arendt's Theory of Totalitarianism', *Social Research*, vol. 69, no. 2.

UNFAO (2010) *The State of Food Insecurity in the World: Addressing Food Insecurity in Protracted Crises*. Rome: FAO.

UNHCR (2010) *2009 Global Trends: Refugees, Asylum-Seekers, Returnees, Internally Displaced and Stateless Persons*. Available at http://www.unhcr.org/statistics.html (accessed 23 July 2010)

Villa, D. R. (1992) 'Postmodernism and the Public Sphere', *American Political Science Review*, vol. 86, no. 3.

Villa, D. R. (1999a) *Politics, Philosophy, Terror: Essays on the Thought of Hannah Arendt*. Princeton: Princeton University Press.

Villa, D. R. (1999b) 'Thinking and Judging', in J. J. Hermsen and D. R. Villa (eds.), *The Judge and the Spectator: Hannah Arendt's Political Philosophy*. Leuven: Peeters.

Villa, D. R. (2001) 'Hannah Arendt: Modernity, Alienation and Critique', in R. Beiner and J. Nedelsky (eds.), *Judgement, Imagination, and Politics: Themes from Kant and Arendt*. Lanham, MD: Rowman and Littlefield.

Weber, M. (1949) '"Objectivity" in Social Science and Social Policy', in *The Methodology of the Social Sciences*. New York: Free Press.

Weber, M. (1958) *The Protestant Ethic and the Spirit of Capitalism*. New York: Scribners.

Weber, M. (1970a) 'Politics as a Vocation', in H. H. Gerth and C. W. Mills (eds.), *From Max Weber: Essays in Sociology*. London: Routledge.

Weber, M. (1970b) 'Science as a Vocation', in H. H. Gerth and C. W. Mills (eds.), *From Max Weber: Essays in Sociology*. London: Routledge.

Weber, M. (1970c) 'Religious Rejections of the World and Their Directions', in H. H. Gerth and C. W. Mills (eds.), *From Max Weber: Essays in Sociology*. London: Routledge.

Weber, M. (1978) *Economy and Society: Volumes 1 and 2*. Berkeley: University of California Press.

Weil, S. (2005) 'The Iliad, or the Poem of Force', in S. Weil and R. Bespaloff, *War and the Iliad*. New York: New York Review of Books.

Wellmer, A. (1996) 'Hannah Arendt on Judgement: The Unwritten Doctrine of Reason', in L. May and J. Kohn (eds.), *Hannah Arendt: Twenty Years Later*. Cambridge, MA: MIT Press.

Werth, A. (2000) *Russia at War: 1941–1945*. Second edition. New York: Carroll and Graf.

Whitebook, J. (2002) 'Michel Foucault: A Marcusean in Structuralist Clothing', *Thesis Eleven*, no. 71.

Whiteside, K. H. (1994) 'Hannah Arendt and Ecological Politics', *Environmental Ethics*, vol. 16, no. 4.

Whiteside, K. H. (1998) 'Worldliness and Respect for Nature: an Ecological Application of Hannah Arendt's Conception of Culture', *Environmental Values*, vol. 7, no. 1.

Whitfield, S. J. (1980) *Into the Dark: Hannah Arendt and Totalitarianism*. Philadelphia: Temple University Press.

Wolin, R. (2001) 'Hannah Arendt: *Kultur*, "Thoughtlessness", and Polis Envy', in *Heidegger's Children*. Princeton: Princeton University Press.

Young, I. (2003) 'From Guilt to Solidarity: Sweatshops and Political Responsibility', *Dissent*, no. 48.

Young-Bruehl, E. (1996) 'Hannah Arendt Among Feminists', in L. May and J. Kohn (eds.), *Hannah Arendt: Twenty Years Later*. Cambridge, MA: MIT Press.

Young-Bruehl, E. (2002) 'On the Origins of a New Totalitarianism', *Social Research*, vol. 69, no. 2.

Young-Bruehl, E. (2004) *Hannah Arendt: For Love of the World*. Second edition. New Haven: Yale University Press.

Young-Bruehl, E. (2006) *Why Arendt Matters*. New Haven: Yale University Press.

Index

Compiled by Sue Carlton